W9-AEI-098

DETROIT
PUBLIC
LIBRARY

BIOGRAPHICAL ENCYCLOPEDIA OF
20th-Century World Leaders

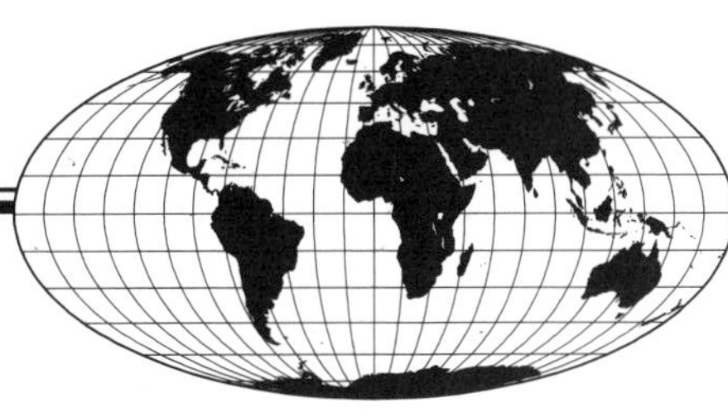

BIOGRAPHICAL ENCYCLOPEDIA OF
20th-Century World Leaders

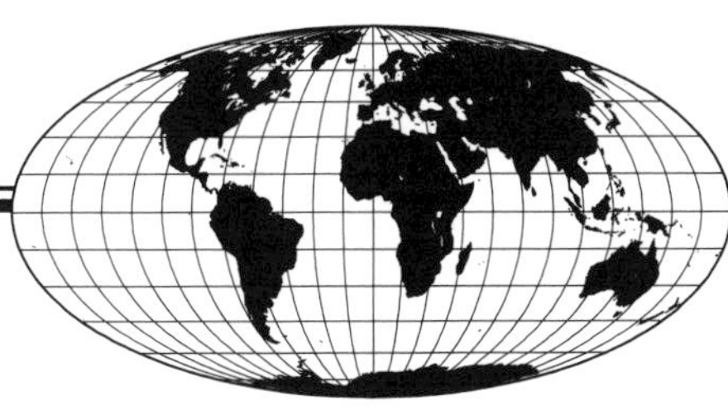

Volume 4

Manley – Rundstedt

Editor
John Powell
Pennsylvania State University, Erie

Marshall Cavendish
New York • London • Toronto • Sydney

Marshall Cavendish Corporation
99 White Plains Road
Tarrytown, New York 10591-9001

Printed in the United States of America
09 08 07 06 05 04 03 02 01 00 5 4 3 2 1

Library of Congress Cataloging-in-Publication Data

Biographical encyclopedia of 20th-century world leaders / John Powell
p. cm.
v. cm.
Includes bibliographical references and index.
1. Heads of state Biography Encyclopedias. 2. Statesmen Biography Encyclopedias. 3. Biography 20th century Encyclopedias. I. Powell, John, 1954- . II. Title: Biographical encyclopedia of twentieth-century world leaders
ISBN 0-7614-7129-4 (set)
ISBN 0-7614-7133-2 (vol. 4)
D412.B56 1999
920'.009'04—dc21

99-34462
CIP

∞ This paper meets the requirements of ANSI/NISO Z39.48-1992 (R1997) Permanence of Paper for Publications and Documents in Libraries and Archives

CONTENTS

Key to Pronunciation

As an aid to users of the *Biographical Encyclopedia of 20th-Century World Leaders,* guides to pronunciation for all profiled leaders have been provided with the first mention of the name in each entry. These guides are rendered in an easy-to-use phonetic manner. Stressed syllables are indicated by capital letters.

Letters of the English language, particularly vowels, are pronounced in different ways depending on the context. Below are letters and combinations of letters used in the phonetic guides to represent various sounds, along with examples of words in which those sounds appear and corresponding guides for their pronunciation.

Symbols	*Pronounced As In*	*Spelled Phonetically*
a	answer, laugh	AN-sihr, laf
ah	father, hospital	FAH-thur, HAHS-pih-tul
aw	awful, caught	AW-ful, kawt
ay	blaze, fade, waiter	blayz, fayd, WAYT-ur
ch	beach, chimp	beech, chihmp
eh	bed, head, said	behd, hehd, sehd
ee	believe, leader	bee-LEEV, LEED-ur
ew	boot, loose	bewt, lews
g	beg, disguise, get	behg, dihs-GIZ, geht
i	buy, height, surprise	bi, hit, sur-PRIZ
ih	bitter, pill	bih-TUR, pihl
j	digit, edge, jet	DIH-jiht, ehj, jeht
k	cat, kitten, hex	kat, KIH-tehn, hehks
o	cotton, hot	CO-tuhn, hot
oh	below, coat, note	bee-LOH, coht, noht
oo	good, look	good, look
ow	couch, how	kowch, how
oy	boy, coin	boy, koyn
s	cellar, save, scent	SEL-ur, sayv, sehnt
sh	issue, shop	IH-shew, shop
uh	about, enough	uh-BOWT, ee-NUHF
ur	earth, letter	urth, LEH-tur
y	useful, young	YEWS-ful, yuhng
z	business, zest	BIHZ-ness, zest
zh	vision	VIH-zhuhn

BIOGRAPHICAL ENCYCLOPEDIA OF
20th-Century World Leaders

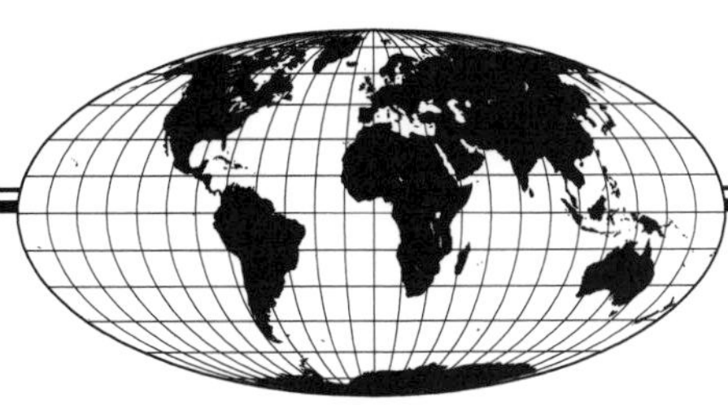

Michael Manley

Born: December 10, 1924; St. Andrew, Jamaica
Died: March 6, 1997; St. Andrew, Jamaica

Prime minister of Jamaica (1972-1980, 1989-1992)

Michael Norman Manley (MI-kuhl NOHR-muhn MAN-lee) was the son of Norman Washington Manley, premier of Jamaica from 1955 to 1962 and founder of one of the nation's major political institutions, the People's National Party (PNP). His mother was a sculptor and patron of the arts. After World War II, Manley studied politics, philosophy, and economics at the London School of Economics. He then worked as a journalist in Britain. He was married four times and had five children.

Early Career

During the 1950's and 1960's, Manley was a leader of the PNP-affiliated National Workers' Union and a champion of Jamaica's working classes. In 1962, the year Jamaica gained independence from Britain, Manley was appointed senator in Jamaica's parliament by his father. He won election to the more powerful House of Representatives in 1967 and became leader of the PNP in 1969. As chief executive of the PNP, Manley inherited a bitter political struggle with the

Michael Manley, with heavily armed security guards, goes to the polls to vote in the 1989 Jamaican elections. Manley's party won, and he became the new prime minister. *(AP/Wide World Photos)*

Michael Manley *(AP/Wide World Photos)*

opposition Jamaica Labour Party (JLP). It had been founded by Norman Manley's cousin, Alexander Bustamante. The PNP and the JLP have alternated as Jamaica's majority party.

Prime Minister

Manley served as prime minister of Jamaica from 1972 to 1980 and then again from 1989 to 1992. Through a belief in democratic socialism, he worked to free Jamaica from neocolonialism, political and economic dependency, underdevelopment, and poverty. Democratic socialists advocate a gradual shift from capitalism to socialism. As prime minister, he worked to transform Jamaica from a poor Third World country with social problems into a country that would be noted for the success of its economic and social reforms and for political independence. He also positioned Jamaica as a leader among nonaligned Third World nations. In 1974, the Manley administration imposed a levy on the mining of bauxite, the claylike ore from which aluminum is made. That action significantly increased Jamaica's national revenues from foreign aluminum companies. The Manley administration's socialist rhetoric, and its close diplomatic ties

The People's National Party

The People's National Party (PNP) of Jamaica was founded in 1938 in the aftermath of nationwide labor protests. It's leaders advocated political independence from Britain. Norman Washington Manley and, later, his son Michael Manley were central figures in the history of the PNP. The PNP's democratic socialist program was first articulated in 1964. Political independence from Britain had brought little improvement in the lives of the vast majority of Jamaicans. Party leaders emphasized the search for economic equality, which widespread unemployment denied, and national independence, which meant wresting control of the economy from multinational corporations. Party leaders believed in participatory democracy and in the need for all Jamaicans to be proud of their national identity and heritage. PNP leaders argued that Jamaica's economic system, not racial problems, perpetuated poverty. They believed that Jamaica would flourish only in a mixed economy—one in which private business and the public sector were partners. Every Jamaican had the right, the PNP stated, to meaningful employment and economic social security.

with communist Cuba, led to difficulties with the United States and the International Monetary Fund, the agency to which nations turn when they run into financial trouble.

Manley's Achievement

The overwhelming achievement of Manley's life was his struggle against colonialism and neocolonialism. Manley kept alive the flame of regional integration and Third World solidarity in the face of economic crises and political strife that compelled Third World nations to struggle separately for survival and democracy. Manley believed that the future of Jamaica depended on broad regional economic and political solidarity. He was a leader of the movement toward self-determination in the Caribbean and the Third World. Manley saw Jamaican foreign policy as offering an alternative to subservient alliances with the United States or a common cause with the nonaligned nations to work for changes in the world's economic system. He worked to change the often-unfair trade relations between the rich, developed nations and the poor relations of the Third World.

In 1978, the United Nations awarded Manley its prestigious gold medal for his uncompromising opposition to racial oppression, especially apartheid in South Africa. Manley played a critical role in the restoration of democracy in Haiti. He championed a commitment to social equity and justice and economic opportunity for all Jamaicans. Moreover, he realized that even a country as small as Jamaica could develop a visionary approach to global economics and politics.

Jamaican prime minister Michael Manley giving a statement after a meeting at the White House in 1990. U.S. president George Bush stands by. *(Reuters/Rick Wilking/Archive Photos)*

Bibliography

Levi, Darrell E. *Michael Manley: The Making of a Leader*. Athens: University of Georgia Press, 1989.

Sherlock, Philip M. *Norman Manley*. London: Macmillan, 1980.

Sherlock, Philip M., and Hazel Bennett. *The Story of the Jamaican People*. Princeton, N.J.: Markus Wiener, 1998.

Fred Buchstein

Carl Gustaf Mannerheim

Born: June 4, 1867; Villnäs, near Turku, Finland
Died: January 27, 1951; Lausanne, Switzerland

Finnish military and political leader, president of Finland (1944-1946)

Carl Gustaf Emil Mannerheim (KAHRL GOOS-tahf AY-meel MAH-nehr-haym) was born on the Finnish estate of his parents, Count Carl Mannerheim and Helene von Julin. A happy early childhood was followed in quick succession by his father's insolvency (1880) and mother's death (1881). Scattered among supportive relatives, Gustaf and his six siblings maintained their mutual loyalty and aspirations. The depleted family fortunes, along with a personal streak of unruliness, dictated Gustaf's choice of an army career.

Because Finland was then part of the Russian Empire, Mannerheim enrolled in St. Petersburg's Nikolaevskoe Cavalry School, eventually attaining a position in the czar's elite Chevalier Guards (1891). In 1892 he married a general's daughter named Anastasia, with whom he had two daughters. Sixteen years were spent pursuing a varied and successful military career which included epic reconnaissance journeys throughout Asia, Manchurian service in the Russo-Japanese War, and multidecorated commands in World War I. Throughout this period, Mannerheim was buffeted by the disparate ideals of military duty and dissatisfaction with the Russian Empire's reactionary policies, which increasingly alienated his Finnish compatriots.

Carl Gustaf Mannerheim *(Library of Congress)*

Revolution and Independence

With disintegration of the Russian government and the successful Bolshevik coup of October/November, 1917, Mannerheim's quandary was resolved. He returned to Finland two weeks after it declared independence (December 6, 1917). The country almost immediately descended, along class lines, into a bitter war between Red Guard (communist) revolutionaries, backed by Russian troops stationed in Finland, and the government's Civil Guard. Mannerheim's political affinity and military abilities were quickly recognized by the Finnish Senate. It appointed him commander in chief and gave him the task of organizing the "White Guard" and fighting the Reds. Only five months later, on May 16, 1918, he paraded his forces through Helsinki, Finland's capital. He was victorious in combat but was still slogging through a political quagmire.

World War I, which began in 1914, was still raging in Europe, although it was in its last year. Pro-German sympathizers in Finland had been successful in having German troops and military instructors brought into the conflict. Mannerheim believed that the move was a bad idea; he feared it would endanger Finland's independence, its relationship with neighboring Sweden, and its international standing should the Western Allies win the war. Because his opinions were disregarded, he resigned in June, 1918.

The Regency

With Germany's defeat in World War I, Mannerheim again became an important Finnish asset. Untainted by the country's misreading of future events and widely esteemed, he was elected interim regent. During seven months as head of state, Mannerheim purged the army of German influences, resumed relations with the Allies, gained recognition from France of Finland's independent status, obtained aid to stave off famine, began the process of national reconciliation with a declaration of amnesty, and formulated a liberal constitution.

Contacts made during his decades of service in Russia, as well as his Allied war record, were used to advantage in many of these efforts. Mannerheim's White Army service and promotion of intervention against the Bolsheviks was, however, viewed as a liability among the newly formed political parties casting about for presidential candidates. Though he ran for the office, he gathered little support. Mannerheim retired to private life. He devoted himself to social services, including chairmanship of the Finnish Red Cross, to extensive travels, and to his villa, where he hunted and worked in his garden.

Return to Public Service

Never far from politics, yet ever more clearly a nonpartisan patriot, Mannerheim was appointed Finland's first armed forces field marshal in 1933. Largely a ceremonial post, the position carried with it self-initiated responsibilities as Europe in the 1930's stumbled once again toward war. Mannerheim correctly predicted that the Soviet Union would be Finland's greatest threat. Accordingly, he planned a defensive campaign based on fortification of the Karelian Isthmus, known as the Mannerheim Line. This strategy was complemented by highly mobile units trained to isolate unwieldly concentrations of enemy troops.

World War II began in September, 1939. When the Soviet invasion of Finland came in November, Mannerheim's preparations proved highly effective. Great sympathy was aroused abroad for Finland's struggle, led by the seventy-two-

The Mannerheim Line

A surprisingly effective deterrent to the 1939 Soviet invasion of Finland, the Mannerheim Line actually consisted of a series of front, intermediate, and rear positions guarding Finland's vulnerable southeastern border. By no means comparable to the massive fortifications of the German Siegfried Line or French Maginot Line, Mannerheim's defenses were primarily pillboxes and dug-in gun positions. They were still being built at the outbreak of hostilities.

Taking advantage of forest and tundra terrains to protect much of Finland's northern territories allowed Carl G. Mannerheim to mass most of his forces along the line, which he deployed just before the unannounced invasion. Initial Soviet assaults failed to penetrate the defenses. A new offensive in February, 1941, however, revealed the line's vulnerability to sustained artillery, air bombardment, and repeated frontal attacks. Lacking reserve forces and sufficient armaments, the Finns had to fall back. The strategy of the Mannerheim Line had not been to win a war, but to buy time for negotiations. In this it succeeded. When Norway and Sweden refused transit of British and French troops to assist in the war, Finland finally capitulated, but not before holding out for 105 days.

year-old general. Yet Soviet numerical superiority was inevitably overwhelming. Mannerheim recommended acceptance of a harsh armistice agreement, signed on March 13, 1940, over problematic Allied intervention. Soon further demands—as well as Soviet incorporation of the Baltic states—made it clear that the Soviet Union was not prepared to accept Finnish sovereignty. The situation became more complex as Germany demanded that its troops based in Norway be allowed to travel through Finland. Rebuffed in its attempts to retain neutrality, Finland was pulled into the war as a German ally.

Dangerous Liaisons

Mannerheim was faced with the delicate task of cooperating with Germany, directing a renewed Soviet campaign without incurring their wrath, and making discreet overtures to the Allies in preparation for Finland's postwar status in Europe. Avoiding German demands to participate in the battle of Leningrad, he held his Finnish army stationary from 1942 to 1944 once it regained territories ceded in the 1940 armistice. He left rail routes to the Soviet's vital Murmansk port uncut. He refused all attempts to implement Adolf Hitler's racial policies, most particularly the persecution of Jews. After being elected president in 1944, Mannerheim negotiated yet another armistice with the Soviet Union and managed to break Finland's covenants with Germany with a minimum of German retribution. The war was over in 1945. Mannerheim, citing ill health, resigned on March 4, 1946.

The Final Years

Decades of responsibility, aggravated by the late-life demands of the war years, brought on stomach ulcers that plagued Mannerheim until his death in 1951. He chose increasingly to spend his time in the quiet and political security of Switzerland. Returning to a hero's burial in Helsinki, Mannerheim was eulogized as the central figure in the history of independent Finland, "a great soldier, a great statesman, a great citizen."

Bibliography

Jagerskiold, Stig. *Mannerheim: Marshall of Finland*. London: C. Hurst, 1986.

Mannerheim, Carl G. *The Memoirs of Marshall Mannerheim*. New York: E. P. Dutton, 1954.

Screen, J. E. O. *Mannerheim: The Years of Preparation*. London: C. Hurst, 1970.

Warner, O. *Marshall Mannerheim and the Finns*. London: Weidenfeld and Nicolson, 1965.

Michael W. Tripp

The White Guard

Immediately after declaring independence from Russia in late 1917, Finland was plunged into a bitter struggle between its new independent government and communist forces fighting for control. The White Guard was the force fighting against the Red Guard, or communist revolutionaries attempting to overthrow the government. Carl G. Mannerheim's White Guard forces were formed from volunteer Civil Guard garrisons, supplemented by conscription and the return of Finnish *Jäger* troops trained in Germany. The war in Finland between Reds and Whites did not escape the unique brutality of civil wars. Atrocities and equally vicious reprisals escalated. When it was over, the victorious White Guard executed thousands of Reds and jailed more than eighty thousand. More than twelve thousand of those jailed died. Though Mannerheim vigorously opposed the mistreatment of prisoners or civilian populations, as commander in chief he came to symbolize for the defeated side the "illegal tyranny of the bourgeois butchers."

Preston Manning

Born: June 10, 1942; Edmonton, Alberta, Canada

Founder (1987) and leader of Reform Party of Canada

Preston Manning (PREHS-tuhn MA-nihng) was born into a prairie populist family in Edmonton, Alberta. His father, Ernest Manning, a radio minister, was premier of Alberta for twenty-five years. Preston Manning spent his early life in Edmonton and his adolescence living and working on a dairy farm on the outskirts of the city. Ernest Manning groomed his son in the fundamentalist, populist beliefs of the Social Credit Party, of which he was leader. Preston followed his father's example, becoming involved in his father's political work and even preaching on his father's radio program, the *Back to the Bible Hour*.

When the elder Manning retired in 1968, Preston launched a career as a management consultant based in Edmonton. He did not enter politics on his own until 1987. In that year he founded the Reform Party of Canada. His first elected seat was won in the 1993 election, when he was voted into Parliament for the riding (district) of Calgary Southwest. The Reform Party has become an influential conservative movement dedicated to lowering the national debt, reducing taxes, making the political system more democratic, and providing for constitutional equality for all Canadian citizens and provinces.

Preston Manning *(Reuters/Peter Jones/Archive Photos)*

A "New Canada"

When Manning founded the Reform Party of Canada in 1987, the regional group sought political power and economic gain for the western provinces. Manning wrote a book in 1992 entitled *The New Canada*, which describes his vision for political reform. When the Reform Party voted to expand into a national force, they adopted as their mission many of the goals in Manning's book—mainly to work for a balanced, democratic federation of provinces. Since Manning founded the group and defined many of its principals and policies, his own conservative, fundamentalist Christian views dominated. He described the populist views of the party as "common sense for the common people."

Canada was ripe for changes when Manning and the Reform Party campaigned in 1993. The country was in a deep recession, and issues regarding constitutional reform were causing increasing agitation. The province of Quebec was considering seceding from Canada if special provisions were not made to protect its French culture, history, and language. In many ways it seemed as though the Canadian people were undergoing an identity crisis. Manning's views on a "unified right" among right-wing political parties and on reforms that would lead to equal treatment among the provinces brought supporters to the Reform Party. By the start of the 1993 election year, the party boasted more than 100,000 members, and it had associations organized in all 220 federal ridings outside Quebec.

The 1993 Reform Party Platform

During the campaign for the 1993 national elections, the Reform Party focused on two areas—taxes and equality among the provinces. They proposed to cut taxes by 15 percent. It was the party's view on the possible secession of Quebec from Canada, however, that caused the party the most criticism. Though the loss of the province of Quebec went against Preston Manning's idea of a unified new Canada, he and the Reform Party opposed special treatment for the Québécois, as the French-speaking quarter of the population is called. He argued that Quebec should not have any privileges the other provinces did not also enjoy. Manning viewed conducting business in both English and French as unnecessary in a majority of the provinces, which have few business dealings with Quebec. During the campaign, the Reform Party hoped to win between thirty and fifty seats in Parliament. They exceeded their expectations, winning 52 seats.

Critics and Supporters

Manning's critics called him a manipulator, but his supporters noted that he manages to express his views while presenting both sides of an issue. Supporters also appreciated his ability to remain unflappable and concentrate on the tasks he assigns himself. His sense of humor also won him supporters.

In 1987, when the Reform Party had established Manning as its leader, it also pledged to disband in the year 2000. However, after claiming fifty-two seats—18 percent of the national vote—in 1993 and sixty seats—19 percent of the vote—in 1997, the party voted to postpone disbanding until 2007. It also strongly encouraged Manning to continue as party leader.

Reform Party leader Preston Manning in 1997, after the party won sixty seats in the Canadian elections and became the official opposition party. *(Reuters/Patrick Price/Archive Photos)*

Bibliography

Dobbin, Murray. *Preston Manning and the Reform Party.* Toronto: J Lorimer, 1991.

Dobbs, Frank. *Preston Manning: The Roots of Reform.* Vancouver: Greystone Books, 1997.

Flanagan, Tom. *Waiting for the Wave: The Reform Party and Preston Manning.* Toronto: Stoddart, 1995.

Mackey, Lloyd. *Like Father, Like Son: Ernest Manning and Preston Manning.* Toronto: ECW Press, 1997.

Lisa A. Wroble

Mao Zedong

Born: December 26, 1893; Shaoshan, Hunan Province, China
Died: September 9, 1976; Beijing, China

Chinese revolutionary and political leader, chairman of People's Republic of China (1949-1959) and Chinese Communist Party (1935-1976)

Born into a family of moderately wealthy peasant farmers, Mao Zedong (MOW DSEH-DOONG) preferred reading to working the farm with his authoritarian father. He enlisted in the Chinese army in 1911, but he left after six months in order to resume his studies. After receiving his degree in 1918, Mao taught school and published articles as he became steadily more involved in politics. Influenced by the Russian Revolution (1917) and Marxist thought, he turned to communism in 1920. The following year he attended the first meeting of the Chinese Communist Party.

Rise to Power

During the 1920's, Mao Zedong (also written as Mao Tse-tung) held numerous positions within the party. However, his theory of a revolution dependent upon a rural peasant uprising brought him into conflict with other party members, who sought an urban movement. During this period the Communists allied with the Kuomintang (KMT, the Nationalists), a relationship that had soured by mid-decade and eventually resulted in civil war. In 1927 Mao led a peasant revolt in his home province of Hunan. When this movement failed, Mao and his followers established a base in the Chingkang Mountains that soon became a refuge for Communists.

The growth of the Communist Party alarmed the Kuomintang, which sought to crush its opponents in a series of military offensives. These offenses resulted in the celebrated Long March of 1934-1935: Mao and his fellow Communists traveled more than 6,000 miles (9,700 kilometers) from Jiangxi to Yan'an, enduring severe hardship and battling Kuomintang forces all the way. The Long March marked a turning point in Mao's career. It allowed him to assert his authority as the leader of the Communist Party, and it provided him with valuable political and military experience. Mao spent the next fourteen years consolidating his power, expanding his party's influence, and fighting the Kuomintang. The long years of struggle culminated in the found-

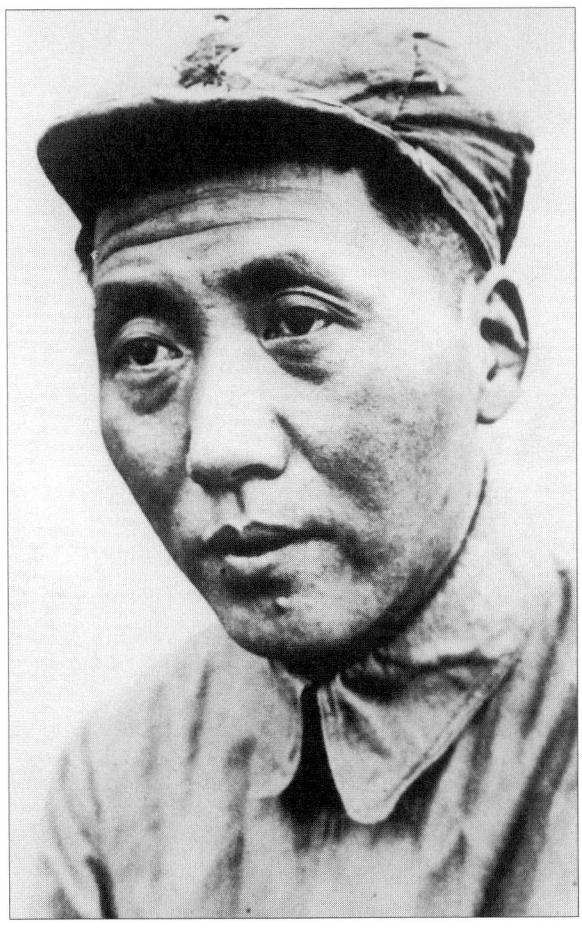

Mao Zedong as a revolutionary leader in the 1940's. *(National Archives)*

A copy of Quotations from Chairman Mao Zedong, or the "Little Red Book." *(Library of Congress)*

ing of the People's Republic of China on October 1, 1949, with Mao as chairman of the new government.

Chairman Mao

In the area of foreign policy, Mao formed an uneasy alliance with the Soviet Union and fended off perceived external threats, sending troops to fight in Korea in 1950. At home, he attempted to solve his nation's considerable economic woes, focusing his efforts on agrarian reforms. He rid the government of potential opponents and worked to solidify loyalty to the new regime among the Chinese people. Granted broad powers in a 1954 reorganization of the government, Mao pushed a rural collectivization program in 1955 that failed, resulting in famine in many parts of the country. Communist Party leaders then sought to curb his authority by reorganizing the party structure in 1956 in order to reduce his influence. Mao responded with the Hundred Flowers campaign, in which intellectuals were encouraged to criticize the government. This apparently liberal move was actually in-

The Little Red Book

A prolific writer, Mao Zedong authorized the collection of several passages from his writings in a pocket-sized booklet entitled *Quotations from Chairman Mao Zedong*. More commonly known as the "Little Red Book" because of its size and red plastic cover, it was originally published in 1964 for use in a political education movement within the military. Soldiers carried it in their packs in order to study and memorize its lessons regarding class struggle and the value of hard work. The book proved to be effective, and a regular edition for distribution outside the army was issued in August, 1965. Periodically revised and reissued, the book became an important symbol during the Cultural Revolution, when people attending mass meetings would wave copies of their book to signal their approval of government policies. By 1967, the Chinese were claiming that more than 350 million copies were in circulation. The book's influence spread beyond China, as radicals in countries including the United States turned to it for ideological guidance. Although the book contributed to the official personality cult that appeared at that time, Mao seems to have believed that the enthusiasm for the book outweighed its importance. The move away from the Cultural Revolution at the end of the 1960's marked the decline of the Little Red Book and its importance in Chinese life.

In the 1950's and 1960's, Chairman Mao Zedong was both a powerful leader and a symbolic figure. The Chinese characters at the bottom roughly translate as "Long live the victory of Chairman Mao's revolutionary line." *(Library of Congress)*

tended to weaken the party after its attack on the chairman.

Mao adhered to the belief that revolution must be a permanent political and social reality. Accordingly, in 1958 he announced the Great Leap Forward, an effort to bring more than 120 million families into collectives (group farming endeavors) in order to increase rural productivity. The movement proved disastrous, resulting in great economic and social dislocation. Mao left the position of chief of state in April, 1959, and his influence on the government and the party waned. However, he remained a powerful figure in Chinese and global affairs, growing increasingly harsh in his criticisms of the Soviet Union during this period.

Final Years

During the early 1960's Mao bided his time, working closely with Lin Piao, China's defense minister, in order to increase his influence over the military. When the Chinese economy improved after 1962, Mao began to criticize his enemies and attack cultural institutions—including the opera—which he argued were not in keeping with revolutionary ideas. These moves presaged the Cultural Revolution of 1966-1969, an era of extraordinary social turmoil during which Mao

The Chinese Communist Party

Founded in 1921, the Chinese Communist Party (CCP) led the opposition to the Kuomintang government (the Nationalist government) during China's civil war, which began during the late 1920's. The party was not monolithic in its ideology; frequent disputes over the nature of revolution caused splits and dissension during the 1920's. After the Communists' victory in 1949, the party, with Mao at its head, played an important political and ideological role in Chinese life. However, the party and the government were not identical, as evidenced by the conflicts between party leaders and Chairman Mao during the 1950's. Although the party was linked to the Soviet Union's Communist Party and often followed Soviet directives in the early years of its existence, it was an independent organization that asserted its differences in the 1950's.

became a cult figure in Chinese life.

The main phase of the Cultural Revolution ended in the late 1960's with the party and the government in disarray. Mao's designated successor to head the party attempted a coup that included an assassination attempt, both of which failed. In 1974, Mao began another of his revolutionary social programs, this one aimed at destroying the role of Confucianism in Chinese life and thought. However, Mao's health was poor, and by 1975 he had disappeared from the public eye. When he died in 1976, he left no clear successor.

A master politician and theorist who understood the realities of Chinese life, Mao played a central role in bringing the Communist Party to power in China. He successfully unified a nation that had suffered a brutal, decades-long civil war, and he made China an important nation in international affairs. As such, he stands as one of the preeminent figures of the twentieth century. However, his commitment to permanent revolution created economic and social chaos that brought great suffering to many of the Chinese people.

Bibliography

Bouc, Alain. *Mao Tse-tung: A Guide to His Thought*. New York: St. Martin's Press, 1977.

Chou, Eric. *Mao Tse-tung: The Man and the Myth*. New York: Stein and Day, 1980.

Howard, Roger. *Mao Tse-tung and the Chinese People*. New York: Monthly Review Press, 1977.

Karnow, Stanley. *Mao and China: A Legacy of Turmoil*. 3d ed. New York: Penguin Books, 1990.

Thomas Clarkin

Ferdinand E. Marcos

Born: September 11, 1917; Sarrat, Philippines
Died: September 28, 1989; Honolulu, Hawaii

President of the Philippines (1965-1986)

Ferdinand Edralin Marcos (FAYR-dee-nahnd e-DRAH-leen MAHR-kohs) was born in the province of Ilocos Norte, in the northwestern Philippines. His father, Mariano Marcos, was a public school supervisor who served two terms in the Philippine Congress. Josefa Marcos, Ferdinand's mother, exercised great influence over her son, instilling high ambitions in him and pushing him to excel in his studies.

Early Success and Fame

In 1935 Mariano Marcos lost an election for Congress to a rival, Julio Nalundasan. The race was a bitter one, and three days after Nalundasan's victory he was shot dead. At the end of 1938, the police identified a target pistol from the University of the Philippines as the murder weapon, and Marcos, a student at the university, was arrested. While on bail, he received his diploma and studied for his bar exams. In the midst of the trial, Marcos received the highest score in the history of the Philippine bar on his exam. After he was found guilty, Marcos appealed to the Philippine Supreme Court, acting as his own lawyer. His brilliant defense convinced the Supreme Court that he had been convicted by false testimony. The victory made the young Marcos a national celebrity.

World War II

After the Japanese defeated Philippine and U.S. troops and occupied the country in 1942, Marcos became head of a paramilitary group. He later claimed that this group had been a guerrilla organization connected to the American armed forces. Many historians believe, however, that the band headed by Marcos at various times fought with the Japanese, collaborated with them, and engaged in banditry.

With the end of the war, Marcos used his image as a war hero to begin a political career. He also managed to get hundreds of men from his province of Ilocos certified as guerrilla fighters, making them eligible for American financial payments. This created a political base, which helped him win election to the Philippine House of Representatives in 1949, 1953, and 1957.

Marriage and Politics

In 1954 Marcos married Imelda Remedios Romualdez. The bride helped to extend his political appeal because she was from Leyte, in the central part of the Philippines, and could thus

Ferdinand E. Marcos *(Archive Photos)*

help win votes outside his northern province. In 1959 Marcos was elected to the Senate, and in 1963 he became Senate president. He expected that his political party, the Liberal Party, would nominate him for the country's presidency in the 1965 election. When the Liberal Party did not nominate him, he switched to the rival Nationalist Party and won the presidency. In 1969 he was reelected, becoming the first Philippine president to serve two terms.

As elected president, Marcos helped to build the industry, agriculture, and social institutions of his nation. However, the country also saw increasing social disruption. Moreover, Marcos had no wish to step down when his second term ended. In order to retain power, he and his followers staged a number of public bombings and other incidents, which Marcos blamed on the communists. Claiming that the country was in danger of a communist takeover, Ferdinand Marcos declared martial law on September 21, 1972. Opposition leaders, such as the outspoken Benigno Aquino, were jailed, and the Marcos government became a virtual dictatorship.

Philippine president Ferdinand Marcos addressing reporters during a trip to the United States. *(Library of Congress)*

Martial Law in the Philippines

On September 21, 1972, President Ferdinand Marcos issued Proclamation 1081, in which he claimed that the country was in a state of emergency. He placed it under martial law—rule by the military under the president's command. The armed forces immediately arrested all those suspected of being threats to national security, including opposition politicians, political activists, and outspoken journalists as well as criminals and revolutionaries. Many Filipino politicians were in the practice of maintaining their own private security forces, essentially small armies. These were made illegal and disbanded. The military and the Philippine Constabulary, a military-style police force, confiscated privately held weapons and brought the media under the control of the government. Marcos closed the Philippine Congress and governed by issuing decrees for the rest of the period of martial law. In January, 1981, Marcos officially ended martial law. However, he had sufficient control to maintain authoritarian power behind the appearance of an elected, constitutional government. After the end of the Marcos regime, it became evident that many of the shootings, bombings, and other episodes he had used to justify declaring martial law had actually been staged by Marcos in order to enable him to stay in power.

Philippine Insurgent Movements

Muslims compose only 5 percent of the population of the Philippines, and they are overwhelmingly concentrated in the south. Tensions between Christians and Muslims increased during the 1950's and 1960's, when large numbers of Christians settled in the Muslim southern regions. After Ferdinand Marcos declared martial law in 1972 and ordered all privately held weapons to be turned in to the government, an open rebellion broke out in the south, with most of the various Muslim groups uniting in the Moro National Liberation Front (MNLF).

In December, 1968, José Maria Sison organized the Communist Party of the Philippines (CPP). Sison and a young antigovernment guerrilla, Bernabe Buscayno, then organized the New People's Army (NPA), the military wing of the CPP. The declaration of martial law drew many people opposed to Marcos into the NPA. By 1986, when the Marcos era ended, the NPA had more than twenty-two thousand fighters and controlled about 20 percent of the country.

The Downfall of Marcos

By the early 1980's, the economy had worsened and Marcos was in poor personal health. Imelda Marcos had become an increasingly influential part of the government and was criticized for appointing her relatives to political offices. The communist New People's Army and the Muslim separatist movement had grown steadily during the period of martial law. In 1983 Benigno Aquino, who had fled to the United States after years in prison, returned to the Philippines. Aquino was shot and killed as he got off the plane. Many Filipinos believed that Marcos was responsible for Aquino's death.

In early 1986, under pressure from the United States and from public opinion in the Philippines, Marcos called an election. Aquino's widow, Corazon, became the candidate of the opposition. Marcos was declared the winner of the election, but evidence of cheating caused the middle class and portions of the army to turn against him. Marcos sent troops to put down a rebellion by Defense Minister Juan Ponce Enrile and General Fidel Ramos. However, Catholic Cardinal Jaime Sin broadcast a radio call for citizens to form a human barricade around the headquarters of Ramos and Enrile. Government troops refused to fire on the civilians, and many soldiers switched to the rebel side. With encouragement from U.S. officials, Marcos fled the country for exile in Hawaii, where he died three years later.

The Marcos Legacy

During the early years of the Marcos era, the Philippine government engaged in extensive public works, expanding the basis for economic growth. However, the corruption of the later Marcos regime may have been responsible for many of the economic problems of the Philippines. The Marcos years also left the Philippines a divided society. Martial law stimulated the growth of communist and Muslim insurgencies. After the end of the Marcos regime, Filipinos continued to be divided into Marcos opponents and Marcos supporters.

Bibliography

Celoza, Albert F. *Ferdinand Marcos and the Philippines: The Political Economy of Authoritarianism*. New York: Praeger, 1998.

Seagrave, Sterling. *The Marcos Dynasty*. New York: Harper & Row, 1988.

Slack, Gordy. *Ferdinand Marcos*. New York: Chelsea House, 1988.

Carl L. Bankston III

George C. Marshall

Born: December 31, 1880; Uniontown, Pennsylvania
Died: October 16, 1959; Washington, D.C.

U.S. military leader and secretary of state (1947-1949), winner of 1953 Nobel Peace Prize

George Catlett Marshall (JOHRJ CAT-leht MAHR-shuhl), American soldier and statesman, was born into a middle-class family. After completing high school, he enrolled in the Virginia Military Institute (VMI), where an older brother had preceded him. At VMI, Marshall excelled in athletics and the cadet corps. Following graduation in 1901, he was commissioned a second lieutenant (infantry) in 1902.

George C. Marshall *(Library of Congress)*

Early Career

Marshall served briefly in the Philippines, where he trained soldiers, and then attended advanced infantry school at the army's command and staff college at Fort Leavenworth, Kansas, becoming an instructor there in 1908. Following a second assignment to the Philippines, he accompanied the American 1st Division to France in 1917 to take part in World War I. Marshall served as chief of operations for the 1st Division and, later, on the general headquarters staff, heading operations for the First American Army.

As a staff officer, temporarily a colonel, he planned the American offensive at Saint-Mihiel and the logistics portion of the Meuse-Argonne attack, carried out in the fall of 1918. The linked operations required movement of nine divisions, about 400,000 men, over difficult terrain for 60 miles (97 kilometers). It further required them to attack almost immediately after arrival. Marshall's plan worked so effectively that he became widely respected as a master of logistics. After the war, he served as senior aide to General John J. Pershing, American commander during World War I.

During the period between the two world wars, Marshall held battalion, brigade, and regimental commands and served both in China and in the Illinois National Guard. He was promoted to brigadier general in 1936. For his future career, however, his most important assignment was as chief instructor at the army's infantry training school at Fort Benning, Georgia (1927-1932). In that position he met and was able to evaluate the young officers who were to become senior field commanders during World War II.

Army Chief

As World War II approached, Marshall was summoned to Washington, D.C., and appointed chief of war plans in 1938. (World War II broke out in Europe in 1939, and the United States entered—fighting both Germany and Japan—at the end of 1941.) Marshall became deputy chief of staff of the army in 1938 and chief of staff in 1939. After the beginning of World War II, he worked to build and supply an army adequate to assure victory. This task meant growth from an army of 200,000 to one exceeding 8 million soldiers.

Marshall selected its most important commanders, often passing over his contemporaries in favor of younger, more aggressive officers. During the buildup, he was the most effective representative of the military to the Congress, where he testified on numerous occasions. In addition, he planned the war strategy that gave priority to the defeat of Germany, believing that Germany posed greater danger to the world than did Japan. He participated in all the major Allied conferences concerning the war and its aftermath. In 1944 Marshall was promoted to general of the army.

Statesman

At the end of World War II in 1945, having reached retirement age, Marshall resigned as army chief of staff. Although he did not realize it, he was to begin a second career as a diplomat, cabinet member, and statesman. In 1946 President Harry S Truman sent him to China as a special ambassador in an unsuccessful attempt to end China's state of civil war. Although Marshall prepared a peace agreement signed by warring nationalists and communists, the accord lasted only briefly. He became secretary of state (1946-1949) in the Truman administration just as the Cold War was beginning. In that capacity he attempted, without success, to reach an understanding with Russian dictator Joseph Stalin, whom he had met during World War II conferences. After their discussion, Marshall realized that Stalin believed that time was on the Soviet Union's side in Europe and that no concessions were needed.

American soldiers testing German telephone equipment after driving German troops back at Saint-Mihiel in France in September, 1918. *(National Archives)*

U.S. president Harry S Truman (left) with his secretary of state and creator of the Marshall Plan, George C. Marshall, in 1948. *(National Archives)*

As secretary of state, his major achievement was the Marshall Plan (1948-1952) for the economic recovery of Europe, officially known as the European Recovery Program. In a speech delivered at Harvard University on June 5, 1947, he outlined a proposal to use the United States' resources to rebuild the economies of European nations ravaged by war. The plan, enacted by Congress in 1948, was also designed to help European nations withstand communist aggression, yet in principle it was open to nations on both sides of the Iron Curtain. For his role in formu-

The Marshall Plan

On June 5, 1947, in an address to graduates of Harvard University, secretary of state George C. Marshall proposed a plan to provide American aid to Europe. (World War II had ended two years before.) American officials had studied the war-torn European economies, and they saw that the standard of living had fallen severely below prewar levels. Marshall proposed to invite governments to identify their most pressing needs and apply for assistance. In April, 1948, Congress approved the European Recovery Program (ERP). Over four years (1948-1952), it provided thirteen billion dollars in grants and loans to European governments.

The plan was motivated by the desire to help Europe rebuild following World War II, to stop the spread of communism into Western Europe, and to strengthen the economies of the United States' most important trading partners. European nations were required to set their own priorities for economic needs, to accept measures that assured the effectiveness of aid provided, and to modify business practices that inhibited free trade. Although the ERP was open to nations of the Eastern (communist) bloc, including Russia, those nations refused to lift the secrecy surrounding their economies and accept outside scrutiny. The principal beneficiaries were the United Kingdom, France, West Germany, and Italy.

The aid met a variety of needs, including restoring infrastructure, rebuilding heavy industry, improving agricultural production, and providing humanitarian aid. Most of the money was spent in the United States and thus had a secondary effect of improving U.S. production. By the end of the ERP, dramatic progress had been made toward restoring European economies to their prewar levels.

The Attack on Saint-Mihiel in World War I

In September, 1918, south and east of Verdun, France, a salient (an outward projection or bulge) of the German lines extended 18 miles (29 kilometers) to Saint-Mihiel, offering German commanders a passageway along the French Army's flank. Situated on high ground that favored defense, the German position had held against earlier French attacks. General John J. Pershing, the U.S. commander, considered the reduction of the pocket a fit test of his American divisions, but he agreed to link the operation to a second attack against the German Hindenburg Line, coordinated with French forces. Colonel George C. Marshall had prepared the plan for Saint-Mihiel as a staff officer with the First Division. It was carried out at two points by divisions of the I, IV, and V American Corps. The attack (September 12-14, 1918) proved an unqualified success, as American divisions quickly overran German positions. Because German artillery was being repositioned, the defenders fought without artillery support. After the victory, French reserves replaced American infantry, and nine American divisions began relocating to the Argonne Forest. American casualties at Saint-Mihiel were much lighter than had been expected: seventy-five hundred out of a force exceeding a half million. German losses included fifteen thousand captured and more than four hundred artillery pieces seized.

lating and implementing the Marshall Plan, Marshall was awarded the Nobel Peace Prize for 1953, the only professional military man to receive that honor.

After resigning as secretary of state in 1949, Marshall became chairman of the American Red Cross and, in 1950, rejoined the cabinet as secretary of defense. He served for a year, building American defenses during the Cold War, contributing to the development of the North Atlantic Treaty Organization (NATO) and, at the same time, working for world peace.

Bibliography

Cray, Ed. *General of the Army: George C. Marshall, Soldier and Statesman*. New York: W. W. Norton, 1990.

Mosley, Leonard. *Marshall: Hero for Our Times*. New York: Hearst, 1982.

Pogue, Forrest C. *George C. Marshall*. 4 vols. New York: Viking, 1963-87.

Stoler, Mark A. *George C. Marshall: Soldier-Statesman of the American Century*. Boston: Twayne, 1989.

Stanley Archer

Thurgood Marshall

Born: July 2, 1908; Baltimore, Maryland
Died: January 24, 1993; Bethesda, Maryland

First African American Supreme Court justice (1967-1991)

Thurgood Marshall (THUR-good MAHR-shuhl) was born Thoroughgood Marshall, named for his paternal grandfather, a freedman. The son of a waiter and a schoolteacher, the younger Thoroughgood shortened his given name when he first began attending grade school. In his final year at Lincoln University, Marshall married Vivian Burey. After graduating in 1930, Marshall attended law school at Howard University, receiving his J.D. in 1933.

Thurgood Marshall *(Library of Congress)*

Civil Rights Leader

Marshall began practicing law in his hometown, and he started his own law firm. This occurred during the depths of the Great Depression, and many of Marshall's clients could not afford to pay even the modest fees he charged. Then Marshall was offered the opportunity to act as the attorney for the local chapter of the National Association for the Advancement of Colored People (NAACP). Soon working for the NAACP would be a full-time job.

During law school, Marshall had been in close contact with members of the NAACP leadership, including Charles Houston. When Houston retired as chief counsel to the organization in 1938, Marshall was asked to replace him. Marshall accepted, and he and Vivian moved to New York City.

Marshall had for some time been trying cases—usually successfully—for the NAACP. As chief counsel, he continued these activities. He also traveled throughout the South to investigate lynchings and other offenses perpetrated against African Americans. In 1939 the NAACP created a new legal organization, the Legal Defense and Education Fund, to handle its lawsuits. Marshall was named as the fund's first director. He served in that capacity for twenty-one years, a period during which the NAACP scored some of its most significant victories. For many blacks, Marshall *was* the NAACP, and he was sometimes referred to as "Mr. Civil Rights."

However, Marshall experienced troubles as well as victories during this period. In 1955 Vivian Marshall died of cancer on her forty-fourth birthday. When Marshall married for the second time ten months later, he caused a minor scandal in the African American community: not only had he remarried quickly, but his new wife, Cecilia Suyat, was not black, but a Hawaiian of Filipino ancestry.

Thurgood Marshall (standing) in court in 1935, successfully bringing suit to allow a black student named Donald Murray admission to the University of Maryland's law school. *(Library of Congress)*

Government Service

Marshall's talents and activism did not go unnoticed among government leaders. In 1951 President Harry S Truman asked him to investigate allegations of discrimination leveled at the army by black soldiers serving in the Korean War. In 1962 President John F. Kennedy named Marshall to the U.S. Second Circuit Court of Appeals.

The Law and the NAACP

Formed in 1910 to combat violence perpetrated against blacks, the National Association for the Advancement of Colored People (NAACP) first sought to appeal to the conscience of Americans. Then, in the 1930's, the NAACP changed tactics, seeking to overcome racism through legal means. In their effort to overturn the 1896 Supreme Court ruling that "separate but equal" facilities for blacks and whites were legally acceptable, NAACP lawyers focused on public education. NAACP lawyers, Thurgood Marshall chief among them, sought to outlaw racial segregation in state-supported educational institutions. They won several victories in the U.S. Supreme Court that gradually improved the lot of African Americans. Then, in 1954, the Supreme Court ruled in favor of the NAACP and their client in the now-famous case *Brown v. Board of Education*. In this case the Court ordered school integration and sparked the Civil Rights movement. In a matter of a few decades, the NAACP's legal maneuvers, combined with the civil disobedience practiced by followers of the Reverend Martin Luther King, Jr., resulted in national civil rights legislation that outlawed segregation in virtually every area of public life.

Marshall thus became only the second African American to serve as a federal appeals court judge. In 1965 President Lyndon B. Johnson nominated Marshall as U.S. solicitor general; Marshall was the first African American to hold this position. On October 2, 1967, Marshall made history again when he was sworn in as the first African American justice of the U.S. Supreme Court.

Marshall served under three chief justices, Earl Warren, Warren Burger, and William Rehnquist, and over the nearly twenty-four years he sat on the Supreme Court, he found himself increasingly voting with the minority as the Court grew more conservative. Toward the end, beset by illness and old age, he held on as long as he could, hoping that a Democratic president would be elected so that his replacement on the Supreme Court might share his concern about civil rights. In the end, Marshall did not get his wish, and he retired from the Court in June, 1991. He died nineteen months later.

Bibliography

Davis, Michael D., and Hunter S. Clark. *Thurgood Marshall: Warrior at the Bar, Rebel on the Bench.* New York: Birch Lane Press, 1992.

Kluger, Richard. *Simple Justice: The History of Brown v. Board of Education and Black America's Struggle for Equality*. New York: Alfred A. Knopf, 1976.

Rowan, Carl T. *Dream Makers, Dream Breakers: The World of Justice Thurgood Marshall*. Boston: Little, Brown, 1993.

Lisa Paddock

Paul Martin

Born: August 28, 1938; Windsor, Ontario, Canada

Canadian political leader

Paul Edgar Philippe Martin, Jr. (PAWL EHD-gur fih-LEEP MAHR-tihn JEW-nyur), was born into a Canadian political family. His father was a member of Parliament who represented a Windsor area riding (district) for more than thirty years. Paul Martin, Sr., held many important cabinet portfolios in the Liberal governments of William Lyon Mackenzie King, Louis St. Laurent, and Lester B. Pearson. He was also a perennial contender for leadership of the party. Paul and his younger sister, Mary Anne, grew up in Windsor, Ontario, and in the Canadian capital of Ottawa, where the family also maintained a residence. He contracted polio in 1946 but was not left with any serious disability.

Early Accomplishments

After earning a bachelor of arts degree in 1962 and an LL.B. in 1965 from the University of Toronto, Paul married Sheila Ann Cowan. Their family grew eventually to include three sons: Paul, born in 1966, Robert (1969), and David (1970). During his younger days Paul Martin worked as a merchant seaman on salvage operations in the Arctic and as a roustabout in the Alberta gas fields. He was admitted to the Ontario bar in 1966.

For the most part, the city of Montreal in Quebec has been home for the Martins. Before entering politics Martin was a business executive, serving as a director of Redpath Industries, Fednov Limited, CB Pak, and the Manufacturers Life Insurance Company. He was a vice president at Consolidated Bathurst and Power Corporation of Canada, and he became the CEO of Canada Steamship Lines. He was also active in community affairs, serving on the boards of advisers for the School of Community and Public Affairs at Concordia University, Amnesty International, and the Centre for Research and Action on Race Relations. Martin ran for Parliament in the election of 1988 and was elected by a large majority. He became the member of Parliament for the riding of Lasalle-Emard, a predominantly working-class area along the St. Lawrence River in the southern part of Montreal.

Minister of Finance

The Liberal Party of Canada formed the government in 1993, and the newly elected prime minister, Jean Chrétien, appointed Martin as his finance minister. Until 1996, he also served as minister for Quebec in the Federal Office of Regional Development. His primary accomplishment as finance minister was the elimination of the yearly deficit in the national budget. This feat was accomplished in 1998 for the first time since the early 1960's. Martin's fiscal policy might be

Canadian finance minister Paul Martin answering budget questions from reporters in 1996. *(Reuters/John Hryniuk/ Archive Photos)*

described as compassionate fiscal restraint. Martin also has an interest in foreign relations; he has advocated a low-key style of Canadian assertion in the world. He coined the expression "nationalism without walls" to describe this approach. In the late 1980's and 1990's Paul Martin was often mentioned as a possible successor to Jean Chrétien as leader of the Liberal Party, and he was the front-runner in most polls. He finished a strong second to Chrétien in the leadership race of 1990.

Paul Martin with Vietnamese finance minister Ho Te in Hanoi, Vietnam, marking the opening of Hanoi offices of two Canadian companies. *(AP/Wide World Photos)*

Bibliography

Barlow, Maude, and Bruce Campbell. *Straight Through the Heart*. Toronto: HarperCollins, 1995.

Dunn, Christopher J. C. *Canadian Political Debates*. Toronto: McClelland and Stewart, 1995.

Gwyn, Richard. *Nationalism Without Walls: The Unbearable Lightness of Being Canadian*. Toronto: McClelland, 1995.

Steven Lehman

Recession in the 1990's

The Liberal Party was swept into office in 1993 in reaction to a serious recession. In Canada, the downturn of 1990 to 1992 was blamed on the goods and services tax, which had been introduced by the Conservatives, and the North American Free Trade Agreement (NAFTA), which the Conservatives had negotiated with the United States and Mexico. Once in office, the Liberals actually made no changes to these policies because they began to bear fruit. The other major legacy from the recession was the huge federal deficit, which had reached the highest level ever in 1992—some $42 billion. Paul Martin attacked the deficit with imagination and resolve, and he achieved spectacular results.

Four important factors contributed to Martin's success. First, approximately $6 billion was cut from the amount annually transferred to the various provincial and territorial governments. Second, a number of loopholes were closed in the income tax system, significantly increasing the tax base. Third, rules for unemployment insurance eligibility were tightened, and large cuts were made in benefits. Finally, interest rates fell worldwide, reducing the payments necessary to finance the federal debt. The Liberal Party lost a certain amount of support on the left of the political spectrum because of these measures. In particular, unions and groups representing the poor felt deserted. However, polls showed that support for the Liberals, and Martin personally, remained strong.

Tomáš Masaryk

Born: March 7, 1850; near Göding, Moravia, Austrian Empire (now Hodorín, Czech Republic)
Died: September 14, 1937; Lány, Bohemia, Czechoslovakia

First president of Czechoslovakia (1918-1935)

Tomáš Garrigue Masaryk (TOH-mahsh ga-REEG MAH-sah-rihk) was the son of a Slovak father and a Germanized Czech mother who worked on imperial estates in Moravia close to the Slovak border. Originally trained to be a teacher, Masaryk received a doctorate in philosophy from the University of Vienna in 1876. He pursued postdoctoral work at the University of Leipzig, where he met Charlotte Garrigue, an American music student. The couple were married in 1878 in the United States, and he took her maiden name as his middle name. They had four children, Alice, Herbert, Olga, and Jan.

University and Political Life

Beginning in 1879, Masaryk taught philosophy at the University of Vienna until he accepted a teaching post at the newly established Czech University in Prague in 1882. He quickly became a popular professor who influenced not only Czech and Slovak students but also Slavs from other regions of the Austro-Hungarian Empire. He wrote many works dealing with important social issues of the day, including suicide, capitalism, and Marxism. He also helped establish such critical journals as *Athenaeum* and *Čas*, which became outlets for his ideas.

A prolific writer and activist, Masaryk at one time or another alienated various sections of Czech society by championing unpopular causes. In 1886 he withstood a backlash from Czech nationalists when he exposed as forgeries two early medieval Czech poetry manuscripts that supposedly proved Czech literary primacy over German. Between 1899 and 1900, Masaryk resisted powerful strong anti-Semitic forces in the empire when he proved the innocence of a Jew accused of the ritual murder of a Christian. As a member of the Young Czech Party, he was elected to the Austrian Parliament in 1891, resigning in 1893 due to philosophical differences. Also dissatisfied with the Young Czech Party, Masaryk established his own Realist (Progressive) Party in 1901. Reelected as a deputy to Parliament, he worked for federalization of the empire, universal suffrage, and equity of all languages in official life. He defended the rights of Slovaks and South Slavs in Hungary while attacking the empire's alliance with Germany and Austria-Hungary's forays into the Balkans.

The Agram treason trial and the Friedjung trial both took place in 1909; they were attempts to justify the empire's annexation of Bosnia and Herzegovina. Masaryk proved the crown's cases to be based on forged documents. As a result, official circles disliked him, while abroad he earned a solid reputation for fairness and justice.

Tomáš Masaryk *(Library of Congress)*

World War I

In December, 1914, making use of his parliamentary immunity, Masaryk fled Austria-Hungary with his daughter Olga when he learned that he was to be arrested for treason because of his political activity. Two years later he was condemned to death *in absentia* by a governmental tribunal.

Once abroad, he attempted to convince the World War I Allies that the antiquated Habsburg monarchy of Austria-Hungary should not be continued after the war. He argued that the creation of an independent Czechoslovak state from the ruins of the empire was feasible and would be viable. Masaryk took control of the liberation movement abroad in 1916 as president of the Czechoslovak National Council, which served as a propaganda organization and as a quasi government-in-exile. His crusade took him around the world. He eventually triumphed, starting in the summer of 1918, when the Allies recognized the cause of Czech independence. Finally, on October 28, 1918, Czechoslovakia was formally established.

Czechoslovakia's First President

The "father of Czechoslovakia" became its first president upon the formation of the country. He arrived amid great celebrations in Prague to assume his duties in December, 1918, to consolidate the new state. Standing above party politics, he was reelected in 1920, 1927, and 1934. Although the presidency was largely a ceremonial post, Masaryk's great prestige gave it strength. He worked to ensure the success of democracy and attempted to reconcile the various ethnic groups by stressing equality in the multinational state of Czechoslovakia. He continued to be controver-

The Founding of Czechoslovakia

In December, 1914, Tomáš G. Masaryk fled the Austro-Hungarian Empire and began his quest for an independent Czechoslovakia. In 1915, in Paris, he joined with the Czech Edvard Beneš and the Slovak Milan R. Štefánik to form the Czech Action Committee, a propaganda organization to champion their cause in Allied capitals. World War I was then raging in Europe. Calling for the independence of the Czechs and Slovaks in one state, Beneš and Štefánik stayed in Paris while Masaryk moved to London. The committee published several journals to support their cause and maintained communication with people in Austria-Hungary through the Maffia, an underground network based in Prague. In early 1916, the committee transformed itself into the Czechoslovak National Council: The council was a quasi government-in-exile with Masaryk as president, Beneš the secretary-general, and Štefánik representing Slovakia. In May, 1917, Masaryk went to Russia to organize Czech and Slovak prisoners of war into a legion to fight on the side of the Allies. Following the Bolshevik Revolution later that year, he negotiated the legion's transfer to the western front via Siberia. Traveling back to Europe by way of Japan, Masaryk arrived in the United States. There, in May, 1918, he wrote and signed the Pittsburgh Pact, approved by the Slovaks. This agreement promised autonomy for Slovakia within a common state. With this document in hand, Masaryk was able to convince Allied leaders, especially U.S. president Woodrow Wilson, that the Czechs and Slovaks desired their own country. Starting in the summer of 1918, the Allied countries recognized the Czechoslovak National Council as a *de facto* government. Prior to the armistice that ended the war, the Czechoslovak Republic was proclaimed in Prague on October 28, 1918, and in Slovakia two days later.

The University of Leipzig

Founded in 1409 with four faculties (arts, medicine, law, and divinity), the University of Leipzig is among the oldest universities in Europe. The first German scholarly journal was published there in 1682. Prior to World War I, it was the third-ranking German institution of higher learning, known particularly for its music program and medicine. After World War II, it languished under the strict doctrinal control of communist East Germany, being renamed Karl Marx University in 1953. Its original name was restored in 1991, and by the late 1990's it was the second-largest institution of higher education in the German state of Saxony. Among its past students were Johann Wolfgang von Goethe, Robert Schumann, Richard Wagner, Friedrich Nietzsche, Tomáš G. Masaryk, and his wife, Charlotte Garrigue.

sial, however. He alienated many Slovaks by his persistent pursuit of a centralization of power rather than the agreed-upon federal organization and by his insistence on the idea of one Czechoslovak nationality instead of separate Czech and Slovak ones. He also strained his relations with devout Roman Catholics by attending, reportedly as a private citizen, the 510th anniversary of the martyrdom of Jan Hus, the Czech burned as a heretic by Roman Catholic authorities. In the early 1930's, he was one of the first leaders to warn about the dangers of Nazism.

Czechoslovakian president Tomáš Masaryk (center) with members of the Czechoslovak Legion, formed in exile in Russia. *(Library of Congress)*

In his late eighties, Masaryk—frequently known as the Liberator-President or Philosopher-President—resigned from office in December, 1935. First he picked his successor: his friend and protégé Edvard Beneš. Masaryk died at his country house less than two years after his retirement. Following the communist seizure of power in Czechoslovakia in 1948, Masaryk became the subject of official criticism. He was returned to this proper place in history after the fall of communism in 1989.

Bibliography

Masaryk, Tomáš G. *The Making of a State: Memories and Observations, 1914-1918*. New York: Stokes, 1927.

______. *Talks with T. G. Masaryk*. North Haven, Conn.: Catbird Press, 1995.

Selver, Paul. *Masaryk: A Biography*. Westport, Conn.: Greenwood Press, 1975.

Zeman, Zbyněk. *The Masaryks: The Making of Czechoslovakia*. New York: Barnes & Noble, 1976.

Gregory C. Ference

Marcel Massé

Born: June 23, 1940; Montreal, Quebec, Canada

Canadian civil servant and politician

Marcel Massé (mahr-SEHL mah-SAY) spent his childhood and youth in Montreal. He received a bachelor of arts degree from the University of Montreal in 1958 and his LL.B. from McGill University in 1961. He was admitted to the Quebec bar in 1963, but his law practice did not interfere with his continuing education. Massé spent a year in Poland on a World University Service scholarship and received a diploma in international law from the University of Warsaw in 1962. He was a Rhodes Scholar in 1963 and then received a Nufield College Scholarship to study at Oxford University in England, receiving a bachelor of philosophy in economics in 1966. Marcel Massé was married in 1965 and has four children.

Marcel Massé *(Corbis/Bettmann)*

Continuing Travels

In 1967 Massé moved to Washington, D.C., to work for the World Bank. He remained there until 1971. During this period he did a study of international investment, which was published in 1970 by the World Bank under the title *An Evaluation of Investment Appraisal Methods*. It became an important reference for measuring the performance of World Bank initiatives. (It subsequently was retitled *Secondary Effects and Project Appraisal.*) Massé returned to Canada in 1971 to become an economics adviser to the Privy Council Office in Ottawa. He then moved to New Brunswick, where he became deputy minister of finance for the province in 1973. From 1974 to 1977, Massé was chair of the Cabinet Secretariat in New Brunswick.

Moving back to Ottawa in 1979, he worked in the Federal Provincial Office until 1979, then again joined the Privy Council Office. From 1980 to 1982 he served his first tour as president of the Canadian International Development Agency. He was an undersecretary of state for external affairs in Ottawa from 1982 to 1985. Massé represented Canada on the Board of Directors of the International Monetary Fund (IMF) from 1985 to 1989. He then became the president of the Canadian International Development Agency again until 1993.

Electoral Politics

In 1993 Massé ran for Parliament as a Liberal in the Hull-Aylmer riding (district) in Quebec, which is across the river from Ottawa. He was well known in this area because of his distinguished career in the Canadian civil service, and he won the election easily. During Prime Minister Jean Chrétien's first mandate from 1993 to 1996, Massé served in the cabinet as president of the Queen's Privy Council, minister of intergovernmental affairs, and minister responsible for public service renewal.

Massé was reelected in Hull-Aylmer in 1997, and his cabinet responsibilities increased during Chrétien's second mandate. Massé became the minister responsible for infrastructure, in charge of the maintenance of basic transportation and communications in Canada. He also became the president of the Treasury Board, an extremely important position in the Canadian system. As one of the four standing cabinet committees of the Queen's Privy Council, the Treasury Board is considered the employer and general manager of the government of Canada. It sets financial, personnel, and administrative policies: it examines and approves proposed spending plans of government departments: and it reviews the development of approved programs. Basically, the president of the Treasury Board is responsible for translating the policies and programs approved by the federal cabinet into operational reality.

Marcel Massé at House of Commons committee hearings in 1988, at which he responded to questions concerning his campaign spending in 1984. *(Corbis/Bettmann)*

Bibliography

Barlow, Maude, and Bruce Campbell. *Straight Through the Heart*. Toronto: HarperCollins, 1995.

Greenspon, Edward, and Anthony Wilson-Smith. *Double Vision: The Inside Story of the Liberals in Power*. Toronto: Doubleday, 1996.

Van Loon, Richard J., and Michael S. Whittington. *The Canadian Political System*. Toronto: McGraw-Hill Ryerson, 1987.

Steven Lehman

An Evaluation of Investment Appraisal Methods

The International Bank for Reconstruction and Development, known as the World Bank, was founded in July of 1944. It opened for business on June 25, 1946. The goal of the World Bank is to fight world poverty and to improve living conditions by promoting sustainable growth and investing in people. It provides people in developing countries with loans and technical assistance through programs developed in consultation with member countries. In 1970 Marcel Massé published a valuable study of ways to assess the relative effectiveness of the bank's programs. It was first printed under the title *An Evaluation of Investment Appraisal Methods*. Until then, the World Bank had no consistent methods for studying and evaluating its approaches. The study later became known as *Secondary Effects and Project Appraisal*, World Bank staff working paper 58 (SWP58). This contribution is typical of Massé's career as a public servant. He has specialized in dealing with the difficult practical details of administration and government. He developed an extraordinary ability to understand and address the essence of a problem and showed himself to be content to work behind the scenes, out of the limelight.

Vincent Massey

Born: February 20, 1887; Toronto, Ontario, Canada
Died: December 30, 1967; London, England

Canadian statesman, first governor-general of Canada (1952-1959)

Charles Vincent Massey (CHAHRLZ VIHN-sehnt MA-see), older brother to actor Raymond Massey, was born into a family that had a thriving corporate business selling farm implements. After earning his B.A. in Toronto in 1910 and M.A. from Oxford University in 1918, he served a brief stint as history lecturer and dean of residence at Victoria College, University of Toronto. He then joined the army as staff officer in Canada. He ultimately worked for the Privy Council Office in Ottawa. His marriage to Alice Parkin in 1915 produced two sons, Lionel and Hart.

A Diplomatic Role

At Oxford, Massey was a member of two debating societies, and he turned his thoughts to his future role in society. After a brief academic career in Toronto, he served as president of the family business, traveling to Europe—particularly to Russia, which he found gloomy and depressed. He stood for election as a federal Liberal in 1925 but lost. However, he accepted a seat in Prime Minister William Lyon Mackenzie King's cabinet as minister without portfolio. He acted as liaison with various government agencies and preparing propaganda pamphlets describing Canada's war efforts. Massey was appointed Canada's first diplomat to Washington in 1927, when Calvin Coolidge was U.S. president. In this period, Massey also became the first president of the National Liberal Federation, conducting the first summer school devoted to studying political methods and issues.

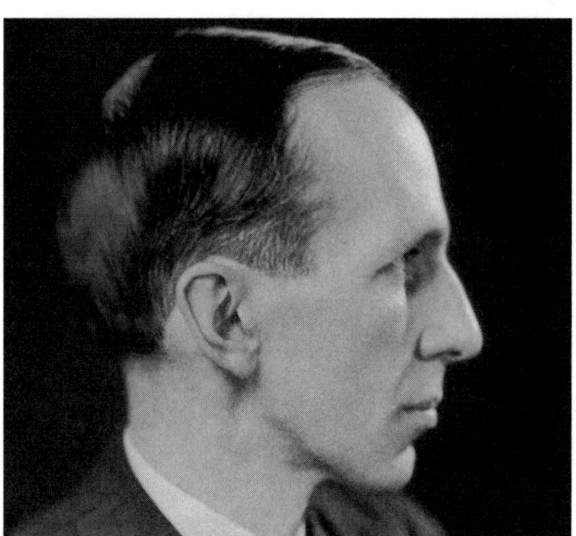

Vincent Massey *(Library of Congress)*

In 1935, during Herbert Hoover's U.S. presidency, Massey was made high commissioner to London. There he became a business and trade agent for his government, a patron of the arts, and a cultural representative who could eliminate English misconceptions of Canada. His staff included future governor-general Georges Vanier and future prime minister Lester B. Pearson. Massey was both an Anglophile and a monarchist, but he and his wife were much beloved by Canadian servicemen in Britain during the eleven years he was high commissioner. Because King did not grant him a platform at international meetings, Massey had little impact on Canadian foreign policy. He supported appeasement in the years before World War II because he believed that any peace settlement was better than war, and he raised controversy by being more sympathetic to English concerns than to Jewish ones.

First Canadian Governor-General

When Massey returned to Canada in 1946, his hope of a cabinet post was dashed by King, so he accepted the chancellorship of the University of

The Massey Commission

In 1949, after William Lyon Mackenzie King appointed him head of the Royal Commission, Vincent Massey quickly recruited fellow commissioners. Each was given a specific area of investigation. Arthur Surveyor was handed television and radio, and Norman A. M. Mackenzie, federal scholarships and research. Hilda Neatby, the Very Reverend Georges Henri-Levesque, and Massey examined major cultural institutions and the proposal for an arts council. Advisory committees of external experts were also established, each chaired by a member of the commission. Massey orchestrated the themes and conclusions. Realizing that a long, drawn-out investigation would lead to public skepticism or indifference, the commission issued its final report in June, 1951. Its chief recommendations were that the Canadian Broadcasting Corporation be entrusted with the development of radio and television, that there be a Canada Council to foster government patronage of the arts, and that there be a clarification and strengthening of the National Film Board and National Archives.

Toronto. He was also made chairman of the Board of Trustees for the National Gallery of Canada (1948-1952). However, his two greatest achievements were his supervision of the Royal Commission on the National Development of the Arts, Letters, and Sciences and his service as the first Canadian governor-general. In this ceremonial role, he insisted on opening Parliament in both official languages, making numerous visits to Quebec, urging English Canadians to learn French, and calling for reforms in school language instruction. He made numerous national tours, especially to the far north, in an effort to unite the country. After he ended his tenure in 1959 at the age of seventy-two, he became the first master of Massey College, Toronto, and published his views on major Canadian issues.

Massey was never a mere mouthpiece for British official opinion or imperialist propaganda, and his service during World War II as high commissioner ensured that Canada had an eloquent spokesman at the very heart of the Allied world. Massey's planning and building of Hart House at the University of Toronto, his patronage of Canadian painters, his chairmanship of the Massey Commission, his founding of Massey College, and his work on behalf of national unity all justified the inscription on his grave: *Patriae proficit* (he was useful to his country).

Canadian governor-general Vincent Massey greeting Indian children in British Columbia in 1956. *(Library of Congress)*

Bibliography

Bissell, Claude. *The Imperial Canadian*. Toronto: University of Toronto Press, 1986.

_______. *The Young Vincent Massey*. Toronto: University of Toronto Press, 1981.

Massey, Vincent. *What's Past Is Prologue: The Memoirs of Vincent Massey*. Toronto: Macmillan, 1963.

Keith Garebian

William Ferguson Massey

Born: March 26, 1856; Limavady, County Londonderry, Ireland
Died: May 10, 1925; Wellington, New Zealand

Prime minister of New Zealand (1912-1925)

William Ferguson Massey (WIHL-yuhm FUR-guh-suhn MA-see) was born into an Irish farming family that immigrated to New Zealand in 1862. Massey, who remained in Ireland to complete his schooling, arrived in New Zealand in 1870. He married Christina Allen Paul in 1882. They had seven children, two of whom died in infancy. Two sons, Walter and William, later served as members of the New Zealand Parliament.

Entry into Politics

A farmer like his father, Massey took an interest in local affairs, serving on the road board and chairing a school committee. In 1891 he became president of the Auckland Agricultural Association. Two years later he narrowly lost his attempt to win the Franklin district seat in Parliament. In 1894 he won the Wiatemata seat, which he held for two years until he won the Franklin seat in 1896. He represented Franklin for the remaining twenty-nine years of his life.

Massey allied with members of Parliament opposed to the policies of the dominant Liberal Party. In 1904 they formed the Political Reform League, later known as the Reform Party, with Massey as their leader. A conservative organization with the support of farmers who demanded the right to title of lands they leased, the Reform Party remained out of power until the Liberal government fell in July, 1912, and Massey became prime minister.

Because the Reform Party lacked a majority in

William Ferguson Massey *(Library of Congress)*

Parliament, Massey had to vie for votes from members of the Liberal or Labour parties, a political reality which limited his actions. Moreover, he encountered difficulties—particularly with labor unions—soon after taking office. Although he received criticism for his handling of militant unions in 1913, the incidents earned him increased popular support. When World War I began in 1914, he made it clear that New Zealand would fight as a member of the British empire. Once again he had the people's backing, but in order to lead the war effort he formed a coalition government in 1915. During the war Massey visited England several times to coordinate the war effort, and in 1919 he attended the peace conference in Paris.

Postwar Years

After the coalition government dissolved in 1919, the Reform Party gained control of Parliament for the only time during Massey's tenure as prime minister. The transition to a peacetime economy created turmoil in New Zealand. Faced with the possible loss of rural support, Massey had to institute export controls on meat and dairy products. Urban voters expressed their disdain to a reduction in the minimum wage by offering support to the Labour Party, and in 1922 the Reform Party lost its majority. His years in office had weakened Massey's health, which began to fail in 1923, although he remained in office until his death.

Often known as Farmer Bill, Massey always adhered to the conservative principles that had brought him to office in 1912. However, he was not opposed to all reform measures; for example, he supported pensions for the blind and a generous loan program that assisted workers in buying homes. Some critics accused him of narrowmindedness and a lack of vision, but Massey offered steady leadership during the wartime era and showed considerable political skill in running a government without a parliamentary majority for most of his time in office.

Bibliography

Barber, Laurie. *New Zealand: A Short History*. Auckland, New Zealand: Century Hutchinson, 1989.

Oliver, W. H., and B. R. Williams, eds. *The Oxford History of New Zealand*. Oxford, England: Clarendon Press, 1981.

Sinclair, Keith. *A History of New Zealand*. London: Oxford University Press, 1961.

Thomas Clarkin

Militant Industrial Unionism

Frustrated by low wages and a government unresponsive to their demands, industrial workers in New Zealand turned to militant tactics in the early years of the twentieth century. They engaged in strikes to achieve reform and higher wages. When he became prime minister in 1912, William Ferguson Massey responded to a contentious miners' strike in Waihi with force. He brought police officers from throughout the country to the town and prosecuted some miners. In 1913 Massey ended a general strike in Wellington with mounted police, many of them recruited from rural areas where the unionists were hated. The police opened the city's port by force. Although Massey's Cossacks, as the police were known, were accused of using unnecessary violence, Massey's actions received the support of many New Zealanders. He also approved legislation that limited the right to picket and to strike. His "law and order" stance ended the period of militant unionism.

Joseph R. McCarthy

Born: November 14, 1908; Grand Chute, near Appleton, Wisconsin
Died: May 2, 1957; Bethesda, Maryland

U.S. senator (1947-1957) and anticommunist crusader

Joseph Raymond McCarthy (JOH-sehf RAY-muhnd ma-KAHR-thee) grew up in the rural Midwest. He was an ambitious young man who studied law and became a circuit judge in 1940, the year before the United States entered World War II. McCarthy served in the army during the war. Leaving the army with the rank of captain, he made a myth out of his wartime exploits as Tailgunner Joe. McCarthy was first elected as a Republican to the U.S. Senate in 1946. A man of great excesses, he was never able to curb his alcoholism, and he died from alcohol-related causes.

Reelection in 1952

Until 1950, Joseph McCarthy had had little to say about communism and the Cold War—the state of tension that had existed between the competing superpowers, the Soviet Union and the United States, since World War II. Other Republicans had garnered attention by suggesting that the U.S. government had been infiltrated by communists and their collaborators (or "fellow travelers"). These infiltrators, they insisted, had encouraged the United States to permit the communist takeover of China and to tolerate the spread of communism throughout the world. McCarthy saw the opportunity to seize the issue of communist subversion, and in February, 1950, he gave a speech in Wheeling, West Virginia, declaring that the U.S. State Department was rife with communists.

McCarthy claimed to have a list of several hundred names. His bold and uncompromising statements attracted considerable press attention and aroused the public. To some, McCarthy was a hero, willing to take on the life-and-death struggle between the United States and the Soviet Union in a forthright way, as no other politician had dared. To others, he was a demagogue who thrived on people's fears and exaggerated the communist threat.

Joseph R. McCarthy *(Library of Congress)*

The Anticommunist Campaign

McCarthy easily won reelection, pursuing publicity by holding hearings that called witnesses to account for their supposed communist activities or connections. McCarthy used insinuation and innuendo, im-

McCarthyism

"McCarthyism" has become a catch-all term to describe a type of unethical, immoral, and dangerous political conduct. McCarthyism means making irresponsible charges against political opponents and making them scapegoats; it includes blaming people, without proof or adequate justification, for programs, policies, or ideas that have failed or have harmed others. McCarthyism employs campaigns filled with insinuation and innuendo, in which a person's integrity is questioned; the person's attackers point out alleged friendships or associations with others who are widely perceived to be unethical, immoral, or untrustworthy, or simply to hold unacceptable opinions. The term is associated not only with communism: It can be applied to any political situation—in the broadest sense of the word "political."

McCarthyism thrives on publicity, on making people aware that they are under some kind of attack. People are led to believe that their way of life is being threatened or that un-American or otherwise unacceptable views are infiltrating schools, governments, or other institutions. Above all, McCarthyism is a form of persecution. The persecutors may believe that they are righteous, or, as in Senator McCarthy's case, they may be capitalizing on people's fears.

plying that he knew much more about his witnesses' supposed disloyal actions than they were willing to admit. Yet he never published his list of communists and communist sympathizers. Moreover, none of his investigations led to convictions of the people he accused of being subversives intent on undermining the U.S. government.

Senator Joseph R. McCarthy (center) with his investigator, Roy Cohn, at U.S. Senate anticommunist hearings. *(Archive Photos)*

McCarthy's charges were disturbing to many Americans. They occurred during the Korean War, when the U.S. was engaged in repelling a North Korean communist invasion of South Korea. To many Americans, it did seem as though their country was under siege by a foreign ideology attempting to dominate the world. President Harry S Truman instituted a loyalty program under which government employees had to swear their allegiance to the country. State Department officials, such as Alger Hiss, had been exposed as communists or sympathizers, and the Soviet Union certainly did have spies in the United States. In other words, McCarthy was responding to a real phenomenon even if he did

The Censure of McCarthy

To be censured, a U.S. senator must have engaged in behavior considered beyond the bounds of civilized conduct and outside the limits of lively and contentious debate, which the Senate prides itself on encouraging. Joseph McCarthy was not censured for his political views, but rather for undermining the foundations of civilized political discourse. For example, he had no evidence of the man's disloyalty, yet he actively campaigned against fellow senator Millard Tydings. He was also censured for showing contempt for the very Senate committee that was investigating his own conduct and financial affairs. In other words, he insulted the Senate itself, undermining its authority. Censure does not mean expulsion from Congress. Rather, it is the strongest form of disapproval that the Senate can express without actually depriving someone of his or her seat. The action of censure is so rare that, in McCarthy's case, it effectively demolished his credibility and influence.

Joseph R. McCarthy pointing to a 1950 map headed "Communist Party Organization U.S.A." during 1954 hearings in Washington. *(AP/Wide World Photos)*

not care to gauge its true level of importance.

By 1950, when McCarthy seized on the anticommunist issue, schoolteachers suspected of disloyalty had been fired from their jobs. The entertainment industry, especially the film industry, kept "blacklists" and refused employment to any actor, director, or writer involved in left-wing or progressive causes associated with the Communist Party. Suspected communists were called as witnesses before congressional committees, such as the House Committee on Un-American Activities. Witnesses were expected to expose friends whom they knew were, or suspected of being, communists or "fellow travelers." Many witnesses refused to cooperate with the House committee or with McCarthy's Senate hearings. Other witnesses did cooperate, either because they feared the loss of their livelihoods or because they genuinely felt duped by communists or ashamed of their participation in supposedly subversive activities. Such witnesses seemed to make McCarthy's charges credible: There seemed to be a hidden conspiracy to weaken America's institutions.

McCarthy finally discredited himself by his utter recklessness. First he viciously campaigned against and helped to defeat Senator Millard Tydings of Maryland, accusing him of being soft on communism. Then he made his greatest mistake: He attacked the U.S. Army, claiming that in its ranks a "fifth column"—a group of spies—was compromising the nation's ability to defend itself from both its internal and external enemies. His charges against the Army were so flimsy that the Army's attorney, Joseph Welch, asked McCarthy in televised hearings, "Have you no shame, Senator? At long last, have you no shame?" The tone of disgust and dismissal in Welch's voice, and McCarthy's inability to respond to Welch's vigorous defense, brought about McCarthy's downfall. It was a complete collapse of his power that had already begun with the editorializing against him by influential television commentators such as Edward R. Murrow. McCarthy lost his committee chairmanship in 1954, when the Democrats retook Congress. With his influence waning and then shattered, he became a symbol of the demagogic politician, dying in disgrace.

Bibliography

Cohen, Daniel. *Joseph McCarthy: The Misuse of Political Power*. Brookfield, Conn.: Millbrook Press, 1996.

Goldston, Robert C. *The American Nightmare: Senator Joseph R. McCarthy and the Politics of Hate*. Indianapolis, Ind.: Bobbs-Merrill, 1973.

Griffith, Robert. *The Politics of Fear: Joseph R. McCarthy and the Senate*. Lexington: University Press of Kentucky, 1970.

Matusow, Allen J., ed. *Joseph R. McCarthy*. Englewood Cliffs, N.J.: Prentice-Hall, 1970.

Sherrow, Victoria. *Joseph McCarthy and the Cold War*. Woodbridge, Conn.: Blackbirch Press, 1998.

Carl Rollyson

William McMahon

Born: February 23, 1908; Sydney, Australia
Died: March 31, 1988; Sydney, Australia

Prime minister of Australia (1971-1972)

William McMahon (WIHL-yuhm mak-MA-uhn) was born a member of a prosperous Sydney family and educated at Sydney Grammar School and the University of Sydney. He practiced law until he signed up for the Australian military in World War II in 1939. In 1949, he entered politics as a Liberal member for the constituency of Lowe, which he was to represent for thirty-three years.

William McMahon *(Library of Congress)*

A Contender for Leadership

During the 1950's and 1960's, the Liberal Party was continuously in office on the national level. McMahon assumed several posts in these governments, including minister of labor, treasurer, and foreign minister. He accumulated experience in an unusual variety of areas that helped qualify him for future leadership. As long as Sir Robert Menzies remained prime minister, however, no politician could seriously contemplate replacing Australia's most prominent politician. When Menzies retired in favor of Harold Holt in 1966, McMahon began to be mentioned as an eventual prime minister. Some observers saw his marriage to Sonia Hopkins in 1965, after decades of being a bachelor, as a politically timed action.

When Holt drowned in 1970, McMahon was a strong candidate to succeed him, but Country Party opposition doomed his effort. McMahon also had other detriments as a political figure. He was generally held to be physically unattractive, and his nickname, Big Ears, added little to an already uncharismatic image. However, McMahon began to appear steady when compared to the often erratic behavior of the man who had beaten him, John Gorton. Gorton backed centralizing policies that seemed socialist in nature to some Liberals, and he failed to control vicious rivalry and infighting among his cabinet. On March 10, 1971, McMahon was elected Liberal Party leader and prime minister. Party elders urged McMahon to present himself as a steady figure above petty politics and personalities, but continued divisiveness within the party doomed this effort.

Belated Cold Warrior

Whereas the rhetoric of anticommunism had served Robert Menzies well in the 1950's, the divisiveness brought on by the ongoing Vietnam War, in which many Australian troops had already served, meant that the Liberal Party could no longer rely automatically upon staunch Cold Warriorism. The crucial blow in this regard came when the United States began a rapprochement with communist China, indicating that Cold War polarities were no longer so firmly in place.

The Election of 1972

For many years, the Labor Party had seemed to be knocking on the door of power in Australia. In 1970, Labor had come close to ousting Prime Minister John Gorton. William McMahon, following Gorton as prime minister, did not succeed in broadening his Liberal Party's electoral base. The global economic boom of the past twenty-five years was finally coming to an end—both inflation and unemployment were on the rise in Australia. In addition, McMahon and his party seemed outdated and out of touch. Labor's new leader, Gough Whitlam, was charismatic and had finally managed to unite the badly divided Labor Party. McMahon could no longer appeal to the same anticommunist sentiment that had aided his Liberal predecessors, as his opponents were now clearly social democratic rather than radical leftist in nature. Though McMahon made a last-ditch effort to inject religion as an issue in his campaign, he and the Liberals went down to defeat on December 10, 1972.

China's growing prominence as a trade partner of Australia seemed to be a good reason for a more realistic diplomatic attitude toward the huge Asian state.

McMahon, though, was politically or psychologically unwilling to take this step. The fact that Gorton, whom McMahon had initially appointed foreign minister in a compromise gesture, resigned in anger increased a sense of uncertainty in the area of foreign policy. McMahon's hesitancy seemed to exemplify an overreliance on the status quo, a perception that also applied to the McMahon government's policies on race and labor relations.

By this time, the Liberal Party had been in power for twenty-three years. Australian voters desired a change, and McMahon was more a symbol than a cause of his party's electoral defeat in December, 1972. McMahon received a knighthood from the queen in 1977. He remained a Liberal member of Parliament until 1982. McMahon's years of energetic and dignified public service to his country were not reflected in his short and troubled tenure as prime minister.

Australian prime minister William McMahon proclaiming victory. *(Camera Press Ltd./Archive Photos)*

Bibliography

Henderson, Gerard. *Menzies' Child: The Liberal Party of Australia*. New York: HarperCollins, 1998.

Mathews, Russell L. *Federal Finance: Australian Fiscal Federalism from Federation to McMahon*. Melbourne: Centre for Strategic Economic Studies, Victoria University, 1997.

Rickard, John. *Australia: A Cultural History*. New York: Longman, 1988.

Ward, Russel. *The History of Australia: The Twentieth Century*. New York: Harper, 1977.

Nicholas Birns

Arthur Meighen

Born: June 16, 1874; near Anderson, Ontario, Canada
Died: August 5, 1960; Toronto, Ontario, Canada

Prime minister of Canada (1920-1921, 1926)

The parents of Arthur Meighen (AHR-thur MEE-ehn) were farmers who lived near Anderson, Ontario. He graduated from the University of Toronto in 1896. He then moved to Manitoba where he studied law. Meighen became a lawyer in 1903. The next year he married Isabel Cox. They had three children. In 1908 he was elected a Conservative member of Parliament in Portage-Neepawa, Manitoba.

Early Political Career

When Arthur Meighen gave his first speech in Parliament in 1908, Liberal prime minister Wilfrid Laurier was so impressed by his eloquence that he predicted a brilliant political career for him. Meighen also impressed Robert Borden, who became the prime minister of Canada in 1911. Meighen's fierce defense of Borden's policies endeared him to Conservatives but permanently alienated large voting groups in Canada. As the minister of the interior, he pushed through Parliament the Wartime Elections Act, which disfranchised Canadians of German and Austrian heritage who had become citizens after 1902. Before the passage of the Military Service Act in 1917, he referred to the people of Quebec as a "backward people" because of their opposition to military conscription. French Canadians and ethnic Canadians never forgave Meighen for questioning their intelligence and patriotism.

In 1919 Wilfrid Laurier died, and the Liberals selected as their leader William Lyon Mackenzie King, whom Meighen had known and disliked since their student days at the University of Toronto. For health reasons, Borden resigned in July 1920. He designated Arthur Meighen as his successor.

Service as Prime Minister

When he became prime minister on July 10, 1920, Arthur Meighen was only forty-six years old and supremely confident. He badly underesti-

The Anglo-Japanese Alliance

As a part of the British Empire, Canada participated in imperial conferences, which were held every few years in London. Until 1921 Canadian prime ministers had basically deferred to the British in matters related to foreign policy. At the 1921 conference, British prime minister David Lloyd George wanted to renew the Anglo-Japanese Alliance of 1901, which had been designed to prevent war between Britain and Japan. Canadian prime minister Arthur Meighen argued that an unintended result of the Anglo-Japanese Alliance was that Britain tolerated Japanese expansion into China. He persuaded Lloyd George and other leaders at the conference that it was essential to include the American government in all efforts to maintain peace with Japan and China. Meighen's actions at this conference represented the first significant Canadian effort to determine its own foreign policy. Meighen understood that it was in Canada's best interest to have good relations with both Britain and the United States.

mated the political skills of King, whom he ridiculed in the House of Commons. The personal enmity between King and Meighen was real and long-lasting. Meighen demonstrated superb diplomatic skills at the 1921 London Imperial Conference by persuading the British prime minister, David Lloyd George, that renewing the Anglo-Japanese Alliance would offend Americans. Nevertheless, he did not impress Canadian voters. He called a general election for December, 1921.

Canada was then experiencing an economic downturn, and Liberal Party leader King blamed Meighen for all of Canada's problems. The Liberals won the election. In the 1925 general election, Meighen's Conservatives won a plurality but not a majority in the House of Commons. King therefore formed a temporary government with support from Progressives, but the Progressives soon withdrew their support. He then asked Lord Byng, the governor-general of Canada, to dissolve Parliament and call new elections. (The Canadian governor-general was appointed by the government of England.) Lord Byng rejected this request and asked Meighen to form a new government. A Canadian law (later changed) required the new prime minister and members of his cabinet to resign their seats and run for reelection before they could assume power. Once Meighen became prime minister, he resigned his seat in Parliament, but his ministers remained in Parliament and became "acting ministers." King responded by arguing that Meighen had usurped power and that Lord Byng had violated the sovereignty of Canada by refusing the prime minister's request to dissolve Parliament. These arguments proved persuasive to enough Progressives for Meighen to lose a vote of confidence. Meighen then lost the general election to King. Meighen served in the Canadian Senate until 1941. After his retirement from politics, he became an investment banker in Toronto. Meighen died in 1960.

Bibliography

Brebner, J. Bartlett. *Canada: A Modern History*. Ann Arbor: University of Michigan Press, 1970.

Hutchison, Bruce. *Macdonald to Pearson: The Prime Ministers of Canada*. Don Mills, Ontario: Longmans Canada, 1967.

Ondaatje, Christopher, and Robert Catherwood. *The Prime Ministers of Canada: 1867-1967*. Toronto: Canyon Press, 1967.

Edmund J. Campion

Arthur Meighen *(Archive Photos)*

Golda Meir

Born: May 3, 1898; Kiev, Ukraine, Russian Empire
Died: December 8, 1978; Jerusalem, Israel

Prime minister of Israel (1969-1974)

When Golda Meir (GOHL-dah MAY-eer) became Israeli ambassador to Russia in 1948, she said she wished that the Russian czar who had ruled during her childhood years could see the Israeli flag flying proudly. When she became Israel's prime minister (1969-1974), she recalled a childhood of suffering that the czar imposed. With her parents—Bluma and Moshe (Morris) Mabovitch (Mabovitz), a skilled carpenter in Kiev—and two sisters, Meir endured the poverty, discrimination, and instability faced by most Russian Jews. Like many others, they moved frequently to escape pogroms—bloody massacres and mass destruction of property that could involve slaughtering or deporting entire Jewish communities.

To escape, the family immigrated to the United States in 1906, moving to Milwaukee, Wisconsin. In 1912 Meir escaped to freedom from parental conflicts by moving to Denver to live with her sister. Reunited with her parents at sixteen, she graduated from high school as class vice president and valedictorian. In 1915 Meir joined the Zionist movement and dedicated herself to the dream of establishing a Jewish homeland. Two years later she married penniless sign painter Morris Myerson; included in their marriage vows was the promise that they would live in Palestine.

Pioneer in Palestine

Having worked for three years to earn enough money, the Myersons finally arrived in Palestine in 1921 to live at the Merhavia kibbutz (Hebrew for "group"). In this agricultural cooperative members contributed labor according to their abilities and received according to their needs, without the exchange of money. The kibbutz had communal housing, dining, education, culture, recreation, health, and child-rearing.

Initially distrusted as a pampered American, the spirited Meir soon became "our Goldie," known for working hard without complaint and admired for her initiative, dedication, and leadership. Meir loved communal living, but Morris hated it. The more important she became to the kibbutz, the more distanced she became from him. After he was hospitalized with malaria and was advised to leave the kibbutz, she chose to go

Golda Meir *(Library of Congress)*

with her husband. She would not admit that the marriage had failed, but fifty years later, she confessed that sacrificing kibbutz life for Morris still upset her.

From Merhavia, they moved to Tel Aviv and then to Jerusalem, where their two children were born: Menachem (Hebrew for "comfort") in 1924 and Sarah in 1926. Meir had returned to Merhavia with her son in 1925 for six months but ultimately chose Morris over her intense pioneering spirit. He had refused to have children on the kibbutz because there children were raised by communal housemothers and lived in separate houses from their parents. Parents could visit only at certain hours.

Israeli prime minister Golda Meir with U.S. president Richard M. Nixon at the White House in 1969. *(Archive Photos)*

A Leader in Training

Because her husband would not give her a divorce, they separated but remained close, because of the children, until his death in 1951. Talented and driven, Meir rose quickly to leadership positions in the Labor Party (the Mapai). She led missions to the United States and Europe for the World Zionist Organization and the Jewish Agency for Palestine. A delegate to the chief branch of Jewish self-government under the British rule of Palestine, she also served on the British

The Pogrom of 1903

Golda Meir always remembered the terror of czarist Russia's pogroms: organized massacres by ruthless Cossack soldiers to persecute Jews. She never forgot the helplessness that she felt one day in Kiev in 1902 as her father hammered boards on doors and windows before a feared pogrom. Although no pogrom occurred that day, Cossacks rampaged in 1903 in Kishinev, killing forty-five Jews and looting and destroying more than a thousand homes and businesses. The Jews of Kiev protested the way the czar was terrorizing them, making them scapegoats for the country's troubles. When they staged a day's fast in the synagogue, five-year-old Meir insisted upon fasting also, despite her parents' objections that she was too young. The havoc wrought by pogroms shaped Meir's loyalty to a Jewish homeland. The frightening sounds of hammering and the ominous hoofbeats of the Cossacks' horses on cobblestone streets haunted her life. Yet the pogroms that tattooed such violence, anger, frustration, poverty, and insecurity onto Meir's childhood also forged her iron will to establish Israel.

War Economic Advisory Council. Zionist leader David Ben-Gurion, having heard her deliver an impassioned speech in 1930, mentored her career. A British white paper (policy statement) in 1939 limited the number of Jewish refugees from Nazi persecution that would be allowed into Palestine. Frustration over this policy led to Meir's work with the Haganah (a militant, anti-British organization) to settle Palestine with illegal immigrants.

Six million Jews (of Europe's eighteen million) were exterminated by the Nazis in concentration camps. When in 1946 the British imprisoned Jewish male leaders in Palestine, Meir headed the Jewish Agency's political department and negotiated with the British to create Israel.

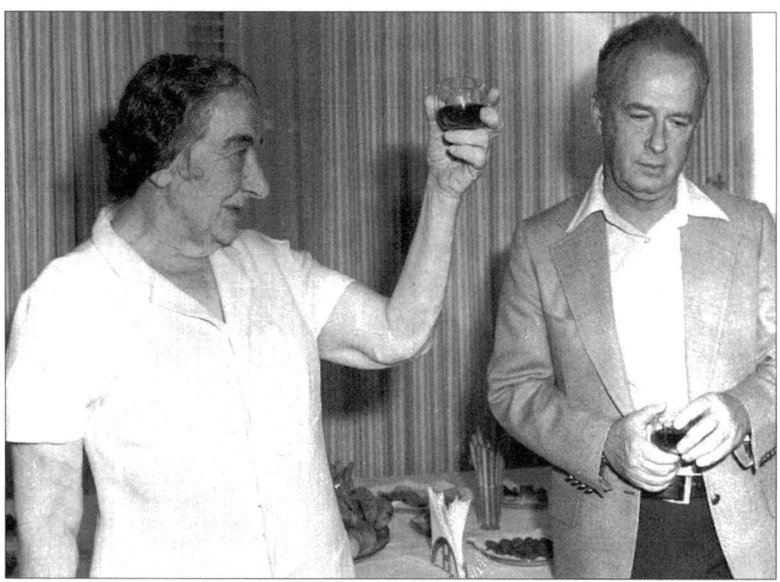

Golda Meir toasts her successor as Israeli prime minister, Yitzhak Rabin, in Jerusalem in 1974. *(AP/Wide World Photos)*

Leader of Israel

Meir signed Israel's declaration of independence on May 14, 1948. Twelve hours later, Egypt bombed Tel Aviv; Lebanon, Syria, Iraq, and Transjordan (Jordan) joined the attack from all sides. The United Nations mandated a truce a month later—a cease-fire that was broken many times in the war-torn years ahead. Meir continued to serve her country—as its first ambassador to the Soviet Union in 1948; as minister of labor, 1949-1956; as minister of foreign affairs, 1956-1966; and as

The National Insurance Institute

National health insurance became a reality in Israel in 1953, marking a historic event in the new nation. From the time Golda Meir joined the Labor Zionists at seventeen, she had envisioned a socialist state that met its people's socioeconomic needs. On January 5, 1952, as Israel's minister of labor, she introduced the first National Insurance Bill to the parliament (the Knesset), calling for comprehensive social insurance that covered benefits for sickness, industrial accidents, other disabilities, unemployment, maternity, widows, orphans, and senior citizens.

In November, 1953, Meir praised the unanimously passed institution of national insurance. Israel, she said, would no longer tolerate the shame of poverty. People could live out their old age in happiness, assured that the country for which they labored many years would now support them. When she turned sixty-six in 1964, Meir applied for benefits under the National Insurance Law. Yet since her country still needed her and would not let her retire, she continued to work in the government every day.

secretary-general of the Labor Party, 1966-1969. In 1956, at Prime Minister Ben-Gurion's request, she changed her name from Meyerson to Meir. In 1969 the seventy-year-old Meir became prime minister. Reelected to office in 1973, she resigned in 1974 amid bitter criticism for allowing the heavy early losses of the Yom Kippur War in October, 1973.

Achievements of the Meir Years

Meir's legacy includes raising money to establish Israel, encouraging large-scale immigration, supporting major construction programs, developing vocational education, and instituting national insurance. She led Israel through conflicts with the ruling British and with warring Arab neighbors. Fearless in negotiating with Arabs, Meir once disguised herself as an Arab to travel secretly to Transjordan, hoping to persuade King Abdullah not to attack Israel. Peace was not to come in her lifetime, however. Arab countries attacked Israel in the Sinai campaign, 1956; the Six-Day War, 1967; the Yom Kippur War, 1973; and a number of other hostilities. Three months after Meir's death, Israel and Egypt signed a peace treaty known as the Camp David accords on March 26, 1979, in Washington, D.C., mediated by President Jimmy Carter.

Bibliography

Agress, Eliyahu. *Golda Meir, Portrait of a Prime Minister*. New York: Sabra Books, 1969.

Hitzeroth, Deborah. *Golda Meir*. New York: Lucent, 1997.

Martin, Ralph G. *Golda Meir: The Romantic Years*. New York: Charles Scribner's Sons, 1988.

Meir, Golda. *A Land of Our Own: An Oral Autobiography*. Edited by Marie Syrkin. New York: G. P. Putnam's Sons, 1973.

Morris, Terry. *Shalom, Golda*. New York: Hawthorn Books, 1971.

Laura M. Zaidman

Carlos Saúl Menem

Born: July 2, 1930; Anillaco, province of La Rioja, Argentina

President of Argentina (took office 1989)

Carlos Saúl Menem (KAHR-lohs sah-EWL MEHN-eh), son of Syrian immigrants to Argentina, completed secondary school in La Rioja and attended the law school at the University of Córdoba in Córdoba, Argentina. Menem graduated in 1955 and returned to his native province, where he became a supporter of President Juan D. Perón. When the military overthrew Perón in September, 1955, and jailed many of his followers, Menem defended these political prisoners.

Carlos Saúl Menem *(Archive Photos/Popperfoto)*

Opposition to Military Regimes

Menem was an active opponent of the military government. In 1956 he was arrested for supporting an unsuccessful coup against the regime. In 1957 he formed the Peronist Youth Party of La Rioja and became legal counselor to the General Labor Confederation (CGT) in La Rioja. After the end of the military dictatorship in 1973 and Perón's return to Argentina, Menem was elected governor of La Rioja Province as the Peronist candidate.

When Perón died in 1974 his widow, Isabel, as vice president, assumed the presidency. In 1976 a military coup ousted the Peronists, and Menem was arrested, spending the next five years in prison. Menem was released from jail in 1981. In 1982, after Argentina's Falkland Islands War with Great Britain, the military regime relinquished power to a civilian government. In 1983 Menem was elected governor of La Rioja Province with 54 percent of the vote. In 1987 he was reelected, this time winning 63 percent.

Menem as President

In 1989, with runaway inflation reaching 5,000 percent in Argentina, Menem defeated the Radical Party candidate to become the first Peronist president since the military coup in 1976. He promptly set in motion two economic programs to benefit Argentina. First, Congress passed the Convertibility Law, which set the Argentine peso at par with the U.S. dollar, effectively ending inflation. Next came Mercosur, a common market of

The Falkland Islands

In 1982 Argentina and Britain fought a war over the Falkland Islands, known in Argentina as the Islas Malvinas. Britain had maintained possession of the islands since 1833, but Argentina claimed sovereignty. During long periods of negotiations, the British government always deferred to the wishes of the island residents, known as Kelpers, who wanted to remain under British control. After losing the Falkland Islands war, Argentina slowly resumed diplomatic and commercial relations with Britain but did not give up its claim to the islands.

Carlos Menem, as president of Argentina, attempted to uphold Argentine claims to the Falkland Islands. His support for the 1993 addition to the Argentine constitution regarding sovereignty angered the British, and no one with an Argentine passport was allowed on the islands except relatives visiting the graves of soldiers killed in the war. Nevertheless, Menem maintained negotiations with Britain, especially regarding oil exploration and fishing rights.

Argentina, Brazil, Uruguay, and Paraguay. Mercosur began in 1995 with the goal of integrating the economies of the four nations and stimulating economic expansion.

Despite his political success, Menem endured tragedies and a number of scandals. In 1995 his son, Carlos Menem, Jr., died in a helicopter crash. Soon after, a woman claimed that Menem's son was the father of her child and demanded the bulk of the young man's estate. There was much speculation as to how Menem's son had amassed a multimillion dollar estate. Also in 1995 Menem himself was named as the father of a fourteen year-old boy. The affair had occurred in 1981 when Menem was a prisoner in northern Argentina.

Argentine president Carlos Saúl Menem (center) in an official procession in 1996 to commemorate the 186th anniversary of the Republic of Argentina. *(Reuters/Zoraida Diaz/Archive Photos)*

Menem's Legacy

Carlos Menem projected a strong and confident leadership style and exhibited a charisma that made him popular. In 1994 he asked that the Argentine constitution be changed to allow him to run for a second consecutive six-year term. The Radical Party strongly opposed the measure, but it was approved. In 1995 Menem was reelected with 50 percent of the vote. Carlos Menem changed the political landscape of Argentina

Carlos Saúl Menem inaugurates the 115th period of Argentina's Legislative Assembly in 1997. *(AP/Wide World Photos)*

during his presidency. He was elected as a Peronist and stabilized the country's economy, even though it created unemployment among laborers, who were the backbone of the party. Although his personal life became the subject of scandal, his political charisma led him to two terms in office. The specter of a military coup and political instability diminished under Menem. Argentina became a successful democracy, and Menem's leadership endowed his country with stability, something Argentina lacked through much of the second half of the twentieth century.

Bibliography

Epstein, Edward C., ed. *The New Argentine Democracy: The Search for a Successful Formula.* Westport, Conn.: Praeger, 1992.

Erro, David G. *Resolving the Argentine Paradox: Politics and Development, 1966-1992.* Boulder, Colo.: Lynne Reinner, 1993.

Skidmore, Thomas E., and Peter H. Smith. *Modern Latin America.* New York: Oxford University Press, 1992.

James A. Baer

Robert Gordon Menzies

Born: December 20, 1894; Jeparit, Victoria, Australia
Died: May 15, 1978; Melbourne, Victoria, Australia

Prime minister of Australia (1939-1941; 1949-1966)

Robert Gordon Menzies (RO-burt GOHR-duhn MEHN-zeez) was raised in a political family. His father was a member of the state parliament, and his mother's brother was a member of the federal House of Representatives. In 1916 Menzies graduated from the law school of the University of Melbourne. After a decade as a successful lawyer and another decade as a politician, Menzies went on to serve his country as prime minister for a record eighteen years.

Menzies's First Term

As a member of the United Australia Party, Menzies became prime minister for the first time in April, 1939. World War II broke out later that year. When Great Britain declared war on Germany, the Menzies-led Australian government followed suit. Consequently, much of Menzies's first term was devoted to war-related issues. The country was ill prepared for war: Military equipment was scarce, and recruitment was extremely slow.

Compounding Menzies's problems was the inability of his government to govern in its own right, having failed to win a majority of seats in the election. In addition, it was unable to form a successful coalition with any of the other parties. Menzies held another election in 1940, but again his party received less than one-third of the seats. This time a tenuous coalition was formed with the Country Party.

During his first term, Menzies spent many months overseas and was widely criticized, even by his own party, for failing to transform his war plans into reality. By August of 1941 his ministers called for his resignation. Eventually he agreed to this, and it appeared that his political career had come to an end.

Second Term

During the eight-year period between his first and second terms as prime minister, Menzies helped create a new political force in Australian politics: the Liberal Party. Campaigning for the 1949 election, Menzies and the new Liberal Party pledged to address two issues of national concern: postwar rationing and the fear of spreading communism. Once installed as the prime minis-

The ANZUS Pact

Robert Gordon Menzies was prime minister when Australia, New Zealand, and the United States signed the ANZUS Pact in September, 1951. According to the treaty, each country agreed to support the others if they were subjected to a military attack. The pact was significant, since it marked the beginning of a close military alliance between Australia and the United States. The omission of Britain as a signatory of the ANZUS Pact reflected a weakening in the connection between the two countries. Although Menzies was intensely loyal to Great Britain, he recognized that Australia would need assistance from the great military power of the United States in the event Australia was ever attacked.

The Liberal Party

In November, 1944, Robert Gordon Menzies led the formation of the new Liberal Party in Australia. Its members included many disenchanted United Australia Party members, as Menzies himself was. Menzies was adamant that the Liberal Party would accept only small financial donations from individuals rather than large amounts from influential organizations and unions. Although the 1946 election was a victory for the Labor Party, the Liberal Party did manage to win two seats.

Postwar rationing and the fear of communism were only two factors that helped defeat the Labor Party in the 1949 election, again returning Menzies to the prime minister's office. In later years, the Liberal and Country Parties would frequently form coalitions to defeat their mutual rivals, the Labor Party. In 1954 the Labor Party split into two groups. One of these, eventually called the Democratic Labor Party (DLP), was devotedly anti-Labor. The DLP consistently supported the Menzies coalition as a means of defeating the Labor Party. When the DLP disintegrated as a political party in the 1970's, the conservative Liberal-Country Party coalition and the Socialist Labor Party continued as the dominating political philosophies in Australia.

Robert Gordon Menzies *(Library of Congress)*

ter for a second time, Menzies soon ended rationing of gasoline, butter, and tea and led the introduction of a bill to dissolve the Communist Party in Australia.

Although the idea of banning the Communist Party was popular, it seemed extreme to many: People accused of being communists could not hold government positions, nor could they have major interests in industries involved in national security. Although the Communist Dissolution Bill passed with Labor Party support, the High Court ruled that it was an infringement of civil liberties and property rights and was therefore inappropriate in peacetime.

In September, 1951, a federal referendum demonstrated that the Australian voters supported the High Court decision, although only by the slimmest of majorities. The fear of communism was kept alive into the 1950's by the Korean War and the widely publicized Petrov affair. Vladimir Petrov was a Russian diplomat who defected. When Russian authorities attempted to take his wife back to the Soviet Union, they were thwarted by the Australian police. The government convinced Mrs. Petrov to defect with her husband. To many, Menzies was viewed as a hero rescuing a helpless woman from evil communists.

Two major international treaties were created during

the Menzies administration: the 1951 treaty between Australia, New Zealand, and the United States (ANZUS) and the 1954 treaty between Australia, New Zealand, the United States, Britain, France, Pakistan, the Philippines and Thailand (SEATO, a Southeast Asian counterpart to NATO, the North Atlantic Treaty Organization). Since Australia possessed only limited military resources, these treaties enhanced the country's confidence at a time when expanding communism was perceived as a real threat in the region.

Accompanying the Korean War was a growing demand for commodities. As a result, inflation levels had reached more than 20 percent by 1952. A three-year freeze on the minimum wage did much to stabilize prices, and the late 1950's saw a greatly improved economy. By late 1960, Menzies had introduced a series of banking and taxation measures to slow the economy down again, but the boom turned into another recession. Later in the 1960's, Menzies was determined to support the United States in the Vietnam War and sent Australian troops to the region. Despite the swings in the country's economy and the controversy over Vietnam, the Menzies-led Liberal-Country Party coalition remained in power until 1966, when Menzies retired at the age of seventy-one.

Menzies the Statesman

Menzies was an eloquent and stirring speaker, and he was frequently praised as a great statesman, particularly by the foreign press. Like U.S. president John F. Kennedy, he was the first political leader of his country to use television extensively as a medium to communicate to the people. Menzies's wit and humor were legendary, and many a political heckler fell victim to his sarcasm. When one of his speeches was interrupted by a vocal coal miner who shouted, "Tell us all you know, Bob, it won't take long!" Menzies quickly replied, "I'll tell you everything we both know—it won't take any longer." Although he is not without his detractors, many regard Menzies as Australia's greatest statesman.

Bibliography

Baker, Richard W., ed. *Australia, New Zealand, and the United States: Internal Change and the Alliance Relations in the ANZUS States.* New York: Praeger, 1991.

Henderson, Gerard. *Menzies' Child: The Liberal Party of Australia, 1944-1994.* St. Leonards, New South Wales, Australia: Allen and Unwin, 1994.

Martin, Allan William. *Robert Menzies: A Life.* Carlton, Australia: Melbourne University Press, 1993.

Robinson, Ray. *The Wit of Sir Robert Menzies.* London: Frewin, 1961.

Weller, Patrick, ed. *Menzies to Keating: The Development of the Australian Prime Ministership.* Carlton, Australia: Melbourne University Press, 1992.

Nicholas C. Thomas

Slobodan Milošević

Born: August 29, 1941; Požarevac, Serbia, Yugoslavia

President of Serbia (1989-1997) and Yugoslavia (took office 1997)

Slobodan Milošević (slo-BO-dahn mih-LO-sheh-vihch), of Montenegrin origin, grew up in the town of Požarevac, about 62 miles (100 kilometers) southeast of Belgrade. His communist schoolteacher parents separated when he was a child. As a youth he was a loner, but he was a diligent student and was active politically. After secondary school he enrolled at the Belgrade University Faculty of Law, graduating in 1964.

Early Influences

The most important influences in the career of young Milošević were his high school sweetheart and later wife, Mirjana Marković, of an influential Communist Party family, and Ivan Stambolić, five years older and son of another illustrious Communist Party family. He assumed the role of mentor to Milošević, paving the way for his rapid rise in the party hierarchy. At eighteen, Milošević joined the League of Communists and became active in political work.

Yugoslavia in the early 1960's was characterized by reforms under the leadership of Josip Tito, who also kept the liberalizing elements, many in Belgrade's Law Faculty, under control. The 1960's also saw the beginning of the ethnic and national issues that were to plague Yugoslavia later. Milošević was not atypical among party members of his generation. His attitude toward career advancement was practical and far from idealistic. He was happy to climb the ladder as his friend Stambolić successively turned over to him leadership positions in business, banking, and politics.

The Practical Politician

Milošević became immersed in politics in the 1980's. He continued to follow the career path of Stambolić, who became Serbian prime minister in the late 1970's. In 1982 Milošević joined the presidency of the Serbian League of Communists, and in 1984 he became president of its City Committee. He faced numerous problems inherited from Tito, including a deepening economic crisis, nationalist conflicts, particularly with Kosovo Albanians, and general political dissatisfaction caused by the purging of the party's liberalizing elements in the 1970's. The 1974 federal constitution, which gave greater powers to the autonomous regions of Kosovo and Vojvodina, contributed to the general malaise, particularly among the Serbs, who formed a plurality of the population.

Kosovo

The Serb leadership discouraged the militant Serb nationalism that was growing stronger, but

Slobodan Milošević *(Reuters/Neal C. Lauron/Archive Photos)*

Ethnic Cleansing

"Ethnic cleansing" is a term for a government policy in which people belonging to an ethnic group the government considers undesirable are expelled from a country or region. It stems from a desire to live only with others who share ethnic origin, language, or religion. It is also frequently born of ethnic hatred and deep prejudice, so a policy of ethnic cleansing easily leads to atrocities such as murder—including mass murder—rape, theft, and wholesale destruction of property. Ethnic cleansing is not new to the Balkans. During the nineteenth century, ethnic atrocities occurred in Bosnia, where Serb, Croat, and Muslim populations shared territory. In the Balkan Wars of 1912-1913 and in both world wars of the twentieth century, much ethnic conflict took place, ranging from relatively peaceful population exchanges to wholesale massacres. The burning of villages, rape, and the driving of minority groups from their homes affected Kosovo Albanians, Serbs, and Croats alike. Yugoslavian leader Josip Tito tried to end ethnic conflict after World War II by establishing a slogan of "unity and brotherhood" to enable the Yugoslavs to coexist.

When Yugoslavia fell apart in 1991, memories of ethnic strife resurfaced under the nationalistic regimes of Serb president Slobodan Milošević and Croat president Franjo Tudjman. Both leaders encouraged ethnic cleansing within their countries, and in Bosnia, in an endeavor to achieve a greater Serbia or a greater Croatia at the expense of minority populations. This callous policy caused great suffering to peoples who had been neighbors, friends, and even married couples for almost half a century.

an eruption of ethnic unrest in Kosovo in 1981 led to increased Serb antagonism. The Serbs believed that the Albanians' continued predominance in Kosovo would ultimately mean that the Serbs would be expelled from the area. Kosovo has historical importance to Serbs as the cradle of their civilization: It was the center of the thirteenth century Serbian Empire and was closely associated with the history of the Serbian Orthodox Church as a center of national awareness. The 1389 Turkish conquest at the Battle of Kosovo subsequently pushed the Serbs northward. Kosovo was then settled by Albanians, many of whom converted to Islam—a fact that did not improve relations between Serbs and Albanians.

Milošević the Nationalist

In 1986 Milošević ran unopposed for president of the Central Committee of the Serbian League of Communists. Shortly after this election, a "memorandum" was put out by the Serbian Academy of Arts and Sciences in Belgrade. It made wide-ranging accusations against various elements in Yugoslavia, alleging a host of anti-Serb activities. The publication elicited much public comment, including condemnation of its contents by the party leadership.

Milošević represented the leadership at a political meeting in Kosovo in April, 1987. During the meeting, Albanian police accosted a crowd of Serbs and Montenegrins. Milošević broke up the confrontation and promised the crowd that they would not have to leave Kosovo. He stated that Yugoslavia could not exist without Kosovo. From this confrontation Milošević realized the power that he could muster by appealing to nationalistic sentiment. In 1989, as president of Serbia, after having ousted his old friend Stambolić, he staged a massive rally in Kosovo for the six-hundredth anniversary of the famous battle. He sought popular support for a pro-Serb policy.

NATO Forces in Bosnia

U.N. peacekeeping forces were first dispatched to former regions of Yugoslavia in 1992, but in general they were not able to enforce cease-fires between Serbs, Croatians, and Bosnians. Even the imposition of U.N. sanctions failed to end the conflict, and at one point U.N. forces were taken hostage. They were released only after intervention by Serb leader Slobodan Milošević.

Following the establishment of the Dayton Peace Accords, signed in Ohio in December, 1995, a North Atlantic Treaty Organization (NATO) Implementation Force of sixty thousand NATO troops was responsible for enforcing their provisions. The task was made difficult because nationalist elements within each region continued to gravitate to their state of primary allegiance. A protracted period of uneasy peace and continued animosity between Serbs, Croats, and Muslims in 1996 and 1997 made the removal of the NATO troops inadvisable. Issues concerning the resettling of refugees caused U.S. president Bill Clinton and NATO to decide on the continued presence of NATO forces.

Civil War

In 1991, because of widening economic and political dissatisfaction, the republics of Slovenia and Croatia expressed their immediate intention of seceding from the Yugoslav federation. The Slovenians did so after only a brief confrontation with the Yugoslav National Army. Plebiscites held in Bosnia and Macedonia resulted in these areas declaring independence as well. In 1992 Yugoslavia re-formed as a federation of only Serbia and Montenegro.

A bitter civil war ensued between the Serbs and the Croats, particularly in areas of Croatia with large Serb populations. Milošević seized control of the Yugoslav National Army and the media. Fighting took place in which hundreds of thousands were killed or made homeless. Numerous attempts were made by the European Community, and later by the North Atlantic Treaty Organization (NATO), to arrange cease-fires and stop the fighting, but to no avail. Between 1992 and 1995 the war spread to Bosnia, where nationalist reprisals and media manipulation were particularly apparent.

Serbian president Slobodan Milošević during a 1995 meeting with U.S. envoy Kofi Annan to discuss the situation in war-torn former Yugoslavia. *(Reuters/Stringer/Archive Photos)*

Both Serbia and Croatia carried out policies of ethnic cleansing of areas of mixed eth-

Hundreds of thousands of refugees fled the Yugoslavian province of Kosovo in the spring of 1999 after NATO air strikes provoked Yugoslavian Serb forces to increase their persecution of Kosovo's ethnic Albanians. *(AP/Wide World Photos)*

nic population in Bosnia, causing untold misery to civilians. Attempts to stop the war seemed fruitless, and Milošević became the target of political demonstrations, even by some fellow Serbs, for his nationalistic excesses, election fraud, and leading his country into devastation. Milošević nevertheless remained popular with huge numbers of Serbs. He served two terms as president of Serbia (from 1989 to 1997). The country's constitution barred him from seeking a third term, but he retained power by having the legislature of Yugoslavia elect him to the Yugoslavian presidency in 1997. The Bosnian war had receded into an uneasy peace in 1995, but soon ethnic violence was increasing in the Serbian province of Kosovo.

Western leaders, including U.S. president Bill Clinton, repeatedly urged, then demanded, that Milošević halt persecution of the ethnic Albanian people (Kosovars) who composed most of the province's population. In 1998 NATO threatened to launch missile and bombing attacks against Yugoslavia if Milošević would not compromise in the Kosovo crisis. In early 1999 NATO launched a sustained campaign of air strikes against the country. Hundreds of thousands of refugees fled from Kosovo to neighboring Macedonia and Albania as the Serbs intensified their anti-Kosovar campaign in response to the bombing. The bombing continued until June, when Milošević suddenly agreed to pull Yugoslavian Serb army forces from Kosovo. NATO forces, soon joined by Russian troops, immediately moved into Kosovo to remove land mines and prepare for the return of the province's ethnic Albanian population. Meanwhile, shortly before the Yugoslavian withdrawal, the United Nations War Crimes Tribunal in The Hague indicted Milošević for war crimes committed in Kosovo. The action set a precedent: Milošević was the first sitting head of state to be indicted for war crimes in modern history.

Bibliography

Djilas, Aleksa. "A Profile of Slobodan Milošević," *Foreign Affairs*, v. 72, no. 3, 1993, p. 81-96.

Judah, Tim. *The Serbs: History, Myth, and the Destruction of Yugoslavia*. New Haven, Conn.: Yale University Press, 1997.

Radan, Peter, and Aleksandar Pavković, eds. *The Serbs and Their Leaders in the Twentieth Century*. Aldershot, England: Ashgate, 1997.

Ramet, Sabrina P. *Nationalism and Federalism in Yugoslavia, 1962-1991*. 2d ed. Bloomington: Indiana University Press, 1992.

Gloria Fulton

William Mitchell

Born: December 29, 1879; Nice, France
Died: February 19, 1936; New York, New York

U.S. Army officer and advocate of airpower

William Lendrum Mitchell (WIHL-yuhm LEHN-druhm MIHT-chehl) was born the son of an influential U.S. senator from Wisconsin. Raised in Milwaukee and educated at Columbian (George Washington) University, he joined the Wisconsin Volunteer Infantry in 1898 and subsequently transferred to the regular U.S. Army. An attentive officer, he became the army's youngest captain in 1903 and served under General John J. Pershing's Mexican expedition in 1912. There Mitchell first witnessed military aviation, and it fired his imagination. Four years later he was posted with the aviation section of the Signal Corps. He earned his flying wings at the age of thirty-six. For the next two decades, airpower became the driving force of his life and legacy.

William Mitchell *(Library of Congress)*

Leading Airman

Though competent as an officer, Mitchell was a self-centered, impolitic, and outspoken individual. His conduct so irritated superiors that in 1917 he was transferred to France as a military observer. This move, viewed as punishment by many, proved fortuitous. When the United States entered World War I in June, 1917, Mitchell was appointed air officer of the American Expeditionary Force (AEF) with a rank of lieutenant colonel. By May, 1918, he had risen to colonel and became the first American airman to fly over enemy lines. In September Mitchell organized and executed a mass aerial offensive involving 850 American and French aircraft against the Saint-Mihiel salient (a bulge in enemy lines). This offensive was executed in concert with ground forces and presaged the close air support so common in World War II. That October, Mitchell became a brigadier general and called for bombing of the German homeland and parachute drops behind enemy lines. When the armistice was signed, he returned home a decorated war veteran. He was totally convinced of the primacy of airpower.

Aerial Avatar

Mitchell's career as an aviation prophet was stormed-tossed and controversial. As assistant chief of the Air Service, he boldly predicted that aircraft had rendered surface vessels—hence navies—obsolete. His bombers underscored this argument by attacking and sinking the captured German battleship *Ostfriesland* off the Virginia Capes in a well-publicized test on July 21, 1921. Navy officials loudly protested, claiming that Mitchell was overstating the case for aviation and that he was out of bounds in denigrating another armed service. Furthermore, when the Navy's

Airpower in the 1920's

The airplane was invented by Americans, but the U.S. government ignored its military potential for many years. Consequently, when World War I erupted, American airmen had to be equipped with French aircraft. The government finally established the U.S. Air Service in 1920, but it was poorly funded, undermanned, and badly equipped. This neglect occurred because the Army still believed that airpower was simply an adjunct to traditional land forces. Men such as Mitchell, Carl Spaatz, Henry Arnold, and Ira Eaker remained convinced of the airplane's potential as a weapon, however, and agitated for greater budgets and research. Charles Lindbergh's 1927 transatlantic flight aroused public interest in aviation, and American airpower finally received greater attention.

dirigible *Shenandoah* was lost with its crew in a storm, Mitchell publicly condemned them for "incompetency, criminal negligence, and almost treasonable administration of the National Defense." The result was a much-publicized court-martial that found Mitchell guilty of insubordination and sentenced him to five years' suspension on half pay. Rather than submit to this humiliation, Mitchell resigned his commission in 1926 and returned to his home in Middleburg, Virginia.

As a civilian, Mitchell continued his personal crusade for airpower. He used his celebrity status to appear before Congress, give speeches, and write numerous books and articles. In them he warned of America's growing vulnerability to air attack, of Germany's rearmament program, and of the inevitability of a Japanese air assault against Pearl Harbor, Hawaii. Mitchell died of a heart attack in New York City in 1936, but events in World War II confirmed the accuracy of his predictions. Another idea for which he had argued, the creation of an independent air force equal to the other armed forces, came to pass in 1947. That July, Congress granted him posthumous promotion to major general and a peacetime Congressional Medal of Honor, a distinction he shares only with Charles Lindbergh. "Billy" Mitchell was the first significant proponent of American airpower.

Bibliography

Burlingame, Roger. *General Billy Mitchell: Champion of Air Defense*. New York: McGraw-Hill, 1952.

Davis, Burke. *The Billy Mitchell Affair*. New York: Random House, 1967.

Hurley, Alfred. *Billy Mitchell: Crusader for Air Power*. New York: Franklin Watts, 1964.

John C. Fredriksen

William Mitchell while stationed in Alaska as a captain in the U.S. Army's Signal Corps. *(Archive Photos)*

François Mitterrand

Born: October 26, 1916; Jarnac, France
Died: January 8, 1996; Paris, France

President of France (1981-1995)

Born into a middle-class Catholic family in western France during World War I, François Mitterrand (frahn-SWAH mee-teh-RO) studied political science and law at the University of Paris. The outbreak of World War II found Mitterrand serving as a soldier. He was captured by the Germans and interned as a prisoner of war. During the Nazi occupation of France, Mitterrand played an active role in the antifascist resistance after his escape from a prisoner-of-war camp. With the liberation of France, he campaigned for and won a seat in the first postwar national assembly of France's Fourth Republic. In 1947, the youthful Mitterrand was appointed minister for veteran affairs, the first of a long series of national offices he would hold during various governments of the Fourth Republic.

From Center to Left

François Mitterrand began his political career as a rather centrist member of the Radical Party. He soon grew more left-wing in his ideas, being one of few noncommunists to oppose General Charles de Gaulle's return to power in 1958 as head of the Fifth Republic. Like most who opposed de Gaulle at that time, Mitterrand was defeated in the 1958 elections. Within five months, however, he had been chosen to be a member of the Senate, France's less-powerful upper chamber. By the 1962 general election, Mitterrand was able to be reelected as a deputy in the National Assembly, where he became an articulate critic of the new regime.

After becoming a Socialist, Mitterrand realized that opposition to de Gaulle required the revitalization of the noncommunist Left. Further, the Socialists had refused to work with the Communists, a situation that resulted in a bitter split within the Left. This divisiveness virtually guaranteed the perpetual rule of France by conservative-dominated governments. He therefore made cooperation among the entire Left a major part of his strategy.

With the president of the Fifth Republic elected by universal suffrage, the Left had to face the logic of Mitterrand's unity arguments. Thus, in the 1965 presidential election, with the prospects for defeating de Gaulle dim, Mitterrand was able to be selected as the joint Left candidate by the Socialists, Communists, and Radicals. Although the campaign was a losing effort, Mitterrand surprised many by receiving 45 percent of the vote against the popular General de Gaulle. Two years later, the Left came within a hair of winning a majority in elections for the National Assembly, losing only because of a lopsided margin for the conservatives in the overseas constituencies.

François Mitterrand *(Archive Photos/Imapress)*

Road to the Presidency

Mitterrand's seemingly straight path to power was forced to take a detour when the traditional Left was surprised by the student-worker revolt of May and June of 1968. These events revealed the weakness of the Socialists, and the ensuing reaction gave de Gaulle a new political lease on life. With the establishment of a new, more dynamic Socialist Party (PS) in 1971, Mitterrand's strategy of union of the Left brought increased membership and greatly increased vote totals. In 1974, he came close to defeating Valéry Giscard d'Estaing for the presidency. Receiving 49.2 percent of the vote in the run-off, Mitterrand was well placed for the future until his alliance with the Communist Party fell apart in September of 1977. In May, 1981, after repairing his alliance with the Communists, a rematch

French premier François Mitterrand (right) with Lech Wałęsa of Poland answering questions from reporters. *(Archive Photos/Imapress)*

The Socialist Party

By the late nineteenth century, four major French socialist organizations were competing for members. Two of these saw themselves as revolutionary, while the others believed primarily in working for reforms within the capitalist system. In 1904, the two most popular factions joined together to form a new socialist party, the Section Francaise de l'Internationale Ouvriere (SFIO). The new organization was led by the pragmatic Jean Jaures until his assassination by a militarist fanatic upon the outbreak of World War I. The SFIO supported France in World War I, although it argued that the conflict was an evil of the capitalist system. Under impact of the war and the Russian Revolution, the SFIO grew in membership and moved leftward until a large number of members split to form the French Communist Party (PCF) in 1920. In 1936, in response to the worldwide depression and the rise of fascism, SFIO leader Léon Blum led a Popular Front Left coalition to power. The following year, this government was removed by the Senate, and the SFIO refused to rally popular support.

With France's defeat in World War II, the Socialists were further weakened, as the PCF's stronger apparatus made it more effective in resistance work. With the liberation of France in 1945 and the new Fourth Republic, the SFIO found itself supported increasingly by the better-paid workers, while their poorer fellows backed the Communists. Unwilling to work with the PCF, the socialists were further weakened by compromising deals with parties to their right. The weakness of the SFIO by the 1960's was clear to many, including François Mitterrand. He devoted himself to the reorganization of the apparatus and a new orientation to a united Left strategy. In June, 1971, a founding congress replaced the old SFIO with a new party, the Socialist Party (PS).

The Defferre Law

Named for Gaston Defferre, the veteran Socialist mayor of Marseilles who was President François Mitterrand's interior minister, this measure moved France toward becoming a more decentralized state. Since before the French Revolution, government had been strongly organized, with power concentrated in Paris. With the Defferre Law, much decision-making power and financial resources were transferred from Paris to twenty-three directly elected regional assemblies. This change is generally considered among the most significant administrative reforms of the Mitterrand presidency. It was partly an attempt to prove that socialism is not inherently encumbered by a strong central state apparatus.

François Mitterrand welcomes Chad president Idriss Deby to the presidential palace in Paris in 1991. *(Reuters/Gareth Watkins/Archive Photos)*

with President Giscard d'Estaing gave Mitterrand an upset victory in the presidential race. The following month, the Socialists won a majority in the parliament.

President Mitterrand

Mitterrand undertook a number of reforms, including the nationalization of several large banks and corporations. He also oversaw the passing of the so-called Defferre Law, which abolished the old centralized prefectoral system and gave more power to local government. In 1986, the opposition won control of the National Assembly, and Jacques Chirac, the Gaullist leader, became prime minister. Mitterrand survived this conservative period and was easily reelected over Chirac in 1988. A month later, the Socialists regained control of the legislature. In 1991, France's first woman prime minister, Edith Cresson, a Socialist, was appointed by Mitterrand. Parliamentary elections in March, 1993, restored the conservative opposition to power, and it was thought that a cancer-stricken Mitterrand would be forced to resign. Once more, however, Mitterrand amazed critics by serving out his term, which ended in 1995. At fourteen years, it was the longest term of any French president to date. He died in Paris in 1996.

Bibliography

Baumann-Reynolds, Sally. *François Mitterrand: The Making of a Socialist Prince in Republican France*. New York: Praeger, 1995.

Cole, Alistair. *François Mitterrand: A Study in Political Leadership*, London: Routledge, 1997.

Friend, Julius Weis. *The Long Presidency: France in the Mitterrand Years, 1981-1995*. Boulder, Colo.: Westview Press, 1998.

Giesbert, Franz-Olivier. *Dying Without God: François Mitterrand's Meditations of Living and Dying*. New York: Arcade, 1998.

Singer, Daniel. *Is Socialism Doomed? The Meaning of Mitterrand*. New York: Oxford University Press, 1988.

William A. Pelz

Mobutu Sese Seko

Born: October 14, 1930; Lisala, Belgian Congo (now Congo)
Died: September 7, 1997; Rabat, Morocco

Dictatorial president of Zaire (1965-1997)

A Cold War icon, Zairian leader Mobutu Sese Seko (moh-BEW-tew say-say SAY-koh) was charismatic, and he was a masterful political manipulator. As head of state he has been described as a "kleptocrat," a reference to his severe mismanagement of Zaire's economy. *The Wall Street Journal* at one point attributed to Mobutu $5 billion personally (in Swiss bank accounts), thirteen foreign residences, and twenty plantations. When Mobutu was born, his country was called the Belgian Congo, and it was a colonial possession of Belgium. It gained independence in June, 1960, becoming the Democratic Republic of the Congo. Mobutu himself renamed the country Zaire after he took power.

Mobutu, who was christened Joseph Désiré Mobutu (zhoh-SEHF day-zee-RAY moh-BEW-tew), entered middle school at eighteen, but he was promptly expelled for theft. In military school, his proficiency at speaking French led him to attain the highest rank in the army of the Belgian Congo. He moved to Belgium while serving with the colonial propaganda agency.

Independence

After the Congo gained independence from Belgium in 1960, leftist prime minister Patrice Lumumba appointed Mobutu defense minister. Crises immediately beset the new country, and in September, 1960, Mobutu took power from Lumumba and president Joseph Kasavubu. Lumumba was assassinated in February, 1961. For the next few years Mobutu wielded power as the head of the country's military, although he let others—including Kasavubu—hold political office as long as they did not get in his way. At this time, in the middle of the Cold War, the United States cultivated any Third World leader who was anticommunist, however corrupt he might be, and Mobutu fit the bill.

Taking Power

Mobutu took over the government completely in 1965, bringing order to the general chaos that had existed since independence. Mobutu's stability was supported by the U.S. Central Intelligence Agency (CIA). Consequently, Zaire was hostage

Mobutu Sese Seko *(Library of Congress)*

Authenticité

In May, 1966, a year after taking power, Mobutu Sese Seko introduced *authenticité,* his attempt to "de-Europeanize" Zaire. All citizens were expected to farm. Mobutu dropped his "Christian" name, Joseph Désiré, in favor of traditional names: Mobutu Sese Seko Kuku Ngbendu Wa Za Banga (which may be loosely translated as "a rooster that leaves no hen intact" or "all-conquering hero"). Citizens were expected to do the same, despite church resistance. Belgian-named cities such as Elisabethville and Leopoldville were renamed—Lubumbashi, Kinshasa. Foreign businesses were taken over by the state. Mobutu began wearing a leopard-skin cap and carrying a scepter. The country was renamed Zaire. European dress was replaced by the *abascos,* a buttoned-up, collarless coat. Women wore *le pagne,* a traditional wrap. Belgian public statues were removed. In 1974 this effort became Mobutuism; the Christmas holiday was eliminated. Mobutu was designated "father of the nation" and "helmsman." By 1976 Mobutuism had been reversed.

Mobutu Sese Seko in 1960, shortly after taking control of the Congo government as head of the nation's military. *(Archive Photos)*

to U.S. support. The United States was also hostage to Zaire, however, relying upon Mobutu as the premier anticommunist African leader as well as relying on certain strategic minerals produced by Zaire.

Belgium had left the Congo with only a dozen university graduates to manage a country of fourteen million. Belgium had also usurped the Congo's resources while transferring Belgium's debt to the colony. In 1958, two years before independence, 1 percent of Congo's population had controlled 95 percent of its assets and earned half its wages. Later, after Mobutu took complete control, he claimed a percentage of all Zairian mineral production—copper, cobalt, diamonds, oil, tin, zinc, and gold.

Mobutu's system of government was highly centralized, autocratic, and elitist. He constructed a personalized oligarchy in which resources of the state were exploited as his own. No institution was free from interference. Tribal chiefs, ignored since independence, were reinstated, but they were rotated to prevent them from developing power bases. Mobutu never evinced a coherent political philosophy. His pronouncements were eclectic and made on the spur of the moment. The populace was excluded from political life; at any rate, poverty left the people little opportunity to think politically. Zairian peasants were not a single social class but a complex group of 250 ethnicities. Mobutu encouraged his subjects to see him as a benign and beneficent patron—a common African role in traditional systems in which chiefs provide guidance and protection and subjects provide loyalty and resources.

Embattled Zairian president Mobutu Sese Seko in 1997 at a press conference on a South African naval vessel. Under the guidance of South African president Nelson Mandela, Mobutu was meeting with rebel leader Laurent Kabila. *(Reuters/Philippe Wojazer/Archive Photos)*

Style of Rule

Mobutu maintained control through his party, Mouvement populaire de la revolution (MPR). Created in 1967 by the Declaration of N'Sele, it lacked ideology. Executives directed both political and party administration. At birth, every Zairian became a member. Mobutu's rule was predicated upon a coterie of family, fellow tribesmen, and an administrative group of fifty, backed by a youth group. During these years, Mobutu was generally held in high repute for Zaire's stability.

Economic progress was not being made, however, so Mobutu introduced "radicali-

Union Minière du Haut-Katanga

This Belgian mining monopoly was created in 1906 to exploit copper, cobalt, tin, zinc, and gold in Shaba Province, transferring immense wealth home to Belgium. In 1925 it began a "stabilized-labor" policy, intended to keep workers on the job for longer periods of time. The company improved conditions and encouraged miners to bring their families with them to live near the mining sites, where towns grew. The policy was quite successful into the 1950's. This paternalistic type of management inhibited employees from developing a unified response to the system imposed by the Belgians. Union Minière du Haut-Katanga later became a subsidiary of Société Générale, partly owned by the Belgian royal family. In the 1960's, anarchy following independence precipitated a decline in efficiency. Nationalization in 1968 drove the Belgians out of the company. The company was renamed Générale des Carrières et des Mines du Zaire and was commonly called Gécamines.

zation." The Catholic Church, which provided two-thirds of the country's primary education, was compelled to surrender control of schools, and Mobutuism became the state religion. Individual actions further diminished effectiveness of the state system: Farmers converted production from export (cotton, peanuts, coffee) to food crops for bartering, returning rural Zaire to subsistence agriculture. Local churches supplanted European churches.

Crises

By 1977 Zaire's external debt was $3.5 billion. *The New York Times* reported, "Politically [Mobutu] is a genius. Economically he is an illiterate." The minimum wage sank to 4 percent of its 1960 level. The economy was faring so poorly that expropriated businesses were returned to their former owners. Infrastructure deteriorated, and telephone service vanished. Financial institutions forced Mobutu to reschedule the country's debt six times. An international team of bankers, finding it impossible to stem endemic pilfering by the elite, resigned. During the 1960's and 1970's, inflation was as high as 47,000 percent. Government deficits rose, and currency became worthless. Most Zairians were undernourished. In the 1980's the rampant spread of acquired immunodeficiency syndrome (AIDS) compounded the misery.

Mobutu experienced problems caused by mutinies, the civil war in Angola, and invasions in Shaba (formerly Katanga Province). Soldiers' loyalty degenerated as they served without pay. Shaba opposition persisted, supported by Belgian mining interests; in 1984 rebellion erupted. Mobutu constructed the Inga-Shaba dam on the Congo River, providing power to Shaba, where copper smelting consumed 75 percent of the country's electric power. The dam's location, however, required a 1,100-mile (1,750-kilometer) American-built transmission line. The system was under Mobutu's control: If Shaba rebelled, he could turn off its power.

Mobutu's Demise

In 1992 dissatisfaction erupted more strongly; Mobutu's control was challenged by the Catholic hierarchy as well as the United States. The Sovereign National Conference convened, and multiparty elections were promised. Opposition leader Etienne Tshisekedi was nominated prime minister after being imprisoned for condemning misrule. An interim assembly was created, and it accused Mobutu of "high treason." However, soldiers attacked Tshisekedi's home and arrested his supporters, and nothing changed.

As Mobutu battled cancer in the 1990's, reports of his death circulated. The constitutional convention meandered toward multipartyism, but Mobutu created multiple parties to fragment opposition. He managed to preserve his position until 1997, when long-time Marxist opponent Laurent Kabila finally triumphed. In the last years before his removal, Mobutu spent his time in his marble retreat, nicknamed "Versailles of the jungle." He fled to Morocco, where he succumbed to cancer within a few months.

Bibliography

Kelly, Sean. *America's Tyrant*. Lanham, Md.: American University Press, 1993.

Shatzberg, Michael G. *Mobutu or Chaos*. Lanham, Md.: American University Press, 1991.

Richard A. Fredland

Mohammad Reza Pahlavi

Born: October 26, 1919; Tehran, Iran
Died: July 27, 1980; Cairo, Egypt

Shah of Iran (1941-1979)

Mohammad Reza Pahlavi (mo-HAH-mahd reh-ZAH PAH-lah-vee) was the oldest son of Reza Shah Pahlavi, the first Iranian ruler in the Pahlavi Dynasty. Mohammad and his two sisters and brother therefore received a royal upbringing. Reza Shah arranged a private palace education for his son and then permitted him to study in Switzerland. Mohammad Reza Pahlavi also graduated at the head of his class from the Iranian Military College. As he was being prepared for kingship, World War II erupted. Britain and the Soviet Union refused to accept Reza Shah's declaration of neutrality and subsequently invaded Iran. Brief skirmishes and resistance followed, but eventually Reza Shah was forced to abdicate the throne in favor of his son. On September 16, 1941, Mohammad Reza Pahlavi became the second shah in the Pahlavi Dynasty.

Mohammad Reza Pahlavi *(Archive Photos)*

Oil and Nationalism

Under the Iranian constitutional system, the shah shared power with the Iranian parliament, or Majles. After World War II, several officials exerted pressure on the shah to eliminate foreign ownership of the Iranian oil fields. Led by Mohammad Mossadegh, various nationalists urged the shah to confiscate Western holdings and evict foreign companies. They maintained that revenues from local oil supplies should be used to support economic modernization. If Western companies continued to dominate the industry, they argued, Iran would remain an underdeveloped and impoverished state. However, because of the growing Western dependency on Arab oil and the threat of Soviet expansion during the Cold War, the United States and its partners refused to abandon their holdings.

In order to stall the momentum of nationalization, the shah appointed Mossadegh prime minister in 1951. This move only intensified the struggle between competing political factions in Iran. Great Britain responded to Mossadegh's threats by freezing all Iranian assets and implementing an international trade embargo that deepened anti-Western sentiment and widened the gap between the two sides. In 1952, the shah and Mossadegh clashed over control of the mili-

Mohammad Reza Pahlavi, in full military dress, with his third wife, Farah Diva Pahlavi. *(Camera Press/Archive Photos)*

tary. Mossadegh resigned in protest but was reinstated following days of rioting and violent demonstrations.

With the country on the verge of civil war, the shah turned to the United States for protection and support. Well aware of the fact that the West viewed him as a potentially valuable ally in a Middle Eastern security system, the shah agreed to participate in a covert operation planned by the U.S. Central Intelligence Agency (CIA) to eliminate Mossadegh's power base. In August, 1953, the shah's forces clashed with Mossadegh's followers. The shah subsequently arrested all opposition, Mossadegh was sentenced to three years' imprisonment for treason, and several key political and military officials were executed.

Following this military coup, the shah acquiesced to foreign oil interests in exchange for the most sophisticated technologically advanced weaponry in the American arsenal. His relationship with the United States, moreover, allowed him to continue to rule Iran through terror and intimidation. While Iranian oil reserves continued to spark postwar Western economic reconstruction in Europe, Japan, and the United States, internal unrest and protests against the shah and his allies continued to grow.

The Baghdad Pact

Some of the shah's political longevity can be attributed to his diplomatic relationship with the United States. After the 1953 CIA-backed coup, the shah agreed to join the Baghdad Pact. This alliance created a collective security agreement between Great Britain, Iraq, Turkey, Iran, and Pakistan. Although the United States did not become a permanent member, it provided diplomatic recognition and military support. After Iraq withdrew in 1958, the pact was renamed the Central Treaty Organization, or CENTO, and the shah emerged as one of its most ardent defenders. His participation in this agreement allowed him to build one of the world's strongest arsenals. While other allies often received outdated and obsolete technology, the shah was able to purchase some of the most advanced weaponry available from the United States. Iran eventually emerged as the linchpin for American security interests in the Middle East, serving as both a barrier to Soviet expansion and ensuring that, even in the face of Arab oil boycotts, the United States could rely on access to Iranian oil.

The White Revolution

In early 1963, the shah attempted to promote himself as a reformer. He introduced a six-point program calling for significant economic changes in Iran. Referred to as the White Revolution, his plan introduced various proposals for land reform, sale of government controlled industries, women's suffrage, nationalization of forests, increased literacy campaigns especially in the rural areas, and salary increases for workers. These reforms, however, did not fundamentally alter the balance of power in Iran or lead to any significant redistribution of land and capital to the working classes. Many tribal and pastoral people, in fact, lost their land as urban landlords became more prominent in the countryside. Foreign manufacturers profited by large-scale Iranian imports of farm equipment, and many of the shah's loyal bureaucrats prospered by pilfering bribes and kickbacks from foreign investors. While mechanized farming was intended to increase food production, it actually enhanced the country's need for agricultural imports. The White Revolution, moreover, did not diminish the control of SAVAK (the shah's internal security force) over internal affairs, nor did it strengthen indigenous political forces.

Life Under the Shah

Despite the advantages of possessing some of the world's richest oil reserves, Iran failed to achieve an economic boom during the shah's regime and remained dependent upon American consumer goods and foreign markets. While the shah built lavish public works projects and frequently displayed his vast military arsenal, the majority of Iranians failed to benefit from his economic modernization schemes. Once he established himself as a royal dictator in 1953, he also utilized all his resources to suppress and eliminate all of his opposition. He created an internal security force, SAVAK, to monitor political activity, and adversaries were often tortured, jailed, or murdered. In fact, SAVAK created such a culture of fear that Iranians became increasingly reluctant to participate in any form of political discussion.

The Fall of the Shah

Economic difficulties and long-standing political repression eventually generated an outbreak of opposition in 1977 and 1978. With the shah

Mohammad Reza Pahlavi (left), the shah of Iran, meeting with U.S. president Franklin D. Roosevelt. *(Library of Congress)*

suffering from cancer, his ability to monitor and eliminate dissent dwindled. Dissidents who had previously been silenced following their association with Mossadegh resurfaced and called for significant reforms. Several lawyers demanded an end to the shah's executive privilege and insisted that he adhere to international law and cease the human rights violations that were rampant in Iran. During a trip to the United States, despite a public show of support from President Jimmy Carter, the shah encountered spirited demonstrators who called for his resignation. Iranian student associations also became increasingly militant. Meanwhile the Iranian religious right, which favored a return to traditional Islamic practices and values—and who associated the shah with the westernization of Iran—obtained growing support throughout the land.

The shah responded by instituting martial law in 1978. Riots followed, and government troops massacred hundreds of protesters. From Paris, Ruhollah Khomeini (Ayatollah Khomeini), the spiritual leader of Iran's thirty-two million Shiite Muslims, called for a general strike and urged his followers to overthrow the government. The shah desperately attempted to discredit Khomeini, but by the end of the year, the majority of Iranians favored a new jihad, or traditional Islamic revolution. On January 16, 1979, the shah left Iran, paving the way for the ayatollah's return. After the shah entered the United States for cancer treatment, a group of Iranian students organized an attack on the American embassy in Tehran in November. They held fifty American hostages until January, 1981. The shah was later forced to leave the United States and succumbed to cancer in Cairo on July 27, 1980.

Bibliography

Keddie, Nikki R. *Roots of Revolution: An Interpretive History of Modern Iran*. New Haven, Conn.: Yale University Press, 1981.

Pahlavi, Mohammad Reza. *Answer to History*. New York: Stein and Day, 1980.

Sick, Gary. *All Fall Down: America's Tragic Encounter with Iran*. New York: Random House, 1985.

Zonis, Marvin. *Majestic Failure: The Fall of the Shah*. Chicago: The University of Chicago Press, 1991.

Robert D. Ubriaco

Vyacheslav Mikhailovich Molotov

Born: March 9, 1890; Kukarka, Russia
Died: November 8, 1986; Moscow, U.S.S.R.

Soviet prime minister (1930-1941) and foreign minister (1939-1949)

Vyacheslav Mikhailovich Molotov (vyih-cheh-SLAHF myih-KI-luh-vyihch MO-lo-tof) was the son of a well-to-do estate steward. While studying in Kazan, Russia, in 1906, Molotov joined the Bolsheviks. Thereafter, the young revolutionary took the pseudonym "Molotov" (Russian for "hammer"), substituting it for his real surname, Scryabin. In 1907 he went to St. Petersburg and, besides enrolling in the St. Petersburg Polytechnical Institute, began an active association with the Bolsheviks' St. Petersburg party committee. After suffering numerous arrests and imprisonment by czarist officials, Molotov cofounded the party's newspaper, *Pravda* ("truth" in Russian) and played a significant role in the Russian Revolution in November, 1917.

Stalin Loyalist

A lifelong staunch supporter of Joseph Stalin, Molotov was appointed to the Communist Party

Soviet foreign minister Vyacheslav Mikhailovich Molotov (right) and Joseph Stalin (center) with German foreign minister Joachim von Ribbentrop at the August, 1939, signing of the German-Soviet Nonaggression Treaty. *(National Archives)*

Secretariat in 1924 and to the ruling Politburo in 1926. As a loyal Stalinist, Molotov energetically supported the purging of Stalin's opponents during the 1920's and early 1930's. He was rewarded for his loyalty to Stalin in December, 1930, becoming the Soviet prime minister (premier). Molotov also played an important role in Stalin's murderous agricultural collectivization campaign in Ukraine and later was intimately involved in the Great Purges of the late 1930's.

Appointed foreign minister in May, 1939, Molotov was instrumental in the signing of the Nazi-Soviet Nonaggression Pact in August of that year. During World War II, Molotov became Stalin's deputy on the powerful State Defense Committee. Hence, during the 1930's and early 1940's, Molotov was probably the second most powerful man in the Soviet Union, after Joseph Stalin. Toward the end of his life, however, Stalin grew to distrust Molotov and even had Molotov's Jewish wife imprisoned in a concentration camp in 1949. It seems likely that Molotov would have been purged as well had it not been for Stalin's death in March, 1953.

Molotov's Power Declines

After Stalin's death, Molotov continued for a time to be an important Soviet leader. Increasingly, however, Molotov was viewed with suspicion by the Soviet Union's new party leader, Nikita Khrushchev, as policy and ideological differences between the two men came to the fore. Along with several other Stalinists, Molotov attempted in June, 1957, to overthrow Khrushchev. Lacking military and regional support, Molotov and his associates failed.

The Nazi-Soviet Nonaggression Pact, 1939

Throughout the 1930's, the Soviet Union (U.S.S.R.) under Joseph Stalin had endeavored to fashion an agreement with Britain and France in order to avert war with Adolf Hitler's Germany. After much diplomatic maneuvering by Stalin's foreign minister, Maksim Litvinov, and prime minister Vyacheslav Molotov, the Soviet leadership decided that efforts to achieve a secure alliance would never succeed. Britain and France allowed Germany to incorporate western Czechoslovakia (the Sudetenland) at the Munich Conference in September, 1938. This event alarmed Stalin and caused the Soviet Union to enter into serious negotiations with Hitler.

These efforts gained renewed vigor after Germany swallowed the remaining portions of Czechoslovakia in 1939 and after the Jewish Maksim Litvinov was replaced as foreign minister by Molotov in May, 1939. By August, 1939, Molotov and his German counterpart, Joachim von Ribbentrop, succeeded in composing a mutual nonaggression pact that satisfied the needs of both parties. For their part, the Soviets wanted to avoid war with Germany because they were ill-prepared for hostilities. For his part, Hitler wanted to avoid a two-front war in Europe. As a result of the signing of the fateful pact by Molotov and Ribbentrop on August 23, 1939, their two countries divided eastern Europe into "spheres of influence"; Germany and the Soviet Union conspired to carve up Poland, among other things. Hitler's invasion of Poland in September signaled the onset of World War II, as Britain and France declared war on Germany two days later. Though the Nazi-Soviet Nonaggression Pact, sometimes called the Molotov-Ribbentrop pact, temporarily achieved peace between Germany and the Soviet Union, it did not allow the Soviet Union to escape Hitler's wrath: Less than two years later, Hitler betrayed his word and launched a military offensive against Stalin's regime.

Khrushchev did not have Molotov eliminated, but he reassigned him to lowly postings—such as ambassador to Mongolia (1957-1960) and Soviet representative to the International Atomic Energy Agency (1960-1961). After criticizing Khrushchev's Party Program in 1962, Molotov was relieved of all his remaining duties and expelled from the Communist Party. Thereafter he lived as a pensioner in Moscow until he died at the age of ninety-six in 1986.

Vyacheslav Mikhailovich Molotov *(Library of Congress)*

Bibliography

Conquest, Robert. *Stalin: Breaker of Nations*. New York: Viking, 1991.

Duranty, Walter. *Stalin & Co.: The Politburo—the Men Who Run Russia*. New York: William Sloane, 1949.

McCauley, Martin. *Stalin and Stalinism*. 2d ed. London: Longman, 1995.

Medvedev, Roy. *All Stalin's Men*. New York: Doubleday, 1984.

Shearer, David R. *Industry, State, and Society in Stalin's Russia, 1926-1934*. Ithaca, N.Y.: Cornell University Press, 1996.

Thomas E. Rotnem

Bernard Law Montgomery

Born: November 17, 1887; London, England
Died: March 24, 1976; near Alton, Hampshire, England

British military leader during World War II

Bernard Law Montgomery (BUR-nurd LAW mont-GUH-meh-ree)—widely known by the nickname Monty—was the fourth child of an Anglican clergyman who later became bishop of Tasmania. His earliest known ancestor, Roger de Montgomery, had fought in the Battle of Hastings in 1066, and his grandfather had distinguished himself in the Indian Mutiny.

An Army Career

Bernard attended Westminster School, London. Though naturally rebellious, he entered the Royal Military College, Sandhurst, in 1907. He joined an infantry regiment stationed on the northwest frontier of India in 1908 and did not return to England until 1913, still a first lieutenant. While involved in front-line fighting in World War I, he became critical of the preparation and conduct of the war. He was appalled by the huge number of casualties and the lack of contact between generals and troops. By the end of the war, he had risen to divisional chief of staff.

Montgomery's war experiences made him determined to become a more professional officer. He went through Camberley Staff College in 1920, where, after a brief spell in Ireland, he was appointed to teach. During this period he met a widow, Betty Carver, and they married in 1927. She died ten years later, leaving him with one son, David. Just before World War II, Montgomery was posted to Palestine. He returned to England to command the Third Division, part of the British Expeditionary Force to France. He again was critical of the British army's lack of preparation as well as its leadership. In the field, he managed to lead his men out of the Dunkirk defeat in 1940.

British field marshal Bernard Law "Monty" Montgomery watching his troops advance in northern Africa in November of 1942. *(National Archives)*

World War II General

After Montgomery served in several postings in southern England, in 1943 Prime Minister Winston Churchill promoted him to command the Eighth Army in North Africa. He was still unknown outside army circles. For the first time he had an opportunity to put his theories of leadership and command into operation. Montgomery was prepared to withstand Churchill's impa-

The British Eighth Army

The British Eighth Army was formed on December 18, 1941, from British and Commonwealth units fighting on the Libyan-Egyptian border against the Axis (German-Italian) army under General Erwin Rommel. Its first commander was Sir Claude Auchinleck.

After initial setbacks, the Eighth Army forced Rommel to retreat westward but was then driven backward to El Alamein, Egypt, in July, 1942. The next month, Montgomery took command. He was able to reequip the Eighth Army and restore its morale quickly. Adapting previous counteroffensive plans, he broke through the Axis lines between October 23 and November 4. The Eighth Army advanced steadily to Tunis, where it joined with the American First Army. Together they expelled all enemy forces from North Africa in May, 1943. Montgomery led the army through Sicily in the summer, then into southern Italy. At the end of 1943, General Oliver Leese took over. The army spent the rest of the war slowly fighting up the eastern flank of Italy until a breakthrough in the last month of the war swept it to Venice and Trieste.

tience, then and later, to prepare fully. The preparations proved effective: Britain badly needed a victory, and Montgomery's victory at El Alamein in Egypt could be seen as a turning point of the war.

After this victory he led the Eighth Army into Italy. Montgomery was then recalled to England to help plan the D day invasion of Normandy, France, under American general Dwight D. Eisenhower. Montgomery, now promoted to field marshall, was put in charge of the landings; he handed overall command back to Eisenhower, however, becoming commander of the British and Canadian forces on the left flank of the Allied advance. The German army eventually surrendered to him in northern Germany. At war's end, Montgomery was appointed to oversee the British occupation zone of a partitioned Germany.

In 1946 Montgomery became Viscount Montgomery of Alamein and was appointed chief of the imperial

Bernard Law Montgomery *(Library of Congress)*

general staff, the highest office in the British army. In this capacity, he toured the world speaking on the need for military cooperation, and he planned the shape of the modern British army. As the Cold War developed, his emphasis on the unity of the West made him a natural appointment to the newly formed North Atlantic Treaty Organization (NATO), as deputy under Eisenhower. Montgomery went into an active retirement in September, 1958.

Achievement

Montgomery was a radical military leader who helped make the British army a modern, efficient fighting force. His populist and humanitarian approach to the common soldier made him popular with his men, though he was often controversial and unpopular with his peers. His views on the need for Western military strength bore fruit in the development of NATO.

Bibliography

Gelb, Norman. *Ike and Monty: Generals at War*. New York: William Morrow, 1994

Hamilton, Nigel. *Monty: The Making of a General, 1887-1942*. London: Hamish Hamilton, 1981.

_______. *Monty: The Master of the Battlefield, 1942-1944*. London: Hamish Hamilton, 1983.

_______. *Monty: The Field Marshall, 1944-1976*. London: Hamish Hamilton, 1986.

Home, Alistair, with David Montgomery. *Monty: The Lonely Leader*. New York: HarperCollins, 1994.

Montgomery, Field Marshall the Viscount. *The Memoirs*. London: Collins, 1958.

David Barratt

Henry Morgenthau, Jr.

Born: May 11, 1891; New York, New York
Died: February 6, 1967; Poughkeepsie, New York

U.S. secretary of the treasury (1934-1945)

Henry Morgenthau, Jr. (HEHN-ree MOHR-gehn-tow JEW-nyur) was U.S. secretary of the treasury under President Franklin D. Roosevelt. He had the formidable task of supervising the spending of $370 billion to finance the New Deal programs devised to bring the United States out of the Great Depression. Morgenthau has been described as one of the hardest working men in President Roosevelt's administration.

Henry Morgenthau, Jr. *(Library of Congress)*

Early Years

Henry Morgenthau, Jr., was born in New York City in 1891. His father, a German-Jewish immigrant, was self-made. A lawyer, he had started with little but had become rich by the time his only son was born. Father and son were constant companions and loved the outdoors. Henry attended the prestigious Phillips Exeter Academy. While the junior Morgenthau was away at school, his father became ambassador to Turkey under President Woodrow Wilson.

In 1913 Henry Jr. began to engage in farming. His farm was only a few miles from Roosevelt's Hyde Park estate north of New York City, and the two men became friends. Morgenthau married Elinor Fatman of New York in 1916. In 1922 he bought a farm journal, the *American Agriculturist*. He ran the publication until 1933, when his duties as chairman of the Farm Board took precedence. As chairman he was responsible for running the Farm Credit Administration, one of the first New Deal programs to provide mortgages and relief for farmers. He made it a point to travel across the country, visiting farming communities to explain in person and in simple language the programs devised to help the United States out of the Great Depression.

Loyalty to the President

Morgenthau was a personal friend of the president, having assisted Roosevelt in his campaigns for the governorship of New York. He also served as state conservation commissioner and as chairman of the agricultural advisory committee while Roosevelt was governor of New York. Roosevelt appointed Morgenthau secretary of the treasury in 1934. Because Morgenthau was conservative in his belief that a balanced budget was necessary for national welfare, he was often torn between his loyalty to a friend and problems with the ambitious financing of domestic recovery programs.

Most observers expected Morgenthau's tenure as secretary of the treasury to be a short-lived position, since Morgenthau's background showed no preparation for the task. His first, somewhat minor changes, occurred within the Department of the Treasury and were accepted with ridicule and discontent. Morgenthau wanted all publicity and press coverage to go through his publicity assistant. He believed that it was important to stop leaks and rumors about Wall Street. He also shaped up his staff, expecting neat and businesslike attire, professional attitudes, and efficiency. Morgenthau expected the whole department to run like clockwork and it did.

During World War II, a memo came to Morgenthau's attention that caused him great distress. A young Treasury Department lawyer had discovered a portion of correspondence regarding the extermination of Jews in Germany. Being Jewish himself, Morgenthau worked overtime piecing clues together. He discovered that the United States had known of Germany's plan for the Jews and had chosen inaction. Morgenthau was horrified. In January, 1944, he presented Roosevelt with a report on the circumstances and pointed out the political repercussions should the facts become known to the general population. President Roosevelt died in April, 1945, not long before the defeat of Germany. Shortly thereafter, Morgenthau resigned, devoting his time to farming and philanthropy.

Bibliography

Berenbaum, Michael. *The World Must Know*. Boston: Little, Brown, 1993.

Block, Maxine, ed. *Current Biography*. New York: H. W. Wilson, 1940.

Blum, John Morton. *From the Morgenthau Diaries: Years of Crisis, 1928-1938*. Boston: Houghton Mifflin, 1959.

Botting, Douglas. *The Aftermath: Europe*. Alexandria, Va.: Time-Life Books, 1983.

Davis, Kenneth S. *Experience of War: The United States and World War II*. New York: Doubleday & Company, Inc., 1965.

Lisa A. Wroble

The Morgenthau Plan

Secretary of the Treasury Henry Morgenthau, Jr., proposed a plan in 1944 for the treatment of Germany once World War II was over. Called the Morgenthau Plan, it called for the "pastoralization" of the German economy. In effect, this meant returning Germany to a preindustrial state by leveling its factories and destroying its mines. Morgenthau, of Jewish descent, argued that this was the only way to prevent Germany from attempting war again. One problem with the plan was that, although it was directed at Germany, it would affect all of Europe, whose economy was in a devastated, fragile state. President Roosevelt at first endorsed the plan, but he later buried its implementation when other advisers argued that it was too harsh. Some of the plan's ideas were incorporated into Joint Chiefs of Staff directive 1067, which called for Germany to be disarmed and de-Nazified. Because of the controversy surrounding the plan, postwar reconstruction of Germany was delayed until 1948. By this time many German civilians had perished from starvation and exposure.

Mohammad Mossadegh

Born: June 16, 1882; Tehran, Persia (now Iran)
Died: March 5, 1967; Tehran, Iran

Prime minister of Iran (1951-1953)

Mohammad Mossadegh (moo-HAH-muhd mo-sah-DAY) was the son of the finance minister for the ruling Qajar Dynasty of Iran. His mother was related to the royal family. Mossadegh (also spelled Mosaddeq and Masaddiq) left Iran in 1902 to study political science and economics in Paris. In 1914, he earned a doctor of laws degree from the University of Lausanne in Switzerland. During his visits back to Iran, he was elected in 1906 to the first Majles (the national assembly) as deputy for Isfahan under the newly granted constitution. By the outbreak of World War I in 1914, Mossadegh was back in Iran, writing law books.

Following the war, Mossadegh was appointed governor of Fars (1919), minister of finance (June-December, 1921), and governor of Azarbayjan (1922). Mossadegh's strict anti-corruption policies antagonized other government officials and local notables. In June, 1923, he was appointed foreign minister. However, the increasingly dictatorial nature of the regime of Reza Shah Pahlavi (original name Reza Khan) caused him to resign. Reza Shah Pahlavi was the newly declared first shah of the Pahlavi Dynasty. Mossadegh rejoined the Majles, where he continued his opposition to foreign concessions, corruption, and constitutional infringements by Reza Shah Pahlavi. Such opposition caused Mossadegh's arrest in 1930 and his exile for the next six years.

At an emotional May 25, 1951, news conference, Iranian prime minister Mohammad Mossadegh announces that Iran will "fight to the end" to achieve nationalization of its oil production. *(AP/Wide World Photos)*

The Anglo-Iranian Oil Company

The Anglo-Iranian Oil Company (AIOC) was formed in 1901 and discovered oil in 1908. By 1913, British interests held 51 percent of the company's shares. Low wages, low royalties, and the company's unwillingness even to show its books to the Iranian government destined British-Iranian relations to be hostile from the start. An Iranian move to revise the agreement with the company in 1927 led to the agreement of 1933; it only slightly improved royalties paid to Iran. Following World War II, the American-Saudi Arabian agreement for a 50-50 split led to increased Iranian pressures for a better deal from the British. A national front developed over the oil issue, catapulting Mohammad Mossadegh to power.

Nationalization was met with British noncooperation, threats, and plots to overthrow Mossadegh. The end result was an explosion of Iranian nationalism. A new oil agreement was reached in the summer of 1954: AIOC (renamed British Petroleum) and U.S. companies would each broker 40 percent of Iranian oil.

Mohammad Mossadegh on trial after his removal as Iranian prime minister in 1953. *(Archive Photos)*

Rise to Power

During World War II, following the Allies' forced replacement of Reza Shah Pahlavi by his son Mohammad Reza Pahlavi, Mossadegh was again permitted to enter politics as deputy from Isfahan. He rapidly became a leading spokesman for nationalism, constitutional reform, and the elimination of corruption. By 1951 Mossadegh had been appointed to head a Majles commission to investigate the oil industry. The committee recommended nationalization (taking over by the government) of the oil industry. The Majles voted to nationalize the industry on March 20, 1951. Amid widespread public celebration, the oil industry was nationalized on the Persian New Year's Day. The sixty-nine-year-old Mossadegh became a hero. One month later, a closed session of the Majles recommended him as prime minister. The shah was undoubtedly horrified, but he had little choice but to accept.

Facing a U.S.-British oil boycott and maneuvers by the British fleet in the Persian Gulf, Mossadegh accepted U.S mediation on the oil issue; however, such efforts proved fruitless. In 1952 he brought the case to the

Mohammad Mossadegh in February, 1953, when he took refuge in an American compound after being driven from his home by angry mobs. *(AP/Wide World Photos)*

World Court at The Hague, which ultimately decided in Iran's favor. Mossadegh also attempted to define the parameters of the shah's powers and to investigate the origins of his personal wealth. In addition, he pledged to institute labor, land, electoral, and judicial reforms. To the U.S. government, his program sounded much like Marxism, and the United States made plans to overthrow Mossadegh.

Mossadegh's Fall

Kermit Roosevelt (the son of Theodore Roosevelt) was sent to Tehran by the Central Intelligence Agency (CIA) to organize a coup in 1953. The U.S. embassy became the center of operations. To frighten Iranian traditionalists, rumors were spread that the shah was leaving Iran. Anti-Mossadegh demonstrations were organized. The shah did in fact flee Iran, after Mossadegh learned of the plan to have the shah replace him with General Fazlollah Zahedi and took preventive actions. However, a military coup launched six days later, as part of a back-up plan, resulted in the storming of Mossadegh's residence and his arrest.

Mossadegh's next three years were spent in solitary confinement, and the remainder of his life was spent under house arrest. With Mossadegh removed, the shah went on to consolidate his power, attempting to establish a dictatorship that would bring modernization to Iran. The United States, which in 1954 obtained a 40 percent interest in Iranian oil for American oil companies, established close relations with the shah's regime.

Bibliography

Diba, Farhad. *Mossadegh: A Political Biography.* London: Croom Helm, 1986.

Katouzian, Homa. *Musaddiq and the Struggle for Power in Iran*. London: I. B. Tauris, 1990.

Zabih, Sepehr. *The Mossadegh Era*. Chicago: Lake View Press, 1982.

Irwin Halfond

Louis Mountbatten

Born: July 25, 1900; Frogmore House, Windsor, England
Died: August 27, 1979; off Mullaghmore, on Donegal Bay, Ireland

British naval commander and viceroy of India

Louis Francis Albert Victor Nicholas Mountbatten (LEW-ihs FRAN-sihs AL-burt VIHK-tur NIH-koh-lahs mownt-BA-tuhn), British military leader and statesman, held close ties to British royalty throughout his lifetime. A great-grandson of Queen Victoria, he was the son of Prince Louis of Battenberg (1854-1921), a name later anglicized to Mountbatten. He was a cousin of both King Edward VIII and King George VI as well as an uncle of Prince Philip, the husband of Queen Elizabeth II. His father served as first sea lord before World War I but resigned his position because his German family background made him a target of intolerance. Louis followed his father's example, entering the British navy as a cadet in 1913 and receiving a commission as ensign in 1916. Early in his career, he determined to rise to the top of his profession.

World War II

A student of military history and tactics, Mountbatten became known for his innovations

British vice admiral Louis Mountbatten (right) in 1943, with British prime minister Winston Churchill between meetings at the Casablanca conference. *(Library of Congress)*

during the interval between World Wars I and II. He was instrumental in establishing and improving radio communications in the British navy. At the outbreak of World War II, he commanded a British destroyer flotilla in the Mediterranean. His ship, the *Kelly*, was sunk by German dive bombers. In 1941 he became captain of the aircraft carrier *Illustrious*. Later appointed chief of British combined operations, he oversaw the invasion of Madagascar and commando attacks on Norway and France. On August 18, 1942, a brigade-strength attack across the English Channel on Dieppe,

Louis Mountbatten *(London Times/Archive Photos)*

The British Legacy in India

After two centuries of colonial rule, the British government decided in principle to grant independence to India following World War II. England was grateful that India had supplied large numbers of fighting forces during both world wars, more than a million in World War II alone. Further, world opinion had turned against colonialism. Decades of strikes and civil disobedience, led by Mahatma Gandhi, had made retention of India too costly. After previous efforts at diplomacy had failed, Lord Louis Mountbatten was appointed viceroy in March, 1947, and was given full authority to make decisions. He set a short deadline for independence, August 15, 1947.

His greatest challenge was resolution of the conflict between the Congress Party, led by Jawaharlal Nehru and Vallabhbhai Patel, and the Muslim League, led by Mohammed Ali Jinnah. Even before Mountbatten's arrival, this conflict had led to widespread rioting and to large-scale killing of Muslims and Hindus. Faced with Jinnah's demand for a separate Pakistan, Mountbatten and the Congress Party reluctantly agreed to partition the country. After boundaries had been charted for the two separate nations, millions of people began to migrate—Muslims living in Hindu areas to Pakistan, Hindus living in Muslim areas to India. A second major problem was the more than five hundred independent principalities that existed within the new nations' boundaries. Mountbatten managed to persuade most of the rulers to join either India or Pakistan. Independence for India meant a legacy of disputed borders, notably in Kashmir, yet Mountbatten managed to persuade both nations to remain in the British Commonwealth. The legacy of the English language, education, civil service, and military tradition has continued strong in both nations.

France, proved a disaster. It taught the Allies that coastal invasions could not succeed without air supremacy.

Appointed supreme Allied commander for Southeast Asia (1943-1946), Mountbatten assumed responsibility for turning back a Japanese threat against India. His territory included hundreds of millions of people and extended from Indochina to India. Taking responsibility for strategy, Mountbatten suggested that his field troops, who had normally retreated when encircled, hold their ground and fight, assuring the commanders of support and resupply from the air. He also decreed that the fighting would continue through the monsoon period, a break with precedent. His undersupplied, multinational forces stopped the Japanese advance and, following battles at Imphal, drove them from Burma (Myanmar) before the war ended.

Postwar India

In March, 1947, Mountbatten became the last English viceroy of India, appointed by Prime Minister Clement Atlee's Labour government to guide the colony to independence. As viceroy, he showed remarkable skill in diplomacy by working out a complicated settlement over a few months. At midnight, August 14, 1947, the agreement left India divided along religious lines into two nations, India and Pakistan. With his mission achieved, Mountbatten was named a British peer as Earl Mountbatten of Burma. Following a year as governor-general of India, a largely ceremonial position, he returned to naval command.

Late Accomplishments

Toward the end of his career, Mountbatten's major appointments included command of the Mediterranean Fleet (1952-1954), first sea lord (1955-1959), and chairman of the Chiefs of Staff Committee (1959-1965). After retiring in 1965, he held largely ceremonial positions, including the lord lieutenancy of the Isle of Wight and the colonel of the Queen's Guards. Mountbatten died after an Irish Republican Army (IRA) terrorist planted a bomb aboard his private boat off Mullaghmore, County Sligo, Ireland.

Louis Mountbatten (center) in Karachi, Pakistan, in August, 1947, the month India and Pakistan were granted independence from England. Second from left is Mohammed Ali Jinnah, governor-general of Pakistan. *(Library of Congress)*

Bibliography

Campbell-Johnson, Alan. *Mission with Mountbatten*. New York: Dutton, 1953.

Hoey, Brian. *Mountbatten: The Private Story*. London: Sedgwick & Jackson, 1994.

Hough, Richard. *Mountbatten*. New York: Random House, 1981.

McGeoch, Ian. *The Princely Sailor: Mountbatten of Burma*. Washington, D.C.: Brassey's, 1996.

Mountbatten, Louis. *Mountbatten*. New York: Viking, 1979.

Ziegler, Philip. *Mountbatten*. New York: Knopf, 1985.

Stanley Archer

Hosni Mubarak

Born: May 4, 1928; Kafr el-Musaliha, Menufiyya Governorate, Egypt

President of Egypt (took office 1981)

Mohammed Hosni Said Mubarak (moo-HAH-muhd HOOS-nee sah-YEED mew-BAH-rahk), a Muslim belonging to Egypt's Sunni sect majority, was born in a village in the Nile Delta. He was one of five children of a minor court officer. Being a good student at Shebin el-Kom, the provincial seat, he gained admission to Cairo's Military Academy in 1947. From there he transferred, in 1949, to the Egyptian Air Academy, graduating in 1952. In 1958, Mubarak married Suzanne Sabet, the daughter of an Egyptian physician and a British nurse. They had two sons.

Military and Political Career

After serving as an air force flight instructor from 1952 to 1959, Mubarak's military ascendancy was rapid. By 1961, he was the commander of the important Cairo West air base. In 1967, he became the director-general of the Egyptian Air Academy, and in 1969, air force chief of staff. In 1972, he was made commander in chief of the air force, having reached the rank of air vice-marshal. As such, he was in charge of the preparations for the air strikes during the October War (the Yom Kippur War) of 1973 with Israel. Despite heavy losses, Egypt's air force performed creditably, and Mubarak was promoted to air marshal. In 1972 Mubarak had also been appointed deputy defense minister, and in April of 1975, Egyptian president Anwar el-Sadat made Mubarak his vice president. In 1978, he became the vice chairman of the ruling National Democratic Party (NDP).

Mubarak was known as a self-effacing, even dour, but efficient technocrat who led an unostentatious life, in marked contrast to Sadat. During their six years working together, Mubarak passively followed his chief's domestic and foreign policy lines. Even after Mubarak became president following Sadat's assassination by Muslim extremists in October, 1981, it was easier to determine what Mubarak was against than what he was for.

On the home front, President Mubarak maintained his predecessor's hard-line policy vis-à-vis opponents, especially beginning in 1992. In that year, extremist wings of the Muslim fundamentalist movement began to stage terrorist attacks against foreign tourists—a major source of Egypt's hard-currency revenues—and the country's Coptic Christian minority. Mubarak simul-

Hosni Mubarak *(AP/Wide World Photos)*

taneously tried to distance himself from some of Sadat's more liberalizing policies, which had led to widespread graft and corruption in his entourage, while juggling the forces still loyal to Sadat, the legal opposition parties, and the outlawed Muslim fundamentalists. In February, 1986, a riotous mutiny by seventeen thousand underpaid and desperate army conscripts threatened his regime.

Foreign Policy

Mubarak supported Sadat's peace initiative regarding Israel, culminating in the two countries' 1979 peace accords. Mubarak also strived to involve other Arab states and the Palestine Liberation Organization (PLO) in the process. After Israel's invasion of Lebanon in 1982 and its reluctance to return occupied territories in the West Bank and the Golan Heights, Mubarak's relations with the Jewish state cooled considerably.

This "cold peace," as some observers labeled the situation, called for some clever balancing maneuvers on Mubarak's part. He was desirous of close cooperation with the United States, Israel's major backer, from which Egypt received a yearly $1 billion in aid as a reward for signing the 1979 peace treaty with Israel. (In addition, Egypt later received from the United States the forgiveness of part of its debt for joining the U.S.-led coalition against Saddam Hussein's Iraq in the 1991 Persian Gulf War.) On the other hand, Mubarak also worked hard to be reinstated into the good graces of other Arab countries following Cairo's "treasonable" unilateral peace with Israel. In April, 1986, he refused the American invitation to join in the punitive air strike being planned against Colonel Muammar al-Qaddafi's Libya for its alleged aiding and abetting of terrorism, even though the Egyptian president had earlier agreed to hold joint U.S.-Egyptian maneuvers in the area. In 1996, Mubarak was again warning the United States against any possible

The Taba Dispute

After completing the return of the Sinai Peninsula to Egypt in 1982, called for by the 1979 peace accords, Israel failed to return Taba, a tiny beach resort on Sinai's east coast. Taba is located 5 miles (8 kilometers) south of the Israeli Red Sea port of Eilat.

The 700-yard (640-meter) beachfront continued to be a bone of contention, particularly because an Israeli entrepreneur had built a popular luxury hotel there during Israel's occupation of the strip following the Six-Day War of 1967. Israel's reluctance to give Taba back to Egypt was also based on the ambiguity or error of a British surveyor who, in 1906, had delineated the border between the Ottoman Empire, then ruling Palestine, and British-controlled Egypt. For its part, Egypt argued that Taba had been returned to it after Israel's first occupation of the Sinai in the 1956-1957 Suez War, and it should therefore be returned again.

The first four years of the Taba dispute in the 1980's led nowhere. In September, 1986, however, Israeli prime minister Shimon Peres agreed to international arbitration of the dispute. The arbitration panel voted mostly in Egypt's favor in September, 1988. Accordingly, on March 15, 1989, after some last-minute hitches involving the resort's continued accessibility to Israeli tourists without a need for visas, the use of Israeli currency, and compensation of $37 million for the hotel, the Egyptian flag was raised. While enhancing Hosni Mubarak's prestige in Egypt and his claim that the 1979 peace treaty with Israel had advanced his country's interests, Israel's return of Taba had little overall effect on long-term Egyptian-Israeli relations.

Egyptian president Hosni Mubarak in 1997 looking at the early phase of construction of a massive irrigation canal project. *(AP/Wide World Photos)*

new military action against Libya. Along the way, the United States had clashed with Egypt because of Cairo's reluctance to renew the Nuclear Nonproliferation Treaty in April, 1995.

A Third Term

During his third six-year presidential term, beginning in 1993 (his was the only name on the ballot, as in 1981 and 1987), Mubarak faced a

Mubarak at the Frunze Military Academy

In 1960-1961, Hosni Mubarak spent a year at the Soviet General Staff Academy. More significant, however, was the 1964-1965 period, during which he received postgraduate jet flight training at the Frunze Military Academy in the Kirgiz Soviet Socialist Republic in Central Asia. There he learned to fly Soviet Ilyushin-28 and Tupolev-16 bombers, squadrons of which he was to command on his return to Egypt. Such training supplemented his initial studies at Egypt's Air Academy, where, first as a student pilot and then as a flight instructor, Mubarak had handled primarily British-made propeller aircraft. During his Soviet visits, Mubarak also learned some Russian. This facility was to serve him well at a time when the Soviet Union was still Egypt's major military supplier and political backer.

Hosni Mubarak waves to cheering crowds during a 1996 speech on Egypt's Labor Day. He criticized recent Israeli attacks on Lebanon. *(Reuters/Aladin Abdel Naby/Archive Photos)*

number of economic and foreign-policy problems. He was the target of a terrorist assassination attempt in Ethiopia in 1995. Religious extremists were able to turn some of Egypt's distress to their own advantage. In his attempts to deal with such problems, Mubarak's repressive actions led to some flagrant fundamental rights violations.

Mubarak's generally pro-American foreign policy was often criticized by Egyptians and other Arab countries as unfruitful. This was especially true following the return of the hardliner Israeli Likud coalition under Benjamin Netanyahu in May, 1996, and its reluctance to relinquish occupied territories to the Palestinians and Syrians. Mubarak also had to contend with being viewed as an uncharismatic leader under the long shadows of his predecessors, Gamal Abdel Nasser and Anwar el-Sadat.

Bibliography

McDermott, Anthony. *Egypt from Nasser to Mubarak: A Flawed Revolution*. New York: Routledge, Chapman and Hall, 1988.

Solecki, John. *Hosni Mubarak*. New York: Chelsea House, 1991.

Springborg, Robert. *Mubarak's Egypt: Fragmentation of the Political Order*. Boulder, Colo.: Westview Press, 1989.

Tripp, Charles, and Roger Owen, eds. *Egypt Under Mubarak*. London: Routledge, 1989.

Peter B. Heller

Robert Mugabe

Born: February 21, 1924; Kutama, Southern Rhodesia (now Zimbabwe)

First prime minister of independent Zimbabwe (1980-1987), then president (took office 1987)

When Robert Gabriel Mugabe (RO-burt GA-brih-ehl mew-GAH-bay) was born, Zimbabwe was a British colony called Southern Rhodesia. A carpenter's son, Mugabe attended Jesuit schools. After teaching for a few years, he earned a bachelor's degree in 1951 at the Fort Hare University in South Africa. He worked in Zambia then Ghana, where he taught at St. Mary's College from 1958 until 1960. While there he met Sally Hayfron, and they married in 1961.

Political Activism Begins

In 1960 Mugabe joined with other activists who sought equality for the black people of Southern Rhodesia. Blacks constituted about 95 percent of the population but had virtually no political or economic power. Mugabe's first position was as the publicity secretary of the National Democratic Party (NDP), led by Joshua Nkomo. The NDP opposed a new Southern Rhodesian constitution proposed by the British in 1961 because it did not grant enough power to blacks.

The NDP was banned by the government of Southern Rhodesia in December. Nkomo, Mugabe, and other leaders immediately formed a new group called the Zimbabwe African People's Union (ZAPU) to carry on the work of the NDP. During the next two years, Mugabe aggressively called for racial equality and was jailed twice. Disappointed with the leadership of Nkomo, Mugabe left ZAPU in July, 1963, to form the Zimbabwe African National Union (ZANU).

Mugabe continued his outspoken criticism of the Southern Rhodesian government, advocating voting rights for all blacks immediately. He was again jailed briefly in late 1963. When Ian Smith, a conservative white, became prime minister in April, 1964, Mugabe denounced him. In August, 1964, Mugabe was imprisoned yet again, and this time he remained in custody for ten years. During that period he earned several degrees from the University of London and instructed his fellow inmates in history and other subjects. Tragically, his four-year-old son died while Mugabe was in prison. The government did not allow him to attend the funeral.

Freedom, War, and Victory

Ian Smith illegally declared Southern Rhodesia's independence from Britain in November of 1965. Smith was intent on maintaining white rule. The United Nations imposed sanctions, but

Robert Mugabe at a press conference in 1979. *(Archive Photos)*

Smith circumvented them with help from South Africa and the Portuguese colony of Mozambique. In 1974 Mozambique gained independence, and Samora Moisès Machel became its first black president. Having lost an important white ally in Mozambique, South African prime minister John Vorster pursued better relations with the region's black leaders. As part of this strategy, Vorster pressured Smith into releasing several of the leaders of ZAPU and ZANU in December, 1974, including Mugabe.

Mugabe immediately began traversing Southern Rhodesia, recruiting people to fight against Smith's regime. Early in 1975 he went to Mozambique to help organize the blacks who were leaving Southern Rhodesia. This Zimbabwe African National Liberation Army (ZANLA) became the largest army battling the security forces of Smith. The fighting escalated throughout 1975 and in 1976 attracted the attention of Henry Kissinger, the U.S. secretary of state.

In South Africa in September, Kissinger convinced Smith to accept the principle of majority rule. A conference to consider the Kissinger plan convened in Geneva in October, 1976. For the conference Mugabe and Nkomo forged a loose alliance known as the Patriotic Front (PF). Discussions between the PF and Smith at Geneva broke down, however, and the war continued. During 1977 and 1978, British and American diplomats continued working for a settlement. Some of the sessions were useful, particularly talks between Mugabe and Andrew Young at Malta. Smith and the PF disagreed completely about who would control the security forces during a transition period, however, so the war continued.

Meanwhile, Smith negotiated a settlement with Abel Muzorewa, a black minister who was not in the liberation war. In May, 1979, Muzorewa was elected the first black prime minister of Southern Rhodesia. Mugabe and Nkomo refused to recognize Muzorewa, judging him a puppet of Smith, and the fighting escalated. U.S. president Jimmy Carter refused to lift sanctions, concluding that Muzorewa's election was not free and fair. Partly because of Carter's decision, and partly because Muzorewa was unable to end the war, the British arranged a conference in London.

The Lancaster House Agreement

On September 10, 1979, a peace conference to negotiate an end to the war in Zimbabwe (which was then still a British colony called Southern Rhodesia) began at the Lancaster House in London. Directed by the British foreign secretary, Peter Carrington, the conference included representatives from all sides in the conflict. The fight was between the government of Southern Rhodesia, led by new prime minister Abel Muzorewa, and two black "liberation armies" that refused to recognize Muzorewa's government. Muzorewa was black, but the liberation forces contended that the constitution reserved too much power for whites.

The larger army was represented by Robert Mugabe, and his stubbornness threatened to undermine the Lancaster conference. Carrington skillfully managed the agenda, however, focusing on one issue at a time. First he got the sides to agree on a constitution that reserved twenty seats for whites. Then he resolved the issue of new elections. Finally he turned to the question of how the cease-fire would be handled, and Mugabe grudgingly approved. On December 21, 1979, all sides signed the Lancaster House Agreement. A cease-fire started one week later, and elections took place in February. Mugabe triumphed and was sworn in as the first prime minister of independent Zimbabwe on April 17, 1980.

Zimbabwe president Robert Mugabe (right) in 1997, speaking as chairman of the Organization for African Unity. At left is the organization's secretary-general, Salim Ahmed Salim. *(Reuters/Howard Burditt/Archive Photos)*

It began in September, 1979, at Lancaster House. Under pressure from Mozambique's Machel, Mugabe joined with Nkomo in signing a settlement in December. The war was over, and elections were scheduled for February.

In January, 1980, Mugabe began campaigning. Election results were announced in early March. Twenty of the one hundred seats in Parliament were reserved for whites. Of the remaining eighty, Mugabe's party won fifty-seven, a stunning majority. On April 17, the country officially became the independent nation of Zimbabwe, and Mugabe was sworn in as prime minister.

Results of Mugabe's Rule

Mugabe initially earned praise with his conciliatory attitude toward whites. He encouraged wealthy whites to stay in Zimbabwe by embracing capitalism in spite of his personal preference for Marxism. He improved education and health care for Zimbabwean blacks. On the other hand, he ousted Nkomo from the government in 1982 and used troops to brutally suppress dissent in 1983. Mugabe's chief contribution to international relations during the 1980's was helping to overthrow apartheid in South Africa.

Mugabe served as prime minister until 1987, and then became president under a revised constitution. He consolidated his rule as Zimbabwe became a virtual one-party state in the early 1990's. The white population steadily decreased as Mugabe considered redistributing land. By the late 1990's, Mugabe's international reputation suffered, partly because of his criticism of homo-

The ZANU Liberation Army

The military arm of Robert Mugabe's Zimbabwe African National Union, the ZANU Liberation Army (ZANLA) was the largest force battling against the white government of the British colony known as Southern Rhodesia. Led by Josiah Tongogara, ZANLA had training bases in Mozambique and began fighting in northeastern Southern Rhodesia in 1972. Supplied mainly by China, ZANLA lacked high-powered weaponry. Yet they enjoyed the support of the people in rural areas, and they pressured the Southern Rhodesian government in Salisbury up to the end of the war in December, 1979. Their votes were then instrumental in the election of Mugabe as the first prime minister of Zimbabwe.

Robert Mugabe addresses the fifty-second session of the U.N. General Assembly in 1997. *(Reuters/Ray Stubblebine/Archive Photos)*

sexuals. He also faced grave circumstances at home, as 25 percent of Zimbabwe's people were suffering from acquired immunodeficiency syndrome (AIDS) by 1998. The AIDS tragedy, combined with his autocratic rule and verbal attacks on gays, cast a shadow over Mugabe in the late 1990's. These developments will be as much a part of his legacy as his long and admirable fight for racial justice as a teacher, activist, and politician.

Bibliography

Martin, David, and Phyllis Johnson. *The Struggle for Zimbabwe*. New York: Monthly Review Press, 1981.

Smith, David, and Colin Simpson. *Mugabe*. London: Sphere Books, 1981.

Worth, Richard. *Robert Mugabe of Zimbabwe*. Englewood Cliffs, N.J.: Julian Messner, 1990.

Andy DeRoche

Muhammad V

Born: August 10, 1909; Fès, Morocco
Died: February 26, 1961; Rabat, Morocco

Sultan (1927-1953) and king (1957-1961) of Morocco

Sidi Muhammad Ben Yusuf (SEE-dih moo-HAH-muhd behn YOO-soof) was the third and youngest son of Moroccan sultan Mulay Yusuf, who reigned from 1912 to 1927. Upon the death of his father he was chosen to be sultan from among his brothers by the Muslim ulema at the urging of the French (who had established their protectorate over Morocco in 1912). The French believed that he would be the easiest for them to manipulate. The comparatively enlightened colonial administration of Resident-General Hubert-Louis Lyautey had been frustrated by less-tolerant colonialists, and the notorious Berber Dahir (Berber Decree) was pronounced in 1930.

Nationalist Hero

Until 1934 Muhammad fulfilled his intended role as a tool of the French authorities. During that year, however, he displayed a suddenly independent spirit: He strongly urged the French to rescind the Berber Dahir and organized an annual festival (Fete du Throne) to mark his accession to the sultanate. Through subtle references encouraging Moroccan nationalist feelings in the speeches he delivered on these occasions, he became a rallying point for all groups who advocated independence.

During World War II Muhammad supported the Allies in defiance of the Vichy authorities (the German-supported government ruling unoccupied France). At the Casablanca Conference in 1943, he secured the support of U.S. president Franklin D. Roosevelt for Moroccan independence. In 1944 the Istiqlal Independence Party was established. It issued a manifesto for self-government under the sultan.

On April 10, 1947, in a speech at Tangier, Muhammad openly supported nationalist aspirations and refused to sign any further laws decreed by the French resident-general. In a coup engineered by the French government, assisted by conservative Moroccan leaders Abd al-Hayy Kittani and T'Hami al-Glavi, Muhammad was deposed in favor of his uncle, Muhammad lbn

The Berber Dahir

When the officials of the French protectorate of Morocco announced the Berber Dahir (Berber Decree) on May 16, 1930, they could not have anticipated the repercussions. The Berber Dahir transformed Moroccan nationalism from an intellectual sentiment of the urban elites to a mass movement rooted in the Islamic faith. The decree was intended to create a wedge between the Berbers and the Arab population in Morocco by placing each ethnic group under separate legal systems. Attempting to remove the Berbers from the strictures of Islamic law, the French took away the sultan's jurisdiction over the Berbers in criminal matters and assumed it for themselves. They also vested minor judicial powers in the hands of Berber village councils. The ensuing nationalist furor centered on both the perceived attack on the Muslim religion and the desire to culturally assimilate the Berbers.

Arafa in 1953. He was exiled to Corsica, and thence to Madagascar.

Widespread resistance, punctuated by acts of terrorism, broke out almost immediately, and by 1955 the Liberation Army had been formed. A bloody attack by the Liberation Army at Oued Zem precipitated the August Conference of Moroccan leaders with French authorities at Aix-les-Bains to arrange for ending the protectorate. In November, 1955, Muhammad returned, his uncle abdicated, and he was restored to power.

Independence and Kingship

On March 2, 1956, the French protectorate over Morocco was ended, and in 1957 the sultan became king under the title Muhammad V (moo-HAH-muhd thuh FIHFTH). On April 7 the Spanish protectorate over Northern Morocco was terminated, and its territories were absorbed into the Moroccan Kingdom. On October 26 the internationalized city of Tangier was also restored to Muhammad's dominions.

During the early years of independence, King Muhammad attempted to steer a middle course between royal authority and limited democracy. Under pressure from the National Union of Popular Forces (UNFP) Party, he set a 1962 deadline for the establishment of constitutional monarchy. In 1958 a rebellion broke out in the northeastern Rif region over living conditions; it was put down by Crown Prince Mulay Hassan. Despite the holding of local government elections in 1960, the crown prince was critical of what he saw as too slow a pace for reform. He was accordingly granted a larger role in governmental decision making by his father. By the end of 1960, Muhammad V had taken for himself the title of prime minister, designating the crown prince as his deputy. On February 26, 1961, the king died suddenly while undergoing a tracheotomy, and the crown prince acceded to the throne as King Hassan II.

Muhammad V *(Corbis/Bettmann-UPI)*

Bibliography

Bernard, Stephane. *The French-Moroccan Conflict: 1943-1956*. New Haven, Conn.: Yale University Press, 1968.

Hoisington, William A. *The Casablanca Connection: French Colonial Policy, 1936-1943*. Chapel Hill: University of North Carolina Press, 1984.

Scham, Alan. *Lyautey in Morocco: Protectorate Administration, 1912-1927*. Berkeley: University of California Press, 1970.

Raymond Pierre Hylton

Robert Muldoon

Born: September 25, 1921; Auckland, New Zealand
Died: August 5, 1992; Auckland, New Zealand

Prime minister of New Zealand (1975-1984)

Robert David Muldoon (RO-burt DAY-vihd muhl-DEWN) grew up near Auckland and started training as an accountant at the age of eighteen. In 1951 he married Thea Dale Flyger, and eventually they had a son and two daughters. Muldoon rose quickly in the accounting profession, becoming president of the New Zealand Institute of Cost Accountants in 1956. In 1960 he chose to enter politics, standing and being elected as a National Party member of Parliament in 1960. In 1967 he joined the cabinet as minister of tourism, later being promoted to minister of finance and deputy prime minister.

Dominant Presence

The National Party was voted out in 1972, and Muldoon became leader of the opposition soon after. His tremendous charisma as a public speaker soon made him a dominant presence in politics, and he became a figure of considerable appeal to New Zealand voters. The National Party won the 1975 election by a landslide, and Muldoon became prime minister. Muldoon's political base, popularly termed "Rob's mob" by supporters and opponents alike, was largely rural and middle-class and responded to his personal vigor and simplicity of manner. Muldoon, unusually for a New Zealand politician, did not attempt to govern by consensus. He was unafraid to take a position that he knew would be opposed by many in the media and in Parliament, confident that his sway over the people at large would eventually prevail.

As soon as he took office as prime minister, Muldoon took the position of minister of finance as well. He reversed most of the previous government's anti-inflation policy. His first priority was to ensure that New Zealand voters had money in their pockets and felt financially secure. To this end, he introduced a national "superannuation" (government pension) plan in 1977. All New Zealanders over age sixty received government support, whatever their own financial means. Even though Muldoon was a conservative, he strongly favored government intervention in the economy, not as much for purposes of redistributing the wealth but to give people a sense of collective well-being. Although he introduced energy conservation measures after the world oil-supply crisis in 1979, he was more devoted to

Robert Muldoon *(Corbis/Reuters)*

The National Party

The National Party of New Zealand emerged in the 1930's to redress the exhaustion of earlier conservative parties. It stood for protecting the rights of the small rural farmer (as opposed to the urban worker favored by the opposition Labor Party), and loyalty to the British crown, which in the time of the Cold War adapted itself to include anticommunism. Through the late 1990's, the National Party had held office for three major stretches, of which Muldoon's tenure was the second. In Muldoon's day, the National Party was socialist in economic terms, giving out large amounts of government aid to most New Zealand citizens, yet traditionalist in its anticommunist foreign policy and its dedication to the conservative values of rural New Zealanders. By the late 1990's, under the leadership of Prime Minister Jenny Shipley, the National Party had become far more free-market in its economic policy and had become more socially liberal in its recognition of Maori land rights (the Maoris are New Zealand's indigenous people) and environmental concerns.

finding new sources of energy, and spent a huge amount of money on a large synthetic fuel plant.

Assertiveness Abroad

New Zealand, traditionally a peace-minded nation, participated aggressively in world politics during Muldoon's tenure. His staunch anticommunism was behind his strong condemnation of the Soviet invasion of Afghanistan in late 1979, and he secured a reputation as one of the most vigilant world leaders with regard to the Soviet threat. Less popular was what seemed his softness on the apartheid government in South Africa. In 1981 he permitted the South African rugby team to tour sports-crazed New Zealand. This decision did not keep him from winning reelection in 1981, but it cost him some international stature. Muldoon's position at home was vulnerable. In 1980 several National Party ministers, desiring a less confrontational and more free-market approach, conspired to oust Muldoon and replace him with his deputy, Brian Talboys. The plot failed when Talboys would not cooperate. Muldoon retained control of the National Party until it was defeated by the Labor Party under David Lange in the election of 1984.

The End of an Era

Muldoon was restless outside politics, working as a radio talk show host and feeling that his vision of New Zealand had been shunted aside. In the judgment of most historians, Muldoon's government represented the end of a distinct period in New Zealand history. Future governments would diverge from New Zealand's previous foreign policy and would turn toward a more free-market economic model. Muldoon's vision of the positive role that government could play in the lives of New Zealanders was thus eclipsed to a large degree.

Bibliography

Muldoon, Robert. *Number 38*. Auckland, New Zealand: Reed Methuen, 1986.

Rice, Geoffrey. *Oxford History of New Zealand*. 2d ed. Auckland: Oxford University Press, 1992.

Sinclair, Keith. *A History of New Zealand*. 4th rev. ed. New York: Penguin Books, 1991.

Templeton, Hugh. *All Honourable Men: Inside the Muldoon Cabinet, 1975-1984*. Auckland, New Zealand: Auckland University Press, 1995.

Nicholas Birns

Brian Mulroney

Born: March 20, 1939; Baie-Comeau, Quebec

Prime minister of Canada (1984-1993)

Martin Brian Mulroney (MAHR-tihn BRI-uhn muhl-ROH-nee) was the son of the chief electrician for the paper mill that was opened in Baie-Comeau, Quebec, in 1938. Brian was the third of six children in the family. Growing up in this small, isolated community on the north shore of the St. Lawrence River, he took an active interest in sports and music. He went to Antigonish, Nova Scotia, after finishing secondary school and obtained a B.A. degree from St. Francis Xavier University in 1959. His law degree came from Laval University in Quebec City in 1964. As a student during these years Brian Mulroney became active in the Progressive Conservative Party of Canada through campus clubs. He even managed to cultivate a personal relationship with the thirteenth prime minister of Canada, John Diefenbaker. Mulroney married Mila Pivnicki in 1973, and they have had three children together.

Brian Mulroney *(AP/Wide World Photos)*

Early Career

In 1964 Mulroney began working with the law firm of Ogilvy, Renault in Montreal. Soon after Mulroney was called to the Quebec bar in 1965, his father died. His mother and his youngest brother and sister moved to Montreal, where he took over responsibility for their support and education. Mulroney felt the financial pressure keenly.

A strike broke out at the Canadian British Aluminum plant in Baie-Comeau in the spring of 1967, and Mulroney was crucial in working out a settlement. His career as a labor negotiator, usually but not always representing management, was launched. Mulroney soon became involved in resolving disputes at the Montreal waterfront that had been escalating all through the 1960's. He was also important in resolving a violent dispute at *La Presse* newspaper in 1972. His efforts won him the future support of Quebec industrialist Paul Desmarais. Finally, Mulroney sat on the Cliche Commission, whose daily hearings into corruption in the Quebec construction industry throughout 1974 and 1975 were televised. This media exposure made him a prominent public figure. Throughout this period he continued active participation in the Conservative Party, but a bid for the national leadership failed in 1976. Afterwards, he accepted an offer to become a vice president of Iron Ore Company of Canada. He later served as president of that company before returning to full-time political involve-

The Meech Lake Accord

Two First Minister's Conferences were held in Meech Lake, Quebec, in 1987. The second resulted in a conditional agreement designed to clearly integrate Quebec within the Canadian Confederation. The accord contained five main provisions. First, Quebec would be recognized as a distinct society. Second, three judges of the Canadian Supreme Court would be chosen from nominees supplied by Quebec. Third, Quebec would have a veto on constitutional changes. Fourth, provinces would have the right to opt out of certain new federal programs. Fifth, certain immigration powers in the future would be shared. A deadline of June 22, 1990, was established for provincial parliaments to ratify the Meech Lake Accord. It was accepted by seven provinces within a year, but the process then stalled. In the end neither Newfoundland nor Manitoba signed the accord, and it never went into effect. The discussions leading to the Meech Lake Accord were perceived to have been conducted too personally and in secret—a holdover from the style Mulroney had developed as a labor lawyer. In addition, many Canadians believed that other problems in the country as a whole—not just those of Quebec—needed to be addressed.

The Mulroney government went back to work on another deal with the ten provincial premiers, the two heads of territorial government, and four aboriginal chiefs. The Charlottetown Agreement resulted: It provided for a reformed Senate, changes in the division of legislative powers, a form of self-government for aboriginal peoples, and the recognition of Quebec as a distinct society. It was defeated in a national referendum on October 26, 1992.

Canadian prime minister Brian Mulroney (right) shakes hands with U.S. president Ronald Reagan at a 1988 economic summit in Toronto. British prime minister Margaret Thatcher looks on. *(AP/Wide World Photos)*

ment in 1983. This time his bid for leadership of the Conservatives was successful.

Prime Minister of Canada

The retirement of Pierre Elliott Trudeau in 1984 set the stage for a major shift in Canadian politics. After sixteen years of Liberal Party rule, interrupted for only a few months by the Conservative government of Joe Clarke, Canada was ready for something new. Quebec led a national landslide in 1984 for its native son, Brian Mulroney, defeating John Turner, who had succeeded Trudeau as Liberal leader. Mulroney became the new prime minister.

At least since the 1960's, domestic politics in Canada had been dominated by the issue of national unity. The country had been founded largely as an informal alliance between the British Empire and the Roman Catholic Church to limit U.S. expansion north. Both of those major world powers were losing influence after World War II, and Canada was going through a process of redefinition. The national unity initiatives of the Trudeau government had ended in ambivalence and confusion. Quebec had refused to sign the Constitution Act of 1982 which "repatriated" amending power—that is, it made changes to the Canadian Constitution possible without the participation of the British crown. Attempts by the Mulroney government to address the growing alienation of Quebec were unsuccessful. Both the Meech Lake Accord and the Charlottetown Agreement were ultimately defeated.

On the economic front, however, things appeared to go better. At least the Mulroney government was able to get its economic program enacted. A 7 percent goods and services tax (GST) was introduced in

Brian Mulroney (right) meeting in 1990 with Cyprus president George Vassiliou. *(Reuters/Gilles Landry/Archive Photos)*

The North American Free Trade Agreement (NAFTA)

The Canadian government had considered free trade with the United States before the Mulroney government. It was considered under Sir Wilfrid Laurier, for example, who lost an election on the issue in 1911. Prime Minister William Lyon Mackenzie King flirted with the idea during the Great Depression but finally shelved it after World War I. NAFTA was signed on December 17, 1992, by Prime Minister Brian Mulroney of Canada, President Carlos Salinas of Mexico, and President George Bush of the United States. It went into effect in 1994. NAFTA governs trade in agricultural products, automobiles, energy, textiles, investment, financial services, transportation, intellectual property, and government procurement, and has provisions for dispute resolution. Many of its terms are only gradually being put into effect, and it contains many exceptions to free-trade policies. Therefore, the name of the agreement notwithstanding, NAFTA really represents "freer" trade rather than free trade, as well as an improved mechanism for dealing with trade disputes quickly and efficiently.

1990 to replace the 11 percent manufacturer's tax. Unfortunately, the high visibility of the GST made it extremely unpopular and proved to be a political disaster for the Conservative Party. Likewise, a five-year phase-in period began in 1989 for the Free Trade Agreement with the United States. This agreement was later expanded to include Mexico in the North American Free Trade Agreement (NAFTA).

Reversal of Fortune

In 1993 Mulroney resigned as prime minister and as leader of the Conservative Party. The electorate despised the GST and interpreted NAFTA as a sell-out of Canadian national interests to the overwhelming power of the United States. The Conservative Party under the leadership of Kim Campbell was decimated in the 1993 election, reduced to only two seats in the Canadian Parliament. This negative reaction was slightly muted in the next few years by the economic boom of the 1990's.

Bibliography

Cameron, Stevie. *On the Take.* Toronto: Macfarlane Walter & Ross, 1994.

Gratton, Michel. *"So, What Are the Boys Saying."* Toronto: McGraw-Hill Ryerson, 1987.

MacDonald, L. Ian. *Mulroney: The Making of the Prime Minister.* Toronto: McClelland and Stewart, 1984.

Mulroney, Brian. *Where I Stand.* Toronto: McClelland and Stewart, 1983.

Murphy, Ray, Robert Chodas, and Nick Auf der Maur. *Brian Mulroney: The Boy from Baie-Comeau.* Toronto: James Lorimer, 1984.

Steve Lehman

Yoweri Kaguta Museveni

Born: 1944; Mbarara district, Uganda

Ugandan revolutionary leader, president of Uganda (took office 1986)

Yoweri Kaguta Museveni (yoh-WAY-ree kah-GEW-tah moo-seh-VEH-nee) was born during the period of British colonial administration of Uganda. He came of age at about the time of Uganda's independence in 1962 and served in the government of Milton Obote during the late 1960's. He fled into exile during the coup led by Idi Amin in 1971, fought with forces that toppled Amin in 1979, served in interim military governments, opposed the reelection of Obote in 1981, and fought a successful guerrilla war as leader of the National Resistance Army against Obote and Obote's successors until 1986. In 1986 he became president of the country.

Young Leader and Guerrilla

In 1966, while a student in secondary school, Museveni distinguished himself as a political activist by helping Rwandan herders resist eviction from their lands in western Uganda. While at the Tanzanian University of Dar Es Salaam, where he studied as a foreign student from 1967 to 1970, he was a founder and leader of the University Students' African Revolutionary Front. He spent time in northern Mozambique collaborating with the Mozambican Liberation Front in 1968. Milton Obote, Uganda's first president, took note of Museveni's talents and engaged his services as an aide. After the coup by Idi Amin in 1971, Museveni fled to Tanzania, where he formed the Front for National Salvation to oppose Amin's regime. When the Tanzanian army invaded Uganda to punish Amin for his seizure of Tanzanian territory, Museveni was among those who fought alongside the Tanzanians to overthrow Amin.

After the fall of Idi Amin, several interim governments attempted to prepare Uganda for new elections. Museveni served in several ministerial positions in these governments, including as minister of defense. After Obote's reelection in 1980, Museveni declared the elections fraudulent and invalid. In 1981 he formed the National Resistance Army, which fought a five-year guerrilla war in southern and western Uganda before seizing control of Kampala, Uganda's capital and largest city, in January, 1986. He accomplished this feat without any substantial foreign support.

Yoweri Kaguta Museveni *(AP/Wide World Photos)*

Presidency and Peace

Museveni fought a long and bloody war against Obote and subsequent military governments. Unlike his predecessors, Obote and Amin, he was determined to establish a just and lasting

The National Resistance Movement

Founded in 1981 by Yoweri Museveni, the National Resistance Movement (NRM) was the guerrilla army that fought for five years against successive governments for control of Uganda's capital and largest city, Kampala. During most of that time, the NRM was in control of the Luwero Triangle, a region in the southwestern part of Uganda. The disciplined and orderly behavior of NRM forces—in contrast to the brutality practiced by Milton Obote's army—led people to respect and support the NRM. It drew increasing strength from disaffected units of the Ugandan military and from Banyarwandans and Tutsi exiles from Rwanda, among many other groups. With little outside help, the NRM drew on this popular support to defeat the national armies. Reconstituted after its victory, the NRM army has actively promoted domestic order since the end of the civil war.

peace in his homeland. He promised to restore security, to promote economic growth, to respect human rights, to encourage humanitarian aid, to rebuild damaged infrastructure, and to supply badly needed social services. He indicated that these priorities would have to be met before the country could seriously discuss a return to democratic rule.

Ugandan president Yoweri Kaguta Museveni (right) welcoming South African president Nelson Mandela to Uganda in 1998. *(Reuters/Antony Njuguna/ Archive Photos)*

Museveni enjoyed some success in keeping his promises. He reached out to a several opposing factions and included them in his newly formed government. He privatized the economy, invited Asians who had been expelled from Uganda by Amin to return, and generally pursued enlightened economic policies. By the late 1990's Uganda had become a relatively stable country with an improved economy and higher levels of education and development. The return to democracy has been slow but largely unhampered by political violence. Museveni took seven years to revise and promulgate a new constitution, which was formally adopted in 1995. In the elections that followed, he won nearly three-quarters of the popular vote as president, indicating the popularity of his policies and personal legitimacy among the electorate.

Museveni's Importance

Museveni has been included among the so-called new leaders of Africa because of his suc-

Yoweri Kaguta Museveni, in his hometown of Mbarara, casts his vote in Uganda's 1996 elections. *(Reuters/George Mulala/Archive Photos)*

cess in bringing peace, stability, and prosperity to a country that had previously been ravaged by fifteen years of civil war. His policy of slow and guided reforms toward democracy have proved beneficial for Uganda, but the true test of his legacy will rest on whether this peace and stability survives his tenure as Uganda's best-loved and most effective leader.

Bibliography

Museveni, Yoweri K. *Selected Articles on the Uganda Resistance War*. 2d ed. Kampala, Uganda: NRM Publications, 1992.

Ofcansky, Thomas R. *Uganda: Tarnished Pearl of Africa*. Boulder, Colo.: Westview Press, 1996.

Rupesinghe, Kumar. *Conflict Resolution in Uganda*. Athens: Ohio University Press, 1989.

Robert F. Gorman

Benito Mussolini

Born: July 29, 1883; Predappio, near Forli, Romagna, Italy
Died: April 28, 1945; Giulino di Mezzegra, near Lake Como, near Dongo, Italy

Fascist dictator of Italy (1925-1943)

Benito Mussolini (bay-NEE-toh mew-soh-LEE-nee) was born Benito Amilcare Andrea Mussolini to a poor blacksmith/social journalist father and schoolteacher mother. Undisciplined and violent, Mussolini was expelled from several strict boarding schools wherein he embraced fervent socialist views. He modified his early enthusiasm for Karl Marx's doctrines with philosophies he formulated from writings by Immanuel Kant, Friedrich Nietzsche, Auguste Blanqui, Peter Kropotkin, Karl Kautsky, and Georges Sorel. In 1910 Mussolini married the peasant Rachele Guidi, the daughter of his father's widowed mistress, with whom he had five children. When World War I broke out in 1914, Mussolini initially joined other socialists in condemning Italian involvement.

Benito Mussolini (left) riding through Munich, Germany, with German chancellor Adolf Hitler in June, 1940. *(National Archives)*

Influenced by Marx's aphorism that social revolution follows war, however, Mussolini dramatically changed his viewpoint and began promoting Italian involvement via the newspaper he founded called *Il Popopo d-Italia.* He waited for the societal collapse that would make him twentieth century Europe's first totalitarian dictator. His 1922 march on Rome occurred one year before Adolf Hitler's first failed attempt to seize power in Germany: By the time Hitler became the führer (leader) of Germany, Mussolini had been Italy's Il Duce for more than ten years.

The Rise of Fascism

Mussolini officially founded the Italian Fascist movement in turbulent postwar Milan on March 23, 1919. He rose to power following a march on Rome in 1922, and he ruled as dictator from 1925 until 1943. "Fascism" refers to a centralized and highly nationalistic type of totalitarian government that regiments social and economic life and suppresses opposition—brutally if necessary.

Like Hitler, Mussolini had been a young soldier during World War I. Both returned to countries in political and economic shambles and formed extremist political organizations that

The March on Rome

The October 28, 1922, march on Rome was the first milestone in Benito Mussolini's totalitarian rise to power. Several riots followed by a general strike during the summer of 1922 had greatly angered the common people of Italy. The politically minded Mussolini used his well-polished journalistic and speaking abilities to declare that if the government would not curtail the strike, the Fascist Party would. Forty thousand black-shirted fanatics at a Fascist rally in Naples responded to Mussolini's declaration that "either the government will be given to us or we will seize it by marching on Rome" by chanting "Roma! Roma! Roma!" Although the march was far less orderly than Fascist propaganda later declared, the Fascist militia descended on Rome in four columns, later known as the Quadrumvir. The next day, King Victor Emmanuel III introduced Mussolini as the youngest prime minister in Italian history. Within four months, Mussolini's coalition government outlawed all political parties except the Fascists, enabling him to rule Italy as dictatorial premier until 1943.

overthrew the existing government. Discharged from the military following wounds inflicted during grenade practice in 1917, Mussolini utilized his considerable journalistic and public-speaking abilities to manipulate the media and promote himself as the only man who could bring order to Italy's economic and political chaos. Mussolini craftily convinced the public via press, radio, films, and personal appearances that he was Italy's man of destiny and that fascism was "the doctrine of the twentieth century." Following Italian socialist leader Giacomo Matteotti's assassination and Mussolini's victory in the undoubtedly fraudulent 1924 election, Mussolini abolished the parliamentary system and imposed a single-party totalitarian regime. He formulated a corporate state and gained international acclaim by settling numerous internal conflicts, most notably those with the Roman Catholic Church.

The Lateran Treaty

The Lateran Treaty was signed for Italy by Mussolini and for the papacy by Cardinal Pietro Gasparri on February 11, 1929, to resolve a dilemma known as the Roman question. The papacy had repeatedly objected to its loss of religious and political supremacy, Rome itself, and the

Benito Mussolini addressing the people of Carbonia, Italy, in 1938. *(Library of Congress)*

papal states. This process had begun during the Protestant Reformation period of the early 1500's. Pope Pius VI had even been imprisoned in 1798 by Napoleon Bonaparte in the last months of the French Revolution. The Lateran Treaty, Mussolini's most enduring legacy, negotiated acceptance of the loss of the papal states by the Holy See by declaring Roman Catholicism as the only state religion of Italy and creating the new sovereign state of Vatican City.

Military Aggression and World War II

The middle 1930's saw Mussolini conquer the African country of Ethiopia. It was a ruthless invasion using poison gas, and it was strongly opposed by the League of Nations. Mussolini also joined Hitler's support of the Nationalists in the Spanish Civil War, thus gaining an ally in General Francisco Franco. When British and French leaders condemned his aggression, Mussolini sought military alliances with Germany and Japan. In May, 1939, Mussolini signed an agreement (the "pact of steel") with Hitler and adopted Nazi racial policies of persecuting the Jews. Italy did not officially enter World War II until Mussolini was convinced that Germany would win. He probably desired to conquer some territory in southern France before Germany controlled it—in case Italy should become the next target of Nazi aggression.

On June 10, 1940, Mussolini joined Hitler against France but did not win even a token victory before France surrendered. He was clearly the junior partner in his alliance with Hitler, and his opinions had little value in later wartime planning with Hitler.

Historians recount Mussolini's union with Germany and entry into World War II as his biggest mistake, as the Italian army and navy—about which he had boasted for fifteen years—were unprepared and ineffective in battle. Italian forces soon found themselves fighting the British in Africa and invading Greece. They joined the Germans in annexing Yugoslavia, attacking the Soviet Union in June, 1941, and declaring war on the United States in December, 1941. Because Hitler did not notify Mussolini prior to his surprise invasions, Mussolini attacked Greece through Albania without notifying Germany. He openly admitted that this aggression was to "pay back Hitler in his own coin." Following military defeats on every front and the Anglo-American landing at Sicily, Mussolini's former Fascist colleagues joined the non-Fascists against him at the July 25, 1943, Grand Council. There King Emmanuel, whom Mussolini had reduced to a figurehead, dismissed him and obtained an armistice with the Allies.

The sickly Mussolini was imprisoned in a hotel high in the Abruzzi Mountains. Hitler sent Ger-

Corporatism

Benito Mussolini's "corporate state" organized employers and workers into professional groups that could be easily controlled by the Fascists. Italy's corporatism introduced laws forbidding laborers to strike, abolished free trade unions, and, in a famous phrase, "made the trains run on time by shooting someone if they did not." All teachers had to swear an oath to defend Mussolini's economic policies, and no one could practice journalism who did not possess a certificate of approval from the Fascist Party. Many corporatism ideas that made Mussolini popular during the early 1930's are being reconsidered in Italy during the 1990's as inefficient social systems and political parties, widespread government corruption, and strikes are again emerging.

Benito Mussolini's fascist government attempted to control almost all aspects of Italian life, giving rise to the saying that he "made the trains run on time." *(National Archives)*

man paratroopers to rescue him and then forced him to organize a brutal puppet socialist "Republic of Salo" in German-occupied northern Italy. There Mussolini executed Fascist leaders who had previously abandoned him, including his son-in-law, Count Galeazzo Ciano, and he meditated on how he would be viewed in history. As World War II was ending, Mussolini attempted to escape from Allied forces disguised as a German soldier in a truck retreating toward Austria. However, he was recognized and captured along with his mistress, Clara Petacci. She insisted on remaining with him until the end. Imprisoned and tried at Giulino di Mezzegra, Mussolini was shot and hung upside down in the Piazza Loreto in Milan on April 28, 1945, by Italian communists.

Bibliography

Absalom, Robert. *Mussolini and the Rise of Italian Fascism*. New York: Roy, 1969.

Halperin, Samuel W. *Mussolini and Italian Fascism*. Princeton, N.J.: Van Nostrand, 1964.

Hibbert, Christopher. *Il Duce: The Life of Benito Mussolini*. Boston, Mass.: Little, Brown, 1962.

Hoyt, Edwin P. *Mussolini's Empire: The Rise and Fall of the Fascist Vision*. New York: John Wiley, 1994.

Kirkpatrick, Ivone. *Mussolini: A Study in Power*. New York: Avon, 1968.

Mussolini, Rachele. *Mussolini: An Intimate Biography by His Widow*. New York: Morrow, 1974.

Ridley, Jasper. *Mussolini*. New York: St. Martin's Press, 1997.

Daniel G. Graetzer

Alva Myrdal

Born: January 31, 1902; Uppsala, Sweden
Died: February 1, 1986; Stockholm, Sweden

Swedish diplomat and peace activist, winner of 1982 Nobel Peace Prize

Alva Reimer (AL-vah RAY-mehr) was the first of five children born to middle-class parents active in local politics and reform movements in Eskilstuna, a small city in south central Sweden. She attended primary school there, and even though secondary education was unavailable to girls at that time, she struggled to obtain private instruction. This instruction prepared her to complete a bachelor of arts degree at Stockholm University in only two years, graduating 1924. In that same year she married Gunnar Myrdal (MEER-dahl), a young economist, and together they were the parents of two daughters and a son.

Alva Myrdal *(The Nobel Foundation)*

Social Reform

In their academic and public careers, Alva and Gunnar Myrdal focused on issues of social and economic justice, often working together on projects. Alva Myrdal especially focused on such matters as population control, women's issues and child care. In 1934 the publication of her first book, coauthored with Gunnar, *Crisis in the Population Question*, caused considerable controversy in Sweden and established Alva and Gunnar Myrdal as important voices in social reform in their country in the 1930's and 1940's. Alva's proposals for improving working conditions and the welfare of families and children were highly influential on government policy and the development of the Swedish welfare state.

Myrdal's career became more international in 1949 when she became head of the United Nations Department of Social Affairs, then later that year was named director of the Department of Social Studies of the United Nations Educational, Scientific and Cultural Organization (UNESCO). These positions allowed her to apply her many years of work on social issues to the world stage, and she again concerned herself with matters of human rights and social and economic justice.

Working for World Peace

From 1955 to 1961, Myrdal was Sweden's ambassador to India, where she saw firsthand the serious tensions that existed among nations armed with nuclear weapons. She returned from India resolved to work for world peace and nuclear disarmament. From 1961 to 1973 she was chief of the Swedish delegation to the United Nations' conference on disarmament in Geneva, Switzerland. In 1966 she became Sweden's minister for disarmament; she was only the third

The Arms Race

After the United States used nuclear weapons at the end of World War II, other countries quickly developed nuclear weapons programs of their own. The Soviet Union, the United States' Cold War adversary, was first, exploding an atomic bomb in 1949. Britain, France, and China later followed suit. By the 1950's tensions ran high as the United States and the Soviet Union competed for nuclear superiority. The development of long-range missile technology and the far more destructive hydrogen bomb increased the fear of global nuclear warfare. World outcry against amassing such destructive power brought about the Nuclear Test Ban Treaty of 1963, which prohibited most forms of nuclear testing. By 1969 the United States and the Soviet Union had agreed to Strategic Arms Limitation Talks (SALT), which produced two arms-reducing treaties, SALT I and SALT II. Although superpower tensions continued through the 1980's, fear of world nuclear destruction abated with the end of the Cold War and the breakup of the Soviet Union in the early 1990's.

woman to hold a Swedish cabinet post. Even after ill health forced her to resign her positions in the early 1970's, she continued to write and lecture internationally about the nuclear arms race. Those efforts were recognized in 1982 when she shared the Nobel Peace Prize with her fellow disarmament negotiator, Mexican diplomat Alfonso Garcia Robles. Alva Myrdal died in Sweden in 1986.

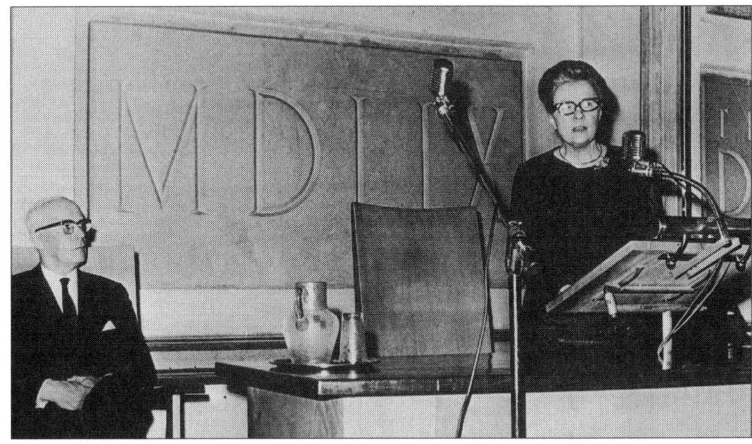

Swedish delegate Alva Myrdal speaks at the 1968 peace and disarmament conference in Geneva, Switzerland. *(Express Newspapers/G407/Archive Photos)*

Championing the Underdog

During her long career, Alva Myrdal was a teacher, social reformer, diplomat, politician, cabinet minister, and Nobel laureate. Her work as a sociologist and reformer left a deep imprint upon her native Sweden, and she is often cited as an architect of modern Swedish social policy. Her work as a diplomat allowed her to work for social reform and world peace internationally. In 1975 Alva Myrdal summarized the philosophy that governed her life's activities: "All my life I have been championing the underdog. I have worked for the equality of children with adults, of women with men, of the poor with the rich, of poor countries with rich countries and of lesser powers with strong nations."

Bibliography

Bok, Sissela. *Alva Myrdal: A Daughter's Memoir*. New York: Addison Wesley, 1991.

Myrdal, Alva. *The Game of Disarmament*. Rev. ed. New York: Pantheon Books, 1981.

Catherine Udall Turley

Imre Nagy

Born: June 7, 1896; Kaposvár, Hungary, Austro-Hungarian Empire
Died: June 16, 1958; Budapest, Hungary

Prime minister of Hungary (1953-1955, 1956)

Imre Nagy (IHM-reh NOJ), a Hungarian prime minister and a nationalist communist politician, was the son of devout Calvinist peasants. After graduating from high school, Nagy, an apprentice blacksmith, was drafted to serve in the Hungarian army during World War I (1914-1918). During this conflict he was captured and transported to Russia as a prisoner of war. While in prison, Nagy became a communist and later a member of the Bolshevik Party despite his early exposure to religious doctrines.

He returned to Hungary but was forced to flee his native land in 1929 to avoid arrest for his political beliefs and for organizing efforts on behalf of the banned communist party. Nagy went into exile in Moscow, where he was employed by the Institute for Agrarian Sciences throughout World War II. With much of Hungary under Soviet military occupation by late 1944, Nagy reappeared in Hungary. (He was a pro-Moscow communist, even though he would move away from copying the Stalinist Soviet model in agriculture

Hungarian premier Imre Nagy (center) with two of his cabinet ministers in 1956; they took refuge in the Yugoslav embassy when Soviet tanks invaded Hungary. *(National Archives)*

The Hungarian Revolt

The Hungarian revolt, an anticommunist, anti-Soviet rebellion, shook the world for several weeks in 1956. On October 23, 1956, students in Budapest held street demonstrations. Foremost among student demands was the appointment of Imre Nagy as prime minister once again. Workers and students made other demands, including the withdrawal of Soviet troops from Hungary. Nagy urged the crowds to go home by pledging that the Communist Party would consider their demands immediately. That evening Nagy was selected as prime minister by party leaders and began forming a new government that included noncommunists. Soon thereafter, however, armed workers took over a Budapest radio station; a mass strike developed, and the revolt spread throughout Hungary. Intervention by Soviet troops turned the uprising against the communist regime in Hungary into an anti-Soviet national revolution.

Nagy refused to acquiesce to communist demands to establish a military dictatorship and called the revolutionary events a democratic mass movement. Responding to popular pressure, he argued for the abolition of the one-party system and for negotiations for the withdrawal of Soviet troops from Hungary. By October 30, the Soviet Union appeared to accept Nagy's program. The Hungarian revolt seemed to have triumphed. However, on November 1, Soviet troops and tanks surrounded Hungarian airfields, Budapest, and other cities. After several days of heavy fighting, they effectively crushed the revolt on November 4, 1956. Nagy, along with several associates, was blamed for the Hungarian revolt and executed.

and other domestic policy arenas.) This time Nagy would play a more commanding political and economic role in governing Hungarian society.

Soviet troops invading Hungary in November, 1956. *(National Archives)*

Rise to Power

Imre Nagy helped establish a multiparty postwar coalition government, the Hungarian National Independence Front. Because he was an agrarian economist and because Soviet officials supervised and guided this new government, Nagy was appointed minister of agriculture and served in this cabinet post from December 23, 1944, to November 15, 1945. An honorable politician who argued that socialist objectives could be achieved without resort to police terror, Nagy served as minister of the interior from November 15, 1945, to March 23, 1946, for a weakly organized, independent government led by the noncommunist Smallholders Party.

The Warsaw Pact

The Warsaw Treaty Organization, or Warsaw Pact, consisted of eight communist nations with a shared Marxist ideology and similar governing, economic, and social systems. This mutual defense organization, which extended Soviet political and military domination over East European satellite regimes through a Soviet-led joint military command, was signed by Albania, Bulgaria, Czechoslovakia, East Germany, Hungary, Poland, and the Soviet Union on May 14, 1955.

Imre Nagy wrote of the possibility of an independent Hungarian foreign and defense policy and the dissolution of the Warsaw Pact. During the Hungarian revolution, Nagy initiated negotiations with Soviet officials concerning Hungary's withdrawal from the Warsaw Pact and removal of Soviet troops from Hungary. On November 1, 1956, Nagy declared Hungary's neutrality and withdrawal from the Warsaw Pact. The Soviet response was swift. Russian troops entered Hungary. This action effectively crushed the Hungarian rebellion within two weeks. It also violated Article 8 of the Warsaw Pact, which pledged noninterference in the internal affairs of other pact members. Nagy was forced to flee and seek refuge in the Yugoslav embassy. While no soldier from any East European country fought alongside Soviet troops in Hungary, each Warsaw Pact regime eventually endorsed Soviet intervention against Nagy's short-lived government.

Imre Nagy speaking in 1956, the last year of his prime ministership. *(Archive Photos)*

Although he served as chairman of the Parliament from September 15, 1947, to August 23, 1949, Nagy had become less influential in the Hungarian Workers Party, the renamed Communist Party, which gradually replaced noncommunists in the government. He was censured by Stalinist leaders for advocating moderation in the collectivization of agriculture, and he was relieved of high government office in 1949. Nagy became a professor in the Economic University of Budapest. Rapid and brutal changes in agriculture soon caused unrest, and Nagy was brought back to resolve problems more humanely as minister of crop collection from May 8, 1950, to November 16, 1952. He served as deputy prime minister from November 16, 1952, until July 4, 1953. At that time, at Soviet insistence, he was named Hungary's prime minister.

A New Course

Nagy's program called the New Course alleviated some of the excesses and brutality of communist programs through liberal reforms. Political prisoners were released, peasants could withdraw from or abolish collective farms, writers and journalists were permitted more freedom, and investment in consumer goods increased. Communist Party leaders led by Matyas Rakosi continued to oppose these changes and forced Nagy to resign as prime minister on April 18, 1955, with Moscow's approval. Nagy brought about improved living standards and partial emancipation from Stalinist ideological beliefs before being silenced politically through expulsion from the party and government.

Revolution and Death

Imre Nagy was readmitted to the Communist Party on October 14, 1956, amid public discontent. He was reinstated as prime minister on October 23, 1956. During the Hungarian revolt of 1956, Nagy, the leader of a genuine coalition government which included representatives of noncommunist parties, workers' councils and students, became a reluctant, though heroic, revolutionary as he made numerous concessions to the demands of Hungarian freedom-fighters. The Soviet Union did not support this type of leadership and drove Nagy from power on November 4, 1956, crushing the Hungarian revolt. Nagy was lured from refuge in the Yugoslav embassy by a false written promise of safe passage to his home. He was captured and flown to Romania. Two years later, after a secret trial, he was executed on June 16, 1958, in Budapest.

Nagy had stood for the New Course: multiparty government, greater freedoms, and independence from the Soviet Union. Some criticized Nagy as an ineffective national communist who failed to secure Hungary's national revolt. For decades one could not mention Nagy's name in Hungary, but in 1989 he was reburied with honor as a national hero.

Bibliography

Dornbach, Alajos, ed. *The Secret Trial of Imre Nagy*. Westport, Conn.: Praeger, 1994.

Litvan, György, ed. *The Hungarian Revolution of 1956: Reform, Revolt, and Repression, 1953-1963*. New York: Longman, 1996.

Remington, Robin. *The Warsaw Pact: Case Studies in Communist Conflict Resolution*. Cambridge, Mass.: The MIT Press, 1972.

Unwin, Peter. *Voice in the Wilderness: Imre Nagy and the Hungarian Revolution*. London: Macdonald, 1991.

Zinner, Paul. *Revolution in Hungary*. New York: Columbia University Press, 1962.

Steve J. Mazurana

Gamal Abdel Nasser

Born: January 15, 1918; Alexandria, Egypt
Died: September 28, 1970; Cairo, Egypt

Premier (1954-1956) and president of Egypt (1956-1970)

Gamal Abdel Nasser (jah-MAHL ahb-dool NAH-sur) was the eldest son of a postal clerk and his wife, the daughter of a prosperous coal merchant. Gamal's early schooling was somewhat troubled in that his father's job involved frequent relocation. In 1923 he went to primary school first in Khataba and then in Cairo; he then attended a number of institutions, including El Nahda al Misria (Egyptian Renaissance) school in Cairo.

Since his high school days, Nasser was deeply concerned over the fate of his country; Egypt had been ruled under British mandate since World War I. Along with many other Egyptians, he remained dissatisfied with the state of the government and economy of his country even after its nominal independence in 1922. He actively participated in student demonstrations during 1935-1936. After graduating from high school, he studied law for a time and then joined the Royal Military Academy in 1937, received a commission in 1938, served for a time in the Sudan, and fought against the Jews in the Palestinian War (1947-1949). The defeat of the Arabs in this war exposed the corruption and inefficiency of the royal government of Egypt.

Egyptian Revolution

The Palestinian War stimulated Arabism, leading to the foundation of the Arab League in Alexandria. The war also fostered plots and conspiracies by the newly formed clandestine revolutionary cell within the Egyptian army, the Free Officers, led by Nasser. The Free Officers carried out an almost bloodless coup on July 23, 1952, forcing King Farouk (Egyptian king since 1937) to abdicate. Pending the formation of a new civilian government, power was placed in the hands of a Revolutionary Command Council, composed of the leading Free Officers and nominally headed by General Muhammad Neguib. Neguib became the premier of the Republic of Egypt in June, 1953, with Lieutenant Colonel Nasser serving as the deputy prime minister.

The new regime rapidly settled Egypt's longstanding disputes with Britain. The British concern about Egypt's claim over the Sudan and

Egyptian president Gamal Abdel Nasser addressing air force cadets during the Suez Crisis, September, 1956. *(National Archives)*

Gamal Abdel Nasser *(Archive Photos)*

control of the Suez Canal was somewhat pacified by an Anglo-Egyptian agreement in 1953 that recognized the principle of self-determination for the Sudan. Another agreement in 1954 stated that the British agreed to withdraw their forces from the canal zone by June, 1956.

Seizure of Power

Meanwhile, growing dissension between Neguib and Nasser reached a climax on February 25, 1954, when the former was forced to resign. He was shortly afterward restored to power, and then finally deposed on November 14. The two leaders clashed over the question of transition from the recently dismantled monarchy to a full parliamentary democracy. While Neguib wanted an early parliamentary government, Nasser insisted on a junta regime pending the establishment of social justice for Egypt's farmers and workers and the liberation of the Suez Canal Zone from British occupation.

Arab Nationalist

More than an Egyptian leader, Nasser became a champion of Arab nationalism against Western colonialism. His pan-Arabism was driven by a policy of "positive neutralism" in the Cold War politics in the Middle East, because most Arabs regarded the Cold War as an intra-Western feud that they should avoid. Nasser's stature as a world statesman was recognized at a conference of Afro-Asian leaders in Bandung, Indo-

Defending the Suez Canal

Ever since the revolution of 1952, Gamal Abdel Nasser was intent on liberating the Suez Canal Zone from British occupation and on achieving economic independence for Egypt. In July, 1954, Israel masterminded a plot to subvert the relationship between Egypt and the Western powers so as to foil the projected British plan to withdraw from the canal. The plot failed, but Egypt's relationships with Israel and the Western powers, especially Great Britain and the United States, turned sour. Nasser's plan for the Aswan Dam, to be financed by Great Britain and the United States, came to nothing on July 16, 1956, when the U.S. government reneged on its promise of financial help. Nasser promptly announced the nationalization of the Suez Canal on July 26. The Israelis invaded the Sinai Peninsula on October 29, and French and British planes bombed Egyptian airfields on October 31. In spite of these setbacks, the canal came under Egyptian control, and Nasser's prestige in the Arab world soared.

Arab Socialism

In a televised speech on October 16, 1961, Nasser defined socialism as the "only road to justice." It is difficult to find a clearly defined and consistent ideology in Arab socialism. In general, however, socialism as understood by Nasser or other Middle Eastern ideologues constitutes a program for achieving greater economic growth, stability, and a more equitable distribution of income and wealth under state control. At the same time, it allows the existence of private property. Arab socialism probably is better understood as nationalistic than socialistic, and it is more compatible with Islamic egalitarianism than with European communism.

Norwegian troops aboard a train look out at Egyptian ships blocking the Suez Canal in November, 1956. *(National Archives)*

nesia, in April, 1955. In fact, along with Jawaharlal Nehru of India and Josif Broz Tito of Yugoslavia, Nasser came to be regarded as one of the three pillars of nonalignment. After Bandung, Nasser defied the Western powers by deciding to purchase Soviet arms through Czechoslovakia in July, 1955, and in May of 1956 he tendered his country's formal recognition of communist China. Meanwhile, he was elected president of the Egyptian Republic in January, 1956, and promulgated a constitution making Egypt a socialist Arab state with a one-party political system.

The Suez Crisis

Nasser was acutely aware of his country's economic predicaments. His program of land reform of 1952 resulted in redistribution of 10 percent usable land. His plan for the Aswan High Dam, to be financed by the capitalist West, was aimed at achieving Egypt's economic independence. Great Britain and the United States promised financial help, but on July 19, 1956, the United States reneged on its promise. Nasser then announced the nationalization of the Suez Canal in a public meeting in Alexandria on July 26. This action made him at once a hero of the Arab world and vulnerable to threats from Israel and some Western powers.

Decline

Nasser's political and ideological decline is connected intimately with the failure of his projected United Arab Republic (UAR) and his military failure in direct confrontation with Israel in 1967. Nasser's ideology, partly predicated on socialism, never conflicted with his loyalty to Islam or his attitude toward Christian Egyptians. Thus his Charter of 1962 underscored the "eternal moral values of religion" without making an overt reference to any particular religion. He appealed strongly to Islam, however, after the Arab-Israeli War of June 6-11, 1967 (the Six-Day War). In this war, triggered by the Israeli attempt to divert water from the Jordan River to irrigate land in the Negev Desert, the Egyptians were squarely defeated by Israel. Nasser lost his pride of place in the Arab world. He endured this humiliation for another three years before dying in 1970 of a heart attack.

Bibliography

Lacouture, Jean. *Nasser: A Biography*. New York: Alfred A. Knopf, 1973.

Mansfield, Peter. *Nasser's Egypt*. Baltimore: Penguin Books, 1965.

Nutting, Anthony. *Nasser*. London: Constable, 1972.

Stephens, Robert. *Nasser: A Political Biography*. London: Allen Lane, 1971.

Woodward, Peter. *Nasser*. London: Longman, 1992.

Narasingha P. Sil

Jawaharlal Nehru

Born: November 14, 1889; Allahabad, India
Died: May 27, 1964; New Delhi, India

First prime minister of India (1947-1964)

Jawaharlal Nehru (jah-WAH-hahr-lahl NAY-rew) was the son of a wealthy lawyer from Kashmir. His parents were Brahmans, members of the highest caste in Hinduism, traditionally associated with the priesthood. The Nehru family lived in a huge mansion and led a heavily westernized lifestyle. The young Nehru was educated by private British tutors, one of whom awakened in him an interest in theosophy. Nehru also studied Hindi and Sanskrit with a Brahman teacher (from whom he later claimed to have learned very little). In 1905 he traveled to England to enroll in Harrow, a preparatory school. In 1907 he entered Trinity College at Cambridge University, where he became aware of discrimination against Indians. After graduating in 1910, he studied law in London.

Jawaharlal Nehru *(Library of Congress)*

Indian Nationalist

In 1912, having passed his bar exam, Nehru returned to India, where he found the Indian leaders apathetic about politics. It was easy for him to be apathetic as well, particularly after 1916, when a marriage arranged in the traditional way by his parents made him a family man. In that same year he met Mohandas K. Gandhi (Mahatma Gandhi), who advocated passive resistance to British rule as a way of obtaining India's independence. In 1919, British soldiers violently put down a group of peaceful protesters in the Jalianwallah Bagh massacres. Nehru was so deeply moved by this event that he felt compelled to become active in politics.

Nehru subsequently traveled to various peasant settlements in his area. In the face of the poverty he saw, he became ashamed of his own life of luxury. The experience compelled him to give up his law firm and his wealth. He embraced a far more austere lifestyle in order to devote himself to full-time political activism in the pursuit of Indian independence and development. In this his wife showed particular grace and strength, accepting without complaint the changes although her health was not particularly strong. Two years later, Nehru was arrested and briefly imprisoned for advocating a strike. However, since he was a married man with children, he avoided engaging in activities that would lead to extensive prison terms.

In 1925 Nehru's wife was in failing health, and he took her to Europe in search of treatment.

India's Congress Party

The official name of the Congress Party is the Indian National Congress. It was founded on December 28, 1885, by Allen Octavian Hume, an Englishman. The Congress Party proclaimed its loyalty to the British crown but requested that Indians have a greater role in the colonial government. In 1905 the partition of Bengal led the party's leaders to take a more activist role and support a boycott movement. The following year, Congress Party president Dadabhai Navroji issued a demand for *swaraj* (self-rule).

In 1918, U.S. president Woodrow Wilson spoke of the conditions that he felt should be met at the end of World War I; these were Wilson's famous Fourteen Points. Among them was the principle of national self-determination. The Congress Party urged Britain to apply the Wilsonian principle of self-determination to India. The British colonial administration adamantly refused. The harsh repression of Indian nationalistic feeling following World War I transformed the Congress Party from an elite to a mass movement. Using the principles of nonviolent civil disobedience, Mohandas K. Gandhi (Mahatma Gandhi) mobilized his people against British rule. His opposition to Britain's entry into World War II in 1939 led to a particularly savage suppression of the anticolonial movement. Almost all Congress Party leaders were imprisoned. When India attained its independence in 1947, the Congress Party was India's majority party. It subscribed to moderately socialistic principles.

While there, Nehru gained a new perspective on politics and learned to relate India's problems to a larger international matrix of issues. He no longer saw Indian independence as a goal sufficient unto itself.

Independence Leader

Nehru returned to India determined to use direct political action to gain Indian autonomy. By 1928, Gandhi was warning him not to push too fast, lest he trigger a counterproductive backlash. Two years later, Nehru was imprisoned while taking part in Gandhi's program of civil disobedience. He would be imprisoned nine times before India gained its independence. The final time was the result of his op-

Indian prime minister Jawaharlal Nehru campaigning for the Congress Party in 1951. *(National Archives)*

Jawaharlal Nehru visiting the United States in 1949. He was met at Washington, D.C.'s National Airport by his sister, Vijaya Lakshmi Pandit (the Indian ambassador) and U.S. president Harry S Truman. *(National Archives)*

position to Britain's entry into World War II.

In 1945, the Labour Party came to power in Britain and pledged to increase self-rule for India. On August 17, 1947, India became a free dominion in the British Commonwealth, with Nehru as its first prime minister. This triumph was tarnished by tension between Hindus and Muslims. The tension was exacerbated by the exodus of

Nonalignment

Nonalignment is the political philosophy by which a state does not identify itself with the political ideologies, objectives, or foreign policies of other states. Specifically, the Non Aligned Movement was a group of Third World nations that refused to join forces with either the United States or the Soviet Union during the Cold War. These nations sought to become a third force in the world arena. As a formal organization, the Non Aligned Movement began in September, 1961, when Josip Broz Tito of Yugoslavia called a meeting of twenty-five nations in Belgrade, Yugoslavia. Subsequently the movement grew to more than one hundred countries. Although some were truly neutral states, many leaned toward one or the other superpower, while others tried to play them against each other for national advantage.

Hindus from Pakistan. (Pakistan, previously part of India, had been established as a new, separate Muslim state as part of the independence plan.) There were disturbances and riots, and the unrest culminated in the assassination of Gandhi by a Hindu fanatic in 1948.

Statesman

In 1950 India became a republic, and Nehru was reelected prime minister, a position that he would hold until his death in 1964. As the leader of a fully independent India, he balanced his nation's independence with continued membership in the British Commonwealth. He steadfastly insisted upon the secular nature of the Indian government in spite of calls by various Hindu leaders for a greater role in their country's leadership. In particular, he sought to separate the Hindu caste system from civil law and jurisprudence. Nehru instituted measures to improve life for various impoverished and downtrodden groups, including widows and untouchables (members of the lowest group in the traditional Hindu caste system).

On the international front, Nehru walked a delicate line among the various superpowers. He sought to keep India from alignments with any major power bloc. Although he had socialist leanings, he refused to ally himself with Soviet communism, which he regarded as simply another form of Western imperialism. At the same time, he refused to allow India to be drawn too tightly into the United States' sphere of influence. One of his great disappointments was his failure to attain any form of rapprochement with the People's Republic of China. In 1962, Nehru's health began to deteriorate. In January of 1964 he suffered a stroke, and his health declined steadily until his death in May of that year.

Bibliography

Brown, Judith M. *Nehru*. New York: Longman, 1999.

Edwardes, Michael. *Nehru: A Pictorial Biography*. New York: Viking, 1963.

Morares, Frank. *Jawaharlal Nehru: A Bibliography*. New York: InterCulture, 1959.

Nanda, Bal Ram. *Jawaharlal Nehru: Rebel and Statesman*. New York: Oxford University Press, 1995.

Pillai, R. C. *Nehru and His Critics*. Columbia, Mo.: South Asia Books, 1986.

Leigh Husband Kimmel

Benjamin Netanyahu

Born: October 21, 1949; Tel Aviv, Israel

Prime minister of Israel (1996-1999)

Benjamin "Bibi" Netanyahu (BEHN-yah-meen "BEE-bee" neh-tahn-YAH-hew), third son of Israeli historian Benzion Netanyahu and Cela Segal, grew up in Jerusalem but spent his high school years in the United States. He earned his bachelor's degree in architecture and a master of science in management studies at MIT in Cambridge, Massachusetts. He married three times and had three children—a daughter from his first marriage and two sons from his third.

Netanyahu served as deputy chief of mission in the Israeli embassy in Washington (1983) and as Israeli ambassador to the United Nations (1984-1988). Elected to the Knesset (the Israeli parliament) as a member of the Likud Party, he was deputy foreign minister (1988), Israel's principal representative during the Gulf War (August, 1990-April, 1991), and senior member on the Israeli delegation to the Madrid Peace Conference (October-November, 1991). Elected Likud Party chair on March 25, 1993, he won election as Israel's ninth prime minister on May 29, 1996.

Political Philosophy

Netanyahu's career was strongly influenced by his older brother, Jonathan, who planned and led the raid on the Entebbe airport to free Israeli hostages from terrorists. Jonathan himself was killed on that expedition on July 4, 1976. In 1979, Netanyahu organized an international conference on terrorism under the auspices of the Jonathan Institute, a private foundation in his brother's memory devoted to the study of terrorism. Netanyahu's writings call for governments to ferret out terrorists in their midst. He claims the moral right of injured parties to pursue terrorists anywhere they might be sought. For example, the Israeli military's attack on two terrorists, who died in a shootout in their West Bank hideout in September, 1998, was intended to avenge the August, 1997, suicide bombing of a Jerusalem grocery complex.

The 1996 Election

Events between 1993 and the election of 1996 had created a perception in the Middle East that the Oslo Accords, signed on September 13, 1993, had failed to achieve their purpose. Fifty-nine Israelis were killed in a nine-month period by

Benjamin Netanyahu *(Archive Photos/Popperfoto)*

Land for Peace Agreements

The terms "land for peace agreements" and "land for security agreements" have been applied to agreements between Israel and the Palestinians that involve Israel returning land to the Palestinians in return for promises that terrorism against Israel will be suppressed. The Hebron Agreement was signed by Benjamin Netanyahu and the Palestinians in January, 1997. In it, Israel agreed to withdraw troops from the West Bank town of Hebron. This agreement was hailed as an indication that Netanyahu's government was recognizing the importance of the 1993 Oslo Accords, which dealt with Israel's returning parts of the West Bank to the Palestinians. Israel had occupied the West Bank in 1967 following its victory in the Six-Day War. Further progress quickly bogged down, however, as Israel announced that it would not surrender as much land as the Palestinians sought. Then a wave of terrorist bombings hit Israel, and Netanyahu said that there would be no more land transfers until the terrorism stopped.

In 1998, U.S. secretary of state Madeleine Albright helped fashion a compromise plan that was confirmed in the White House on September 28 in meetings between President Bill Clinton, Netanyahu, and PLO leader Yasir Arafat. It gave the Palestinians control of 40 percent of the West Bank, land that contains 98 percent of the Palestinian population. A month later, on October 23, 1998, a tenuous agreement was signed after nine days of negotiation in Wye Mills, Maryland. Generally termed the Wye River Agreement, it granted the PLO acquisition of 14 percent of the West Bank territory that was formerly under joint Israeli-Palestinian control and 13 percent of the West Bank that was formerly under Israeli control alone. The agreement also called for the establishment of an airport in Gaza and corridors of travel between the West Bank and Gaza, provided that the PLO excises twenty-six anti-Israeli articles from its charter and suppresses terrorist actions against Israel.

suicide bombers of the Islamic Jihad and Hamas; for most Israelis, the killings laid to rest the idea that peace could be delivered by Yasir Arafat's Palestine Liberation Organization (PLO). The PLO had been granted authority over the municipalities of Jericho, Gaza, and Khan Yunis. In addition, the assassination of Yitzhak Rabin by a right-wing Israeli on November 4, 1995, demonstrated the anger of Israel's radical Right over the accords. Not even a demilitarized Palestine state was deemed acceptable by Netanyahu's government. Netanyahu argued that the PLO, despite the Oslo Accords, maintained key points of its charter, adopted in 1964 and revised in 1968, including a call for armed struggle and the liberation of Palestine from Israel.

Netanyahu won election by a narrow popular vote over Shimon Peres by achieving a coalescence of Likud advocates, West Bank settlers, Jerusalem archconservatives, Russian immigrants led by Nathan Sharansky of the Yisrael B'aliyah Party, and the religious ultra-Orthodox, including the Gush Emunim, principal settler groups on the West Bank, and the Habad, devoted to Hasidic tradition. Russian immigrants, 10 percent of the electorate, delivered 65 percent of their vote to Netanyahu. Netanyahu's Likud embraced a pragmatic parliamentary position seeking to maintain maximum territory.

Challenges

Probably the most difficult issue confronting Netanyahu's government in the late 1990's was Palestinian statehood. Arafat set a timetable that

The 1991 Madrid Peace Conference

Israel's endangerment in the 1991 Gulf War and its self-control in not launching strikes against Iraq offered an opportunity to further the peace process. The United States called a conference in Madrid, Spain, October 30 to November 1, 1991. The conference brought together representatives from the Soviet Union, the United States, the European Community, Jordan, the Palestinians, Syria, Egypt, Israel, and Lebanon. U.S. secretary of state James Baker had gained the confidence of Arab leaders. Invitations were issued by U.S. president George Bush and Soviet president Mikhail Gorbachev. The Palestinians arrived as a distinct political delegation, differentiating themselves from the Tunis-based Palestine Liberation Organization (PLO). The PLO was not allowed representation, though the Palestinians maintained communication with Chairman Yasir Arafat. In 1992, eight sets of bilateral sessions and five multilateral groups convened to consider arms control and regional security, water, economic development, the environment, and refugees. Benjamin Netanyahu forcefully stated Israel's opposition to a number of Palestinian demands. The refusal of the Syrians to enter serious negotiations hindered further progress.

Israeli prime minister Benjamin Netanyahu meeting with Palestinian president Yasir Arafat in 1996. *(Reuters/Ahmed Jadallah/Archive Photos)*

targeted May 4, 1999, as the date for the proclamation of a Palestinian state. Netanyahu, on the other hand, supported Palestinian autonomy rather than statehood. Netanyahu's arguments against statehood included the difficulties it would produce in foreign alliances, water control, and airspace control. The Netanyahu government also expressed skepticism over the PLO's ability to establish a stable democratic government in Gaza and the West Bank. Israeli officials assumed, for example, that Arafat's secular operation would find growing opposition among Muslim fundamentalists.

The efforts of Palestinian police to disperse a protest of two hundred Hamas activists in Gaza City, as well as a parade of forty thousand or more Israeli peace protesters against Netanyahu's policy, indicated that proponents of the peace process sought a voice in negotiations. U.S. envoy Dennis Ross sought to revive the peace process in September of 1998, asking Israel to withdraw from 13 percent of the West Bank. Meetings in the White House in September and October resulted in the signing of an agreement between Israel and the Palestinians that would surrender land in the West Bank to the Palestinians in return for assurances that the PLO would suppress terrorism against Israel. In April of 1999, Arafat postponed his deadline for the establishment of a Palestinian state. Holding to the May 4, 1999, deadline would have created severe hostility with Israel. In addition, Israeli elections were approaching.

The 1999 Election

The Israeli elections of 1999 were bitter and hard-fought. Netanyahu's primary opponent for prime minister was Labor Party leader Ehud Barak. Barak's party won the election with a wider margin than anyone had expected; the defeated Netanyahu immediately stepped down as leader of the Likud Party. Israeli observers saw the election results as a strong repudiation both of Netanyahu personally and of the desire of far-right factions within his party's coalition to move slowly on the peace process with the Palestinians. Many analysts noted that Barak was better positioned politically than Netanyahu had been to move the peace process forward.

Benjamin Netanyahu addressing the Israeli Knesset (parliament) in December, 1998, after the signing of the Wye River peace agreement caused a storm of protest. *(AP/Wide World Photos)*

Bibliography

Netanyahu, Benjamin. *Fighting Terrorism: How Democracies Can Defeat Domestic and International Terrorism*. New York: Farrar Straus Giroux, 1995.

______. *A Place Among the Nations: Israel and the World*. New York: Bantam Books, 1993.

Netanyahu, Benjamin, ed. *Terrorism: How the West Can Win*. New York: Farrar Straus Giroux, 1986.

Netanyahu, Jonathan. *Self-Portrait of a Hero: The Letters of Jonathan Netanyahu (1963-1976)*. Notes and afterword by Benjamin and Iddo Netanyahu. New York: Random House, 1980.

Irving N. Rothman

Nicholas II

Born: May 18, 1868; Tsarskoye Selo (now Pushkin), near St. Petersburg, Russia
Died: July 16 or 17, 1918; Yekaterinburg, Russia

Last czar of Russia (1894-1917)

In 1894, at age twenty-six, Nicholas II (NIH-koh-lahs thuh SEH-kuhnd), born Nicholai Aleksandrovich (nyih-kuh-LI uh-lyihk-SAN-droo-vy-ihch), became the Russian monarch, or czar. He married Princess Alexandra the same year, and they became the parents of five children (four girls and a boy). Nicholas ruled the Russian Empire during the final decades of the czarist system, under which Russia had been ruled for three hundred years by the Romanov Dynasty. The catastrophic effects of World War I resulted in the 1917 Russian Revolution that ousted Nicholas from power. In July of 1918, Bolshevik revolutionaries executed the royal family.

Governing Principles in Russian History

Three major principles had long shaped Russia's history. The first, autocracy, represented the unlimited power of the Russian monarch. Famous Russian rulers who governed as absolute monarchs included Ivan the Great, Ivan the Terrible, Peter the Great, and Catherine the Great. The second, orthodoxy, refers to the Russian Orthodox Church, which dominated the lives of the Russian people. The third, nationalism, emphasized love of country, closeness to the land, and acceptance of the traditional social system. The population's obedience to these principles was expected, and the state and church maintained nearly absolute control.

With the premature death of his father in 1894, Nicholas became the czar of Russia. He was ill-prepared to govern successfully. Even his father, not long before his death, had questioned his son's ability to rule as his successor. Nicholas had been taught to accept "official nationality" as essential to the continued success of his nation. Inheriting the state's institutions and traditional values, he saw no reason to govern differently. His statements and policies emphasized the continuation of the autocratic policies of his predecessors.

Although he was a loving husband and father, Nicholas usually is interpreted as a weak and

Nicholas II *(AP/Wide World Photos)*

ineffective monarch: indecisive, vacillating, and dominated by others. Yet he also could be self-centered, determined, and stubborn, unwilling to accept advice or consider the needs of his nation and his subjects. The czar's advisers and government officials rarely questioned his conservative outlook, and their policies generally supported the status quo. This led to a growing split between the monarchy and the population.

Conditions by 1900

Russia by the late nineteenth century faced significant changes and challenges that complicated Nicholas's efforts to maintain the status quo. Russia embarked on its Industrial Revolution, creating a large urban workforce that altered the nation's traditional peasant society and agricultural economy. Poor working and living conditions in cities and factory towns created frustration and unrest. Millions of illiterate peasants faced widespread poverty and hardship.

Reform movements and antigovernment groups proved increasingly difficult for the government to control or eliminate. Some opponents used terrorism; Nicholas's grandfather, for example, Czar Alexander II, had been assassinated. The repressive responses of the government included press censorship, creation of a secret police, arrests and prison sentences, and executions of opponents. Russian expansion into eastern Europe, southern and central Asia, and the Far East occasionally created friction with its neighbors. Imperialistic advances in China and Korea caused the disastrous Russo-Japanese War (1904-1905), which resulted in substantial Russian military defeats and its surrender to Japan.

The Final Collapse

Widespread revolutionary ferment in 1905 was caused by unstable domestic conditions and the disastrous war with Japan. In January, soldiers fired into unarmed crowds in St. Petersburg in the event known as Bloody Sunday. This event ignited revolutionary activity that lasted many months, including public unrest, strikes, the growing militancy of opposition groups, and scattered violence. The continued existence of the monarchy itself was uncertain.

Nicholas had to make a decision: to restore order by the massive use of force or to make

The December Revolution of 1905

The political concessions that Czar Nicholas II promised in his October Manifesto of 1905 met the objectives of many of the government's opponents. The promise of reforms failed to satisfy everyone, however. Radicals did not trust the regime to fulfill its promises. They demanded more sweeping political, economic, and social changes. Some opponents, including Vladimir Lenin, sought the end of the monarchy itself.

Factory workers also were dissatisfied that working conditions, salaries, and legal rights did not improve despite assurances of economic reforms. Employers opposed making further concessions to workers' demands. This situation led to scattered outbreaks of violence in December, 1905, notably in Moscow, where workers and radicals erected street barricades and fought against the authorities. Government forces soon crushed these disorganized efforts, however, and many workers and radicals were sent to prison or exile in Siberia. Some were executed. Although the revolutionaries failed to achieve their objectives in 1905, their sacrifices inspired others to continue the struggle against the czarist autocracy. In the communist era (1917-1991) these individuals were celebrated as national heroes.

concessions to the opposition. He chose the latter policy, promising in his October Manifesto to create a parliament with legislative authority and a written constitution with guaranteed civil rights. If these reforms had been implemented, Russia would have become a constitutional monarchy, bringing an end to absolute czarist rule. Anti-government opinion quickly subsided in response to his assurances.

Artist's representation of the first meeting of the Duma, the Russian parliament, in 1906. Nicholas II promised a degree of representative government in his 1905 "October Manifesto," but reforms soon fell by the wayside. *(Library of Congress)*

Nicholas gradually weakened the reforms after 1905, however, and the conservative leadership regained its authority until World War I (1914-1918). An unbroken series of military defeats in the war steadily weakened the czar's credibility and authority. This situation led to serious unrest in the capital in early 1917. Revolutionaries overthrew the government and forced Nicholas to abdicate as the Russian czar a few days later. The former czar and his family were kept under house arrest in several locations throughout 1917 and 1918 before Bolshevik revolutionaries executed them in July, 1918.

The Romanovs

The Romanov Dynasty (or ruling family) governed Russia between 1613 and 1917. Michael Romanov was the first Romanov czar, ruling from 1613 to 1645. The abilities and significance of the dynasty varied widely according to the specific czar in power. The most important Romanov monarchs included Peter I (Peter the Great, who ruled 1694-1725) and Catherine II (Catherine the Great, ruled 1762-1796). Alexander I (1801-1825) successfully led Russian forces against the armies of Napoleon I of France. Alexander II (1856-1881), grandfather of Nicholas II, freed millions of serfs in 1861.

The three-hundred-year dynasty succeeded in making Russia a major military power in Europe and Asia, and the Russian Empire grew in size. This traditional and conservative dynasty governed by the principles of "official nationality" (autocracy, orthodoxy, and nationalism). The major leaders are buried in the chapel of the Fortress of St. Peter and Paul in St. Petersburg, the Russian capital during Romanov rule from the time of Peter the Great. Nicholas II was the last of the Romanov monarchs. Modern descendants of the Romanov dynasty can be found, although none is descended directly from the family of Nicholas and Alexandra.

Various investigations disagreed about the location of the bodies, but DNA tests of skeletal fragments in the 1990's generally have been accepted as satisfactory identification of the remains of the Romanovs.

The Verdict of History

Many scholars have investigated Nicholas's role and responsibility for Russian events of the early twentieth century—Russia's losses in World War I, the overthrow of the Russian government and the end of the monarchy in early 1917, and the subsequent rise of Vladimir Lenin and the Communist Party to power. The consensus is that Russia would have faced major stresses in the twentieth century without Nicholas but that many problems were magnified by his inept rule.

Bibliography

Cowles, Virginia S. *The Romanovs*. New York: Harper and Row, 1971.

Ferro, Marc. *Nicholas II: The Last of the Tsars*. New York: Oxford University Press, 1990.

Massie, Robert. *Nicholas and Alexandra*. New York: Atheneum, 1967.

_______. *The Romanovs: The Last Chapter*. New York: Ballantine, 1995.

Radzinsky, Edvard. *The Last Tsar: The Life and Death of Nicholas II*. New York: Doubleday, 1992.

Taylor Stults

Chester W. Nimitz

Born: February 24, 1885; Fredericksburg, Texas
Died: February 20, 1966; San Francisco, California

U.S. Commander of Pacific naval forces in World War II

Chester William Nimitz (CHEH-stur WIHL-yuhm NIH-mihtz) was the grandson of a retired sea captain who had gone into the hotel business. Nimitz never knew his father, who died before he was born. Although brought up on sea tales, Nimitz originally desired an army career. When he could not obtain an appointment to West Point, he settled for the U.S. Naval Academy at Annapolis. Nimitz excelled in mathematics and graduated seventh in a class of 114. He was remembered for his cheerful disposition.

Early Career

After graduating in 1907, Nimitz joined the crew of the USS *Ohio.* While still a relatively junior ensign, he was given his first command. He subsequently ran aground the USS *Decatur* and was court-martialed. Nimitz then was assigned to duty in submarines, which were still experimental. He commanded several submarines and was awarded the Silver Lifesaving Medal for rescuing a fireman who had fallen overboard and could not swim. During World War I Nimitz served as an aide and chief of staff to the commander of submarines, Atlantic. He then came ashore to serve in the office of the chief of naval operations. In 1922 he went to the Naval War College as a student. Subsequently he became chief of staff to the commander of the battle force.

In 1926 Nimitz took charge of the Navy ROTC program at the University of California at Berkeley. This assignment began a close association with the university that would continue throughout his life. Nimitz then held a number of sea commands before being called ashore to serve as chief of the bureau of navigation. He was in this post on December 7, 1941, the day of the Japanese surprise attack on Pearl Harbor. The United States entered World War II the next day.

Commander in Chief, Pacific Fleet

After the Japanese attack on the U.S. naval base at Pearl Harbor, Hawaii, the Navy decided that it needed a new commander in the Pacific. Amidst the secrecy and near-hysteria of the period immediately after the attack, Nimitz made the trip across the country under an assumed name. Hidden in his wife's sewing bag he carried secret documents that detailed the nature and extent of the damage to the U.S. Pacific Fleet.

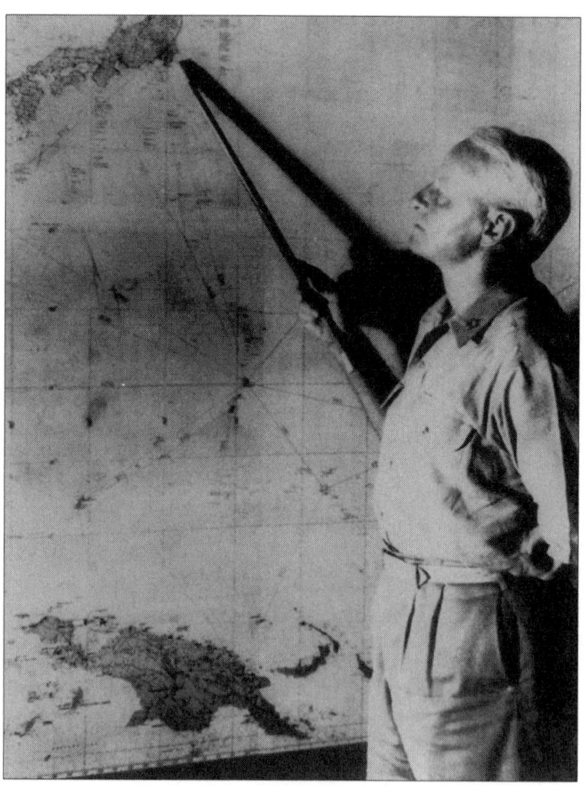

Chester W. Nimitz *(Library of Congress)*

When he arrived at Pearl Harbor, Nimitz did the best he could to restore the confidence and morale of his new subordinates. He kept his predecessor's staff and only gradually brought in his own people as others were promoted to responsible positions. Nimitz immediately set to work organizing his forces to fight the Japanese. With the battleships damaged or destroyed, he relied heavily on his aircraft carriers, and particularly on carrier commander William F. "Bull" Halsey.

In May of 1942 Nimitz had evidence that the Japanese were planning a major offensive, but he could not tell whether they were aiming for Midway Island or Oahu (Hawaii). He gambled on the former and sent his main striking force there. The Battle of Midway turned the tide of the war in the Pacific: From that time, the Japanese were always on the retreat. Under Nimitz's command, American forces retook the various islands of the Central and South Pacific. Finally, in September of 1945, Nimitz went to Tokyo Bay to receive the Japanese surrender. On December 15, 1945, Nimitz relieved Fleet Admiral Ernest J. King as chief of naval operations. After his term, he served in various administrative and diplomatic positions.

Bibliography

Driskall, Frank A. *Admiral of the Hills: Chester W. Nimitz*. Austin, Texas: Eakin Press, 1983.

Hoyt, Edwin Palmer. *How They Won the War in the Pacific: Nimitz and His Admirals*. New York: Weybright and Talley, 1970.

Potter, E. B. *Nimitz*. Annapolis, Md.: Naval Institute Press, 1976.

Leigh Husband Kimmel

American troops wade ashore over mined beaches during the March, 1945, invasion of Cebu Island. *(Library of Congress)*

Island Hopping

World War II in the Pacific posed special problems for American forces. They faced a lengthy struggle to capture many small islands, most of them rugged and covered with tropical jungle that made combat difficult. The Japanese had dug into these islands and boasted that their bases would be "unsinkable carriers" from which they could carry out the war indefinitely. The senior American commanders decided upon the strategy that came to be known as "island hopping." Instead of attacking the strongest Japanese garrisons directly, American forces would bypass them to attack weaker islands. When those were secured, the Americans would cut off the Japanese supply lines from behind, using submarines to sink as much Japanese shipping as possible. This strategy was used to great effect in the campaigns of New Guinea and Hollandia. As American forces increased in strength, major offensives were carried out in both the Central and South Pacific island groups.

Richard M. Nixon

Born: January 9, 1913; Yorba Linda, California
Died: April 22, 1994; New York, New York

President of the United States (1969-1974), the first president to resign from office

Richard Milhous Nixon (RIH-churd MIHL-hows NIHK-suhn) was the son of small businessman from Southern California and a devout Quaker mother. After graduating from Whittier College in 1934 and from Duke University's law school in 1937, he practiced law in California. In 1940 he married Thelma Catherine "Pat" Ryan. They had two daughters, Patricia and Julie. Pacifist by virtue of his Quaker upbringing, Nixon nevertheless served as a transportation officer in the South Pacific during World War II.

Richard M. Nixon *(Library of Congress)*

Controversial Campaigns

Nixon was a moderate conservative but was stridently anticommunist, matching America's Cold War mood. He became famous when he helped secure a perjury conviction against Alger Hiss, a former State Department official accused of being a spy. In 1946 he ran a harsh Republican campaign for U.S. representative from the Twelfth District of California. He was reelected in 1948, and in 1950 he sought a Senate seat, defeating the popular Helen Gahagan Douglas after another controversial campaign in which he labeled her "soft on Communism."

Nixon's youth, hard-line stance, and western origins won him the Republican nomination for vice president in 1952. Presidential candidate Dwight D. Eisenhower did not back Nixon fully, however, until after a dramatic television appearance by the Californian. Challenged to explain his financial background, Nixon made the famous "Checkers speech," in which he noted that the only gift he had ever accepted was the family dog, Checkers. The response to the speech—thousands of pro-Nixon letters and phone calls—made Nixon a political asset. As vice president, Nixon found himself in charge of the Republican Party, admired by party regulars for his loyalty but nicknamed "Tricky Dick" by his adversaries. He served two terms as vice president.

Nixon easily secured the Republican nomination for president in 1960 but lost to Senator John F. Kennedy. In televised debates between the two candidates, Americans could see Nixon sweating and pale, exhausted from campaigning, while Kennedy appeared tanned and healthy. The popular vote was very close, but the deciding electoral college vote favored Kennedy 303 to 219. Nixon returned to California to practice law.

Rapprochement with China

Diplomatic relations between the United States and China were abruptly ended after the communist takeover of China in 1949. In 1972, President Richard M. Nixon and his secretary of state, Henry A. Kissinger, made a historic trip to China. There they met with leaders Mao Zedong and Zhou Enlai. The trip led to a *rapprochement*, or better relations, that paved the way for U.S. trade with China. This trade, along with cultural exchanges, gave China a taste of Western life and aided in its modernization. Good relations between China and the United States may also have discouraged the Soviet Union from anti-American actions. Rapprochement with China was one of Nixon's major achievements as president.

He sought the governorship in 1962 but lost to Edmund G. "Pat" Brown. He announced that the press would not have him to "kick around any more."

The Presidency

Nixon changed his mind, however, and in 1968 he again won the Republican presidential nomination. A public disillusioned with the Johnson administration's handling of the war in Vietnam voted against Vice President Hubert Humphrey, and Nixon won 301-191 in the electoral college.

A Cold War president, Nixon focused on foreign policy, believing that the cabinet could look after the country. His administration did little to advance civil rights. In 1972 Congress passed the Equal Employment Opportunity Act to enforce parts of the 1964 Civil Rights Act. Still, Nixon's administration sought the support of southern segregationists. Nixon stressed "law and order" issues, encouraged revenue sharing to shift power to state and local government, and sought welfare reform. His administration did little to curtail the size or power of the federal government or to reduce tax burdens. In 1970 the voting age was lowered to eighteen, fulfilling a Nixon campaign promise.

U.S. president Richard M. Nixon atop the Great Wall of China during his historic 1972 visit to that country. *(National Archives)*

Nixon began to modify his bitter anticommunism. He realized that Americans, wearied by the Vietnam War, would no longer support intervention abroad. Seeking to end U.S. involvement in Vietnam without allowing South Vietnam's collapse, Nixon escalated bombing to apply pressure for a peace settlement. Finally, in January, 1973, the United States and North Vietnam signed an agree-

The Watergate Affair

On June 17, 1972, five men were arrested during a bungled break-in at the Democratic campaign headquarters at the Watergate hotel-apartment complex in Washington, D.C. The crime was later found to have been sponsored by the Committee to Reelect the President (CREEP). Ironically, the break-in, which would ultimately topple Richard M. Nixon, occurred during a campaign that the president was virtually assured of winning and, in fact, did win by a landslide in November.

By then, however, the president and his aides had already instituted a cover-up of Republican involvement in the break-in. The seven Watergate burglars were convicted, and the Senate began investigations into the affair. Tape recordings of the president's conversations with his aides were subpoenaed from the White House in July, 1973. Nixon resisted for months but finally was forced to hand over the tapes, which left little doubt that he had obstructed justice. The House Judiciary Committee voted to present articles of impeachment against the president in July, 1974. Even hard-line Republican senator Barry Goldwater, after hearing these tapes, agreed that they were the "smoking gun" that pointed to Nixon's direct involvement in the scandal. He advised Nixon to resign to preserve the integrity of the office of the president. On August 9, 1974, a disgraced Richard Nixon became the first president to do so.

U.S. president Richard M. Nixon (left) shakes hands with Soviet leader Leonid Brezhnev after the two signed the Strategic Arms Limitation Talks (SALT) Treaty in Moscow in 1972. *(Popperfoto/Archive Photos)*

ment that ended U.S. involvement in Vietnam. The agreement was so loosely worded, however, that the war was not really ended. South Vietnam fell in 1975.

With the Soviet Union, Nixon concluded agreements for grain sales and, most important, arms limitation. A 1972 agreement, the Strategic Arms Limitation Talks (SALT I) treaty, limited antiballistic missiles. During the 1973 Yom Kippur War, Nixon ordered a middle-level alert of U.S. armed forces that probably kept the Soviet Union from intervening in the Middle East conflict. His major triumph, however, came in 1972 with his trip to Beijing, China. He and Secretary of State Henry A. Kissinger effected rapprochement with China. On the other hand, Nixon, through the Central Intelligence Agency (CIA), aided in the overthrow of Chilean president Salvador Allende in 1973, and he supported the government of Pakistan despite that country's murderous behavior toward its own people.

A Second Term

Nixon was reelected in 1972, defeating Democratic senator George McGovern by an overwhelming 520 to 17 electoral votes. Unfortunately, Nixon had been so intent on ensuring his reelection that high officials in his campaign sanctioned a burglary of the national Democratic headquarters in the Watergate building in Washington, D.C. The Watergate affair, as the break-in and subsequent cover-up came to be known, not only tarnished Nixon's accomplishments but also sowed cynicism among U.S. citizens concerning their elected officials. After months of publicized congressional hearings, Nixon was forced to resign in disgrace on August 9, 1974.

In some ways, Nixon represented millions of post-World War II Americans: From a humble background, he achieved much through sheer drive, creating a public image of a patriotic, hardworking, decent young man. Behind the image, however, remained the real man: remote, under tremendous stress in his drive to succeed, angry at those who opposed him, and in the end actively willing to cover up a crime. His intelligence and diplomatic acumen bequeathed a legacy of brilliant and far-reaching foreign policy achievements; his fatal character flaws bequeathed an indelible public distrust of government.

Bibliography

Aitken, Jonathan. *Nixon: A Life*. Washington, D.C.: Regnery, 1993.

Nixon, Richard M. *RN: The Memoirs of Richard Nixon*. New York: Grosset and Dunlap, 1978.

Wicker, Tom. *One of Us: Richard Nixon and the American Dream*. New York: Random House, 1991.

Robert W. Sellen
updated by Christina J. Moose

Kwame Nkrumah

Born: September 21, 1909; Nkroful, Gold Coast (now Ghana)
Died: April 27, 1972; Bucharest, Romania

Pan-Africanist leader, first president of Ghana (1960-1966)

Kwame Nkrumah (KWAH-may ehn-KREW-mah) was raised Roman Catholic in a middle-class family. There was little in his early life to suggest a left-wing political career. His parents, a merchant mother and goldsmith father, were not unduly interested in radical ideology. Yet Kwame Nkrumah became increasingly involved in politics as he reached adulthood. He attended college in the United States beginning in 1935, receiving an undergraduate degree from Lincoln University. He then attended graduate school, earning master's degrees from both Lincoln and the University of Pennsylvania. Besides his official studies, Nkrumah read the works of Karl Marx and Vladimir Lenin as well as other socialist literature and black nationalist writings. Even after he declared himself a Marxist, Kwame Nkrumah described himself as a "nondenominational Christian." Leaving the United States in 1945, Nkrumah traveled to Great Britain, where he helped organize the fifth Pan-African Congress. Two years later he returned home to the Gold Coast to work for self-rule.

Kwame Nkrumah *(Library of Congress)*

Organizing for Independence

As general secretary of the United Gold Coast Convention (UGCC), Nkrumah delivered persuasive and radical speeches. He began to build a mass base for an independence movement that previously had garnered only narrow support. Support came mainly from the educated African elite. Nkrumah and his fellow radicals soon clashed with the moderate leaders of the UGCC. In 1949, he created the Convention People's Party (CPP), committed to immediate freedom from Great Britain. Within a year, Nkrumah had organized militant but nonviolent actions including strikes. In response, the British authorities arrested him, and Nkrumah was sentenced to a year in prison. Early in 1951, the first general election in the history of the Gold Coast showed powerful support for Nkrumah and the CPP. Freed from prison as a result of his election to Parliament, Nkrumah became prime minister of the Gold Coast in 1952.

Leader of an Independent Ghana

In 1957, the Gold Coast and the British trust of Togoland joined to become Ghana, an independent state within the British Commonwealth. Kwame Nkrumah took his place as the nation's first prime minister. His popularity grew as he built new schools, hospitals, and roads while giving Ghanaians jobs that had been filled by European whites. After the election of 1960,

Ghana became a republic with Nkrumah as president; he had wide-ranging powers. The harsh realities of the world capitalist market undermined the new government's development programs, and Ghana became saddled with a huge foreign debt. After 1961, Nkrumah increasingly believed that neocolonialism was thwarting his efforts to develop his nation, and he became friendly with the Soviet bloc nations.

After an attempted assassination in 1962, Nkrumah grew increasingly isolated from everyday life. The assassination attempt (and later attempts on his life) encouraged the authoritarian tendencies that Nkrumah had already exhibited. He encouraged a cult of personality to develop about him, and he strengthened his internal security force. In 1964, Ghana became officially a one-party state, with Nkrumah as president for life of both the country and his party. Nkrumah's once radical party became more and more the tool of self-interested careerists who cared more about their own well-being than about pan-African ideals.

Kwame Nkrumah, president of Ghana (left), greeting Indonesian president Sukarno at the United Nations in 1960. Behind them is Indian prime minister Jawaharlal Nehru. *(Archive Photos)*

Pan-Africanism

The concept of pan-Africanism was first promoted internationally by Henry Sylvester Williams in a 1900 London conference. At this meeting, the young W. E. B. Du Bois noted that "the problem of the twentieth century is the problem of the color line." The concept that all people of African descent, no matter where they might live, share a common struggle against racism and oppression formed the core belief of the movement. The movement also argued that a kinship exists among all African peoples that is cultural, social, and historical. Pan-African Congresses were held later in Paris (1919), London, Paris, and Brussels (1921); London, Paris, and Lisbon (1923), and New York (1927).

In 1945, black leaders from Africa, the Caribbean, the United States, and England gathered in Manchester, England, to issue their "Challenge to the Colonial Powers." This manifesto demanded autonomy and independence for Black Africa. Among the leaders of this congress were W. E. B. Du Bois, George Padmore, and Kwame Nkrumah, who would put these words into practice by leading Ghana to independence.

The Organization of African Unity

The longer Nkrumah continued in power in Ghana, the more he turned to the promotion of pan-Africanism. His key role in the formation of the Organization of African Unity (OAU) in 1963 marks the peak of his success. Despite his—and others'—high hopes, the OAU never became the vehicle that Nkrumah hoped would liberate and unify black Africa. He wanted to develop an ideological cadre of African political activists who would fight not only against outright colonialism (which then still existed in places such as Angola) but also against the neocolonialism that he saw as strangling Africa. Nkrumah believed that the OAU ultimately failed to counter the ability of major nations outside Africa to play one black-ruled nation against another.

Troubles at Home

Nkrumah's commitment to pan-Africanism probably contributed to his failure to see the warning signs back home in Ghana. By the mid-1960's, the nation's economy had worsened dramatically, and corruption existed throughout his governmental apparatus. Discontent grew within the armed forces, while Western governments feared Nkrumah's apparent procommunist slant in foreign affairs. While Nkrumah was visiting Beijing in early 1966, the army and police force seized power. Unable to return home, Nkrumah asked for and received political asylum in Guinea. During his exile, he wrote bitterly, but often insightfully, of his political career and the plight of Africa. In 1972, while undergoing treatment for cancer, Nkrumah died in Romania.

Kwame Nkrumah was a complex historical figure who combined a genuine love for the African people with a tendency toward undemocratic government. His promotion of pan-Africanism as an ideology, along with his long, remarkable record as an anticolonialist, clearly marks him as one of the heroes of twentieth-century African self-determination. Even after his death, Nkrumah has been an inspiration for Africans discouraged by the corruption and pettiness of many postcolonial regimes. Still, in practice, he was unable to reconcile democracy with freedom and self-determination. Moreover, he confronted—and was ultimately brought down by—the West's hostility toward African leaders who refused to follow their lead.

Bibliography

Baynham, Simon. *Military and Politics in Nkrumah's Ghana*. Boulder, Colo.: Westview Press, 1988.

Birmingham, David. *Kwame Nkrumah: The Father of African Nationalism*. Athens: Ohio University Press, 1998.

James, C. L. R. *Nkrumah and the Ghana Revolution*. Bridgeport, Conn.: Lawrence Hill, 1978.

Nkrumah, Kwame. *Consciencism: Philosophy and Ideology for De-colonization*. New York: Monthly Review Press, 1970.

William A. Pelz

The Coup of 1966

As Kwame Nkrumah promoted pan-Africanism, the Ghanaian economy continued to decline. Whether as a result of outside imperialist sabotage, as Nkrumah claimed, or government incompetence, as his critics claimed, by 1966 there was a shortage of food. The economy had all but collapsed. Nkrumah's flirtation with the communist world had alienated the United States and the West. So, on February 24, 1966, while Nkrumah was on a state visit to Communist China, the army revolted and seized power. With its charismatic leader absent, Nkrumah's government offered little resistance to a coup that was supported by the United States.

Philip John Noel-Baker

Born: November 1, 1889; London, England
Died: October 8, 1982; London, England

British political leader and peace activist

Philip John Baker (PHIH-lihp JON NOH-ehl BAY-kur) was one of seven children born to Joseph Allen, a businessman and politician, and Elizabeth B. Baker. Raised in a Quaker household, Baker attended King's College of Cambridge University and graduated with an M.A. in economics. He was an outstanding athlete and in 1912 competed in the Olympic Games in Stockholm. In 1914 he became vice principal of Ruskin College at Oxford University. The following year he married Irene Noel and added his wife's surname to his own name. In World War I Noel-Baker served in the British Ambulance Corps in Italy and was decorated with the Italian Croce di Guerra. He competed again in the Olympic Games in 1920 (winning a silver medal in the 1500-meter run), 1924, and 1928.

Philip John Noel-Baker *(Archive Photos)*

Advocate for Peace

After World War I, Noel-Baker worked on the commission that founded the League of Nations and was a member of the league's secretariat until 1922. A pacifist, he believed ardently in the cause of world peace and disarmament, and he devoted a large part of his life to working for that cause. The two books on disarmament he wrote in 1926 and 1927 established him as an authority, at a time when there were many failed attempts to establish an international framework for reducing armaments.

From 1929 to 1931 Noel-Baker served as a member of Parliament for the Labour Party, and he continued to support the League of Nations, advocating peace through the agency of international law. In 1936, as the political situation in Europe worsened, he published The *Private Manufacture of Armaments,* which argued that governments had abdicated their responsibilities to prevent the spread of weapons. The result, he wrote, was that unscrupulous private arms manufacturers, encouraged by governments, were producing a dangerously escalating arms race.

Cabinet Minister

After World War II, during which Noel-Baker served in Sir Winston Churchill's coalition government, Noel-Baker held several positions in the Labour government of 1945-1951. He was secretary for air in 1946, commonwealth secretary from 1947 to 1950, when he handled negotiations

The Geneva Protocol

In 1924, the League of Nations drew up the Geneva Protocol. It was aimed at establishing machinery for the peaceful settling of disputes between nations. The protocol called for all members of the League of Nations to condemn aggressive war and refrain from using force to settle a dispute. Quarreling nations were to request the mediation of the league, which would refer the case to the Court of International Justice or to a special tribunal. However, the Great Powers failed to agree on the terms of the Geneva Protocol. It was never ratified by the League of Nations and was dropped after its rejection by Britain in 1925. Philip Noel-Baker, who at the time was a university professor in London, worked extensively on the preparation of the Geneva Protocol. In spite of its failure, he later described his work on it as one of the most fulfilling experiences of his life.

with British colonies for their independence, and minister for fuel and power from 1950 to 1951, when the main debate was whether to place major British industries under state control. From 1946 to 1947 Noel-Baker was also Britain's representative to the United Nations.

In 1958, Noel-Baker published his major work, *The Arms Race*. At a time when the tension between the West and the Soviet Union was at its height, he exposed the folly of a continuing nuclear arms race. The book made carefully reasoned proposals for the gradual reduction of weaponry. Noel-Baker did not believe that total disarmament was an impractical goal, although he did oppose the faction in the Labour Party which argued that Britain should unilaterally disarm. Instead, Noel-Baker argued for collective agreements and collective security. *The Arms Race* was acclaimed worldwide and was a factor in Noel-Baker's being awarded the Nobel Peace Prize in 1959. The Nobel Committee cited Noel-Baker's many years of work for disarmament and for the League of Nations, and also for the relief work he organized during the Russian famine in the 1920's.

Noel-Baker retired from politics in 1970, but he continued to advocate the causes he believed in. Unfortunately, he died before he could witness the advances in arms control made during the 1980's.

Bibliography

Brennan, D. G. *Arms Control and Disarmament*. London: Jonathan Cape, 1967.

Ceadel, Martin. *Pacifism in Britain 1914-1945*. New York: Oxford University Press, 1980.

Morgan, Kenneth O. *Labour in Power 1945-1951*. Oxford, England: Clarendon Press, 1984.

Whittaker, D. J. *Fighter for Peace: Philip Noel-Baker*. York, England: William Sessions, 1989.

Bryan Aubrey

Manuel Noriega

Born: February 11, 1938; Panama City, Panama

Leader of Panama as commander of Panamanian Defense Forces (1983-1989)

Manuel Antonio Noriega Morena (mahn-WEHL ahn-TOH-nee-oh noh-ree-AY-gah moh-RAY-nah), former commander of the Panamanian military, drug trafficker, money launderer, and CIA informant, established a reputation as the dominant political power in Panama during the 1980's. From 1985 until 1989, Noriega hand picked Panama's political leaders, including the president, and ensured his candidates victories when necessary. In 1989, Noriega's government was removed by U.S. military forces. He was taken to the United States, where he was convicted of various crimes and sentenced to forty years in prison.

Early Career

Manuel Noriega was born in a poor barrio of Panama City, the son of parents of Colombian descent. He attended the Instituto Nacional, one of the premier high schools in Panama, prior to accepting a scholarship to the Military School de Chorrios in Lima, Peru. Noriega returned to Panama after completing his studies in Peru to join the National Guard as a commissioned sublieutenant. Eventually he attained the rank of first lieutenant. When a military coup brought down President Arnulfo Arias and his government in 1968, Noriega positioned himself as an ally of Omar Torrijos, the emerging dominant political leader in Panama.

After Noriega quelled a failed countercoup in 1969, he was rewarded with a promotion to lieutenant colonel and an appointment as chief of military intelligence. By the 1970's, Noriega had emerged as the chief adviser of Torrijos and was considered the most feared man in Panama. As head of the intelligence service, Noriega harassed and intimidated government opponents and dissidents. As early as 1971, the U.S. government was expressing concern regarding his involvement in drug trafficking. President Richard M. Nixon was so troubled by Noriega's actions that his administration considered assassinating him in 1972.

Political Strongman

Torrijos died in a 1981 plane crash. In 1983 Noriega emerged as his successor following a lengthy power struggle. Promoting himself to the rank of general and commander of the national guard, Noriega consolidated his power by com-

Manuel Noriega in a 1995 news interview at which he claimed that the U.S. government had violated his civil rights. *(AP/Wide World Photos)*

bining the national guard with the navy and the air force. His title became commander of the Panamanian Defense Forces. Beginning in 1986, U.S.-Panamanian relations steadily deteriorated. General Noriega's political repression and illegal activities became an embarrassment for the U.S. government, which had for some time been providing Panama with considerable support. Ultimately, relations between the two countries became so strained that the United States reduced its economic and military aid to Panama.

U.S. agents escort former Panama leader Manuel Noriega aboard an Air Force plane after his capture and arrest in Panama in 1990. *(Department of Defense)*

In 1988 two indictments against the general were handed down by federal grand juries in Florida. They alleged that he had violated U.S. racketeering and drug laws by providing protection for drug traffickers. Noriega responded by ousting the constitutionally elected president of Panama, Eric Arturo Delvalle. In March of 1988, a military coup failed in an attempt to oust Noriega. Unsuccessful in efforts to encour-

The U.S. Invasion of Panama

When Manuel Noriega became commander in chief of the Panamanian National Guard in 1983, he quickly emerged as Panama's most powerful political figure. At first his importance to the U.S. government—for fourteen years, Noriega had been a CIA informant—paid dividends for both the United States and Noriega. Over time, however, his ties to the infamous Medillin drug cartel, as well as to Chinese, Libyan, and Cuban spies and gunrunners, combined with his brutal suppression of his political enemies, became an embarrassment to the U.S. government.

The United States tried to find coup leaders within the ranks of the Panamanian military, but failed. Therefore, the administration of U.S. president George Bush decided that the U.S. military would remove Noriega by force. In the early morning hours of December 20, 1989, twenty-four thousand U.S. troops invaded Panama. Within an hour of the invasion, known as Operation Just Cause, a civilian government under the leadership of Guillermo Endara had been installed. The U.S. government lifted the economic sanctions that had been imposed in 1986. President Bush argued that the invasion of Panama had been necessary in order to protect the lives of Americans in the region, defend democracy in Panama, protect the sanctity of the Panama Canal Treaties, and combat the drug traffickers of Central and South America. Twenty-three Americans died in the U.S. invasion of Panama.

age a second coup attempt from within the ranks of the Panamanian military, the United States removed Noriega by force in December of 1989. Convicted in the United States of cocaine trafficking, racketeering, and money laundering, Noriega was sentenced to forty years in prison. Noriega published his memoirs in 1997, which he coauthored with Peter Eisner, former foreign editor of *Newsday*.

Bibliography

Buckley, Kevin. *Panama: The Whole Story*. New York: Simon and Shuster, 1991.

Coniff, Michael L. *Panama and the United States: The Forced Alliance*. Athens: University of Georgia Press, 1992.

Donnelly, Thomas M. *Operation Just Cause: The Storming of Panama*. New York: Lexington Books, 1991.

Grant, Rebecca. *Operation Just Cause and the U.S. Policy Process*. Santa Monica, Calif.: Rand, 1991.

Leonard, Thomas M. *Panama, the Canal, and the United States: A Guide to Issues and References*. Claremont, Calif.: Regina Books, 1993.

Donald C. Simmons, Jr.

Julius Nyerere

Born: March, 1922; Butiama, Tanganyika (now Tanzania)

President of Tanganyika (1962-1964), then Tanzania (1964-1985)

Julius Kambarage Nyerere (JEW-lee-uhs kahm-bah-rah-GAY ehn-YAY-ray-ray), whose father was a chief of the small Zanaki tribe, graduated from Makere College in Uganda and then became the first Tanganyikan to earn a university degree in the United Kingdom. He was awarded an M.A. degree in history and economics by the University of Edinburgh in 1952. Nyerere intended to follow a career in teaching, but that proved to be impossible once he took leadership of Tanganyika's campaign for independence. Eventually, he became prime minister of an independent Tanganyika and then president of the Republic of Tanzania. In 1954, Nyerere married Maria Magige; they had five sons and two daughters.

Julius Nyerere *(Library of Congress)*

Independence for Tanganyika

Tanganyika was under a British U.N. trusteeship when Nyerere returned from Edinburgh in 1953. Already a member of the Tanganyikan African Association (TAA), Nyerere was made president of the organization in 1953, mostly to honor him for his educational achievements. Although the TAA had made a commitment to eventual independence for Tanganyika, Nyerere concluded that the British colonial administration did not take the association seriously. Thus, on July 7, 1954, he helped to create the Tanganyikan African National Union (TANU), which became the country's principal force behind the drive for independence. Nyerere orchestrated TANU's political activities.

In 1954, the United Nations proposed that Tanganyika should become independent within twenty to twenty-five years. Colonial administrators argued that this was too soon, but TANU endorsed the U.N. position. Nyerere believed that independence might come within ten years, and he was right. Colonial officials tried by various means to weaken TANU and the independence movement, including the creation of the multiracial United Tanganyikan Party in 1955, but these efforts failed. Under the U.N. trusteeship arrangement, Tanganyika was governed by a British governor and a local legislative council. In 1960, TANU controlled seventy of the seventy-one council seats. In September, 1960, Tanganyika gained self-government, with Nyerere as chief minister, and in December, 1961, the country became fully independent.

In January, 1962, Nyerere resigned as prime minister to concentrate on strenghtening TANU.

Effectively, however, he remained in control of the government through his leadership of TANU. In 1962 he was elected president of the Republic of Tanganyika, and in 1964, after Zanzibar joined with Tanganyika, he became president of the United Republic of Tanzania. Nyerere was reelected every three years until he resigned in 1985. During his tenure, Tanzania was a one-party state.

African Socialism

Nyerere is best known for his efforts to establish a successful economy for Tanzania based on *ujamaa*, a Swahili word meaning "of the family." The underlying principles for this effort were contained in Nyerere's 1967 Arusha Declaration. Based on the region's cultural heritage of sharing goods, *ujamaa* placed a heavy emphasis on cooperative farming. It discouraged industry backed by foreign investors. Supported, ironically, by many Western economic development experts, Nyerere intended to prove that an African nation could become self-reliant without the benefit of Western-style capitalism and development. His program, which acquired the name "African socialism," failed abysmally. Little attention was paid to improvements in the country's infrastructure (roads, water supply, electricity, and so on), and one-third of the national budget was supplied by foreign assistance. On the other hand, a concurrent effort to improve literacy through free and universal education proved quite successful. By 1980, the country had the second highest indigenous literacy rate in Africa.

Nyerere refused to surrender his belief that African socialism could succeed. As a result, Tanzania, despite its impressive educational achievements, remained one of the world's poorest countries. It was not until January, 1992—seven years after he resigned as president—that Nyerere ad-

The Arusha Declaration

To a great extent, it was the Arusha Declaration of 1967 that propelled Julius Nyerere into the consciousness of world economic leaders and experts. The Arusha Declaration, named for the town in which Nyerere first read it in public, proclaimed a dramatic new course for economic development in an emerging independent state. Nyerere wanted to avoid the relationship of "dependency" that so many newly independent African countries had with highly developed Western states. Many development experts (mostly academics) had urged the adoption of a limited capitalism for Tanzania, one that emphasized small, regional industries. Nyerere, however, went a step farther: He advocated a socialist economy based on Tanzania's cultural heritage of sharing.

For Nyerere, Tanzanian self-reliance was the primary goal. The Arusha Declaration contained Nyerere's prescription for attaining this objective. The declaration stated that Tanzania would follow the path of rural development through cooperative farming and cooperative industries. Great urban industrial development was rejected, as was the acceptance of foreign investment. All produce and income was to be shared among those involved. Eventually, everyone in the country would achieve social and economic equality and become self-reliant. There would be no need to import expensive material goods from developed countries. Nyerere's experiment, which became known as "African socialism," did not succeed. In 1992, the economic policies outlined in the Arusha Declaration were recognized as unworkable, and Tanzania entered an era of economic reform in which the basic tenets of capitalism were accepted.

The Tanganyikan African National Union

Julius Nyerere established the Tanganyikan African National Union (TANU) in July, 1954, to provide purposeful leadership for the campaign for Tanganyikan independence. TANU succeeded the Tanganyikan African Association (TAA) because Nyerere, after becoming TAA president, believed it to be disorganized, overly cozy with colonial officials, and essentially a social club. Nyerere wanted TANU to have as members only those Tanganyikans (Europeans were excluded) who were committed to self-rule at the earliest possible time. He hoped that TANU would emerge as a dominant political force. Within a decade that hope became reality. When Nyerere announced the formation of TANU, he made it clear that there were certain guidelines to which the organization would adhere. These guidelines included a commitment to peaceful political change, social equality, and racial harmony. Nyere and TANU rejected the tribalism and ethnic divisions that threatened to delay the achievement of self-government.

mitted that Tanzania required economic reform along the lines of Western capitalism.

Julius Nyerere's first public meeting upon becoming the chief minister of a self-governing Tanganyika in September, 1960. *(National Archives)*

Reaction to Nyerere

Nyerere enjoyed strong support from Western European and North American governments. He appeared to be a trustworthy (from the West's viewpoint) African leader who rejected racism and who kept corruption to a minimum. He gained considerable respect in the West when, in 1972, he denounced Idi Amin, leader of neighboring Uganda, for forcing Asians from his country. In 1979, Nyerere sent troops to help bring down Amin's regime.

While Nyerere's personal charm and high level of education made him popular outside Africa, he was looked upon with jealousy and suspicion by many other African leaders. Many wondered why Nyerere commanded such respect in the West as a "democratic" leader when, in actuality, Tanzania had only one political party, and that party was controlled by Nyerere. There were often reports, largely ignored in the West, that Nyerere dealt harshly with anyone who attempted to mount opposition to his government. As early as 1962, he had pressed for laws to outlaw industrial action by workers and which made it possible to detain, without charges, anyone suspected of being a "troublemaker."

Divided Opinions

Historians have mixed views of Nyerere's twenty-three years as president of Tanganyika and then Tanzania. His plan to create an African socialism in Tanzania is now severely criticized, but that economic failure was no greater than those experienced by virtually every other African country following independence. Moreover, Nyerere's plan was endorsed, and to a great extent devised, by Western development experts. Nyerere continues to receive praise for maintaining political stability without resorting to excessive violence, for encouraging an end to racial and ethnic divisions, and for making education accessible to Tanzanians.

Bibliography

Coulson, Andrew. *Tanzania: A Political Economy*. New York: Oxford University Press, 1982.

Fischer, Heinz. *The Influence of Jomo Kenyatta and Julius K. Nyerere on Education and Development in Kenya and Tanzania*. Los Angeles: University of Southern California Press, 1980.

Resnick, I., ed. *The Long Transition: Towards Socialism in Tanzania*. Toronto: University of Toronto Press, 1979.

Samoff, Joel. *Tanzania: Local Politics and the Structure of Power*. Madison: University of Wisconsin Press, 1974.

Smith, William Edgett. "Julius K. Nyerere." *The New Yorker*, Oct. 16, 23, 30, 1971.

Ronald K. Huch

Milton Obote

Born: December 28, 1928; Akoroko, Lango, Uganda

President of Uganda (1966-1971, 1980-1985)

Apollo Milton Obote (a-PO-loh MIHL-tuhn oh-BOH-tay) was the third of nine children of a minor chieftain of the Lango tribe. At age twelve, Obote suffered a spear wound that ended his career as a shepherd and landed him in the Lira Protestant Missionary School. He attended Bugosa College in Mwiri, and later Makere College, but was expelled for his political activities. The British colonial government refused to allow Obote to accept scholarships from foreign colleges, so he left for Kenya in 1950. While in Kenya, Obote became involved in the independence movement and was a founding member of Jomo Kenyatta's Kenya African Union.

Milton Obote *(Archive Photos)*

Moving Uganda Toward Autonomy

Obote returned to the Lango District in 1956 after being asked to join the Uganda National Congress Party to fill the seat of an imprisoned Lango representative. By 1958, he was elected to serve on the legislative council, which gave him a forum from which to criticize British colonial rule. Following factional disputes in the Uganda National Congress in 1960, Obote founded the Uganda People's Congress (UPC) and was chosen president-general.

As Uganda began to move toward independence, its four traditional kingdoms—Buganda, Bunyoro, Toro, and Ankole—resisted. They feared that they would be dissolved under the rule of the competing political parties. In 1961, Obote negotiated agreements with the kingdoms, and the UPC entered into an alliance with the Kabaka Yekka (king only) party of Buganda. On April 25, 1962, this new alliance won sixty-seven of the ninety-one seats in the unicameral National Assembly. Obote was instrumental in constructing a constitution which allowed the kingdoms to exist as separate federal states within Uganda. On October 8, 1962, the Ugandan flag was raised for the first time after sixty-eight years of British rule. The results of the compromise played out in October of 1963, when King Mutesa II of Buganda was sworn in to the ceremonial role of president. Obote served as prime minister.

Consolidation of Power

The uneasy alliance with Buganda was short-lived, as Obote's desire for a socialist one-party

The Uganda People's Congress

Founded in 1959, the Uganda People's Congress (UPC) was built from dissidents who left the Uganda National Conference with Milton Obote in combination with the Uganda People's Union. The original focus of the UPC was the attempt to overcome the power struggles between the new political organizations and the four traditional Ugandan kingdoms. Following a compromise which promised autonomy to the kingdoms, the Kabaka Yekka (king only) party and the UPC entered into an alliance which led to victory in the 1962 elections.

The alliance between the UPC and the Kabaka Yekka collapsed in 1964, but defections from the other parties provided the UPC with the power it needed to maintain a substantial majority in the National Assembly. When Obote was deposed by Amin, the UPC's power went with him, only to return with Obote's return to power. After the second time Obote was deposed, the UPC remained active on the fringes of Ugandan politics seeking ways to return to control in Uganda.

state and his centralizing tendencies made the Kabakas nervous. In August of 1964, the Kabaka Yekka and the UPC split over territory issues. Despite the split, the UPC had garnered enough defectors from other parties to maintain the majority in the national assembly through 1965 and seemed to be moving toward Obote's ideal of a one-party state.

The first major challenges to Obote's power came in 1966. Opposition leaders charged Obote and his deputy commander of the army, Idi Amin, with having misappropriated $350,000 of war booty captured during the revolt in the Belgian Congo. In February of 1966, Obote responded to the charges by suspending the constitution and ordering the arrest of five members of his cabinet who had supported the allegations. He then instituted a new constitution which expanded the government's powers and installed himself as executive president for a five-year term. In May, the Bugandan conflict peaked when Obote sent troops, led by Amin, to attack Mutesa's palace, driving Mutesa into exile in Britain. The bloody engagement eventually led to the defeat of the Bugandan rebellion.

In an effort to solidify his rule, Obote had a new constitution adopted on September 8, 1967. It abolished the hereditary kingdoms and centralized most of the government's power within the presidency. Within a year, there was almost no official opposition to Obote and the UPC. Unopposed, Obote led Uganda through a period of relative stability and prosperity.

Overthrow

In July of 1970, the UPC passed new laws which made the UPC president the president of Uganda. Such a move eliminated virtually all political opposition to Obote. Among the public, Obote's plan for a one-party, socialistic Uganda led to growing discontent in the traditionally pluralistic nation. Obote began to grow wary of his own subordinates, especially Amin. While Amin was abroad, Obote attempted to regain control of the Ugandan army. Amin turned this move and the public discontent against Obote, ensuring continued devotion to Amin from the military. Amin did not wait long to take advantage of this devotion. On January 25, 1971, while Obote was in Singapore, Amin seized control of Uganda in a coup.

Return to Power

In 1979, Ugandan nationalist forces and Tanzanian forces toppled Amin. Obote returned from exile in May and was reelected president on De-

The Bugandan Rebellion

After being charged with misappropriation of gold and ivory in 1966, Milton Obote assumed all the powers of the government and arrested any who opposed him. Obote then installed a new constitution that expanded the role of the central government and diminished tribal autonomy. The ruler of Buganda, King Mutesa II, was outraged. He demanded, in April of 1966, that the Obote government leave Bugandan territory. In May, Obote's forces, led by Idi Amin, surrounded and eventually seized the palace and drove Mutesa into exile in London. After the bloody engagement, Obote enacted "emergency regulations" in Buganda.

Ugandan prime minister Milton Obote with Indian president Sarvepalli Radhakrishnan in New Delhi in 1965. *(Archive Photos)*

cember 9, 1980 in the first popular election in Uganda in eighteen years. Obote's second term as president was plagued by guerrilla attacks, his inability to control the army, tribal unrest, and economic instability. In an attempt to maintain control, Obote reinstated the State Research Bureau, the agency which led the violent repression of the Ugandan people during the Amin regime. Obote's second term ended July 27, 1985, when Lieutenant General Basilio Olara-Okello's National Liberation Army, which had also been instrumental in deposing Amin, took control of Kampala and installed a military government in Uganda. Obote was granted exile in Zambia.

Obote remained active in the workings of the UPC, conducting "external wing" meetings in Toronto, Canada, in July of 1998. Guerrilla groups continued to conduct terrorist operations in eastern Uganda in an attempt to return Obote's regime to power.

Symbol of the State

In many ways, the two terms Obote served as leader of Uganda are a microcosm of the central problem that has plagued the African nation since gaining freedom from Britain: the incessant battle between tradition and modernization. Despite his moves to modernize and unify Uganda and his brilliant political strategies, Obote was never able to overcome the conflict between new and old.

Bibliography

Adoko, Akena. *From Obote to Obote.* New York: Stosius/Advent Books, 1983.

Ingham, Kenneth, and Milton Kenneth Ingham. *Obote: A Political Biography.* New York: Routledge, 1994.

Mittleman, James H. *Ideology and Politics in Uganda from Obote to Amin.* Ithaca, N.Y.: Cornell University Press, 1975.

B. Keith Murphy

Álvaro Obregón

Born: February 17, 1880; Alamos, Sonora, Mexico
Died: July 17, 1928; Mexico City, Mexico

Mexican revolutionary, president of Mexico (1920-1924)

Álvaro Obregón (AHL-vah-roh oh-bray-GOHN) was born on a farm in northern Mexico to Fernando Obregón and Cenobia Salido de Obregón. He was the youngest of eighteen children. At the time of his son's birth Fernando was virtually penniless, having lost his holdings through a variety of political misadventures, fires, floods, and the theft of his livestock. Fortunately for young Álvaro, his mother's family, the Salidos, were well connected in Sonoran society, a fact that would aid him later in his career.

Obregón's father died when Álvaro was still young, so he had to begin working on a part-time basis when he was only ten years old. Even at that early age he demonstrated rare mechanical skills. Later he would build and patent a garbanzo seeder that became a popular farm-equipment item in Sonora's river country. As a young man he made a name for himself locally in the agricultural and contracting fields. His leadership qualities led him to be elected mayor of Huatabampo, Sonora, in 1911.

When the Mexican Revolution of 1910 broke out, Obregón did not become involved immediately. It was only after the overthrow of Mexico's revolutionary president, Francisco Madero, by the reactionary General Victoriano Huerta, that Obregón joined the revolutionary forces. He began his military career by leading a contingent of local Sonorans against the invasion of their state by Pascuál Orozco, a revolutionary turncoat.

Revolutionary General

Obregón and his Sonoran revolutionaries joined the forces of First Chief Venustiano Carranza in a protracted campaign to overthrow Huerta and restore the revolutionary government initiated by the murdered Madero. He and Francisco "Pancho" Villa became the two leading generals in the ensuing struggle. By 1914 the revolutionaries had defeated Huerta's federal army and forced Huerta to leave the country. Unfortunately the victors could not agree on how the government was to be reinstated. Obregón sided with Carranza, while Villa and the peasant leader, Emiliano Zapata, opposed the first chief.

From 1914 until 1920, civil war raged across the country. In a series of pitched battles, Obregón outmaneuvered the impetuous Villa, reducing that leader's formidable army to little more than

Álvaro Obregón *(Library of Congress)*

a small band of raiders. The defeat of Villa and the assassination of Zapata ensured Carranza's accession to the presidency in 1917.

The Rise of the Caudillo

Although the Mexican constitution precluded the reelection of an incumbent president, Carranza sought to select his own successor in order to retain control of the presidency. The Sonoran contingent, which had backed Obregón's bid for the office, ended up in open rebellion against the central government. Obregón's great popularity with the army led that institution to back their former commander. The result was the overthrow and, ultimately, the assassination of Carranza. An interim government, headed by the Sonoran Adolfo de la Huerta, took control until a new national election could be held. In 1920 Obregón himself became president in an overwhelming victory at the polls against only token opposition.

The Presidency

The tasks facing the newly elected caudillo (a Spanish term for a leader who is a powerful, authoritarian political boss) proved to be formidable. The recognition of the new government by the United States was critical. The American government wanted loans that it had made to Mexico repaid and wanted its citizens who had suffered losses during the Revolution reimbursed. The United States also wanted protection for American mining and petroleum interests in Mexico assured. Obregón managed to satisfy U.S. interests and to receive recognition by that government; some behind-the-scenes negotiations were involved in the process.

Internally, Obregón sought to strengthen the power of the executive branch. He was not a supporter of the political party system, and he played one against another in order to further his own political ends. When he attempted to emulate Carranza and select as his own successor Plutarco Elías Calles, another civil war erupted. Nevertheless, he and Calles managed to put down the rebellion. Calles became president in 1924.

Following Calles's victory, Obregón returned to Sonora, ostensibly retiring to civilian life. Soon it became apparent that he planned to campaign once more for the presidency in 1928. The caudillo's popularity with the general public remained so great that Calles had little choice but to support his former chief in the reelection bid. Despite an abortive attempt of a coup by some disgruntled army officers which was quickly suppressed, Obregón won the election handily. On July 17, shortly before he was to take office,

Obregón's War with Pancho Villa

Álvaro Obregón and Pancho Villa were destined to become mortal enemies. They were allied at first in the movement to oust the usurper Victoriano Huerta. After the latter had been deposed, however, the two found themselves on opposite sides of the fence in the dispute to reestablish the revolutionary government. In 1914, when Obregón met with Villa at his camp in an effort to resolve their problems, Villa lost his temper and threatened to execute Obregón on the spot. Obregón managed to calm Villa down and escape with his life.

Obregón had his revenge. In 1923, Villa, now retired and living on his ranch in Chihuahua, publicly announced his support for Adolfo de la Huerta over Obregón's chosen candidate, Plutarco Elías Calles. On July 20 of that year, assassins murdered Villa as he was driving through the town of Parral. Strong suspicions still exist that President Obregón was involved.

The de la Huerta Rebellion (1923-1924)

The Mexican constitution of 1917 specifically prohibits the reelection of the country's incumbent president. In 1923, Álvaro Obregón decided to extend his influence beyond the conclusion of his own term of office by choosing his own successor. He selected Plutarco Elías Calles, a fellow Sonoran and his minister of the interior. A storm of protest greeted this course of action. Opposition to the Calles nomination coalesced behind another Sonoran, Adolfo de la Huerta, who had served as the country's interim president in 1920.

De la Huerta's followers included a number of high-ranking military figures. In December, 1923, de la Huerta and his supporters launched an armed rebellion. The fighting was intense. Although it lasted only four months, fifty-four generals, seven thousand soldiers, and a large number of opposition politicians were executed, killed in action, or forced to flee the country. Critical to the success of Obregón and Calles in smothering the uprising was the refusal by the U.S. government to furnish any aid to the rebel faction. De la Huerta managed to cross the border into the United States without being apprehended. He started a new career as a voice coach in Hollywood, California.

president-elect Obregón was assassinated by a religious fanatic, José de León Toral, who considered the popular leader a major persecutor of the Catholic Church. Obregón's death caused a temporary crisis for Mexico's political leaders, but outgoing President Calles's astute handling of the succession problem saved the country from being plunged into another civil war.

Although Álvaro Obregón proved to be one of Mexico's most popular postrevolutionary leaders, he has also been classified as the last of the country's caudillos. Following his death, the office of the president and the government itself became more institutionalized, with strict limitations placed on the manner in which the president could govern. Obregón will be remembered for his battlefield achievements and the fact that he held Mexico together in the first turbulent years following the Mexican Revolution.

Bibliography

Aguilar Camin, Héctor, and Lorenzo Meyer. *In the Shadow of the Mexican Revolution*. Austin: University of Texas Press, 1993.

Dulles, John W. F. *Yesterday in Mexico*. Austin: University of Texas Press, 1961.

Hall, Linda. *Álvaro Obregón: Power and Revolution in Mexico*. College Station: Texas A&M University Press, 1981.

Hart, John Mason. *Revolutionary Mexico*. Berkeley: University of California Press, 1987.

Machado, Manuel A., Jr. *Centaur of the North*. Austin, Tex.: Eakin Press, 1988.

Carl Henry Marcoux

Sandra Day O'Connor

Born: March 26, 1930; El Paso, Texas

First woman to be named a U.S. Supreme Court justice (named 1981)

Sandra Day O'Connor (SAN-drah DAY oh-KO-nur), born Sandra Day, was born into a ranching family that owned sizable acreage in southern Arizona. She earned her bachelor's degree from Stanford University in 1950 and graduated with honors from Stanford's law school in 1952. She married John O'Connor, an attorney, in 1952, and they had three sons.

Sandra Day O'Connor *(Library of Congress)*

Groundbreaking Justice

Although O'Connor graduated near the top of her class from the Stanford Law School, she had difficulty getting a job because many law firms discriminated against women. For example, one law firm was willing to offer her a job as a secretary but not as a lawyer. Thus O'Connor turned to public service as the avenue for using her legal education to contribute to society.

O'Connor was the first woman to serve as an assistant attorney general in Arizona. When she subsequently ran for political office, she eventually became the first woman majority leader of the Arizona state senate. She was later appointed to serve as a judge on the Arizona Court of Appeals. When President Ronald Reagan sought to fulfill his campaign pledge to appoint the first woman to the U.S. Supreme Court, he appointed O'Connor to be an associate justice in 1981.

O'Connor's Judicial Legacy

O'Connor became a dependable member of the conservative wing that dominated the Supreme Court during the 1980's and 1990's. For example, she joined in many decisions which defined rights for criminal defendants more narrowly than in prior cases. Because of her experience in state government, she emerged as a strong advocate for federalism, the governmental theory that emphasizes the need for state governments to have sufficient authority to handle their own affairs without interference from Congress or the federal courts.

O'Connor developed a role as one of the "middle" justices who could shape the development of important legal issues by deciding in each case whether to join the Court's conservative wing or their more liberal rivals. Although O'Connor voted regularly with the Supreme Court's most conservative justices, she also demonstrated her independence by joining other justices for specific issues such as freedom of religion and gender discrimination. For example, while O'Connor criticized aspects of *Roe v. Wade* (1973), the Supreme Court's controversial decision that established a right of choice for women concerning abortion, she resisted her conservative colleagues' arguments for abolishing the precedent. Despite harsh criticism from conservatives who had supported her Supreme Court nomination, O'Connor wrote a jointly authored opinion in *Planned Parenthood v. Casey* (1992) that preserved a right of choice for abortion. O'Con-

U.S. Supreme Court justices David Souter, Anthony Kennedy, and Sandra Day O'Connor watch President Bill Clinton deliver the State of the Union message in January, 1999. At the time, the U.S. Senate was in the midst of the impeachment trial of Clinton. *(AP/Wide World Photos)*

Religious Freedom Restoration Act, 1993

The First Amendment of the U.S. Constitution guarantees the right to freely engage in religious practices. In 1990 the Supreme Court declared that governments can hinder religious practices if those practices conflict with general laws. The case, *Employment Division of Oregon v. Smith*, upheld a state drug law which prevented Native Americans from using peyote as part of traditional religious ceremonies. Congress reacted to the Supreme Court decision by enacting the Religious Freedom Restoration Act in 1993. The act required governments to provide compelling justifications for laws that hinder religious practices. In 1997, however, the Supreme Court declared the act unconstitutional, saying that Congress lacks the power to enact such a law. In a dissenting opinion in *City of Boerne v. Flores* (1997), Justice Sandra Day O'Connor traced the history of religious freedom rights and argued that *Employment Division of Oregon v. Smith* should be overturned. She argued that the Constitution itself imposes on governments the same requirements that Congress sought to enact in the Religious Freedom Restoration Act.

Sandra Day O'Connor with chief justice of the United States Warren Burger on the day of her swearing in as Supreme Court justice in 1981. *(Ricardo Watson/Archive Photos)*

nor argued that the legitimacy of constitutional law would be threatened if the Court acted too rashly in eliminating established precedents. In *Mississippi University for Women v. Hogan* (1982), O'Connor cast the deciding vote and wrote the Supreme Court's opinion in a case which required federal courts to look more closely at allegations of gender discrimination. In *Thompson v. Oklahoma* (1988), O'Connor cast the deciding vote to prevent the application of the death penalty for crimes committed by defendants younger than age sixteen.

Sandra Day O'Connor will always be remembered as a pioneering role model who helped break down barriers to the success of women in the legal profession. She will also be known for her pivotal role on the Supreme Court. Although she usually supported conservative outcomes, she demonstrated her independence by providing her liberal colleagues with support on specific issues.

Bibliography

Fox, Mary Virginia. *Justice Sandra Day O'Connor*. Hillside, N.J.: Enslow Publishers, 1983.

Lamb, Charles, and Stephen Halpern. *The Burger Court: Political and Judicial Profiles*. Champaign: University of Illinois Press, 1991.

Maveety, Nancy. *Justice Sandra Day O'Connor*. Lanham, Md.: Rowman & Littlefield, 1996.

Christopher E. Smith

Seán T. O'Kelly

Born: August 25, 1882; Dublin, Ireland
Died: November 23, 1966; Dublin, Ireland

President of Republic of Ireland (1945-1959)

Seán Thomas O'Kelly (SHON TO-muhs oh-KEH-lee) was the son of Samuel O'Kelly and his wife, Catherine O'Dea. He was educated in Dublin at the Christian Brothers and O'Connell Schools and from 1898 to 1902 worked at the National Library of Ireland. He joined the nationalist Sinn Féin Party in 1903. By this time, O'Kelly had obtained his credentials as a full-time journalist, becoming editor of the Gaelic League publication *An Claidheamh* and journalistic associate for *United Irishman*, Sinn Féin's official publication. He would hold key positions in both the Gaelic League (general secretary, 1915-1920) and the Sinn Féin Party (honorary secretary, 1908-1910). In 1918, O'Kelly married Mary Kate Ryan of Tomcoole, County Wexford. She died in 1934, and, in 1936, O'Kelly remarried, to his late wife's younger sister, Phyllis.

Early Political Career

O'Kelly was elected to the Dublin City Council in 1906 and was to serve on the corporation until 1932. He was a charter member of the paramilitary Irish Volunteers. He participated in gunrunning operations and, as staff captain to Volunteer commandant Patrick Pearse, played an active role in the 1916 Easter Uprising in Dublin. For this, O'Kelly was incarcerated by British troops at Richmond Prison, Dublin. Spared the death sentences meted out to Pearse and other rebel leaders, O'Kelly was transferred to prison in Wales. By May of 1917 he had escaped to join the staff of the new Irish Volunteers commandant, Eamon de Valera. Running for a seat in Parliament, he was elected representative for County Longford.

In the December, 1918, general election, O'Kelly was Sinn Féin's organizational director. The party achieved spectacular success, captur-

Seán T. O'Kelly (center), long-time president of the Republic of Ireland. *(National Archives)*

ing seventy-three parliamentary seats on 48 percent of the popular vote. On January 21, 1919, these Sinn Féin members of Parliament in effect seceded from the Westminster Parliament and proclaimed themselves "Dáil Éireann," an independent Irish Parliament. O'Kelly was elected its speaker. Almost simultaneously, the Anglo-Irish War of 1919-1921 broke out.

The Irish revolutionary government split over the question of acceptance of the terms of the Anglo-Irish treaty of 1921, which called for the partition of Ireland into an autonomous Irish Free State and Protestant-dominated Northern Ireland, which would remain within the United Kingdom. O'Kelly and de Valera were among those opposing the agreement, and O'Kelly was consequently imprisoned for the duration of the Irish Civil War (1922-1923). Released, he collaborated with de Valera to form the Fianna Fáil Party, becoming its deputy leader in 1926. He was elected once more to Dáil Éireann the following year.

Government Minister and President

When Fianna Fáil assumed power, O'Kelly served in de Valera's cabinet as minister for local government and health (1932-1939), of education (1939), and of finance (1939-1945). In 1945, upon the retirement of President Douglas Hyde, O'Kelly was nominated for the position on the

Seán T. O'Kelly in September, 1949, reviewing an honor guard in ceremonies marking the end of British rule over Ireland. *(National Archives)*

Dáil Éireann

The summary execution of fourteen leaders of the Irish Easter Uprising by British military authorities shocked Irish public opinion into sympathy for the revolutionary nationalism that the rebels and their Sinn Féin Party advocated. By December, 1918, most of the former rebels were at liberty. That month, many ran under the Sinn Féin banner for parliamentary seats in the general election. Among them were Eamon de Valera and Constance de Markievicz, the senior surviving rebel leaders. A Sinn Féin electoral landslide occurred everywhere in Ireland except in the Protestant north. In January of 1919 the seventy-three new Sinn Féin members of Parliament remained in Dublin and convened at the Mansion House. There, on January 21, 1919, in defiance of British authority, they voted themselves the title Dáil Éireann and claimed to be the legitimate parliamentary body of a separate Irish state.

Fianna Fáil ticket and won convincingly. He was reelected without opposition in 1952 and retired in 1959. O'Kelly died in Dublin in 1966, his wife Phyllis surviving him. He left no children. O'Kelly's studiously nonpolitical role as official head of state, despite the highly partisan nature of his pre-1945 career, is credited with establishing the presidency as a respected focal point within the social and governmental structure of the Republic of Ireland.

Irish leader Michael Collins with Irish Free State soldiers in 1922, during the Irish Civil War. Séan O'Kelly was imprisoned for the war's duration because of his opposition to the Anglo-Irish treaty of 1921. *(Archive Photos/Camera Press)*

Bibliography

Bowman, John. *De Valera and the Ulster Question, 1917-1923.* Oxford, England: Clarendon Press, 1982.

Dunphy, Richard. *The Making of Fianna Fáil Power in Ireland, 1923-1948.* Oxford, England: Clarendon Press, 1995.

Lawlor, Sheila. *Britain and Ireland: 1914-1923.* Dublin: Gill & Macmillan, 1983.

Lee, J. J. *Ireland, 1912-1985: Politics and Society.* Cambridge, England: Cambridge University Press, 1989.

MacCardle, Dorothy. *The Irish Republic!* New York: Farrar, Straus & Giroux, 1965.

Raymond Pierre Hylton

Thomas P. O'Neill, Jr.

Born: December 9, 1912; Cambridge, Massachusetts
Died: January 5, 1994; Boston, Massachusetts

U.S. politician, speaker of the House (1977-1986)

Thomas Philip "Tip" O'Neill (TO-muhs PHIH-lihp "TIHP" oh-NEEL) was born into an Irish Catholic family. O'Neill may have inherited his political inclination from his father, who served six years on the city council while directing the Cambridge water department. O'Neill got his nickname from a St. Louis Browns baseball player known for hitting foul tips. He drove a truck and played poker to support himself while attending Boston College. After graduating, he sold insurance; he continued to do so during his early political career. In 1941 he married Millie Miller, and together they had five children.

Thomas P. O'Neill, Jr. *(Library of Congress)*

Political Beginnings

O'Neill began his political career in 1928 when, as a teenager, he campaigned door-to-door for Al Smith's unsuccessful run for the presidency. In his senior year at Boston College, he decided to run for a seat on the Cambridge City Council. He lost by 150 votes. In 1936 he was elected to the Massachusetts state legislature. After serving ten years, he was elected minority leader. In 1948, when the Democrats regained control, he became the youngest majority leader in the history of the state.

The Move to Washington

In 1952, O'Neill successfully campaigned for John F. Kennedy's seat in the House of Representatives. During his second term in the House, he began serving on the Rules Committee, where he helped broker procedural deals that brought major bills to the floor. In his eighteen years on the Rules Committee, O'Neill participated in antipoverty legislation, the Civil Rights Acts of 1956, 1957, and 1964, gun control legislation, and aid to education. On the committee, O'Neill was known more as a loyal follower than as a potential leader of the House.

Before being elected as House majority leader in 1973, O'Neill served as party whip, whose job it is to enforce a party's discipline and ensure that party members vote. In 1967, at the risk of damaging his political career, O'Neill spoke out against Democratic president Lyndon B. Johnson's sending American troops to Vietnam. He decided to support Eugene McCarthy, the Democratic antiwar candidate, in the 1968 presidential election. A few years later, O'Neill was one of the first members of Congress to mention impeachment when the issue of Watergate surfaced. Although he admired President Richard M. Nixon's pre-Watergate politics, he grew concerned over the possibility that Nixon's people would resort to any means they felt necessary to defeat the Democratic Party.

Speaker of the House Thomas P. "Tip" O'Neill, Jr. (left), with minority leader John Rhodes at the start of the ninety-sixth Congress in 1978. *(Archive Photos)*

Speaker of the House

O'Neill was elected speaker of the house in 1977 because of his services to friends and supporters throughout his political career. It was a position to which

Tip O'Neill and the Vietnam War

Despite personal reservations, Tip O'Neill voted to support President Lyndon B. Johnson's original resolution to send troops to Vietnam. After much thought, he decided to lead an investigation of the war. The results of his investigation convinced him that it was a civil conflict, one in which the United States should not be involved. He began to express his disapproval of the war in 1967. O'Neill knew that going against his party, and his president, could endanger his political career. Nevertheless, he drafted a carefully worded newsletter outlining his position and sent it to his constituents. Through his investigation, he had also discovered that many other Washington officials felt as he did. In later years, O'Neill regretted not going public with his opposition sooner.

Thomas P. O'Neill leaving the Capitol in April, 1985, after the House of Representatives denied a request from President Ronald Reagan for $14 million in aid to the Contras, who were fighting against Nicaragua's government. The denial led White House officials to supply aid illegally. *(AP/Wide World Photos)*

he had aspired since his arrival in Washington in 1953. He led congressional trips to other countries to learn about the problems and solutions of other nations. As speaker, O'Neill served under Presidents Jimmy Carter and Ronald Reagan. He served ten consecutive terms as speaker, the longest tenure since Congress first met in 1789.

A cigar-smoking, poker-playing, outspoken baseball fan, O'Neill spent nearly sixty years in state and federal government. He was widely known to have keen political instincts. He stood up for what he believed in, earning himself a place as one of the nation's most respected leaders before retiring in 1986.

Bibliography

Clancy, Paul R., and Shirley Elder. *Tip: A Biography of Thomas P. O'Neill, Speaker of the House.* New York: Macmillan, 1980.

Ehrenhalt, Alan, ed. *Politics in America: Members of Congress.* Washington, D.C.: Congressional Quarterly Press, 1981.

O'Neill, Thomas P., and William Novak. *Man of the House: The Life and Political Memoirs of Speaker Tip O'Neill.* New York: Random House, 1987.

Maryanne Barsotti

Daniel Ortega

Born: November 11, 1945; La Libertad, Chontales, Nicaragua

Sandinista revolutionary leader and president of Nicaragua (1979-1990)

Daniel Ortega Saavedra (dah-NYEHL ohr-TAY-gah sah-ah-VAY-thrah) was born into a poor working-class family, one bitterly opposed to the rule of the then Nicaraguan dictator Anastasio Somoza García. He attended local Catholic schools with his brother, Humberto, two years his junior. The brothers would become close collaborators throughout their political careers.

Ortega joined the FSLN, a political movement created to overthrow the Somozan dictatorship, in 1963. He participated in bank robberies and assassinations designed to compromise and weaken the government. In 1967 he was captured and imprisoned by the Somoza regime and served seven years. He was then released in an exchange of prisoners held by the government and hostages taken by the FSLN.

Ortega and his brother belonged to what was called the *tercerista* faction of the movement, one advocating a broad alliance between the FSLN and other political groups opposed to Somoza. They argued for revolutionary activity in Nicaragua's urban areas and worked to organize active military units in the cities themselves. In 1979 the Sandinistas (FSLN groups) and their allies succeeded in overthrowing Somoza, who fled into exile.

The Sandinista Government

Although the Sandinistas represented only part of the total opposition movement, they quickly seized control of the reins of government. They created a group named the National Directorate, consisting of the Nine Comandantes of the Revolution. Daniel and Humberto quickly assumed leadership roles in this small, concentrated center of power that ran the country.

The Cuban government of Fidel Castro had aided the Sandinistas in their military successes and now provided aid to the new leftist government. Nicaragua, under its National Directorate, quickly declared the country an ally of Cuba and the Soviet Union in the then continuing Cold War with the United States. They began to provide aid to the leftist rebel FMLN movement in neighboring El Salvador, hoping to see that organization overthrow the legally constituted government there as well.

Daniel Ortega *(Archive Photos/Archive France)*

The Ortega Presidency

The Sandinistas called for a national election in 1984 in order to legitimize their rule. Daniel Ortega was elected president, with 67 percent of the votes cast over only nominal opposition. However, under Ortega's government the economy failed to improve. Much of the national product went to support a sixty-thousand-man army that the Sandinistas developed with the help of Cuba and the Soviet Union.

Much of the northern part of the country was under constant attack by the U.S.-supported Nicaraguan Democratic Force (FDN), armed bands composed of former national guardsmen from the Somoza era, disaffected Sandinistas, and local peasants opposed to government agrarian policies. These rebels came to be known as the Contras. In aiding them, the U.S. government under President Ronald Reagan had decided that Central America would be the battlefield to stop the expansion of the Soviet Union and its allies in the Western Hemisphere. Although the Sandinistas were able to contain the Contra movement, they had little success in managing Nicaragua's economy.

Nicaraguan president Daniel Ortega (right) with visiting Cuban president Fidel Castro, at ceremonies in Timal, Nicaragua, for the 1985 opening of a major sugar-processing plant built with Cuban assistance. *(AP/Wide World Photos)*

By 1989, the global picture had changed. The primary Sandinista allies, Cuba and the Soviet Union, lacked the resources to furnish Nicaragua with material aid. Neighboring El Salvador had a popularly

The Contras

The Contra movement, although composed almost entirely of native Nicaraguans, depended completely on the United States for weapons and supplies. In 1986, an American named Eugene Hasenfus was on a supply plane shot down by the Sandinistas. When captured, he readily admitted his role in the clandestine U.S. shipments to the Contras. Although the Contra movement succeeded in disrupting Nicaragua's economy and resulted in the deaths of many innocent civilians as well as troops on both sides, it did not succeed in securing the support of most of the country's population. The Contras gave up their weapons in return for an internationally supervised amnesty program in March of 1988.

Daniel Ortega with supporters in 1990, after conceding defeat in the Nicaraguan elections. *(Reuters/Jorge Nunez/Archive Photos)*

elected government, and Democratic movements were beginning to spread throughout Latin America.

Ortega and the Sandinistas, seeking to arrive at some type of an understanding with the new U.S. administration under George Bush, agreed to an open presidential election in Nicaragua, to be held February 15, 1990. To the surprise of the incumbent, a united opposition party led by a woman, Violeta Chamorro, defeated the Sandinistas with 55 percent of the popular vote to their 42 percent. Democracy had returned to Nicaragua. Although out of power since 1990, Ortega and the Sandinistas remained a potent political force in Nicaragua in the 1990's. Ortega planned to run for president once more in the year 2000 election. In the late 1990's Nicaragua remained one of the poorest nations in Latin America.

Bibliography

Christian, Shirley. *Nicaragua: Revolution in the Family*. New York: Vintage Books, 1986.

Kinser, Stephen. *Blood of Brothers, Life and War in Nicaragua*. New York: G. P. Putnam's Sons, 1991.

Miranda, Roger, and William Ratliff. *The Civil War in Nicaragua*. New Brunswick, N.J.: Transaction Publishers, 1993.

Pastor, Robert A. *Condemned to Repetition: The United States and Nicaragua*. Princeton, N.J.: Princeton University Press, 1987.

Carl Henry Marcoux

Turgut Özal

Born: October 13, 1927; Malatya, Turkey
Died: April 17, 1993; Ankara, Turkey

Prime minister (1983-1989) and president (1989-1993) of Turkey

Turgut Özal (TEWR-geht OO-zahl) was born in the provincial Malatya region of Turkey. His father was an Islamic religious leader, his mother a teacher; these two influences may have contributed to the respect Özal showed for both the religious and secular aspects of the Turkish polity. The Özal family frequently traveled around the country in their work, which gave the young Turgut a chance to meet broad segments of the Turkish population. In 1950, he graduated from Istanbul Technical University, a leading training ground for Western-oriented Turkish scientists and engineers. In 1954, he married Semra Yeginman, whom he met while working in the Electrical Studies Institute in the Turkish capital, Ankara.

Economist Turned Politician

Özal's economic expertise won him positions in various governments in the 1960's and 1970's, particularly those led by the conservative Suleyman Demirel. The maverick strains in his character showed, though, as he spent some years running a private corporation and campaigning for Parliament as a candidate for the pro-Islamic party. With the military coup led by General Kenan Evren in 1980, Demirel and all other traditional politicians were banned from politics. The military encouraged Özal, who had been named deputy prime minister for economics in the military regime, to run in the carefully monitored elections it set up in the fall of 1983. The military assumed that Özal, as an economic technocrat, would not rock the political boat and that he was so little-known he would not win. Indeed, the conservative candidate, Turgut Sunalp, was the generals' favorite to win. However, Özal prevailed in the battle of the two Turguts, partially because he was seen as a new face who did not wholly have the generals' approval.

A Change for Turkey

Özal was an anomaly in Turkish politics, a new force in many ways. Though a pro-Western conservative, his belief in the free market made him more analogous to the then-British prime minister Margaret Thatcher than to the sort of steady conservative politicians Turks had traditionally elected. In addition, Özal had a flamboyant personal style, one labeled egotistical by his critics.

Turkish president Turgut Özal at an August, 1990, press conference discussing the Persian Gulf crisis brought about by Iraq's invasion of Kuwait. *(Reuters/Ratih Saribas/Archive Photos)*

Özal lifted as many economic controls as possible. Especially visible was his repeal of quotas on imports, meaning that Turkish consumers had access to a far wider variety of foreign goods, especially automobiles. In turn, he devalued the Turkish currency, which helped raise exports. Özal also tried to reduce bureaucracy and central control in the civil administration. Despite all these signs of Westernization, Özal made it clear that he was personally committed to Islam and, though hardly abandoning Turkey's secular tradition, that he was open to a public role for the Muslim faith lacking in Turkey's modern traditions.

Consolidating Civilian Rule

By the mid-1980's, it was clear that Özal, rather than the military, was in charge in Turkey. Gradually, civilian rule and multiparty democracy once again became the norm. Yet shadows soon emerged for Özal on the domestic political stage. In 1987, despite his opposition, the politicians banned in 1980 were once again allowed to run

Turgut Özal touring a Kurdish refugee camp in Silopi, Turkey, in 1991. Fifteen to twenty thousand Kurds who had fled persecution by Saddam Hussein's government in Iraq were living at the camp. *(AP/Wide World Photos)*

The Motherland Party

After General Kenan Evren's military coup in 1980, all previous Turkish political parties were banned. New parties, with different leaderships, were ordered set up in their place. One of these was the Motherland Party (*Anavatan* in Turkish), which was founded by Turgut Özal on May 20, 1983. Though in many ways a continuation of the Conservative Party led by the since-banned Suleyman Demirel, it had two important differences. The Motherland Party was more open to free-market economics, yet paradoxically was also more welcoming to Islamic religious elements that had been alienated by Demirel's basically secular orientation. In the 1980's, the Motherland Party played a key role in reestablishing Turkish civil society and laying the groundwork for a truly democratic political sphere. Once Özal became president in 1989, the prestige of the party weakened, as his successor as prime minister, Yildirim Akbulut, lacked his charisma. The Motherland Party lost the October, 1991, election to a centrist coalition and did not return to power in Özal's lifetime. Under the leadership of Mesut Yilmaz, the Motherland Party remained an important factor in Turkish politics through the 1990's.

Turgut Özal (left) meeting with U.S. president George Bush in the White House in 1992. *(AP/Wide World Photos)*

for office. Particularly annoying to Özal was the reemergence of his former mentor and current rival, Demirel.

Secure in his control of Parliament, Özal had himself elevated from prime minister to president in 1989. This office removed him from the fray of daily politics, but it also began to isolate him from public opinion. The lavish entertaining of Özal and his wife, Semra, and their conspicuous ties to the wealthy elite did not endear him to ordinary Turks. When Bulgaria persecuted and expelled its ethnic Turks, Özal welcomed them to Turkey without having a rational plan as to where to house them, raising charges that he was exploiting these refugees for propagandis-

Turkey and the European Community

In April, 1987, Turgut Özal's government applied to enter the European Community (EC). This move signaled an unprecedented wish to be fully integrated with Europe even though most of Turkey is in Asia. The European Community decided not to grant admission to Turkey. Europeans mentioned Turkey's human rights record and its ongoing rivalry with Greece over Cyprus as factors leading to their refusal of Turkey's application. However, most Turks suspected that Europe turned them down primarily because Turkey is a Muslim country. Özal had argued that his free-market reforms made Turkey a natural fit to join the European Community. Many European nations, however (especially Germany, which already housed two million Turkish people known as "guest workers"), feared massive immigration by what they saw as an alien Turkish element. Turkey finally established what was called a "customs union" with the European Union in 1996 (the European Community had become the European Union, or EU, in 1993). This arrangement fell short of full membership. The compromise was seen as necessary because many Turkish politicians did not expect full membership any time soon but did not wish to be excluded in principle from the new Europe. As a number of eastern European nations were approved for membership in the EU in the 1990's, Turkey's frustration with Europe became more acute.

tic purposes. In 1991, Özal's party lost parliamentary control, leaving Özal in office as president but his rival Demirel as prime minister.

Turkey on the World Stage

Özal's economic policies made him something of a protégé of both the Thatcher government in Britain and the administration of president Ronald Reagan in the United States. His trade policies also gave Turkey more respectability in Europe, a situation which led the Özal government to apply, unsuccessfully, for Turkish admission to the European Community (EC) in 1987.

Two unexpected events in the early 1990's made Turkey's geopolitical position more important. First, the breakup of the Soviet Union in 1991 led to the emergence of several independent republics of basically Turkic language and culture, resurrecting an age-old vision of a Turkish sphere of influence extending deep into Central Asia. Second, Iraq's invasion of Kuwait in 1990 placed new emphasis on Turkey as a pro-Western linchpin in the Middle East. Özal played this position to the hilt, frequently appearing on American television as a crucial figure in the anti-Iraq coalition.

An Interrupted Career

Özal died suddenly in April, 1993, leaving a vacuum in the leadership of Turkey. Even though Özal smoked heavily and had undergone several operations in the United States, his demise was unexpected. Despite Özal's internal loss of popularity, most observers believed that he had more to accomplish. Özal's death left Turkey open to continued tension between the military, the political establishment, and various Islamic movements.

Bibliography

Bianchi, Robert. *Interest Groups and Political Development in Turkey*. Princeton, N.J.: Princeton University Press, 1984.

Muftuler-Bac, Meltem. *Turkey's Relations with a Changing Europe*. New York: St. Martin's Press, 1997.

Pope, Nicole, and Hugh Pope. *Turkey Unveiled: Ataturk and After*. London: John Murray, 1997.

Rustow, Dankwart A. *Turkey, America's Forgotten Ally*. New York: Council on Foreign Relations, 1989.

Nicholas Birns

Ian Paisley

Born: April 6, 1926; Armagh, Northern Ireland

Northern Ireland religious and political leader

The parents of Ian Richard Kyle Paisley (EE-ahn RIH-churd KIL PAYZ-lee) were devout Protestants, his father being a Baptist preacher committed to Northern Ireland's continued union with the United Kingdom. Paisley's preaching career began in his teens, as did his crusade against the Catholic Church, the Irish Republic, theological modernism, and any sort of ecumenism that could endanger his fundamentalist Protestant Christianity. By the early 1950's Paisley had become the moderator, or head, of the small Free Presbyterian Church.

Religion and politics were one for Paisley. The paradigm of the outsider, he believed the Unionist Party, which had ruled Northern Ireland since its inception in 1922, was too willing to compromise with both the Catholic Church and the Irish Republic. He also opposed the leadership of the Protestant and unionist Orange Order because of its ties with the Unionist Party.

A tall and physically imposing man, Paisley exuded charisma and power, whether attacking the Catholic Church, the Irish Republic, the Unionist Party, or the British government. His approach was always confrontational, and he led demonstrations in Northern Ireland, in England, and even in Rome at the time of the Second Vatican Council. Charged with creating disturbances, Paisley was arrested several times.

Ian Paisley (center) marching with other Protestant protesters in London in 1967. *(Express Newspapers/Archive Photos)*

Rise to Influence

In the 1960's, Northern Ireland prime minister Terrance O'Neill attempted to reach out to the north's Catholic minority and to the Irish Republic. However, many Protestants and unionists were suspicious of any contacts with their historic enemy. A Catholic civil rights movement began in 1968, dedicated to obtaining equal rights for Northern Ireland's Catholics in housing, employment, and the political arena. Most Protestants and unionists saw the campaign as an attempt to subvert Northern Ireland's ties with Britain and as a stalking horse for the militant Irish Republican Army (IRA).

British troops were dispatched, both communities were polarized, violence increased, and as a defender of Protestant unionism, Paisley rose in prominence. In 1970 he was elected to the Northern Ireland parliament and a few months later to the United Kingdom parliament. He helped found the Democratic Unionist Party (DUP) in 1971, effectively becoming the party's despot. The DUP was frequently in uneasy coalition with other dissident groups, but Paisley was unable to work with others as equals. By the end of the decade Paisley was the leading spokesman for radical Protestant unionism, a position symbolized by his victory in the 1979 European Community (EC) elections: He was elected a member of the European Parliament, ironically because he condemned the EC as being a Catholic conspiracy.

The Democratic Unionist Party

Founded in 1971, the Democratic Unionist Party (DUP) was the successor of earlier groups opposed to the long-governing Unionist Party, and it quickly became the vehicle for Ian Paisley's crusades. The leadership of the DUP was drawn largely from the Free Presbyterian Church, although most supporters, coming mainly from rural areas and from the Belfast working class, were not members of that body. By the 1980's the DUP had emerged to near-parity with the Official Unionist Party, forcing the latter to the political right. Although the DUP became more professional with the addition of many university graduates, it maintained its intransigence, opposing any compromise with Northern Ireland's Catholics, with the governments of the Irish Republic or the United Kingdom, or with Ulster's more moderate Protestant and unionist politicians. In 1998 the DUP was the only major party opposed to the agreement which posited the possibility of peace in beleaguered Northern Ireland.

The Hillsborough Agreement

At times Paisley favored total integration into the United Kingdom. At other times he desired a restoration of the Protestant-controlled Northern Ireland Parliament. Not a constructive statesman, his forte was opposition. In 1980 he objected to British prime minister Margaret Thatcher's consultations with the Irish Republic, and in 1985 he opposed the Hillsborough Agreement, which allowed cross-border cooperation with the Irish Republic, anathema to Paisley. After several abortive truces and years of negotiations, a peace and power-sharing agreement was signed in 1998. Paisley led the opposition to the pact, although it was approved, and in the subsequent elections his DUP won twenty seats in the new assembly.

North Ireland political figure Ian Paisley speaking in Washington, D.C., in 1994. *(Reuters/Bruce Young/Archive Photos)*

Bibliography

Bruce, Steve. *God Save Ulster: The Religion and Politics of Paisleyism*. New York: Oxford University Press, 1986.

Cooke, Dennis. *Persecuting Zeal: A Portrait of Ian Paisley*. Dingle, County Kerry, Ireland: Brandon, 1996.

Moloney, Ed, and Andy Pollak. *Paisley*. Dublin: Poolbeg, 1986.

Smyth, Clifford. *Ian Paisley: Voice of Protestant Ulster*. Edinburgh, Scotland: Scottish Academic Press, 1987.

Eugene Larson

Andreas Papandreou

Born: February 5, 1919; Chios, Greece
Died: June 23, 1996; Ekáli, near Athens, Greece

Prime minister of Greece (1981-1989, 1993-1996)

Andreas George Papandreou (ahn-THREH-ahs yeh-AWR-yay pah-pahn-THRAY-ew) was the son of a politician, George Papandreou, who served as prime minister of Greece during the 1960's. Arrested and tortured in 1939 for his opposition to the government of dictator Ioannis Metaxas, Andreas Papandreou immigrated to the United States in 1940. He earned a doctorate in economics from Harvard University in 1943. He became a naturalized U.S. citizen in 1944 and served for two years in the U.S. Navy. After his first marriage ended in divorce, Papandreou married Margaret Chant in 1951. They had four children.

Andreas Papandreou *(Library of Congress)*

Return to Greece

Papandreou taught at several American universities during the 1940's and 1950's, publishing several books that raised his reputation as a liberal economist. He returned to Greece in 1959 to direct the Center for Economic Planning. In 1964 he renounced his American citizenship in order to run for Parliament. That February he won a seat in Parliament, and his father became prime minister. The elder Papandreou appointed his son to the office of minister to the prime minister, a position of considerable influence. Although the two men had a turbulent relationship, the father was clearly grooming his son for high office. Andreas Papandreou quickly became a controversial figure, and he combined intelligent criticisms of the Greek economy with harsh attacks on the political right. He was soon accused of financial improprieties and forced to resign from the cabinet; however, within six months he was appointed deputy minister of economic coordination.

Allegations that Papandreou was connected to a secret left-wing society within the military contributed to the downfall of his father's government in July, 1965. For the next two years, the Greek government was in constant turmoil, with Papandreou under attack for his leftist views. In April, 1967, right-wing military officers seized control of the government and arrested their opponents. Papandreou spent eight months in jail before the military offered all political prisoners a general amnesty. In January, 1968, he left Greece for a teaching position in Sweden. The following year he moved to Canada, where he remained until 1974.

Panhellenic Socialist Movement

The military junta proved to be both repressive and inept, and it fell from power in 1974. In August of that year, Papandreou returned home to cheering crowds. He quickly formed a new political party, the Panhellenic Socialist Movement (Pasok), committed to national independence and popular sovereignty. In November elections, Pasok captured 14 percent of the popular vote, an impressive showing for a party only two months old.

During the 1970's Pasok grew in popularity with the Greek people, earning nearly 26 percent of the vote in 1977. The party was national, gaining support from Greeks in all regions and from most socioeconomic groups. In truth, however, Papandreou and Pasok were virtually identical. He ruled the party with an iron hand and developed its campaign positions. Papandreou promoted economic development as the best means to raise wages, improve social services, and end dependence on foreign nations. He was especially critical of Greek entry into the European Community (EC, the Common Market) and of cooperation with the United States, which he argued undermined national independence. As the Greek economy faltered during the late 1970's, Papandreou and Pasok gained more support. Using the campaign slogan "Change" in 1981, Pasok received 48 percent of the popular vote. On October 21, 1981, Papandreou was sworn in as prime minister of Greece, the first socialist to hold that position.

Prime Minister

After taking office, Papandreou moderated his positions on many issues. His threat to withdraw from the North Atlantic Treaty Organization (NATO) was forgotten, and, despite anti-American rhetoric, he allowed the United States to lease land for military bases. Nonetheless, he steered an independent foreign-policy course, offering

Greece in the Common Market

In 1961, Greece entered into a treaty of association with the European Economic Community (EEC), also known as the Common Market. The treaty included scheduled tariff reductions. It was assumed that Greece would receive full membership in the EEC in 1984. However, after the fall of Greece's military junta in 1974, Greek entry into the Common Market—then called the European Community (EC)—became an important and contentious issue in domestic politics. Prime Minister Constantine Karamanlis made membership in the EC a top priority. Karamanlis believed that in addition to bringing economic benefits, full EC membership would provide international political legitimacy to the government and to the nation.

While Karamanlis negotiated with other Common Market members, Andreas Papandreou and his Panhellenic Socialist Movement (Pasok) party condemned the move. In 1977 Papandreou declared that should he ever become prime minister, Greece would withdraw from the EC. When Greek officials signed a treaty in 1979 that would make Greece the tenth member of the EC on January 1, 1981, Pasok members boycotted the ratification debates. However, Papandreou moderated his position on the EC as the 1981 elections approached. When he became prime minister in October, 1981, he did not fulfill his earlier promise to withdraw from the EC. In 1984 Papandreou told Pasok members that withdrawal would have a negative impact on the Greek economy.

Greek prime minister Andreas Papandreou voting in Greece's 1990 national elections. *(Reuters/Yannis Behrakis/Archive Photos)*

his support to groups such as the Palestine Liberation Organization (PLO) and the Nicaraguan Sandinistas.

Papandreou supported liberal social measures, including a national health system and a lower voting age. In the economic sphere, he called for the development of rural areas, which lagged behind urban growth. However, government spending contributed to a high inflation rate, and in 1985 Papandreou announced austerity measures. Although this move curbed inflation, it also slowed the growth of the Greek economy.

Pasok earned 46 percent of the vote in the 1985 elections, but Greek voters soon soured on Papandreou's leadership. In addition to concerns about the economy, Greeks were troubled by scandals in his public and personal life. Although his health was poor, he refused to delegate authority while he was hospitalized in 1988. News that he was divorcing his wife to marry an airline flight attendant half his age did not please his constituents. Finally, charges of financial wrongdoing ensured that Papandreou and Pasok would not be returned to power in the 1989 elections.

The Cyprus Question

Cyprus is a large island off the coast of Turkey that has both Greek and Turkish populations. By the 1960's, conflict between Greece and Turkey over control of Cyprus had existed for generations. The issue was further complicated by the fact that Greece and Turkey were allies under the North Atlantic Treaty Organization (NATO). Therefore, Cyprus was a significant foreign-policy and domestic-policy issue in Greek politics. Because 80 percent of the island's population is Greek, many Greeks hoped to unite with the island, an idea that the Turkish minority fervently opposed. Andreas Papandreou took a nationalistic position that allowed for little compromise; he supported the Greek Cypriots. During the 1960's, he and his father thwarted a move that would have effectively partitioned the country into Greek and Turkish sections. In a move calculated to anger the United States, he suggested that Greek Cypriots look to the Soviet Union for support. Turkey invaded Cyprus in 1974, and NATO failed to intervene. Turkey ultimately took control of the northern part of the island. Papandreou used the incident to attack American influence and to garner support among Greek voters. In 1982 he became the first Greek prime minister to visit Cyprus.

A Second Term

Papandreou was acquitted of the charges against him in 1992, and the following year he again became prime minister. However, by 1995, worsening health was preventing him from taking an active role in governing, and he resigned from office in January, 1996. He died five months later. Papandreou was remembered as a skilled politician with popular appeal whose internal contradictions limited his effectiveness as a leader.

Andreas Papandreou in Athens in 1974, shortly after returning to Greece from Canada when Greece's ruling military government collapsed. *(AP/Wide World Photos)*

Bibliography

Clogg, Richard. *A Concise History of Greece*. Cambridge, England: Cambridge University Press, 1992.

_______. *A Short History of Modern Greece*. 2d ed. Cambridge, England: Cambridge University Press, 1986.

Legg, Keith R., and John M. Roberts. *Modern Greece: A Civilization on the Periphery*. Boulder, Colo.: Westview Press, 1997.

Theodoracopulos, Taki. *The Greek Upheaval: Kings, Demagogues, and Bayonets*. London: Stacey International, 1976.

Woodhouse, C. M. *Karamanlis: The Restorer of Greek Democracy*. Oxford, England: Clarendon Press, 1982.

Thomas Clarkin

Franz von Papen

Born: October 29, 1879; Werl, Westphalia, Germany
Died: May 2, 1969; Obersasbach, Baden-Württemberg, West Germany

Chancellor of Germany (1932) and Nazi diplomat

Descended from prosperous Catholic landowners in the Saar valley, Franz von Papen (FRAHNTZ fon PAH-pehn) received a military education and in 1911 was accepted for General Staff duties. However, late in 1913 he was appointed military attaché for the German embassy in Washington, D.C., with subordinate functions in Mexico. Papen was, in fact, organizing German and Austrian participation in Mexico's revolutionary politics when World War I broke out in Europe in August of 1914. Papen returned to the United States, but his intelligence work left a paper trail connected to espionage and sabotage against American war production for the Allies, as well as a private letter referring to "idiotic Yankees." In 1915 he was recalled from the United States as *persona non grata.* He subsequently served as an officer on the western front and in the Middle East.

Politics

After the war, Papen rejoined his wife and children and became a gentleman farmer representing agricultural interests, religious values, and anticommunism in the Prussian assembly (the Landtag) during the 1920's. Germany's national governing coalition crumbled as the 1929 depression and unemployment drove voters into the ranks of the communists or the Nazis, and in 1932 presidential confidant Kurt von Schleicher proposed Papen's appointment as chancellor, heading an anticommunist administration. As an individual Center Party member without an organized following, Papen was understandably pessimistic about his chances for success, but he let himself be persuaded by President Paul von Hindenburg. He was appointed chancellor on May 31, 1932. His cabinet, already selected by Schleicher, was so conspicuously upper class that critics soon dubbed them the "barons."

Papen's political plan was to gain major concessions from France and Britain at the Lausanne Conference on postwar reparations, opening on June 15, 1932. He would thereby win German votes in the Reichstag elections set for July 31. However, the predominantly hostile German press minimized Papen's gains at Lausanne while attacking his overtures to the Nazi Party

Franz von Papen *(Library of Congress)*

and his suspension of the Social Democratic government in Prussia. In addition, as a nonparty chancellor, Papen had no space on the July ballot, in which the greatest gain went to the Nazis. Their führer, or leader, Adolf Hitler, refused to join a cabinet except under his own leadership.

Papen was prepared to change the constitution by presidential decree, ultimately restoring the monarchy, but Hindenburg demurred. On December 2 Hindenburg replaced Papen with Schleicher in the search for a right-wing coalition government. Papen, however, on January 4, 1933, negotiated a bargain with Hitler by which the Nazi leader would become chancellor in a predominantly non-Nazi cabinet, with Papen as vice chancellor. However, when Hindenburg appointed Hitler chancellor on January 30, Papen discovered that as vice chancellor he had no specific duties or authority. Hitler, moreover, could decide policy himself without taking a vote in cabinet.

Diplomacy

Nevertheless, Hitler found a useful task for his vice chancellor—special emissary to the Vatican for negotiating with Cardinal Pacelli a 1933 Concordat defining the status of the Catholic Church in the Third Reich (Hitler's government). Papen's grasp of the issues made it easy for him to arrive quickly at a practical compromise between Catholic and state interests. Hitler gained credit for a step favoring moderation and traditional values, and Cardinal Pacelli (later Pope Pius XII) observed that the Concordat provided Catholics at least a measure of legal protection.

In the spring of 1934, as tension rose in Germany between left-wing and right-wing Nazis, Papen on June 17 delivered a speech at Marburgh University deploring the increasing intolerance of political criticism. This speech coincided with the conflict between rival Nazi factions that led to the bloody Röhm purge of June 30. Several members of Papen's staff were killed, and it appears that Papen himself was spared partly by confusion. This event ended his membership in the cabinet but not his diplomatic career.

When local Nazis assassinated Austrian chancellor Engelbert Dollfuss on July 25, 1934, Hitler appointed Papen "minister on special mission" to Vienna as a gesture toward a peaceful solution

Mexico and the Central Powers

World War I began in 1914. A major goal of the diplomacy of the war's Central Powers (led by Germany) was a Mexican-American war that would distract the United States from intervention in Europe, divert American military production, and interrupt the supply of Mexican petroleum to Britain and the Royal Navy.

At the outset of 1914, Germany was supplying arms to General Victoriano Huerta, who seemed to be the emerging "strongman" following the Mexican Revolution of 1910. However, U.S. president Woodrow Wilson found an excuse to send American Marines to Veracruz, crippling Huerta by cutting off his supplies. Within months, Venustiano Carranza became Mexico's leader, accepting German or Austrian funds while resisting Wilson's political discipline.

Neither Wilson nor Carranza wanted war, despite the tensions produced in 1916 by U.S. general John J. Pershing's unsuccessful pursuit of Francisco "Pancho" Villa into Mexican territory. Certainly there was no practical basis for the fanciful alliance of Germany, Mexico, and Japan that was proposed by the 1917 "Zimmerman telegram," a piece of Germany's Mexican policy that helped produce the April 6, 1917, U.S. declaration of war against Germany.

of the crisis. His negotiations with Chancellor Kurt Schussnigg were, in Papen's account, aimed at improved relations leading to an eventual union of Germany and Austria. However, Papen can hardly have been surprised when Hitler and Hermann Göring expedited this process with the forced annexation of Austria in March, 1938.

In April, 1939, Hitler appointed Papen ambassador to Turkey. There he negotiated a ten-year Turko-German agreement. The agreement did not bring Turkey into Hitler's war against Britain and Russia, but it did keep the Turks neutral even as Axis forces occupied the Balkans in 1941. Papen also made good use in 1943 and 1944 of the diplomatic papers photographed at the British embassy in Ankara by the famous spy "Cicero." Ultimately the Turks yielded to Allied pressure and broke relations with Germany, leading to Papen's retirement.

The Allied invasion of Germany made Papen a fugitive until he was arrested and imprisoned by U.S. Army authorities on April 20, 1945. He

Franz von Papen was among the Nazi leaders tried at the war-crimes trials at Nuremberg, Germany, in 1946. He is seated third from right in the row immediately in front of the military police standing at rear. *(AP/Wide World Photos)*

Reparations for World War I

The 1932 Lausanne Conference, attended by Franz von Papen, was a ragged end to the bitter wrangling over post-World War I reparations. The European countries that had defeated Germany in World War I demanded, in the 1919 Treaty of Versailles, that Germany pay war reparations: payments for damages that would also serve to punish Germany's aggression. To many Germans the imposition of reparations came as an unjust surprise, but to many Frenchmen and Britons, it seemed a logical prize for winning the war.

The amount of damages claimed, initially $56.5 billion, later $33 billion, was of less immediate concern than finding the interest costs in gold. After all, no sensible private financier would invest gold in a German economy liable for extensive gold reparations payments. German failure to make the 1922 payments led to the French occupation of the Rhur region of Germany in 1923 and to runaway inflation, which wiped out German savings. With the 1924 Dawes Plan and the 1929 Young Plan, American loans funded German reparation payments, which in turn financed Allied war-debt payments to the United States. The Hoover moratorium of 1931-1932 marked the end of American support for this circulation of funds. The 1932 Lausanne Conference reduced Germany's obligation to 3 billion Reichsmarks (about $750 million) in gold bonds. In 1933, Adolf Hitler disavowed the bonds.

was tried at Nuremberg from October, 1945, to October, 1946, as one of the major Nazi war criminals. He was charged with aggression and conspiracy to commit aggression. Acquitted by the International Military Tribunal, he was subsequently arrested, tried, convicted, fined, and sentenced in several German denazification proceedings. Released in 1949, he published his memoirs in 1952 and died on May 2, 1969.

Franz von Papen chose to believe that serving Germany and opposing communism justified his working for Hitler and the Nazis. German books and articles on Papen reflect many different views on the man. Most English-language sources have been critical.

Bibliography

Katz, Friedrich. *The Secret War in Mexico*. Chicago: University of Chicago Press, 1981.

Papen, Franz von. *Memoirs*. London: Andre Deutsch, 1952.

Rolfs, Richard W. *The Sorcerer's Apprentice*. Lanham, Md.: University Press of America, 1995.

K. Fred Gillum

Park Chung Hee

Born: September 30 or November 14, 1917; Taegu region, Korea
Died: October 26, 1979; Seoul, Korea

President of South Korea (1963-1979)

Park Chung Hee (PAHRK CHUHNG HEE) was born in 1917 during Korea's Japanese colonial period (1910-1945). In his twenties he attended the Japanese-run Manchuria Military Academy and began a career as a soldier, initially in the Imperial Japanese Army. After the liberation of Korea in 1945, he continued his military career in the South Korean army. After a brief involvement in a military uprising in Yosu in 1947, Park continued to rise through the ranks. His service included a six-month stint in the United States at Fort Sill, Oklahoma.

During the 1950's, many officers, including Park, were upset by the corruption and cronyism that characterized the Syngman Rhee regime (1948-1960). When demonstrations broke out against Rhee in 1960, the military refused to support him. As a result, Rhee was forced to resign, and a new democratically oriented government took power. The new government, however, made little progress economically. Political process seemed chaotic, and many anticommunist army officers feared that South Korean students would link up with their counterparts in communist North Korea. After one year of this state of affairs, Park, along with his relative Kim Jong-p'il and other high-ranking military officers, overthrew the civilian government and established military rule. By this time Park had become a major general.

Park Comes to Power

The military coup, in May of 1961, was upsetting to the United States, South Korea's most important ally. It was especially embarrassing to the new liberal democratic president, John F.

The Coup of 1961

The military coup of May, 1961, was led by Kim Jong-p'il and Park Chung Hee, both high-ranking officers in the South Korean military. The coup overthrew a civilian government that had been in power for only a year following the forced resignation of Syngman Rhee, the country's previous leader. In part, the coup's leaders were motivated by factionalism within the armed forces. The junior officers involved in the coup saw their senior officers as corrupt. Since senior military officers controlled the allocation of American military aid, their power was extensive. Many of the coup leaders were also concerned about the poor economic record of the civilian government and worried about the threat of communism. Others were convinced that a democratic form of government—which had operated since the overthrow of Rhee in 1960—was too chaotic and invited military aggression from communist North Korea. Park was a major general at the time, but he had the confidence of many of the junior officers. The coup itself was relatively bloodless, and the result was the elevation of Park to power. Kim was later named to head South Korea's Central Intelligence Agency. The coup placed the military in the forefront of Korean politics, where it would remain for the next three decades.

Economic Growth in South Korea

In the early 1960's, South Korea was one of the poorest countries in the world, with a per-capita income of about $100 a year. Despite large amounts of American aid, the Syngman Rhee administration had been unable to stimulate economic growth. Under Park Chung Hee (head of the South Korean government from 1961 to 1979), the economy began to grow. There were many reasons for this growth, including the conclusion of a normalization treaty with Japan, the economic stimulation provided by the Vietnam War, and a construction boom in the Middle East. In addition, Park's government followed a policy of promoting export manufacturing by giving preferential treatment to those companies that could lead the way. These companies became huge corporations and received government assistance; they later became known as *chaebol*, or conglomerates, and included Daewoo, Hyundai, Samsung, and Lucky Goldstar.

Economic development was impressive in South Korea in the 1960's and 1970's under the Park Chung Hee government; a plywood plant is shown. *(Library of Congress)*

Kennedy, who put enormous pressure on Park to liberalize and civilianize his rule. To that end, Park resigned from the military, agreed to elections, and eased restrictions on the press and political activities. Under these conditions, Park won election for president in 1963 and was reelected four years later in 1967.

In addition to providing for national security, Park endeavored to put South Korea on a sound economic footing. To that end, in the mid-1960's he began an export-led manufacturing program to raise the living standards of the Korean people. This program led to growth that was later called the "Korean miracle" or the "miracle on the Han River." The Korean economy grew at double-digit rates. By the mid-1970's, Korea no longer required assistance aid from the United States.

Park Chung Hee *(Library of Congress)*

Dictatorship and Downfall

Politically, however, Park was similar to his predecessor, Syngman Rhee, in his desire to rule indefinitely. To that end, in 1971 he proclaimed the Yushin Constitution, which effectively would allow him to rule as long as he desired while silencing his critics. The United States disapproved but needed South Korea's support for its military efforts in Vietnam. It was generally believed that most Koreans would support Park as long as their living standards were going up. When Jimmy Carter became U.S. president in 1977, there were tensions between the two administrations. A bribery scandal nicknamed Koreagate tarnished the image of the Korean government. Moreover, Park was outraged at Carter's proposal to remove U.S. ground troops from Korea.

Domestically, Korean citizens were becoming more critical of their lack of democratic freedoms. In 1979, Park was assassinated by the head of the Korean Central Intelligence Agency, who had turned against him. In a poll taken in the late 1990's by a leading South Korean daily newspaper, Park was named the greatest political figure in modern Korean history.

Bibliography

Oh, John Kie-chiang. *Korea: Democracy on Trial*. Ithaca, N.Y.: Cornell University Press, 1968.

Park, Chung Hee. *To Build a Nation*. Washington, D.C.: Acropolis Books, 1971.

Wayne Patterson

Vallabhbhai Jhaverbhai Patel

Born: October 31, 1875; Nadiād, Gujerāt, India
Died: December 15, 1950; Bombay, India

Indian nationalist leader and political figure

"Sardar" (leader) Vallabhbhai Jhaverbhai Patel (vuh-lah-BAH-ee jah-VAYR-bah-ee pa-TAYL) was born in a small town to a lower-middle-class agricultural family. He was married in 1892 and he had a son and a daughter. Patel studied law in England, beginning in 1910, and was called to the bar in 1913. Back in India he practiced law in Ahmedabad and entered politics.

Early Career in Gujerāt

In 1917 Vallabhbhai Patel was elected a municipal councillor at Ahmedabad. In 1918 he joined Mahatma Gandhi in his civil disobedience campaign. Gandhi believed the movement was becoming successful because of Patel's work, and Patel became a prominent figure in the Indian National Congress in Gujerāt. In 1920 Patel gave up his legal practice to devote his life to politics. During the 1920's he continued his work in Ahmedabad. In 1928 he was a leader of the successful mass peasant revolt against the increased tax assessment in the Bardoli district of Gujerāt; he was called the "victor of Bardoli" and given the title of "Sardar."

Vallabhbhai Jhaverbhai Patel *(Library of Congress)*

National Politics

Patel became a national figure in the 1930's. He joined Gandhi's civil disobedience campaign in 1930 and spent most of the next four years in prison. For sixteen months of this period he was in the same jail that Gandhi was, and the two men became close. In 1935 Patel was appointed chairman of the Congress Parliamentary Board. Over the next fifteen years he became one of the most powerful figures in the party and became known as the "strong man" or "iron man" of the congress. In 1937 he organized the election campaigns for the Indian National Congress. In 1940 and 1941 he spent nine months in prison. He was imprisoned once again in August, 1942, and spent most of the next three years in jail. After his release from jail he was part of the congress group that negotiated with the British over the terms of independence. In late 1945 and early 1946 he ran the congress campaigns in the general elections. In May and June, 1946, he was part of the Indian National Congress negotiating team with the British; in September he became the minister of home affairs and information and broadcasting in the interim government. In 1947 he was a member of the Partition Council.

The Government of India Acts

The British passed three Government of India Acts in the twentieth century; they established a democratic constitution. The first was passed in 1909 and is popularly known as the Minto-Morley Reforms. The act increased the number of seats in the legislative councils, and separate electorates were established for Muslims.

The second Government of India Act was passed in 1919 and is known as the Montagu-Chelmsford Reforms. It expanded on the reforms of 1909 and introduced the concept of "dyarchy," a system under which Indian ministers, responsible to the legislature, held charge of a number of subjects "transferred" to popular control. The British were responsible for the "reserved" subjects. The Government of India Act of 1935 continued the move toward responsible government. It established Indian control in the provinces of India and envisaged a federal structure of government. The central government was made up of a lower house, the House of Assembly, and an upper house, the Council of States, which would also include representatives of the Indian states.

A Leader of India

India became independent on August 15, 1947, and Patel became deputy prime minister. During this period he acted very firmly, including the use of military intervention, to bring some 562 Indian princely states into the Union of India. He worked tirelessly to help restore order and to take care of the Hindu refugees streaming into the country in the summer and fall of 1947. He reorganized public services and established the Indian Administrative Service as a successor to the Indian Civil Service. He is remembered as a party boss who controlled the Congress Party effectively and with a firm hand. He is also remembered for his close connections with Indian businessmen, as a staunch Hindu, and as a conservative. In spite of his reputation as a tough politician he is also known as an idealist and as a kind and gentle man who harbored no bitterness toward the British.

Bibliography

Chopra, P. N. *The Sardar of India: Biography of Vallabhbhai Patel*. New Delhi, India: Allied Publishers, 1995.

Gandhi, Rajmohan. *Patel: A Life*. Ahmedabad, India: Navajivan Publishing House, 1990.

Krishna, B. *Sardar Vallabhbhai Patel: India's Iron Man*. New Delhi, India: HarperCollins, 1996.

Roger D. Long

George S. Patton

Born: November 11, 1885; San Gabriel, California
Died: December 21, 1945; Heidelberg, Germany

U.S. military leader during World War II

George Smith Patton, Jr. (JOHRJ SMIHTH PA-tuhn JEW-nyur), was born into a wealthy and prominent family whose Virginia-based ancestors had played significant roles in American military history. As Patton grew up, he was strongly influenced by a sense of his military heritage, and he longed to be a great commander someday. In 1903 he entered the Virginia Military Institute but left a year later to attend the U.S. Military Academy at West Point, New York. He graduated in 1909, a year late owing to deficiencies in mathematics. However, he ranked a respectable 46th in his class of 103. A superb athlete, he represented the U.S. Army and the United States in the 1912 Stockholm Olympic Games, competing in the modern pentathlon.

Early Career

During World War I, Patton served with General John J. "Black Jack" Pershing, first in Mexico (1916) and then in France (1917). There he developed a keen interest in tank warfare and led an

General Patton (left front) in Belgium in November, 1944, with Generals Omar Bradley and Dwight D. Eisenhower. *(AP/Wide World Photos)*

George S. Patton *(Library of Congress)*

armored brigade in the Saint-Mihiel offensive. After the war, however, he rejoined the cavalry (1920), sensing that the Army's interest in armored weapons was evolving slowly. Between World Wars I and II he forcefully promoted the importance of the tank. He went back to the armored branch in 1940, when the Army showed a renewed interest in armored warfare. By then Patton had also graduated from the Army's top advanced-officer-training programs, including the Cavalry School (1924), the Command and General Staff School (1925), and the Army War College (1931).

Career Apex

Once back in the tank corps, Patton rose quickly to division command. By 1941 he was a major general and commander of the 2nd Armored Division. By January, 1942, he was recognized as one of the Army's top tank men and appointed commander of the I Armored Corps. In November, 1942, he led American forces landing at Casablanca, Morocco. In July, 1943, promoted to lieutenant general, he led the U.S. Seventh Army in the invasion of Sicily. However, his career almost came to an end when the press dis-

The U.S. Third Army, 1944

In January, 1944, the U.S. Third Army was activated under the command of General George S. Patton. Seven weeks after the Normandy invasion (at the end of July, 1944), the Third Army was on the European continent, advancing toward Germany with lightning speed. By March of 1945, Patton's Third Army had swept across France and crossed the Rhine into Germany.

One of the greatest tests for the Third Army came in December, 1944, when they were called upon to rescue American forces surrounded by the Germans. The Germans had launched a surprise counterattack that pushed a huge salient, or bulge, in American lines around Bastogne in Belgium. Known as the Battle of the Bulge, the operation was one of the most spectacular of World War II. Almost 250,000 men of the Third Army, along with thousands of tanks and trucks, moved approximately 100 miles (160 kilometers) in less than a week to cut off the last gasp of the German army and rescue the 101st Airborne Division as well as other American units.

covered that he had slapped two hospitalized enlisted men suffering from shell shock (Patton accused them of cowardice). His immediate superior, General Dwight D. Eisenhower, refused to remove him from command because of his value and reputation (among the Germans, no less) as a formidable warrior.

In 1944 Eisenhower put Patton in charge of a mythical army group as a decoy in preparation for the Normandy invasion. In August, 1944, Patton was returned to the actual field to command the U.S. Third Army, which had the task of driving the Germans from north-central France. He performed so aggressively that at one point he outran available supplies and was forced to watch scarce fuel go to British General Bernard Montgomery. Patton regained the headlines in March, 1945, when he drove his Third Army across the Rhine before Montgomery could get there. By the end of the war, he had his troops in Austria.

Trouble continued to follow Patton after Germany's defeat. He proposed a continuation of the fighting—against the Russians, who had been allies of the United States and Britain. Patton was finally removed from command for using former Nazis to help his occupation forces administer Bavaria. Patton died in 1945 as the result of an automobile accident in Germany. Despite his vulgar speech and offensive manner, George S. Patton was a hard-working and courageous commander. His brilliant battlefield performance and flamboyant style (including pearl-handled pistols worn on his hips) made him a national hero. He was feared and respected by ally and enemy alike.

Bibliography

Blumenson, Martin. *Patton: The Man Behind the Legend, 1885-1945*. New York: William Morrow, 1985.

D'Este, Carlo. *Patton: A Genius for War*. New York: HarperCollins, 1995.

Farago, Ladislas. *Patton: Ordeal and Triumph*. New York: Obolensky, 1963.

Andrew C. Skinner

Paul VI

Born: September 26, 1897; Concesio, Lombardy, Italy
Died: August 6, 1978; Castel Gandolfo, the Vatican

Pope of the Roman Catholic Church (1963-1978)

Giovanni Battista Montini (joh-VAH-nee bah-TEES-tah mohn-TEE-nee) was born into an upper-class family of Brescia, Italy. His father, Giorgio, was a Catholic activist, journalist, and politician, and his mother, Giuditta Alghisi, a leader of Catholic women. Montini was educated at the Jesuits' Cesare Arici Institute and entered the seminary in 1916. After ordination in 1920, he studied canon law at Gregorian University, served in the Vatican Secretariat of State, and worked with university students for many years. During World War II he headed Catholic relief efforts under Pius XII, who later appointed him archbishop of Milan in 1954. In 1958, John XXIII named Montini a cardinal, and he participated in the first session of the Second Vatican Council, convened in 1962. Upon the death of Pope John, Montini was elected pope on June 21, 1963.

Paul VI *(Library of Congress)*

Finishing Vatican II

Paul VI (PAWL thuh SIHKSTH) was elevated to the papacy at a momentous juncture in the history of the Catholic Church. The Second Vatican Council had met once, but most of its work remained incomplete at the death of Pope John. It was left to Pope Paul to bring the council to a successful conclusion. The reforms enacted at the council were far reaching. They included liturgical reforms (such as the use of the vernacular instead of Latin in the rite of the mass), encouragement of ecumenical dialogue among churches, and more active lay participation in church decision making and in liturgical and pastoral activities. Theologically speaking, however, the council remained essentially true to past church teaching. The coexistence of reforms and an underlying conservative theology of continuity in the Vatican II documents would later lead to considerable confusion and conflict between Catholics who wanted even more modernization and those who thought that reforms had already gone too far.

The first five years of Pope Paul's papacy were exceptionally productive. He issued seven encyclicals on such subjects as the Catholic Church in the modern world, the preservation of peace, the development of peoples, and the more controversial subjects of birth control (in the *Humanae Vitae* encyclical) and priestly celibacy. He was the first pope to visit five continents, and he made historic visits to the Middle East, South America, India, and the United States, where he addressed the United Nations.

Dogged by Controversy

Although Paul VI was an intelligent and holy man, he proved unable to marshal the forces of change let loose by Vatican II. He disappointed the progressive wing of the church by reaffirming papal infallibility, by reserving certain issues for decision by himself alone rather than in collegiality with the bishops, and by reaffirming the traditional Catholic Church doctrine prohibiting the use of artificial contraception. Although conservative Catholics hailed this teaching of *Humanae Vitae*, they viewed Paul VI as a relatively weak, if pious, man whose indecision in matters of church reform had unleashed a barrage of experimentation, novelty, upheaval, and uncertainty. Reform-minded Catholics bitterly attacked Pope Paul's encyclicals on artificial contraception and on priestly celibacy as outmoded.

The Last Decade

Although the first five years of Paul's papacy were remarkably productive, the last decade was marked by declining vigor. His major encyclicals were issued early in his papacy, and there were only occasional statements thereafter. His natural

Pope Paul VI greeting Catholics in Manila, the capital of the Philippines. *(Archive Photos)*

Pope Paul VI and Birth Control

The most controversial decision of Pope Paul's papacy concerned his prohibition of the use of artificial contraception by Catholics in his encyclical *Humanae Vitae*. Many liberal Catholics and theologians had expected a change in church teaching on this subject. The papal commission on population and family life, consisting of many lay experts and some clergy, recommended a revised teaching. The church hierarchy was divided, however, and Paul decided to take the matter into his own hands. He relied upon the advice of several trusted cardinals, including Karol Wotyła, who would later become Pope John Paul II. Paul decided that the consistent and strong church teachings of the past could not be ignored, so he called upon married Catholics to reject the use of artificial methods of contraception. Natural methods of regulating conception involving abstinence from sexual relations during periods of fertility were not prohibited.

Pope Paul VI with Mother Teresa in 1971; he presented her with the first Pope John XXIII Peace Prize. *(AP/Wide World Photos)*

shyness and humble reserve were accentuated in the later years of his papacy, perhaps as a reaction to the stormy controversies that swept through the Catholic Church in the wake of Vatican II. Pope Paul seemed ill at ease in dealing with this and became increasingly withdrawn into a life of great personal piety. It would be up to a younger and more energetic successor, John Paul II, to grapple with the disputes and divisions unleashed by Vatican II.

Bibliography

Barrett, W. E. *Shepherd of Mankind*. Garden City, N.Y.: Doubleday, 1964.

Hebblethwaite, Peter. *Paul VI: The First Modern Pope*. New York: Paulist Press, 1993.

Holmes, J. Derek. *The Papacy in the Modern World*. New York: Crossroad, 1981.

Murphy, Francis X. *The Papacy Today*. New York: Macmillan, 1981.

Robert F. Gorman

Lester B. Pearson

Born: April 23, 1897; Newtonbrook (now part of Toronto), Ontario, Canada
Died: December 27, 1972; Ottawa, Ontario, Canada

Prime minister of Canada (1963-1968), winner of 1957 Nobel Peace Prize

Lester Bowles Pearson (LEHS-tur BOHLZ PEER-suhn), son of a Methodist minister, grew up near Toronto in Canada. In 1913 he entered the University of Toronto, but World War I intervened, and he did not receive his degree until 1919. During the war Pearson began training as a pilot, but injuries from a plane crash and traffic accident sent him back to Canada to serve as a flight instructor. In 1922 Pearson was offered a fellowship to study history at Oxford University in England. Always an avid athlete, Pearson was a member of the 1922 British Olympic hockey team. He earned a second bachelor's degree and went on to receive a master's degree from Oxford in 1925. While completing his studies, Pearson taught at the University of Toronto and married one of his students, Maryon Elspeth Moody. They had two children, Geoffrey and Patricia.

Public Service

Although Pearson enjoyed teaching and coaching at the University of Toronto, he decided to take the civil service examination in 1928. He did well and was appointed to a position as a first secretary in the Department of External Affairs. He developed an understanding of international matters which led to an appointment with the Office of the High Commissioner for Canada in London. During 1942, Pearson was sent to the Canadian embassy in Washington, D.C., as a minister, and in 1945 he became the ambassador to the United States. Pearson returned to Canada in 1946, first as an undersecretary, then as secretary of state for external affairs. He had reached the topmost office in the area of foreign affairs.

International Affairs

Pearson discovered that he had a gift for quiet diplomacy and resolving international differences. As a member of the Canadian delegation to the League of Nations in 1949, he helped set the groundwork for the creation of the United Nations (U.N.). He acted as head of the Canadian delegation to the third through the eleventh U.N. General Assemblies and served as president of the seventh session in 1952-1953. During his years at the United Nations, Pearson helped shape the politics of the world. He was a chief originator of the North Atlantic Treaty Organization (NATO). He was also active with the U.N. Relief and Rehabilitation Administration and the Food and Agriculture Organization, created to

Lester B. Pearson *(Library of Congress)*

Canadian prime minister Lester B. Pearson speaking at the White House during a 1964 visit to the United States. U.S. president Lyndon B. Johnson is at the right. *(Archive Photos)*

help nations devastated by World War II as well as to assist developing nations.

Pearson was instrumental in creating the nation of Israel, and in 1947 he helped resolve Arab-Israeli conflict over possession of Palestine. He oversaw the division of the area into sections for each side, averting an escalation of armed encounters.

In 1956 the threat of international war arose when the combined forces of Britain, France, and Israel invaded Egypt over use of the Suez Canal. Pearson proposed the creation of a U.N. peacekeeping force to move into the area and allow a cease-fire to be maintained until differences could be resolved. Although Pearson received much criticism at home, where he was seen as siding against Canada's allies, his efforts were acclaimed internationally. He received the Nobel Peace Prize in 1957 in appreciation of his work.

Canada and the British Empire

During Lester B. Pearson's tenure as prime minister, long-standing problems began to surface. French-speaking citizens believed that English-speaking Canadians received preferences in employment opportunities with the government and private corporations. Reminders of the days of British rule, such as the use of the British Union Jack as the basis for the Canadian flag, also irritated Canadians of French heritage. Pearson faced increasing activity from radical groups, including bombings of federal buildings and calls for a separate state for French-speaking people. Drawing on his skill at fostering cooperation and compromise, Pearson established the Royal Commission on Bilingualism and Biculturalism to determine more equitable ways to treat the two dominant Canadian cultures. The province of Quebec, a French-speaking stronghold, received greater autonomy.

Pearson worked diligently to remove reminders of Canada's days as a British colony and to establish a distinctive national identity for his country. He took a personal interest in the creation of a new Canadian flag. The now familiar red-and-white flag displaying the Canadian maple leaf was first flown on February 15, 1965. The national pride nurtured by Pearson's efforts culminated in Expo '67, a world's fair held in Montreal during 1967, when the world was invited to visit the unique country Canada had become.

The Creation of NATO

Following the communist takeover of Czechoslovakia in 1948, Lester B. Pearson proposed a union of Western nations for protection against the Soviet Union's quest for domination of other countries. In April of 1949, a formal agreement created the North Atlantic Treaty Organization (NATO). Pearson envisioned an organization that would allow partners to protect one another from encroachment through a policy of deterrence. Member nations vowed that an attack on any one nation would be treated as an attack on all members and that they would come to the aid of one another. The original members included Belgium, Canada, Denmark, France, Iceland, Italy, Luxembourg, the Netherlands, Norway, Portugal, the United Kingdom, and the United States. Pearson called for cooperation among members not only in military matters but also in economic, health, and social matters.

Politics

Politics captured Pearson's attention, inspiring him to run for office, and in 1948 he was elected a member of the House of Commons for the district of Algoma East in Ontario. He was sent to the House of Commons eight times by his district and served as head of the Liberal Party from 1958 to 1963. His rise to head of the party came just as the Liberals suffered a massive defeat at the hands of the Conservative Party. Using his skills learned as a diplomat, Pearson set about rebuilding his party.

In 1963 the Conservative Party refused to accept atomic warheads from the United States. Pearson and the Liberal Party felt that Canadian acceptance had been promised and that the promise should stand. Pearson's view prevailed, and the Liberals were returned to power. Pearson became the fourteenth prime minister of Canada. During his five years in office, Pearson worked diligently to remove vestiges of Canada's days as a British colony and to turn the nation into a country with a strong national identity. He helped create Canada's national health and pension plans. Directing his attention to Canada's neighbor to the south, Pearson created strong ties with the United States, although he disagreed with U.S. involvement in the Vietnam War and pushed for a peaceful resolution through U.N. intervention.

One of Pearson's greatest problems involved the French separatist movement. Canadians in French-speaking areas felt overwhelmed by Canada's English-speaking majority. Small groups resorted to terrorism, and there were calls for a separate nation of Quebec. Pearson drew upon his skill in compromise and conciliation to try to bring peace among the citizens of Canada.

After retiring in 1968, Pearson turned to teaching at Carleton College in Ottawa, but he maintained his international concerns. He set up a commission for the World Bank to help developing nations and remained active in the international community until his death in 1972.

Bibliography

Bothwell, Robert. *Pearson: His Life and World.* New York: McGraw, 1978.

English, John. *Shadow of Heaven: The Life of Lester Pearson, vol. 1, 1897-1948.* Toronto: Lester & Orpen Dennys, 1989.

_______. *The Worldly Years: The Life of Lester Pearson, vol. 2, 1949-1972.* New York: Knopf, 1992.

Pearson, Lester. *Mike: The Memoirs of the Right Honorable Lester B. Pearson.* 3 vols. Toronto: University of Toronto Press, 1972-1975.

Carol Fox

Peng Dehuai

Born: c. October 24, 1898; Xiangtan County, Hunan Province, China
Died: November 29, 1974; Beijing, China

Chinese revolutionary leader and politician

The early life of Peng Dehuai (PUHNG DUH-HWI), also written P'eng Te-huai, alternated between comfort and hardship as his family's fortunes changed. In 1916 he joined the Hunan army. Later that year Peng was briefly imprisoned for plotting to kill the governor of Hunan. The imprisonment did not prevent him from receiving an officer's commission in 1918, however, and by 1926 he was a regimental commander.

Revolutionary Leader

By 1927, Peng had bee active in the communist-influenced Hunan peasant association, and in 1928 he joined the Chinese Communist Party (CCP), bringing the soldiers under his command into the slowly evolving Red Army. Later that year he joined forces with Mao Zedong and Zhu De. In 1930 his support helped elevate Mao to the leadership of the CCP. Beginning in 1931, Peng held high positions in the CCP, becoming a Central Committee member in 1934. His military forces continued their efforts to gain territory in the interior and to resist the "annihilation campaigns" of the Nationalist government. In October, 1934, he was one of the leaders of the legendary Long March of the Communists; after great hardships, the surviving Communist forces reached a sanctuary in Yan'an in northwest China.

Peng Dehuai in 1949. *(AP/Wide World Photos)*

War and Civil War

During the war against Japan, which began in 1937, Peng was deputy commander under Zhu De of the main Communist unit, the Eighth Route Army. He was the Chinese field commander in the "Hundred Regiments Offensive," which covered a large area in northern China from August to December, 1940. From 1943, Peng remained in Yan'an as one of the top leaders of the CCP. After Japan surrendered in 1945, ending World War II, the Communist military forces were reorganized into the People's Liberation Army (PLA), with Peng still second in command under Zhu De. Peng's forces successfully ousted the Nationalist forces from the northwest provinces between 1947 and 1949.

The Korean War

In October, 1949, the Communist Party's takeover of China was completed by the establishment of the People's Republic of China under Mao Zedong. Peng held several high government and party posts but also functioned as military commander in the northwest. In the summer of 1950, the communist government of North Korea invaded South Korea. A U.N. military force led by the United States aided in resisting this attack. Chinese "volunteers"—really military units of the PLA under Peng's command—moved into Korea in October, 1950. Woefully lacking in arms and equipment, the Chinese troops experienced at least 700,000 casualties. When a truce was finally achieved in July, 1953, Peng returned to a hero's welcome in China. He now held numerous high government posts, including minister of national defense. He led efforts to professionalize the PLA.

Downfall

In July, 1959, Peng prepared a memorandum questioning the economic policies of the Great Leap Forward and the formation of people's communes. Mao Zedong took great offense and denounced Peng as a "rightist." Peng was put under house arrest, and he disappeared from public view. He became a major target of abuse during the Cultural Revolution in 1966. The physical and mental abuse eventually brought about Peng's death in 1974. Peng Dehuai was one of many highly competent

Top-ranking officers of the Communist Chinese army, including Peng Dehuai, at left. *(National Archives)*

The People's Liberation Army

In the summer of 1946, China's Communist military forces were renamed the People's Liberation Army (PLA) and successfully overthrew the Nationalist government. PLA troops were held strictly to proper behavior—treating civilians with respect, helping with relief and reconstruction, paying for all supplies, and avoiding the corruption and arrogance that characterized the Nationalist army. As a result, they were welcomed in many parts of the country.

With the establishment of the People's Republic, the PLA became a major bulwark of the Communist Party leadership. Conscription was instituted in 1955, but army life became a pathway to upward mobility for rural youth. When Lin Biao succeeded Peng Dehuai as minister of defense, the PLA underwent intensive ideological campaigns centered on the Little Red Book of quotations from Mao Zedong. As the Cultural Revolution took shape in 1965, Lin ordered the abolition of all military ranks and their associated insignias. The PLA was not internally disrupted, and it was later able to play a major role in restoring order from the anarchy of the mid-1960's.

Peng Dehuai in 1958, as China's minister of defense, talking with two Soviet officers in Beijing. *(AP/Wide World Photos)*

and dedicated people who helped bring China under Communist rule. His strategy in Korea showed a willingness to accept the slaughter of hundreds of thousands of his countrymen to support communist imperialism. His downfall paralleled the fate of many other revolutionary leaders.

Bibliography

Case of Peng Teh-huai, The. Kowloon, Hong Kong: Union Research Institute, 1968.

Domes, Jurgen. *Peng Te-huai: The Man and the Image.* London: Hurst, 1985.

Peng Te-huai. *Memoirs of a Chinese Marshal.* Beijing: Foreign Language Press, 1984.

Paul B. Trescott

Shimon Peres

Born: August 21, 1923; Vishneva, Poland (now Belarus)

Prime minister of Israel (1984-1986; 1995-1996), winner of 1994 Nobel Peace Prize

Shimon Peres (shih-MOHN PEH-rehs) was born Shimon Perski (PEHR-skee) in Vishneva, Poland, on August 21, 1923. He immigrated with his family to British-run Palestine in 1934, where he was educated at Tel Aviv's Geula school and at the Ben Shemen Agricultural School. Peres studied at New York and Harvard Universities. Then, influenced by his upbringing in the Kibbutz Geva, he became a founder of Kibbutz Alumot in the Jordan Valley.

Early Career

Peres's political career began with his 1943 election as secretary of the Hano'ar Ha'oved Labor-Zionist Youth Movement, followed by his 1947 conscription into the Zionist military organization Haganah by his political mentor, and Israel's founding father, David Ben-Gurion. With responsibilities over recruitment and arms purchasing, Peres held this position until Israel's 1948 War of Independence. Ben-Gurion then appointed him head of naval services of the new nation at age twenty-five. In 1949, Peres assumed the position of director of the Defense Ministry's procurement delegation in the United States. He returned to Israel in 1952 and was appointed deputy director-general of the Ministry of Defense in 1952; he served as its director-general from 1953 until 1959. Peres married Sonya Gelman; they had one daughter, Tzviąa, and two sons, Yoni and Chemi.

Major Government Posts

While director-general of the Ministry of Defense, Peres began Israel's nuclear program after procuring the secret Dimona reactor from France. He also established the country's electronic aircraft industry and guided Israel's "special relationship" with France, which led to France's strategic cooperation during the 1956 Sinai campaign. Peres was elected to Israel's parliament, the Knesset, in 1959, serving as deputy defense minister from 1959 until 1965. Peres then left the Mapai Party and became secretary-general of Rafi, the Israel Workers List. In 1968 the Rafi initiated the uniting of Rafi to Mapai, thus founding the Labor Party.

In 1969, Peres was appointed minister of absorption, with responsibilities over economic development within Judea and Samaria. Peres then

Shimon Peres *(Archive Photos/Laurence Agron)*

Israeli prime minister Shimon Peres (right) confers with his press spokesman in the Knesset, Israel's parliament. *(Reuters/Jim Hollander/Archive Photos)*

became minister of transportation and communications in 1970. After a period as information minister, he was appointed minister of defense in Yitzhak Rabin's government. He played a critical role during the restructuring period following the 1973 Yom Kippur War. Peres then received international acclaim for masterminding the 1976 Entebbe rescue operation. Following Rabin's April, 1977, resignation, Peres was elected party chairman and headed the Ma'arach in the 1977 elections. He functioned as opposition leader from 1977 until 1984.

Upon establishment of the national unity government in September, 1984, Peres served as Israel's eighth prime minister for two years. He worked toward resolving the problems resulting from Israel's incursion into Lebanon during the 1982 Galilee Operation, and rebuilding Israel's failing economy. During this period, Peres en-

The Raid on Entebbe

On June 27, 1976, an airliner departing Athens for Paris was hijacked by Palestinians. The Palestinian terrorists subsequently held one hundred hostages at the Entebbe airport in Uganda. They demanded the release of fifty-four dissidents jailed in six countries as well as a $5 million ransom. Shimon Peres, then serving as Yitzhak Rabin's defense minister, masterminded a raid against the terrorists. On July 3, 1976, Israeli Defense Forces swiftly traveled 2,200 miles (3,500 kilometers), avoiding radar detection, and returned from Entebbe with the mostly Jewish hostages. Jonathan Netanyahu, brother of Benjamin Netanyahu, was killed leading this daring raid, nicknamed the "miracle at Entebbe." It is regarded as one of history's most successful counterterrorist operations. Benjamin Netanyahu later founded the Jonathan Institute, dedicated to abolishing terrorism.

The Elections of 1996 and 1997

Following Prime Minister Yitzhak Rabin's 1995 assassination by a right-wing fanatic, Shimon Peres served as acting prime minister until May, 1996, when he was narrowly defeated by Likud Party hard-liner Benjamin Netanyahu. Netanyahu became Israel's youngest prime minister, born one year after the nation's 1948 founding. Netanyahu's "peace with security" platform advocated a cautious approach to peace during a time of repeated Palestinian suicide attacks against Israeli civilians. Peres's defeat marked his fifth defeat in a national election in five attempts: 1977, 1981, 1984, 1988, and 1996. Opinion polls showed Peres ahead of Netanyahu, but most analysts ascribed this support to feelings about Rabin. As the Labour Party recovered from this 1996 defeat, foreign minister and former army chief Ehud Barak defeated Peres in a June, 1997, election for the Labor Party chairmanship. Voter cynicism about Peres's attempts to negotiate peace was partly to blame for his downfall, as was his ordering of attacks into Lebanon to prevent Hizbollah guerrillas from firing rockets into Israel. Peres's strikes killed more than two hundred mostly Lebanese civilians, motivating disgruntled Israeli Arabs to punish him at the polls.

tered into a power-sharing agreement with Yitzhak Shamir, leader of the Likud (consolidation) Party. From 1986 to 1988 he served as deputy prime minister and foreign minister in Shamir's government. Following a close, inconclusive 1988 general election, Shamir became prime minister and appointed Peres as deputy prime minister and minister of finance. This second Likud-Labor coalition collapsed in 1990 when Shamir fired Peres.

In December, 1995, Shimon Peres meeting Palestine Liberation Organization chairman Yasir Arafat for the first time since Peres became Israeli prime minister. *(Reuters/Jim Hollander/Archive Photos)*

Peres opposed Shamir until Peres's 1992 replacement as Labour Party leader by Yitzhak Rabin. Peres was appointed foreign minister in June, 1992, in the newly elected Labor government. Peres promoted the process that led to the Declaration of Principles that was signed with the Palestinians on September 13, 1993. In 1994, the Norwegian Nobel Committee jointly awarded the Nobel Peace Prize to Peres, Palestine Liberation Organization (PLO) chairman Yasir Arafat, and Rabin for their Middle East peace accords. The accords transferred power in the

Gaza Strip and Jericho to an elected Palestinian administration. Peres was influential in the signing of the Israel-Jordan peace agreement on October 26, 1994, and he promoted relations with Arab countries in North Africa and the Persian Gulf as part of his vision of a "new Middle East."

Brief Second Ministership

On November 5, 1995, Rabin was assassinated by a right-wing Israeli fanatic minutes after embracing Peres at a Tel Aviv peace rally. Peres was then appointed acting prime minister and on November 22, 1995, after approval by the Knesset, was sworn in as prime minister and minister of defense. Peres held these posts until May, 1996, when he was defeated by Benjamin Netanyahu. Peres held his last position, chairman of the Israel Labor Party, until his June, 1997, defeat by Ehud Barak. He remained a member of the Knesset. The Peace Research Institute was established in Peres's honor. Peres has written hundreds of articles and eleven influential books. A statesman and parliamentarian who served two nonconsecutive terms as prime minister of Israel and was awarded a share of the 1994 Nobel Peace Prize, Peres has held every top Israeli cabinet position. U.S. president Bill Clinton hailed Peres as "one of the great peacemakers of our time."

Bibliography

Golan, Matti. *The Road to Peace: A Biography of Shimon Peres*. New York: Warner, 1989.

Guyatt, Nicholas. *The Absence of Peace: Understanding the Israeli-Palestinian Conflict*. New York: Zed, 1998.

Peres, Shimon. *David's Sling*. London: Weidenfeld and Nicolson, 1970.

Peres, Shimon, and Robert Littell. *For the Future of Israel*. Baltimore: The Johns Hopkins University Press, 1998.

Peres, Shimon, with Arye Naor. *The New Middle East*. New York: Henry Holt, 1993.

Sachar, Howard M. *A History of Israel: From the Rise of Zionism to Our Time*. New York: Random House, 1996.

Daniel G. Graetzer

Javier Pérez de Cuéllar

Born: January 19, 1920; Lima, Peru

Peruvian diplomat, secretary-general of the United Nations (1982-1992)

Javier Pérez de Cuéllar (hah-VYEHR PAY-rehs thay KWAY-yahr) attended Catholic schools and university in Lima. He studied law and literature. After graduating, he entered the Peruvian diplomatic service as a third secretary. Because of his fluency in French, his first assignment was in Paris. While there he was posted temporarily to London, where he represented Peru in the work of creating the United Nations (U.N.). Following his Paris assignment he held diplomatic posts in London, La Paz, and Rio de Janeiro. His first ambassadorial post was in Switzerland. In 1968 Pérez de Cuéllar became Peru's first ambassador to the Soviet Union.

Career in the United Nations

Two years later the young statesman was chosen to be Peru's permanent representative to the United Nations in New York. He served two four-year terms in the prestigious position of president of the U.N. Security Council. During his second term, the Cyprus crisis between

U.N. secretary-general Javier Pérez de Cuéllar (center) with Salvadorean rebel leader Joaquin Villalobos (left) and a Salvadorean government official (right) in 1991. The two men are signing an agreement to end El Salvador's eleven-year civil war. *(Reuters/Ray Stubblebine/Archive Photos)*

The 1991-1992 El Salvador Peace Pact

On January 16, 1992, a peace treaty between the Salvadorean government and the rebel Farabundo Martí Front for National Liberation (FMLN) was signed in Mexico City. The treaty concluded almost two years of negotiations under the auspices of the United Nations. U.N. secretary-general Javier Pérez de Cuéllar personally led the discussions in the final meetings between the two opposing sides.

The agreement called for a substantial reduction in the country's military establishment, the disarmament of the FMLN rebel forces, and the establishment of a new national civilian police force. The FMLN converted from a revolutionary army to a political party committed to seeking a peaceful solution to the small country's economic problems. In addition to furnishing peacekeeping troops during the initial phases of the treaty and supervising the disarmament of the FMLN forces, the United Nations carried out an extensive investigation of atrocities committed by both sides during the eleven-year civil war. A number of high-ranking officers were required to take early retirement as a result. The efforts of Pérez de Cuéllar and his U.N. associates in El Salvador proved successful. The country became relatively tranquil although both economic problems and a high crime rate remained major problems.

Javier Pérez de Cuéllar *(National Archives)*

the governments of Greece and Turkey erupted. The U.N. secretary-general, Kurt Waldheim, asked Pérez de Cuéllar to be his special representative for Cyprus. Pérez de Cuéllar spent two years (1975-1977) on the island of Cyprus, coordinating a cease-fire between the two parties.

Pérez de Cuéllar returned to the Peruvian diplomatic service briefly after the Cyprus assignment. For a year he held the post of ambassador to Venezuela. In 1979 Waldheim asked the president of Peru for Pérez de Cuéllar's services once more, this time as one of two undersecretaries-general for special political affairs. He spent two years in that position. In 1981 Peru called him back to assume one of the country's most important diplomatic positions, ambassador to Brazil. Before Pérez de Cuéllar could assume that assignment, he learned that he was being considered for the top post in the United Nations, that of secretary-general. On the recommendation of the Security Council, the U.N. General Assembly named him to that post effective January 2, 1982.

Pérez de Cuéllar as Secretary-General

In the course of the next ten years the new secretary-general found himself involved in attempting to find solutions to a wide variety of global problems. In 1982 the United Nations brought an end to the Falkland Islands conflict between Great Britain and Argentina. In 1988 the war between the Soviet Union and Afghanistan and the war between Iran and Iraq were terminated, largely as a result of the work of Pérez de Cuéllar's negotiating teams. Pérez de Cuéllar demonstrated a high degree of skill in successfully negotiating the termination of a number of serious conflicts; moreover, he was sometimes able to establish peacekeeping arrangements between two opposing parties when he could not achieve a final settlement. Perhaps Pérez de Cuéllar's greatest diplomatic triumph was the negotiation of a peace treaty in El Salvador's civil war, accomplished literally in the final hours of his second term as secretary-general.

Javier Pérez de Cuéllar addressing the press in 1991 a few hours before the U.N. deadline for Iraq to withdraw from Kuwait to avoid war with an international coalition. Pérez de Cuéllar made a final appeal to Iraqi leader Saddam Hussein to withdraw. *(AP/Wide World Photos)*

Bibliography

Meisler, Stanley. *United Nations: The First Fifty Years*. New York: Atlantic Monthly Press, 1995.

Melvern, Linda. *The Ultimate Crime: Who Betrayed the U.N. and Why*. London: Allison & Busby, 1995.

Montgomery, Tommie Sue. *Revolution in El Salvador: From Civil Strife to Civil Peace*. Boulder, Colo.: Westview Press, 1995.

Pérez de Cuéllar, Javier. *Pilgrimage for Peace*. New York: St. Martin's Press, 1997.

Yoder, Amos. *The Evolution of the United Nations System*. New York: Taylor and Francis, 1989.

Carl Henry Marcoux

Eva Perón

Born: May 7, 1919; Los Toldos, Argentina
Died: July 26, 1952; Buenos Aires, Argentina

Argentine political figure, wife of president Juan Perón

Eva Perón (AY-vah pay-ROHN), known almost universally to Argentines as "Evita," rose from poverty to become the powerful first lady of Argentina. To millions of the poor, she was a savior. To her enemies, she was a monstrous dictator. By the time of her death, Perón had become one of the most influential women in the world.

Eva Perón *(Library of Congress)*

Background

Eva María Duarte de Perón was born María Eva Duarte into extreme poverty on an isolated estate in Buenos Aires province. Her mother was Juana Ibarguren, the humble mistress of Juan Duarte, Eva's father, who was a local landowner. Eva was the fifth illegitimate child of Juan Duarte. When Duarte died, the family was not allowed to participate in the funeral. At the age of fifteen, Eva and her family moved to the small town of Junín. Here she allegedly worked as a prostitute with her sisters and mother. As a young teenager, Eva became enchanted by a traveling drama team. The lead singer met Eva and excited her about the possibility of succeeding in Buenos Aires as an actress. After her arrival in Buenos Aires, Eva did not do particularly well in theater or films, but her beauty enthralled people. By 1940 she realized that her avenues for success in acting had become rather limited, and she pursued a new career as a soap-opera celebrity. It has been alleged that Eva also worked as a high-priced call girl. She was certainly promiscuous and became quite close to many in the Argentine military.

Alliance with Juan Perón

During a fund-raiser for victims of a January, 1944, earthquake in the province of San Juan, Eva met Juan Perón and realized that this charismatic and ambitious Argentine army officer could win in a struggle for control of Argentina. She quickly became his mistress. Eva provided Perón with mass appeal by playing nationalistic records on her radio show and discussing Perón's nationalistic ideology. By helping to organize the relief program for San Juan, she also began cultivating an image of social concern. She consolidated this role by speaking to workers while Perón headed the labor department. A fiery speaker capable of providing emotional tirades against the Argentine oligarchy, Eva became the idol of many when she appeared in expensive clothes and jewelry: She symbolized the dreams of many who wanted to rise to the top. On the other hand, unlike Juan, Eva became known for her quick temper, stubbornness, inability to compromise, and desire for revenge when she felt that she had been wronged. Therefore, Eva became feared by those who opposed Perón. Her enemies pointed out that Eva and Juan lived together without marriage, a situation that many Argentines viewed as scandalous. (They were married in 1945.)

The events of October 17, 1945, cemented the relationship of Juan Perón and Eva Duarte. With the end of World War II, the authoritarian Argentine government that included Perón faced considerable opposition. The landed elites opposed the industrialization that Perón and other nationalists sought. Perón had cultivated labor unions, and the United States considered him, incorrectly, a fascist. Conservative officers disliked his mobilization of the poor, as well as his relationship with Eva. The government arrested Perón on October 9, 1945, in preparation for exile abroad. At that moment, a spontaneous social revolution unfolded as hundreds of thousands of working-class Perón supporters marched on Buenos Aires in order to free him. As roughly one million laborers assembled in front of the presidential palace and threatened to tear elegant Buenos Aires apart brick by brick, Perón learned of these events. He wrote to Eva from jail, promising to marry her. The generals weakened. They claimed that they were only "protecting" Perón and then released him. Perón then appeared on the balcony of the Casa Rosada and announced his candidacy for the presidency during elections scheduled for 1946, only four months away. Quite dramatically, he appealed to his *descamisados* (shirtless ones) for support. He married Eva four days later.

Eva in Power

After Perón's election in 1946 and his subsequent reelection, Eva's role in government became paramount. In addition to attending strategy meetings and accompanying Perón on trips to the interior of Argentina, Eva became the unofficial head of the country's national labor union. More important, she also managed the Eva Perón Foundation, which became a mammoth social welfare organization used to build hospitals, low-income housing, schools, and youth hostels, and to distribute goods to the needy. Eva often worked sixteen hours a day, personally handing out candy, cash, and favors. The upper class continued to snub her despite her mass popularity. Therefore, Eva continued to attack the oligarchy. She organized women by means of a movement known as the Peronist

Evita, the Movie

A successful musical film based on the life of Eva Perón, *Evita*, was released in 1996. It won three Golden Globe awards. The film featured the lyrics of Tim Rice; the main stars were Madonna, Antonio Banderas, and Jonathan Pryce. The film was adapted from the 1979 stage production of the same title. Although the film *Evita* is historically accurate in some ways, much in the film is misleading. Perhaps the greatest distortion presented is the idea that Evita wielded more power and influence than Juan Perón. Juan Perón had gone to great lengths to organize working-class Argentines, who would never forget his support of labor unions beginning in 1943. There is no doubt that Eva Perón enjoyed great popularity, but her husband was the real substance of the regime. The events of October 17, 1944—when workers marched on the capital to demand that Juan Perón be released from jail—were not really organized by Eva Perón but by the union leaders themselves. When the regime finally collapsed in 1955, there was no resistance to the army takeover, despite the film's suggestion otherwise. These caveats aside, *Evita* is generally a rousing portrayal of the turbulent period of Peronista rule.

Women's Party. The role of women became crucial to the support of the Perón regime. Eva saw that women could vote (a right granted in 1949) and hold public office for the first time. She publicly stated that economic independence was essential for every woman's dignity. Eva organized *unidades basicas* all over Argentina, which served as social meeting places, day-care centers, and sources of legal as well as medical aid. Eventually, twenty-four women became deputies and seven were senators in the Argentine legislature.

Eva Perón—"Evita"—was tremendously popular with the Argentinian people, drawing attention and crowds wherever she went. *(National Archives)*

The End of Evita

Eva's decline began when the army refused to allow her to become vice president of Argentina in 1951. A misguided attempt to make Eva a saint in the Catholic Church angered the Vatican. Eva died of cancer in 1952. Hundreds of thousands of Argentines filed by to view her embalmed body, many of them becoming hysterical. After being overthrown in 1955, Perón fled Argentina for Spain. Meanwhile, the Argentine military stole Eva's body and hid it in Italy. Even in death, Evita was a potent political rallying point. Unable to rule the country, the army returned Eva's casket to Perón in Spain. Shortly after assuming power for the last time, in 1973, Perón had Eva's body reburied in the famed Recoleta cemetery in Buenos Aires.

Bibliography

Barnes, John. *Evita: First Lady*. New York: Grove Press, 1978.

Fraser, Nicholas, and Marysa Navarro. *Eva Perón*. New York: Norton, 1985.

Montgomery, Paul L. *Eva, Evita*. New York: Pocket Books, 1979.

Taylor, J. M. *Eva Perón: The Myths of a Woman*. Chicago: University of Chicago Press, 1979.

Douglas W. Richmond

Buenos Aires

Founded in 1580, Buenos Aires soon became an important port and enjoyed a rich culture. In 1880 Buenos Aires became the national capital of Argentina, with the executive branch of government located in the Casa Rosada (pink house) on the Plaza de Mayo. Beautiful art nouveau buildings dominate the downtown area. Opera became the main form of artistic expression after the construction of the Colón theater in 1857. Horse racing at the swank Jockey Club, carnivals, and shopping on elegant Calle Florida were principal diversions. Symbolic of the city's pride was the completion of the sumptuous Recoleta cemetery in 1881. Argentina attracted some 670,000 European immigrants from 1875 to 1920, two-thirds of whom stayed in Buenos Aires. By 1914, 80 percent of the city was foreign-born. Immigrants established industries and formed militant labor organizations. They succeeded to the point that foreigners owned 67 percent of the land in Buenos Aires by 1914. Juan and Eva Perón appealed to these newcomers.

Juan Perón

Born: October 8, 1895; Lobos, Argentina
Died: July 1, 1974; Buenos Aires, Argentina

President of Argentina (1946-1955, 1973-1974)

Juan Domingo Perón (WAWN doh-MEEN-goh pay-ROHN) was a charismatic Argentine populist who dominated his country's politics throughout the latter half of the twentieth century. Born into a family of straitened economic conditions, he was raised on a sheep farm in southern Argentina. Deciding to pursue a military career, he obtained entry into the army's military academy in 1911.

Juan Perón *(Library of Congress)*

Military Career

Commissioned as a second lieutenant in 1913, Perón had a good nature and easy manner that allowed him to rise steadily through the ranks. In 1926 he was admitted to the Superior War School. Completing the school's course with distinction, he received an appointment to the headquarters of the army's general staff in 1929.

This appointment brought him into close contact with military leaders who led a coup against the civilian government of President Hipólito Yrigoyen in 1930. As a supporter of one of its leaders, Major Perón was given a faculty appointment at the Superior War School. In the following years he began to publish books on the role of the military and the need for a strong, centralized government to achieve economic prosperity and political stability. In 1929 he married Aurelia Tizón, who died childless in 1938 of uterine cancer.

Perón's career acquired an increasingly international character when he was appointed in 1936 as military attaché in Chile. Three years later he was posted to Italy, where he observed with satisfaction the authoritarian regimes of that country and Germany. Back in Argentina, he was posted in Mendoza as a warfare instructor and in 1941 was promoted to colonel. The following year Perón was posted to Buenos Aires, where, with other officers discontented with the civilian government, he aided in organizing a coup against the government on June 4, 1943.

While two generals successively became president, Colonel Perón was the "power behind the throne," skillfully nurturing the government positions he occupied to expand his political base. As undersecretary for war, he consolidated his support among the military. Becoming secretary of labor and social welfare, he pushed for in-

Peronism

The Peronist Party was founded in 1946 to support the presidential election of Juan Perón. It created an alliance of political parties, the military, and the economically disadvantaged, known as the *descamisados* or "the shirtless ones." Crucial to the allure of the movement was Perón's wife, Evita, who conveyed enormous sympathy for the masses. She founded the Feminist Peronist Party.

Ideologically Peronism intended to be a middle or third way between socialism and capitalism. It depended on a charismatic, commanding leader and emphasized the corporate organization of society. Crucial to such corporate organization was the General Confederation of Labor. The authoritarian character of the Peronist movement was reminiscent of fascism.

The movement was a key element in Argentine politics throughout the latter half of the twentieth century. With Perón in exile after 1955, the movement could no longer use his name and became the Justicialist Party, a change that Perón favored. The party was greatly torn between left- and right-wings and affiliation with terrorist groups such as the *Montoneros*, which were eliminated by the military after the coup of 1976. Although in 1983 the party was defeated in its attempt to return to the presidency, it regained power in 1989 with the election of Peronist candidate Carlos Menem.

Argentinian president Juan Perón (left) speaking as wife Eva looks on. *(National Archives)*

creases in salaries and benefits for workers, giving him a powerful grip on unions and the growing labor movement.

Political Career

In 1944 Perón became vice president, arousing political elements who were suspicious of his demagoguery and approval of authoritarianism. He was forced to resign his office and was arrested in October, 1945. Nevertheless, he was released a few days later after a massive labor demonstration in his favor. A highly significant person among Perón's supporters was his new companion, radio and screen actress Eva (Evita) María Duarte. They married shortly after his release, Evita becoming one of his most astute and loyal advisers.

In elections in early 1946, Perón was elected president with 56 percent of the popular vote. He won largely because of his newly formed Peronist Party, which emphasized social justice and economic independence. During Perón's first administration (1946-1951), Argentina had considerable financial reserves because of its wartime exports. Great prosperity occurred as the government stimulated industrialization, obtained full employment, and supported high salaries. With Peronism dominant, its leader, now a general, became increasingly authoritarian, repressing opposition and criticism.

Perón's second administration was ill-fated. By the early 1950's Argentina had exhausted its reserves and could no longer finance industrialization, especially at the expense of its traditional agricultural economy. With rising unemployment and inflation, the masses to which Perón had so successfully appealed began to be dissatisfied with him. Yet through it all, Evita significantly contributed to his appeal. She had founded a benevolent association, the Evita Perón Foundation, which distributed millions of dollars' worth of food, clothes, medical help, and school materials to the *descamisados* (the poor). However, in 1952, after much suffering, she died of cancer, a great political and personal blow to Perón.

Charismatic populist leader Juan Perón dominated politics in Argentina in the 1940's and 1950's, and Peronism continued to be influential after his death. *(Library of Congress)*

The Argentine Coup of 1943

Early in 1943 it became known that Argentina's president, Ramón Castillo, intended to support as his successor a powerful and corrupt politician whom the military opposed. To thwart this candidacy, Colonel Juan Perón and like-minded officers founded the United Officers Group, committed to opposing electoral fraud, enhancing the military, and combating communism. In addition, Perón and many other officers believed that Argentina should continue to be neutral in World War II, then raging. After the entry of the United States into the war in 1941, they were not sure whether a new civilian government would resist American pressure against Argentine neutrality. On June 4, 1943, the United Officers Group ousted President Castillo. Successive generals occupied the presidency, supported by a group of colonels, including Perón. It was from this base of power that Perón mounted the platform for his own occupancy of the presidency in 1946.

Dissatisfaction with Perón increased because of the deteriorating economic situation and his increasingly authoritarian reaction. Furthermore, because of his personality cult and rumors of immorality in his personal life, he raised the ire of the Catholic Church. In 1955 he was ousted by the military.

Exile and Return

Perón wandered in exile from Paraguay to Panama, Venezuela, and the Dominican Republic, eventually settling in 1961 in Spain. In Panama he met and eventually married a fellow Argentine, María Estela Martínez, known as Isabel or Isabelita. From Madrid, Perón continued to be a significant factor in Argentine politics. Numerous civilian and military governments followed his, each experiencing many difficulties and frustrations; large among them was negotiating with the continuing, powerful Peronist movement in the country.

Finally acknowledging that Argentina could not be ruled without Perón, in 1972 the military allowed him to return to the country. In 1973 the aged Perón ran for election with Isabelita as his vice-presidential candidate and received 62 percent of the vote. However, Argentina had become ungovernable even for Perón, especially with the Peronist movement divided between Right and Left, the latter dominated by the Peronist Youth. Perón died in office the following year and was succeeded by his wife, who was ousted by the military in 1976.

Bibliography

Crassweller, Robert D. *Perón and the Enigmas of Argentina*. New York: W. W. Norton, 1987.

Dujovne Ortiz, Alicia. *Eva Perón*. Translated by Shawn Fields. New York: St. Martin's Press, 1996.

Hodges, Donald C. *Argentina, 1943-1987: The National Revolution and Resistance*. Albuquerque: University of New Mexico Press, 1988.

Kirkpatrick, Jeane. *Leader and Vanguard in Mass Society: A Study of Peronist Argentina*. Cambridge, Mass.: MIT Press, 1971.

Page, Joseph A. *Perón: A Biography*. New York: Random House, 1983.

Turner, Frederick C., and José Enrique Miguens, eds. *Juan Perón and the Reshaping of Argentina*. Pittsburgh: University of Pittsburgh Press, 1983.

Edward A. Riedinger

H. Ross Perot

Born: June 27, 1930; Texarkana, Texas

American businessman and presidential candidate (1992, 1996)

After attending Texarkana Junior College, Henry Ross Perot (HEHN-ree ROS peh-ROH) earned an appointment to the U.S. Naval Academy in 1949. After graduating in 1953, he served in the U.S. Navy for four years as an officer on a destroyer and an aircraft carrier. In 1957, Perot settled in Dallas, Texas, where he worked until 1962 as a computer salesman for the data processing division of International Business Machines (IBM).

Business Career

Convinced that he could succeed on his own, Perot started Electronic Data Systems (EDS), a computer services company, in 1962. EDS expanded rapidly and was soon running entire data-processing departments for insurance companies, banks, and state and national government agencies. Making huge profits with EDS, Perot eventually became a billionaire. In 1984, Perot sold EDS to General Motors for more than two billion dollars. He served as a member of the General Motors board of directors until 1986. Later he was associated with the Perot Group, an investment and real-estate firm in Dallas. He returned to the computer business in 1988, when he founded Perot Systems Corporation in Washington, D.C.

Presidential Candidate

Long interested in politics, Perot was dissatisfied with the leadership and performance of the two major U.S. political parties. In March, 1992, he announced that he would run for president that year as an independent candidate. Promising to go to Washington and fix the country's problems, he attracted widespread grassroots support in a matter of months. The major-party candidates were incumbent Republican president George Bush and Democratic challenger Bill Clinton, the governor of Arkansas. Perot astounded political analysts by pulling ahead of both Bush and Clinton in some national polls. Suddenly, however, to the surprise and dissatisfaction of many of his supporters, Perot dropped out of the race on July 16, stating that his campaign might become too disruptive to the unity of the country.

On October 1, however, Perot reentered the

During the 1992 U.S. presidential campaign, H. Ross Perot was noted for his use of visual aids. Here, in a thirty-minute commercial, he discusses balancing the federal budget. *(AP/Wide World Photos)*

H. Ross Perot during his business years, before his entry into the political arena. In 1984 he sold his company, Electronic Data Systems, to General Motors for more than $2 billion. *(National Archives)*

race, claiming that the Republican and Democratic candidates were not responding to national concerns and that they presented no real choices for the American people. By then, national polls showed that support for Perot had dropped sharply, but his renewed candidacy introduced an unpredictable factor into the political race. In the last stages of his campaign, Perot relied heavily on paid television advertising. Upon his reentry into the political arena in October, Perot stated that the U.S. government had become a "government in gridlock." He declared that he would eliminate the national debt by stimulating the national economy to produce more wealth, while reducing fraud and waste. Although Perot failed to draw any electoral college votes, he did manage to garner a surprisingly strong 19 percent of the popular vote in 1992.

In 1995, Perot formed the Reform Party, and he became its presidential nominee in 1996. Denouncing big government, budget deficits, campaign finance practices, and the existing two-party system, Perot relied on half-hour television infomercials to con-

The Presidential Election of 1992

In 1992, H. Ross Perot was recognized as a serious candidate for the presidency, deserving equal stature with the Republican and Democratic nominees. The presidential debates clearly illustrated the differences between the candidates on such issues as the national debt, gun control, pollution control standards, and free trade with Mexico. President George Bush presented an image of a vigorous leader and an experienced chief executive. Bill Clinton presented himself as a competent leader who understood the national desire for change, particularly economic change. Perot positioned himself as a leader who would fix the government, taking it away from career politicians and special interests and restoring many of its old virtues. By the end of the 1992 presidential campaign, television, radio, and newspapers had inundated the American public with an enormous amount of information about the presidential candidates. A new precedent had been set for informing the American voters and for establishing the viability of a third political party.

George Bush (left) and H. Ross Perot continue talking at the conclusion of the televised U.S. presidential candidate debate of October 15, 1992. Bill Clinton is at right. *(AP/Wide World Photos)*

vey his message. However, Perot's popularity had faded since 1992, and he attracted only 8 percent of the popular vote in 1996.

Impact on American Politics

Perot campaigned on a platform of high ethical standards for American leaders, a balanced budget, campaign reforms, a new tax system, and lobbying restrictions. He demonstrated that a third political party could be viable and could influence American politics. In 1992, Perot had a profound effect on the outcome of the election by taking more votes away from President Bush than from Bill Clinton. Perot's formation of the Reform Party provided a magnet for activist independents in the late 1990's.

Bibliography

Black, Gordon S., and Benjamin D. Black. *The Politics of American Discontent*. New York: John Wiley & Sons, 1994.

Gross, Ken. *Ross Perot: The Man Behind the Myth*. New York: Random House, 1992.

Posner, Gerald. *Citizen Perot*. New York: Random House, 1996.

Alvin K. Benson

John J. Pershing

Born: September 13, 1860; Laclede, Missouri
Died: July 15, 1948; Washington, D.C.

Commander of U.S. military forces during World War I

John Joseph "Black Jack" Pershing (JON JOH-sehf "BLAK JAK" PUR-shihng) was born in Missouri in 1860. Confederate raiders pillaged his hometown when he was four years old, a memory that stayed with him throughout his life. He graduated from West Point in 1886. Trained as a cavalry officer, Pershing served in the Indian Wars and instructed briefly at West Point. As the commander of the 10th Cavalry, a black regiment, Pershing was nicknamed "Black Jack."

John J. Pershing *(Library of Congress)*

Rise to Prominence

Pershing was noticed for bravery leading the 10th Cavalry at Cuba's San Juan Hill in the Spanish-American War. Though horseless during the Cuban campaign, Pershing's unit fought equally bravely on foot, earning respect and admiration from white troops, including volunteer colonel Theodore Roosevelt. From 1899 to 1903, Pershing served in the Philippines as part of the American campaign against Philippine revolutionaries during the bloody Philippine Insurrection. It was in this service that he achieved notice for his command skills.

Pershing was appointed military attaché to Japan and served as the official American observer with General Tamemoto Tamesada Kuroki's Manchurian army in the Russo-Japanese War of 1905. In 1906 Major Pershing was promoted to brigadier general, a rare feat in the American military: His promotion jumped him ahead of eight hundred superior officers. The promotion came as a result of his distinguished leadership in the Philippine campaign and his service in Manchuria. President Theodore Roosevelt personally nominated Pershing for the promotion. Personal tragedy struck in 1915 when Pershing's wife, Frances Warren, and three daughters perished in a fire that destroyed their home at the Presidio, near San Francisco. Only Pershing's son survived.

Pershing led the punitive expedition against Mexican border raiders in 1916. His force of eleven thousand men chased Pancho Villa's band for eleven months across northern Mexico, failing to capture the bandit-revolutionary. Nonetheless, the expedition did end the raids on American border towns in New Mexico and

Texas. The expedition was one of the first American forces to integrate automobiles and airplanes for transport and reconnaissance in a land campaign. Field radios were also used for the first time.

Commander of the AEF

Because of his experience as a field commander and his other command qualities, Pershing, a major general, was chosen to command American forces in Europe upon the American declaration of war against Germany in April, 1917. Pershing and his staff traveled to France before the main force, which would take several months to train, equip, and transport to Europe. Pershing's primary task in preparing for the arrival of the American Expeditionary Force (AEF) was to determine its role in the Allied war effort against Germany. Pershing stubbornly resisted the demands of the Allied high command that the AEF be integrated into already standing French and British armies, an approach that would include wearing French and British uniforms.

General John J. "Black Jack" Pershing leading U.S. cavalry forces into Mexico in pursuit of Pancho Villa in 1916. *(Institute of Texan Cultures)*

The American Expeditionary Force

The American Expeditionary Force, or AEF, was formed in May, 1917, shortly after the American declaration of war against Germany. Commanded and organized by General John J. Pershing, the force represented the largest American military force assembled to that point in history and the first American armed force to serve in a European war. The original mobilization plan called for more than five million troops, but the war ended before roughly half this number could be mobilized. Nonetheless, more than two million American "doughboys," as they were nicknamed, arrived in France by November, 1918. Operating as an independent army in France, Pershing's AEF distinguished itself in intense campaigns at Saint-Mihiel, the Meuse-Argonne sector, and elsewhere. The entry of the AEF into the conflict was one of the decisive factors in leading Germany to seek an armistice. The AEF consisted of army and marine units and included air, artillery, tank, and medical corps. Some forty thousand African American troops served in combat. The AEF suffered 264,000 casualties, including more than fifty thousand killed in combat and twenty-five thousand dead from disease.

Kuroki's Manchurian Army, 1905

General Tamemoto Tamesada Kuroki's First Army of Japan was a crucial part of the Japanese war effort against Russia in the 1904-1905 Russo-Japanese War. Kuroki's force was instrumental in Japanese successes in Manchuria, a region of China. Combined with the great Japanese naval victory at Port Arthur (Lü-shun), China, these efforts forced an end to the war favorable to the Japanese. The First Army achieved fame in its crossing of the Yalu River in May, 1904. A similar engagement in August, 1904, on the Taitzu River also resulted in Japanese success. Kuroki, not a brilliant commander, was criticized for reckless tactics and overstretching his supply lines. However, his tactics, despite some failures, achieved the results necessary for Japanese victory.

The Allies also wanted immediate American intervention, but Pershing resisted this as well, knowing that piecemeal integration of hastily trained and poorly equipped American forces would be detrimental to the overall war effort. Instead, he patiently waited for the AEF to mass in force, reaching some two million men at its greatest number, before leading the AEF into battle. Considering the dire situation of the Allies in western Europe, these demands were understandable. Russian forces had disintegrated during the summer as a result of that country's March revolution. A massive British offensive tragically failed in the fall. Showing his independent nature, Pershing argued for command of an independent American force, fighting under its own flag. By the spring of 1918, the AEF was ready to fight.

The great German offensive of that same time forced the issue; in desperate need of their help, the Allied command agreed to let the AEF fight on its own, giving Pershing the independent American force for which he tirelessly argued. For this reason, among others, the United States was considered an "associated" rather than an "allied" member of the allied Entente forces against Germany. Under Pershing's leadership, the AEF played a decisive role in forcing Germany to sign an armistice in November, 1918. Pershing himself disagreed with the armistice, wanting to continue offensive operations against Germany until Germany surrendered unconditionally.

After the War

Upon his return from Europe, Congress promoted Pershing to "general of the armies." He served as army chief of staff from 1921 until 1924. His war memoir, *My Experiences in the World War* (1931), won the Pulitzer Prize for history in 1932. At the outbreak of World War II, Pershing served as an unofficial military adviser to President Franklin D. Roosevelt.

Bibliography

Pershing, John J. *My Experiences in the World War*. New York: Frederick A. Stokes, 1931.

Smith, Gene. *Until the Last Trumpet Sounds: The Life of General of the Armies John J. Pershing*. New York: John Wiley & Sons, 1998.

Smythe, Donald. *Guerrilla Warrior: The Early Life of John J. Pershing*. New York: Scribner, 1973.

Vandiver, Frank Everson. *Black Jack: The Life and Times of John J. Pershing*. College Station: Texas A&M University Press, 1977.

William Allison

Philippe Pétain

Born: April 24, 1856; Cauchy-à-la-Tour, France
Died: July 23, 1951; Port-Joinville, Île d'Yeu, France

French military leader and premier of Nazi-affiliated Vichy government (1940-1944)

Henri-Philippe Bénomi Omer Pétain (o-REE fee-LEEP bay-no-MEE oh-MAYR pay-TA) was born into an established farming family in northern France. After his mother's death when Philippe was only three, he was raised by relatives. Educated at local schools, he was an above-average student. The army offered the prospect of a secure career, and Pétain entered the military academy at St. Cyr in 1876, embarking upon his long life as a soldier. Even though Pétain was exceptionally hard working and industrious, he lacked the political patronage necessary for rapid advancement. Moreover, his ideas about strategy were in opposition to those that prevailed in the French military. As a result, his rise through its ranks was slow and his early career undistinguished.

Philippe Pétain *(Library of Congress)*

World War I

In 1914 Pétain was a fifty-eight-year-old colonel, preparing for retirement. With the outbreak of World War I that August, everything changed. Both the Allies (France, Great Britain, and Russia) and the Central Powers (Germany and Austria-Hungary) had planned for a nineteenth-century style war of rapid movement and quick, decisive battles. In 1914, however, a stalemate soon developed with both sides dug into trenches facing each other. The battle lines stretched through Belgium and northern France from the English Channel to the Swiss border. Infantry offensives against trenches heavily defended with machine guns resulted in death on a scale that Europeans had never before seen in warfare.

Pétain, almost alone among French commanders, understood the importance of machine guns, artillery, and the need to destroy the enemy's defenses before launching an attack. Given a battlefield command at the war's outbreak, he was rapidly promoted to general on the basis of his organizational and strategic skills. He won the devotion of his soldiers through frequent visits to the front and through his attempts to spare as many of their lives as possible. His original thinking and compassion for common soldiers were important assets when Pétain was given charge of French forces at the Battle of Verdun in 1916, where it appeared that the French faced certain defeat. Pétain reorganized the troops, and even though the loss of life on both sides was staggering, he held the line and emerged a national hero. In 1917 he assumed another difficult assignment in restoring order after a large-scale mutiny nearly caused the French army to collapse. He was successful in his task, which enabled France to persevere until the ultimate Allied victory in November, 1918.

Career Between the World Wars

Pétain emerged from World War I a national hero, beloved for his simplicity, compassion, and patriotism. He was elevated to the rarely conferred rank of marshal of France. In the 1920's and 1930's he held a series of high-level military positions, including minister of war, and played a major role in formulating national military policy. Marked by the experience of the 1914-1918 war, Pétain advocated strong defensive fortifications. He was a strong advocate of the Maginot Line, a series of concrete forts along the French-German border built in the 1930's. He returned to active service briefly in 1925 to command French forces in Morocco, and in March, 1939, he accepted the post of ambassador to Spain.

World War II

In September, 1939, Adolf Hitler's Nazi forces invaded Poland, sparking World War II. By the spring of 1940, Nazi troops had swept across western Europe, invading France in May. Pétain was recalled from his ambassadorial post to sit in the war cabinet. With the Nazis advancing and the government in chaos, Pétain offered himself as prime minister. Unprepared to defend against the new tactics of Hitler's "lightning war," or Blitzkrieg, France fell in June. Pétain was convinced that the nation's survival was again at stake, and he quickly concluded an armistice with the Nazis. Under its terms Germany occupied northern France, and a Nazi-controlled French government led by Pétain ruled the southern part of the country from the city of Vichy. After the Allied victory in 1945, Pétain was arrested and tried for treason. He was found guilty and condemned to death, but his sentence

The Battle of Verdun

The Battle of Verdun, lasting from February to December, 1916, was the result of a plan formulated by the German general Erich von Falkenhayn. His objective, rather than to gain territory, was to weaken the French by inflicting heavy casualties. In his effort to "bleed France white," he chose to attack the fortified city of Verdun on the river Meuse, a place so important to French history and pride that the French would pay any cost in men and materiel to defend it. The Germans sent one million men to the initial attack, which was devastating. France suffered heavy casualties, lost two important forts, and appeared to be on the brink of defeat. In this dire situation, Marshal Joseph Joffre placed Philippe Pétain in charge at Verdun. Pétain quickly reorganized operations, personally commanding the artillery. He instituted an effective new system of supply and rotated units frequently so no soldier had to endure long periods under heavy fire. The Germans continued to launch massive attacks throughout the spring and summer of 1916, but the French, while suffering heavy losses, were able to defend their position. They began to retake lost territory in the fall. In the ten-month campaign, the Germans did seriously weaken the French army, but their own casualties were nearly as great: France lost 542,000 men, Germany 434,000, making Verdun the longest and most deadly battle of World War I.

Vichy France

Convinced of an ultimate German victory in World War II, Pétain, in the name of preserving French autonomy, cooperated with the Nazi invaders. However, the French government he headed at Vichy, which came under increasing German control as the war progressed, looked more like a Nazi-style authoritarian state than Republican France. The Vichy regime emphasized order and authority, and it actively persecuted Jews, communists, and other "undesirables." Politicians and military leaders who chose to leave France and oppose the Nazis in exile, such as Pétain's former protégé, Charles de Gaulle, were branded as traitors by the Vichy government. As the Nazis began to suffer defeats elsewhere, internal resistance to the Vichy regime grew, and the Vichy government quickly fell after all of France was liberated by Allied forces in 1944.

was commuted. He died in prison six years later at the age of ninety-five.

Philippe Pétain (left), premier of France's Nazi-controlled Vichy government of 1940-1945, facing German chancellor Adolf Hitler in 1940. *(TAL/Archive France/Archive Photos)*

Pétain's Legacy

Pétain remains a controversial figure in the history of modern France. He twice saved his country from military disaster during World War I and became a larger-than-life patriotic hero. He was one of France's chief military planners in the interwar period. Unfortunately, his approach to defensive military strategy, which was so effective in World War I, was useless in World War II. The Maginot Line, which he strongly supported, was designed for a World War I-style conflict; it was ineffective against the new tank and airpower technologies used by the Nazis. Pétain is still reviled by many for his collaboration with Nazi Germany, but he is defended by others who believe that he did what he felt necessary to save France.

Bibliography

Atkin, Nicholas. *Pétain*. New York: Longman, 1998.

Horne, Alistair. *The Price of Glory: Verdun, 1916*. New York: Penguin, 1993.

Lottman, Herbert. *Pétain: Hero or Traitor, the Untold Story*. New York: Morrow, 1985.

Ousby, Ian. *Occupation: The Ordeal of France, 1940-1944*. New York: St. Martin's Press, 1998.

Catherine Udall Turley

Henry Petty-Fitzmaurice

Born: January 14, 1845; London, England
Died: June 3, 1927; Clonmel, County Tipperary, Ireland

British politician and diplomat

Henry Charles Keith Petty-Fitzmaurice (HEHN-ree CHAHRLZ KEETH PEH-tee fihtz-MOH-rihs) was born into an old British aristocratic family that possessed some of the largest private land holdings in Britain. He was educated in a manner befitting the heir to a title and large estates, attending school at Eton and then Balliol College, Oxford. He was still at Oxford when his father died in 1866, making Henry, at the age of twenty-one, the fifth marquess of Lansdowne. He was thereafter known in public life as Lord Lansdowne. In 1869 he married Lady Maud Hamilton, and they had two sons and two daughters.

Career in Government Service

Lansdowne's first government appointment came in 1868 when he accepted a position at the Treasury, offered him by Prime Minister William Gladstone. Although only twenty-four and lacking experience in public life, Lansdowne was given the job on the basis of his name and title. Over the next decade, he gained a great deal of political experience, sitting in the House of Lords and accepting other administrative appointments. He was undersecretary for war from 1872 to 1874 and briefly served as undersecretary for India in 1880.

Imperial Administrator

Lansdowne's first major foreign assignment came in 1883, when he accepted the position of governor-general of Canada. His five-year tenure there was relatively quiet and uneventful. Upon returning to England, he accepted another imperial appointment, this time as viceroy of India, and governed Britain's most important colony from 1888 to 1894. While he enjoyed a fairly peaceful time as viceroy, Lansdowne was an active administrator, founding an imperial library and records office, reforming the army system, reorganizing the police and local legislative

England in East Asia

The English first established a presence in East Asia in the 1600's through the British East India Company. The company was originally chartered by the Crown to compete with other European countries for trade with China. The English soon concentrated their attention on the Indian subcontinent. Backed by English troops, the British East India Company brought large areas of India under its direct control, especially after the mid-1700's. By the nineteenth century the English held India, Sri Lanka, Burma, much of the Malay Peninsula, Singapore, and other territories in East Asia. After a serious Indian rebellion against the English in 1857, the British East India Company was replaced by a direct colonial government. Its chief officer or governor was known as a viceroy—the position that Henry Petty-Fitzmaurice (Lord Lansdowne) held from 1888 to 1894. The British maintained their colonial holdings in East Asia until after World War II, when most former colonies gained their independence.

Henry Petty-Fitzmaurice *(Corbis/Bettmann-UPI)*

councils, and enhancing the nation's railway and irrigation systems. He also presided over the British annexation of the kingdom of Sikkim and of Indian border lands with Afghanistan.

Diplomacy and Politics

Home once again in England, Lansdowne was soon appointed secretary of state for war in 1895. As foreign secretary from 1900 to 1906, Lansdowne advocated arbitration treaties with the United States and promoted an English-Japanese alliance. In 1904 he concluded several agreements with France that settled outstanding questions between the two countries, and he renewed the Entente Cordiale, an agreement of friendly relations stopping short of a formal alliance. It was the Entente Cordial that would eventually bring Britain into World War I on the side of France and Russia.

Between his foreign ministry and the outbreak of World War I in 1914, Lansdowne was a Unionist Party leader in the House of Lords. During 1915 and 1916 he sat in Prime Minister H. H. Asquith's wartime coalition cabinet as minister without portfolio. When that coalition government gave way to another, led by David Lloyd George, Lansdowne left government service. As the slaughter of World War I dragged on, a disheartened Lansdowne sent a letter to the editor of a London newspaper suggesting that the British open talks with Germany and find a way to negotiate an end to the war. This controversial "Lansdowne letter" of 1917 met with great hostility, and the episode effectively ended Lansdowne's public career.

As the twentieth century progressed, Britain lost hold of its colonial possessions, and the House of Lords came to play an increasingly smaller role in British political life. In the light of these later developments, Lord Lansdowne stands as one of Britain's last truly powerful and influential aristocratic politicians, diplomats, and imperial governors.

Bibliography

Barker, Dudley. *Prominent Edwardians*. London: Allen & Unwin, 1969.

Misra, Jagannath Prasad. *The Administration of India Under Lord Lansdowne (1888-1894)*. New Delhi: Sterling Publishers, 1975.

Newton, Thomas Wodehouse Legh. *Lord Lansdowne: A Biography by Lord Newton*. London: Macmillan, 1929.

Catherine Udall Turley

Augusto Pinochet Ugarte

Born: November 25, 1915; Valparaíso, Chile

Dictatorial president of Chile (1974-1990)

Augusto Pinochet Ugarte (ow-GEW-stoh pee-noh-CHEHT ew-GAHR-tay) was raised in a middle-class family, the son of a customs officer in Valparaíso. Admitted in 1933 to the National Military Academy, after failing in two previous attempts, Pinochet graduated in 1936 at the bottom of his class. After further study in the army infantry school, he was commissioned as a second lieutenant. Although Pinochet did not distinguish himself academically, he was known for his strict adherence to the regulations and hierarchy of the army. In 1943 he married Lucía Hiriart, the daughter of a senator, with whom he had three daughters and two sons.

Augusto Pinochet Ugarte in 1997. *(Agence France Presse/Archive Photos)*

Military Career

After various military postings in the country, Pinochet studied at the war academy from 1949 to 1952 and was an instructor at the military academy in Ecuador from 1956 to 1959. In 1956 he visited the United States as part of a Chilean military delegation. Upon his return to Chile from Ecuador, he taught and became deputy director of the war academy. He published several books on Chilean military history and geopolitics. Rising steadily through the ranks, he became a division general in 1970 and was appointed to head the pivotal sixth division of the army, in Santiago. In 1970 a Marxist and socialist, Salvador Allende, was elected president of Chile by a narrow plurality. Although Marxism was not to his taste, Pinochet believed in strict adherence to military hierarchy and in the separation of the military from politics.

As unemployment, inflation, and instability grew under the Allende government, there was increasing pressure within and without the armed forces to oust him. At the end of August, 1973, Pinochet became commander of the army. In the following weeks he agreed with the three heads of the other armed forces to overthrow Allende. The president was ousted in a coup on September 11.

The Presidency

As head of the army, the largest and senior armed force in the country, Pinochet presided over the military junta (committee) that assumed power. Awakening to his role as the political savior of Chile, in 1974 he acquired the titles of supreme chief of the nation and then president of the republic. The junta used brutal means to maintain its power and to deal with its enemies and critics. The military and police forces interrogated thousands of people, torturing and murdering many. Power was not returned to civilians. In 1977 Pinochet announced that national elections would be allowed when conditions warranted. In the midst of economic recovery and as a reprisal to the United Nations' (U.N.) condemnation of his regime, Pinochet conducted a plebiscite (vote of opinion) on his government in 1978. Although there were questions regarding how the plebiscite was conducted, his government re-

Chilean president Augusto Pinochet in 1987, saluting with top Chilean military leaders. *(Reuters/J. Asurto/Archive Photos)*

The Coup of 1973

The election of a Marxist government in Chile under Salvador Allende in 1970 was anathema to the many military and reactionary governments in the region. In addition, in the United States, President Richard M. Nixon and Secretary of State Henry Kissinger reduced financial aid to the country and encouraged destabilization of the regime.

There was also dissatisfaction in Chile with the Allende government, which was elected by little more than a third of the vote, because of growing economic, social, and political unrest. In Chilean history, the armed forces were generally restrained, rarely interfering in civilian government. However, the pressure of internal and external forces caused the heads of the army, navy, air force, and national police to oust President Allende on September 11, 1973. The armed forces bombed Santiago and the presidential headquarters, La Moneda Palace. Allende, fighting from the palace with a machine gun, was found dead there. It is generally assumed that he was killed by airplane fire, although some allege that he committed suicide.

The military did not return power to civilians but formed a junta presided over by Augusto Pinochet Ugarte as head of the army. The junta brutally suppressed its opponents and remained in power for more than sixteen years.

ceived approval from a majority of voters, who seemed satisfied with the newfound stability and emerging prosperity in Chile.

In another plebiscite two years later, more questionable than the last, a new constitution was approved. The constitution of 1980 authorized Pinochet to remain as president for an eight-year term from 1981 to 1989. In 1988 a plebiscite would occur regarding whether he or another candidate should have a further eight-year term, lasting until 1997.

Pinochet obtained acceptance of his government by achieving levels of prosperity that came to be termed an "economic miracle." This prosperity was achieved by giving responsibility for the economy to a group of young, free-market Chilean economists. They had been trained under Nobel laureate Milton Friedman at the University of Chicago. Therefore they became known as the "Chicago boys." Prosperity was achieved through reducing public deficits, extensive foreign investment, privatization of state companies, and elimination of union influence regarding wages and prices.

Prosperity, however, was unevenly distributed in society. The gap between rich and poor widened. Moreover, the rapid development had serious environmental consequences. In addition, members of Pinochet's family became exceptionally and noticeably prosperous. The plebiscite of 1988 was held at the end of a decade in which Chileans had recovered from another recession, had begun to mount mass rallies against the regime, and had suffered the consequences of authoritarian reaction to their opposition. Voters overwhelmingly opposed a further term for Pinochet or the continuation of the military government. At the end of 1989, a civilian, Patricio Aylwin Azócar, was elected president, backed by a wide coalition of political parties. In 1990 Aylwin assumed office and Pinochet stepped down as president. Pinochet remained head of the army.

He considered it important to occupy this post in order to protect himself and the military against criticisms of his regime that would undoubtedly arise under succeeding civilian government. In

Demonstrators march in Santiago, Chile, in March, 1999, following a decision by Britain's highest court that Pinochet was not entitled to diplomatic immunity. Pinochet, under house arrest in London, could therefore be extradited to Spain to stand trial for alleged human rights violations. *(AP/Wide World Photos)*

Human Rights Under Pinochet

The violation of human rights by the Pinochet regime began immediately following the coup of 1973. The military junta decreed an end to political parties and union activities, established censorship of the media, and closed Congress. It rounded up nearly fifty thousand of its opponents for interrogation in stadiums, barracks, and other locations.

In 1977 the United Nations condemned human rights abuses in Chile by a vote of 96 to 14. The regime continued its repression nonetheless. Both military and police intelligence agencies spied upon citizens, torturing and killing opponents. Many people were arrested and never seen again, becoming a haunting generation of *desaparecidos*—the "disappeared" ones. In 1991 the National Committee on Truth and Reconciliation reported that it had been able to document almost a thousand cases of individuals who had disappeared after detention by security forces and could identify more than two thousand murders carried out by these forces.

the investigations of human rights violations that ensued, Pinochet used the power of his position to quell any threats to punish members of the military. As had been specified previously in transitional agreements, he left his position as head of the army in 1998 and took a seat in the Chilean senate as a life member. The position gave him legislative immunity against prosecution for crimes committed under his presidency.

Later in 1998 Pinochet was in London for medical treatment when he was detained by British authorities. The government of Spain had issued a warrant, seeking to have him extradited to stand trial for acts he allegedly committed against Spanish citizens while he was leader of Chile. Pinochet appealed the action on the grounds that he had diplomatic immunity, and the case proceeded through the British courts in early 1999. Britain's Law Lords (the country's highest court) upheld Pinochet's arrest, meaning that he would not be allowed to return home immediately. Then British home secretary Jack Straw decided that extradition proceedings could go forward. Pinochet was required to remain in Britain during the proceedings. The Spanish warrant established an extraordinary historic precedent in international law for the prosecution of crimes by military dictators.

Bibliography

Arriagada, Genaro. *Pinochet: The Politics of Power*. Boston: Unwin Hyman, 1988.

Falcoff, Mark. *Modern Chile, 1970-1989: A Critical History*. New Brunswick, N.J.: Transaction, 1989.

Nunn, Frederick. *The Military in Chilean History*. Albuquerque: University of New Mexico Press, 1976.

O'Brien, Phil, and Jackie Roddick, with Jon Barnes and James Painter. *Chile, the Pinochet Decade: The Rise and Fall of the Chicago Boys*. London: Latin American Bureau, 1983.

Spooner, Mary Helen. *Soldiers in a Narrow Land: The Pinochet Regime in Chile*. Berkeley: University of California Press, 1994.

Edward A. Riedinger

Pius XI

Born: May 31, 1857; Desio, Italy
Died: February 10, 1939; Vatican City, Italy

Pope of the Roman Catholic Church (1922-1939)

Ambrogio Damiano Achille Ratti (ahm-BROH-joh dah-mee-AH-noh ah-KEE-lay RAH-tee) was born into the family of a silk-factory manager and was educated in Monza, Milan, and the Gregorian University in Rome. He was ordained a Catholic priest on December 20, 1879, in Rome, and continued a scholarly career that earned him doctorates in canon law, philosophy, and theology. Between 1882 and 1911 he taught theology at the seminary in Padua and worked in Milan's Ambrosiana Library, publishing numerous scholarly works. In 1911 he began work in the Vatican library, of which he became prefect in 1914. Pope Benedict XV sent him to help reorganize the Catholic Church in the new state of Poland near the end of World War I, and in 1919 he was named archbishop of Lepanto, though he stayed in Warsaw until being named archbishop of Milan and cardinal in June, 1921.

A Turbulent Papacy

When elected pope on the fourteenth ballot in February of 1922, Ratti took the name Pius XI (PI-uhs thuh ee-LEH-vehnth) and, for the first time since Italy became a state in 1870, blessed the city of Rome and the world (*Urbi et Orbi*) from St. Peter's basilica (church). This signaled a new openness to the Italian government. Benito Mussolini's seizure of power in October, however, cooled relations until successful secret negotiations resulted in the Lateran Treaty of 1929. Mussolini violated the treaty, however, by disbanding Catholic youth groups in 1939, and he further alienated Pius by adopting Nazi-like racial policies in 1938.

Concordats with twenty other countries helped stabilize the position of the Catholic Church in modern secular states such as France (1924) and Nazi Germany (1933). Pius also intensified the Church's missionary efforts, more than doubling the number of native Asian priests and consecrating the first native Chinese and Japanese bishops. He canonized numerous saints, including Thomas More and Teresa of Lisieux, and modernized both Vatican scholarship—establishing the Pontifical Academy of Sciences in 1936—and the education of priests. He would not agree, however, to ecumenical talks between Catholics

Pius XI *(Archive Photos)*

and Protestants. Pius openly condemned the secularizing influence of "modernism" on morality. He used Jubilee Years (1925, 1929, and 1933), bienniel Eucharistic congresses, radio, and several formal statements (encyclicals) to attack immoral behavior. Encyclicals opposed contraception (*Casti connubi*, 1930), unfair labor practices that lead to unemployment (*Quadregesimo anno*, 1931), and the arms race (*Nova impendet*).

International Affairs

As an international moral leader, Pius sought cooperation with the political leaders of his day but spoke out against the injustices they often visited on their people. He condemned atheistic Soviet communism for its attacks on Christians in 1937. In the same year he ordered his encyclical *Mit brennender Sorge* (composed in German rather than Latin) read from all pulpits. This statement denounced the fundamentally anti-Christian nature of National Socialism (Nazism) and Nazi leader Adolf Hitler's violations of the concordat of 1933. When the Mexican Catholic Church was persecuted by Mexico's socialist government in the 1920's, Pius protested, and in 1937 he recommended the founding of lay Catholic action or-

The Lateran Treaty of 1929 between the Vatican and Benito Mussolini's Italian government made Vatican City a separate state within Italy. Here Mussolini (center) and other Italian government officials pay their first state visit to the Vatican. *(National Archives)*

The Lateran Treaty

Atheistic and anticlerical dictator Benito Mussolini had been treating Catholicism and the papacy rather generously as he established his Fascist state, while the papacy remained aloof. After realizing that Mussolini was not going to disappear from power, papal secretary of state Pietro Cardinal Gasparri signed a treaty, or series of pacts, with Mussolini, on February 11, 1929. These created the independent state of Vatican City on 44 hectares (109 acres) of land around the Vatican and St. Peter's. They also paid the Vatican 750 million lire plus 1 billion lire in state bonds in compensation for papal territories the Italian state had absorbed after 1870. Other agreements allowed religious education in secondary and primary schools, exempted seminarians from military service, and recognized church marriages as valid without a civil ceremony. Nonpolitically affiliated lay Catholic organizations directed by the papacy were also legalized. Mussolini gained papal and Catholic support, and the papacy gained freedom of action. The treaty was written into the postwar Italian constitution as Article 7.

ganizations to promote peaceful coexistence. Ever fearful of communism, Pius supported the Spanish fascist Francisco Franco against the anticlerical Republican forces supported by the Soviet Union in the Spanish Civil War.

Pope Pius XI posing for a portrait in 1924. *(Library of Congress)*

Pius's pontificate spanned the years between the two world wars, a period which saw the rise of dictatorships both fascist and communist, the Great Depression, and the march into the cataclysm of World War II. Scholarly Pius's own Christian faith, energy, and authoritarian personality steeled him for confrontations with these threats to humanity. He also denounced the trend to secular values as a threat to humankind's dignity and spiritual nature, preaching a message of Christian moral life in the modern world. Though unable to stem the tide of totalitarianism, militarism, or secularism, Pius XI provided a voice of conscience while taking positive steps toward modernizing the Catholic Church.

Bibliography

Anderson, Robin. *Between Two Wars: The Story of Pope Pius XI*. Chicago: Franciscan Herald Press, 1977.

Binchy, D. A. *Church and State in Fascist Italy*. London: Oxford University Press, 1941.

Rhodes, Anthony. *The Vatican in the Age of the Dictators*. London: Hodder and Stoughton, 1973.

Joseph P. Byrne

Pius XII

Born: March 2, 1876; Rome, Italy
Died: October 9, 1958; Castel Gandolfo, near Rome, Italy

Pope of the Roman Catholic Church (1939-1958)

Eugenio Maria Giuseppe Giovanni Pacelli (ay-ew-JAY-nyoh mah-REE-ah jew-ZEH-pay joh-VAH-nee pah-CHEH-lee) was the son of an Italian lawyer. He studied at the Pontifical Gregorian University and was ordained a priest in 1899. Under Cardinal Pietro Gasparri, he worked to codify canon law and subsequently served in the Vatican secretariat of state. He became undersecretary of state in 1912 and papal nuncio to Bavaria and archbishop of Sardes in 1917. He was elevated to the status of cardinal in 1929 and became secretary of state to Pope Pius XI in 1930. He negotiated a concordat in 1933 with the Nazi government regarding its treatment of the Catholic Church. In 1937 he collaborated in drafting an encyclical letter for Pius XI condemning Nazism as non-Christian. Cardinal Pacelli was elected to the papacy on March 2, 1939 as the successor to Pope Pius XI. He assumed the name Pius XII (PI-uhs thuh TWEHLFTH) and was the first Roman-born pope since Innocent XIII in 1721.

A World at War

Upon his election to the papacy, Pius XII faced a world descending into war. His attempts to convene peace conferences during 1939 proved fruitless, given the bellicose intentions of German dictator Adolf Hitler and Soviet dictator Joseph Stalin. Germany and the Soviet Union invaded Poland that fall, and Europe was enmeshed in World War II. Still, in his first papal encyclical, *Summi Pontificatus*, Pius XII called for peace and criticized the rise of modern totalitarianism as reflected in Nazi and communist ideologies. Pius unsuccessfully tried to prevent Italy's entry into the war on the side of Germany.

During the course of World War II, Pius XII attempted to retain ties with all of the belligerents, hoping thereby to work for a peaceful resolution to the conflicts. The Vatican, possessing no armies and delicately situated in the midst of fascist Italy, chose to use its moral authority and economic resources prudently. Confronting the evils of the Nazi regime was a delicate exercise. In his Christmas message of 1942, Pius XII condemned Nazi persecution of minorities and was hailed by *The New York Times* as one of the few voices for humanity standing against Nazi brutalities.

In general, however, Pius XII decided that prudence demanded quiet diplomacy rather than public rhetoric. His reluctance to condemn Nazi atrocities consistently led critics to accuse him of silence and apparent toleration of the Jewish Holocaust. His defenders have pointed out that when Nazi policies were specifically condemned,

Pius XII *(Library of Congress)*

ferocious retaliation occurred. In Holland, for example, Catholic bishops publicly denounced the deportation of Dutch Jews. Within weeks, many Catholics of Jewish ethnicity, including any priest or nun with any Jewish background, were deported by the Nazis and sent to concentration camps. With many Jewish groups urging him to avoid public denunciations and with millions of Catholics, including many clergy, suffering persecution, Pius XII opted for quieter forms of resistance.

Shortly after being chosen pope, Pius XII blesses a crowd from Rome's Church of St. John Lateran in May, 1939. *(AP/Wide World Photos)*

Vatican wartime archives document this quiet diplomacy, which included negotiations and ransom payments to prevent deportation of Jewish populations, the issuance of false passports and baptismal certificates, the hiding of Jewish refugees in the Vatican, and quiet pressure on governments collaborating with the Nazis, such as Hungary, to observe fundamental decency and regard for human rights. The Vatican spent more than four million dollars in defense of Jews.

An extensive traveler prior to his papacy, Pius XII remained in his native city of Rome during the entire war. He is credited with saving Rome from all-out destruction by gaining "open city" status for the city, thus protecting its historical monuments and population. The humanitarian work of the Vatican was extended without discrimination to thousands of refugees and displaced people. Millions of inquiries were made by the Vatican to trace the whereabouts of missing persons and to reunify families during the war.

Worker Priests

After World War II, which ended in 1945, workers in many Catholic countries were attracted to Communist Party organizations as a means of confronting capitalist owners of industry. Such workers often ceased practicing their religion, a situation that worried local bishops. To win back such workers, bishops in France and Belgium began training and assigning priests to work in factories and docks as a show of solidarity with workers. About one hundred priests eventually undertook such assignments as "worker priests." This experiment by the French and Belgian bishops came under scrutiny of the Vatican in the early 1950's during the papacy of Pius XII. The worker priests, serving no recognized order, were expected to join unions. Many ended up identifying with communist groups and joining in political activities. The Vatican, fearing that too many of the priests were being converted to communist sympathies rather than succeeding in reconverting former Catholic workers, decided to suppress the movement.

Vatican Neutrality

As a nonmilitary entity, the Vatican pursued a policy of neutrality during World War II in order to more readily serve as a mediator for peace. Thus the Vatican opposed the Allied declaration imposing an unconditional surrender on Germany, despite Allied efforts to gain Vatican support. The Vatican faced pressure from Benito Mussolini, Italy's Fascist dictator, to approve Adolf Hitler's attack on the Soviet Union. The Vatican pointedly refused to do so. This policy of neutrality has been criticized by those who think that an unqualified condemnation of Nazi atrocities was in order. Pius XII, however, refused to do this unless Joseph Stalin's regime in the Soviet Union, then an Allied state, was also condemned for similar atrocities. Neutrality was adopted partly out of fear that the Fascists or Nazis would simply seize the Vatican, thus ending the humanitarian work it was able to pursue quietly under the cover of neutrality.

Postwar Political and Pastoral Activities

Pius XII was an ardent foe of communism. He worked to strengthen Catholic action groups to halt the growth of communist influences in Italy and other West European countries. He issued excommunication orders for Catholics who joined the Communist Party and strongly supported resettlement of refugees fleeing communist regimes.

In matters of theology, dogma, and Catholic Church discipline, Pius XII issued numerous encyclicals, including subjects as diverse as biblical studies and the doctrine of the Mystical Body of Christ. He is perhaps best remembered for his proclamation defining the dogma of the Assumption of Mary (1950). Pius XII was politically and theologically conservative. However, his encyclical on biblical studies cautiously encouraged Catholic scholars to use modern historical methods in their research. He also took steps to reform Church liturgy and to relax fasting rules in relation to reception of Communion. Moreover, he is credited for naming many native bishops in areas under colonial administration rather than assigning foreign bishops to overseas dioceses.

A Legacy of Peace and Reform

Pius XII died after serving for nineteen years as pope. He prepared the way for the Second Vatican Council, which was convened by his successor, John XXIII. He is remembered as a man of great learning and great humanitarian concern. Golda Meir, prime minister of Israel, made the following statement on the event of his death:

> When fearful martyrdom came to our people, the voice of the pope was raised for its victims. The life of our times was enriched by a voice speaking out about great moral truths above the tumult of daily conflict. We mourn a great servant of peace.

Bibliography

Graham, Robert A. *Pius XII's Defense of Jews and Others: 1944-1945*. Milwaukee, Wis.: Catholic League, 1982.

_______. *The Vatican and Communism in World War II: What Really Happened?* San Francisco: Ignatius Press, 1996

Halecki, Oscar, and James Murray. *Pius XII*. New York: Farrar, Straus and Young, 1954.

Hochhuth, Rolf. *The Deputy*. New York: Grove Press, 1964.

Lapide, Pinchas. *Three Popes and the Jews*. New York: Hawthorne, 1967.

Weisbord, Robert G. *The Chief Rabbi, the Pope, and the Holocaust: An Era in Vatican-Jewish Relations*. New Brunswick, N.J.: Transaction Publishers, 1992.

Robert F. Gorman

Raymond Poincaré

Born: August 20, 1860; Bar-le-Duc, France
Died: October 15, 1934; Paris, France

Five-time prime minister of France between 1912 and 1929

The political career of Raymond Poincaré (ray-MO pwa-kah-RAY) included five prime ministerships and the presidency of the Republic during World War I. He was one of the foremost statesman of France's Third Republic. Raymond was born in western Lorraine on August 20, 1860, the only son of a liberal republican civil engineer and a mother who embraced the traditional beliefs that his father lacked. Early family life included toleration of a wide variety of views. Raymond's adolescence was clouded by four years of life under German occupation, as Germany took control of Alsace-Lorraine following its victory over France in the War of 1870. A brilliant student, Raymond went on to earn both an arts and law degree from the Sorbonne. Admitted to the Paris bar in December, 1880, he became the youngest practicing lawyer in France.

As Poincaré began practicing commercial law, he started writing articles on literary and cultural topics. At the same time, he entered government as a chief cabinet staff person. He proved skilled in preparing dossiers and budgets. By 1887 Poincaré was encouraged to run as deputy representing his native Meuse. He became the youngest member of the Chamber of Deputies. While shyness prevented any notable speeches, Poincaré established a reputation as a legal and financial expert, a nonideological moderate republican, and a completely honest individual. Between 1893 and 1896, he would twice serve as education minister and once as finance minister. Yet Poincaré also became disgusted by the inability of the unstable parliamentary system to generate meaningful policies. Although still sitting in parliament, Poincaré redirected energies into his legal and literary careers.

Raymond Poincaré *(Library of Congress)*

Power

In 1903 Poincaré became senator for the Meuse. By 1909 his prolific writing earned him election to the prestigious Academe Française. He traveled widely. Then the unexpected happened. The Moroccan (Agadir) Crisis of 1911 necessitated delicate negotiations to avoid conflict with Germany. Poincaré was appointed head of a Senate Commission to examine a Franco-German Treaty, a task into which he plunged with great thoroughness. The treaty needed to be ratified by the Chamber of Deputies, however, and the premier (Joseph Caillaux) had resigned. In January, 1912, Poincaré seemed to be an ideal choice to replace Caillaux. As prime minister, serving also as foreign minister, Poincaré worked toward strengthening ties with Russia and Great Britain. He campaigned for a three-year conscription law to increase French military reserves in the event of war. With presidential elections planned for January, 1913, Poincaré was encouraged to run. He wanted to use the symbolism of the office to promote seven years of national unity while also increasing the presidential role in foreign policy and in the selection of new governments.

World War I

During the Sarajevo crisis from which World War I began, Poincaré was on a three-week cruise to Russia, accompanied by his premier and foreign minister. The circumstances of the visit gave rise during the 1920's to a conspiracy theory about Poincaré's desire to involve France in war. More recent historical research shows only that Poincaré was anxious to give every appearance that France was fighting a defensive war. By August 1, he did believe that war was inevitable and planned a national unity government (*union sacrée*) while working to guarantee British participation. Although France had seven different governments during the war, the government of national unity prevailed. Poincaré's own leadership role was difficult, since presidential leadership was not part of the Republic's constitution or political traditions. However, Poincaré was in a unique position to mediate between civilian

The National Union Ministry

Having made the decision to mobilize the military in preparation for war on August 1, 1914, Raymond Poincaré also drew up a two-page proclamation. It called for national unity (*union sacrée*, or sacred union) and for a France "heroically defended by all her sons, whose sacred union will never be shattered in the face of the enemy." The national union concept appealed to the whole French political spectrum. The cabinet was widened into a war cabinet to include socialist leftists and Catholic rightists such as Alfred de Mun. For symbolism, all major cabinet decisions were made with the president present. Although there was discord as early as 1915, the national union lasted until the summer of 1917. Then Catholics resigned due to lack of response to papal peace initiatives, and socialists left because they were prohibited from attending an international socialist conference.

The idea for a national union government was resurrected on July 23, 1926, when Poincaré was called on to solve the nation's financial crisis. Taking over the premiership and financial affairs, Poincaré instituted new taxes, stabilized the franc by basing it on the gold standard, and refused new foreign loans. The French economy quickly revived and entered two years of prosperity. By November, 1928, the radical republican Left made clear its desire to leave the national union. Shortly thereafter, the national union came to an end.

needs and military demands. Since all important cabinet decisions were made in his presence, he symbolized unity of purpose.

Aftermath of World War I

In 1918, with victory in sight, Poincaré was not happy about the armistice. He wanted the war to end with the complete destruction of German forces. He was largely excluded from the peace negotiations by his dynamic premier, Georges Clemenceau. Poincaré wanted the Rhineland and Saar regions to be autonomous. He hated the Treaty of Versailles (signed by the war's combatants) not only for its specific terms but also for the lack of enforcement guarantees. With his presidential term ending on February 17, 1920, Poincaré returned to the senate as chairman of the Reparations Committee. He was associated with those who wanted to make Germany pay.

Support for the former president grew, leading in January, 1922, to his appointment as premier and foreign minister. Failing to gain German cooperation for its treaty obligations, Poincaré ordered the military occupation of the valley of the Ruhr River. In the meantime France was plagued with severe economic problems that required new taxes and a readjustment of the value of the franc. Faced with an alliance on the Left, Poincaré was forced to resign on June 1. However, as the crisis grew during the next two years, he was reinstated to form a new national unity government to solve the economic problems of France.

Four European heads of state meeting in London in 1922 to discuss German reparations and Allied war debts from World War I: prime ministers Raymond Poincaré of France, Bonar Law of Great Britain, Benito Mussolini of Italy, and George Theunis of Belgium. *(Library of Congress)*

The Occupation of the Ruhr

Faced with hyperinflation and a crippled economy, Germany evaded its war-reparations payments during 1921 without any serious response by Great Britain or the United States. Raymond Poincaré's return as French premier in January, 1922, signaled a strong French stand on the reparations issue and produced blistering attacks in the German press. After a year of failed negotiations, Poincaré ordered French troops into the Ruhr region of Germany in January, 1923, instructing them to seize mines and railroads. The only German response was passive resistance. As the occupation continued, the cost for French taxpayers soared. The French Left joined the British government in its hostility to this unilateral French action. If Poincaré's ulterior motive was to encourage separatist movements in the Ruhr and the Rhineland, they did not materialize. The year-long occupation did convince Germany to resume reparations payments, however, and moved Britain and the United States to recalibrate German payments under the Dawes Plan (1924). Meanwhile, the French economy was in disarray. In 1924 a coalition of the French Left (*Cartel des Gauches*) narrowly gained control of the Chamber of Deputies, forcing Poincaré's government to resign.

This he achieved with consummate skill. However, once the crisis ended the national unity government unravelled. In the midst of negotiating inter-Allied war debts left over from World War I, Poincaré fell ill. He resigned on July 26, 1929. His last five years were spent completing ten volumes of memoirs (*Au Service de la France*, 1926-1974).

Bibliography

Huddleston, S. *Poincaré: A Biographical Portrait*. London: T. Fisher Unwin, 1924.

Keiger, J. F. *Raymond Poincaré*. Cambridge, England: Cambridge University Press, 1997.

Wright, Gordon. *Raymond Poincaré and the French Presidency*. Stanford, Calif.: Stanford University Press, 1942.

Irwin Halfond

Pol Pot

Born: May 19, 1925 (or 1928); Kompong Thom province, Cambodia
Died: April 15, 1998; Dangrek Mountains, near Choam Ksant, Cambodia

Cambodian revolutionary and premier of Cambodia (1976-1979)

Born Saloth Sar (sah-lot sahr), Pol Pot (pahl PAHT) was the son of an influential small landowner in the Kompong Thom province in central Cambodia. Pol Pot's father had some influence with the Cambodian royal court. Pol Pot was educated in a Catholic institution and a Buddhist monastery. He also trained to be a carpenter at a technical school and was sent to France to study radio electronics.

Lessons in Communism

While in France, Pol Pot joined a small group of Cambodian students who argued against French colonialism. These students studied with members of the French Communist Party. As he focused more on studying Karl Marx and Vladimir Lenin than electronics, Pol Pot failed school and returned to Cambodia in 1953. Upon his return, he joined the Vietminh United Khmer Issarak Front, an underground communist organization, and the Khmer People's Revolutionary Party (KPRP). (The Khmer ethnic group makes up the majority of Cambodia's population.) On September 28, 1960, he met with Tou Samouth and a number of other Khmers to found the Workers' Party of Kampuchea (WPK). Pol Pot was named one of the three Politburo members supporting Samouth as secretary-general. Three years later, at the second congress of the WPK, Pol Pot succeeded Samouth as secretary-general. Samouth would later be found dead, reportedly assassinated by Pol Pot.

Pol Pot *(National Archives)*

From 1954 to 1963 Pol Pot taught at a private school in Phnom Penh. He was eventually forced to leave, as the police began to suspect his ties to the communists and the WPK. In 1965 Pol Pot began traveling to Hanoi and Beijing in attempts to win acceptance from Communist Party leaders in Vietnam and China. The Chinese accepted Pol Pot's overtures, resulting in his pro-China stance upon his return to Cambodia in September of 1966. He also renamed the WPK the Communist Party of Kampuchea (CPK).

People's Revolution

In 1964, Cambodia won independence from the French and was ruled by Prince Norodom Sihanouk. The CPK led demonstrations against Sihanouk. When Sihanouk denounced and then executed a large number of these protesters, whom he described as Khmer Rouge (meaning, literally, "Red [communist] Khmers"), the fragmented communist groups in Cambodia came together to follow the lead of the CPK. In December of 1969, Pol Pot and members of his CPK politburo again visited Hanoi and Beijing in an attempt to gain support for the final push against Sihanouk. Before the CPK could move, however, Sihanouk's government was toppled in a coup and Lon Nol was named president of Cambodia.

In September of 1971, the CPK again elected Pol Pot as secretary-general and commander in chief of the CPK's Revolutionary Army. He continued to antagonize the Vietnamese, refusing to participate in negotiations with the United States, Lon Nol's government, and the Vietnamese. As Vietnamese troops left Cambodia as a part of the Paris Accords, Pol Pot ordered units of the CPK's Revolutionary Army to take over the encampments, thus solidifying its strategic and negotiating positions.

Angka's Killing Fields

Phnom Penh fell on April 17, 1975, after two years of battles between Lon Nol's forces and the CPK. Within a day of the victory, Khmer Rouge soldiers descended upon the hospitals of Phnom Penh and herded the patients who could move into the countryside, leaving the rest to die in the street. Later that day, the rest of the populace was marched out into the fields as a part of the process of re-creating Cambodian society. The empty city was then razed. Civic institutions were de-

Khmer Rouge leader Pol Pot on trial in Cambodia in 1997. *(Reuters/Stringer/Archive Photos)*

The Killing Fields

The 1984 film *The Killing Fields* portrays the wartime travails of Dith Pran (played by Haing S. Ngor), a Cambodian journalist who served as an interpreter for *New York Times* correspondent Sydney Schanberg (Sam Waterston). The film examines events in Cambodia that resulted from the American withdrawal from the Vietnam War in 1975. In the film, Schanberg convinces Pran to remain in Cambodia to continue coverage of the Khmer Rouge's brutal struggle for control of Cambodia. The film provides a chilling account of the massacres and re-education camps that Pol Pot's Angka used in an attempt to purge political opponents from the population. Produced by David Puttnam and directed by Roland Joffe, *The Killing Fields* was nominated for seven Academy Awards in 1985. The film won three of the awards, including a Best Supporting Actor award for Haing S. Ngor. Ngor, a Cambodian physician, had personally lived through the horrors brought about by the Khmer Rouge.

The Domino Theory

The domino theory was named by President Dwight D. Eisenhower. It holds that neighboring countries are so interrelated that, if they are faced with the same threat, if one country collapses, they will all collapse like falling dominoes. The domino theory was employed primarily as part of the attempt to contain the spread of communism. It was used, for example, to justify American intervention in the war between North and South Vietnam.

The argument was that if one country in this region were to fall to communism, all would become communist states. In 1961, Vice President Lyndon B. Johnson cited the domino theory argument when he went to Saigon to show his support for South Vietnam's leader, Ngo Dinh Diem. Johnson argued that if South Vietnam were lost, Americans would soon be fighting the war against communism in Hawaii. Some historians discount the domino theory. Others argue that the consecutive collapses of noncommunist governments in South Vietnam, Cambodia, and Laos stand as proof that the argument is valid.

stroyed. Banks were destroyed; money, now abolished as a form of currency, fell like leaves on the vacant city. This action was the first step in the attempt to achieve the agrarian communist utopia that Pol Pot visualized.

Pol Pot's reform was carried out by his secret inner-party organization, the Angka. They began by systematically killing political enemies and their families. The purges included the wealthy, the educated, even individuals who had the misfortune to wear eyeglasses. The killing continued, and as ammunition became scarce, victims were lined up in the fields and bludgeoned to death. Their bodies were then buried in mass graves. The skeletons of these victims remain, heaped by the thousands, in museums and memorials in Cambodia. By the time the bloodshed stopped, an estimated 1.6 to 2 million Cambodians—one fifth of the country's population—had perished at the hands of Pol Pot and the Angka.

Pol Pot held power in Cambodia until January 7, 1979, when the Vietnamese military forced the CPK leadership to flee to the Cardamom mountains in western Cambodia. The CPK regrouped, and Pol Pot remained in command of a thirty-thousand-man army that waged a guerrilla war against the Vietnamese for years. Pol Pot remained in seclusion for nearly two decades. Part of that time he was under house arrest by the Khmer Rouge. Unrepentant to the end, Pol Pot died of an apparent heart attack in April of 1998.

Bibliography

Chandler, David P. *Brother Number One: A Political Biography of Pol Pot*. New York: Westview Press, 1992.

Pran, Dith, comp. *Children of Cambodia's Killing Fields: Memoirs of Survivors*. Edited by Kim Depaul. New Haven, Conn.: Yale University Press, 1997.

Stefor, Rebecca. *Pol Pot*. New York: Chelsea House, 1990.

B. Keith Murphy

Georges Pompidou

Born: July 5, 1911; Montboudif, France
Died: April 2, 1974; Paris, France

Prime minister (1962-1968) and president (1969-1974) of France

Georges-Jean-Raymond Pompidou (ZHOHRZH ZHO ray-MO po-pee-DEW) was born to parents who were both teachers, and Georges graduated from Paris's École Normale Supérieure, the most prestigious university in France for future teachers. Like his parents, he became a teacher. He taught French and Latin in French high schools from 1935 until 1944. He was a member of the French Resistance during World War II and barely avoided being arrested by the Gestapo. During the Nazi occupation of France, he demonstrated courage and loyalty to General Charles de Gaulle. In 1944, he accepted an invitation from de Gaulle to serve as his special assistant entrusted with reforming French universities. In 1946, de Gaulle asked Pompidou to direct the Anne de Gaulle Foundation, a charitable organization named for his chronically sick daughter. He managed the money of this organization so well that de Gaulle asked him to serve as his chief adviser, a post Pompidou occupied from 1947 to 1954. In July, 1954, the French banker Guy de Rothschild asked Pompidou to become a director of his family bank. From 1954 to 1962, Georges Pompidou was a banker, but he also remained a loyal adviser to de Gaulle, who became president of France in 1958.

Years as Prime Minister

In 1961, President de Gaulle asked Pompidou to undertake secret negotiations with French army officers in Algeria who had undertaken illegal military actions in order to prevent Algerian independence from France. At Pompidou's urging, de Gaulle ordered the French army to crush this revolt and to arrest the traitors. The rule of law was maintained in France. De Gaulle rewarded Pompidou by naming him his prime minister in April, 1962. Pompidou served as prime minister until July, 1968, and directed the successful legislative victories of the Gaullist coalition in the 1967 and 1968 elections. He also directed the successful reelection campaign of de Gaulle in 1965 against socialist candidate François Mitterrand. In France, there are two rounds in presidential elections. There are usually several candidates in the first round. If no candidate receives an absolute majority, the top two candidates compete two weeks later in the second round. In the first round in 1965, de

Georges Pompidou *(Library of Congress)*

Gaulle received only 44 percent of the vote. All indications are that Pompidou had to persuade de Gaulle to campaign vigorously, because de Gaulle was discouraged by his showing in the first round. Pompidou launched especially harsh attacks against the policies of Mitterrand. De Gaulle was reelected with 55 percent of the votes.

Pompidou's role as prime minister was basically to make sure that French legislators implemented de Gaulle's policy decisions. Pompidou was skillful in keeping party discipline, especially after the 1967 elections gave the Gaullists a very small majority in the National Assembly. After the French general strike in May, 1968, Pompidou led the Gaullists to a massive victory in the June, 1968, election, but de Gaulle dismissed him as prime minister the next month. Dismissal proved to be a blessing in disguise, because it meant that Pompidou was not in de Gaulle's government when de Gaulle decided to resign in April, 1969, following the defeat of a referendum dealing with regionalization and the reform of the French senate.

Georges Pompidou during his successful run for the French presidency in 1969. At left is Jacques Chaban-Delmas, whom Pompidou chose as his premier. *(Agence France Presse/Archive Photos)*

The Sixth Plan

During France's Fourth Republic (1946-1958) and also during its Fifth Republic (established 1958), several different French governments created specific plans to establish priorities for economic development and industrialization. These consecutively numbered plans all envisioned significant expenditures of public funds to support private industry and encourage the export of French products and services. When he became president in 1969, Georges Pompidou concluded that such programs were ineffective and too expensive. In a lengthy introduction that he wrote in 1971 for the Sixth Plan, he argued that what French companies truly needed was better-educated workers and more assistance from the French government in marketing their products in foreign countries. The Sixth Plan covered the period from 1971 to 1975. From 1971 until his death in 1974, Pompidou significantly increased spending for education and technical training and expanded the number of university technical institutes so that French workers would be very well prepared to succeed against worldwide competition. He believed that, in the long run, better skilled workers would help French industry much more than corporate welfare.

Gaullism

Gaullism became the name for a political movement created by General Charles de Gaulle in the 1940's. De Gaulle believed that France needed a strong leader whose authority derived directly from the people rather than from the legislature. To attain this goal, he persuaded French voters to approve a new constitution in 1958 that granted the president significant executive powers. De Gaulle created a center-right coalition of several parties. Gaullism has had a significant influence on France long after de Gaulle's retirement in 1969. Members of his coalition dominated subsequent presidential elections. Georges Pompidou won in 1969, Valéry Giscard d'Estaing won in 1974, and Jacques Chirac won in 1995. The only non-Gaullist to serve as the president of France in the late twentieth century was François Mitterrand, who served two seven-year terms between 1981 and 1995.

The Presidential Years

When President de Gaulle resigned, Alain Poher, the president of the French senate, became the temporary president of France until a new election could be held. The Gaullists decided to support Georges Pompidou as their candidate. The other major candidate was the almost unknown Alain Poher. Early opinion polls favored Poher over Pompidou, but the more French voters saw of Poher, the less they liked him; he seemed inflexible and uninspired. Pompidou was well known to French voters because of his more than six years of service as prime minister. People knew that Pompidou would be a moderate conservative, but they did not know what Poher's policies would be. Pompidou easily defeated Poher in the second round on June 15, 1969.

Pompidou continued the general domestic and foreign policies of de Gaulle, but, unlike his predecessor, he was much less supportive of government intervention to support private industry. Under de Gaulle, the French government had devised various plans to make French companies more competitive internationally. French economic growth in the 1960's had surpassed that of other European countries, including West Germany and England, but this corporate welfare had become very expensive for France. Some costly projects, such as the construction of the supersonic Concorde jets, attracted little commercial interest outside England and France. In 1971, Georges Pompidou decided that it was unwise for the French government to continue making massive investments in companies that could probably succeed on their own.

Pompidou believed that French taxes were too high. He was philosophically opposed to taxpayer support for private industry. In foreign affairs, Pompidou strove to preserve and improve relationships with other countries, but he also approved large expenditures to maintain the national defense. Pompidou died of cancer in Paris on April 2, 1974, at the relatively young age of sixty-two. The following month French voters elected Valéry Giscard d'Estaing, a member of the Gaullist coalition, as their new president.

Bibliography

Alexandre, Philippe. *The Duel: De Gaulle and Pompidou*. Translated by Elaine P. Halperin. Boston: Houghton Mifflin, 1972.

Andrews, William G., and Stanley Hoffmann, eds. *The Impact of the Fifth Republic on France*. Albany: State University of New York Press, 1981.

Hauss, Charles. *Politics in Gaullist France: Coping with Chaos*. New York: Praeger, 1991.

Edmund J. Campion

Adam Clayton Powell, Jr.

Born: November 29, 1908; New Haven, Connecticut
Died: April 4, 1972; Miami, Florida

U.S. Congressman (1945-1967, 1969-1971) and civil rights advocate

Adam Clayton Powell, Jr. (A-duhm KLAY-tuhn POWL JEW-nyur), the son of Mattie and Adam Clayton Powell, Sr., was born in New Haven, Connecticut. When he was six months old, his family relocated to New York City. Educated at Colgate University and the Union Theological Seminary, he followed his father into the ministry of the most prestigious African American church in the city. He served as pastor after the retirement of his father in 1936 until his own resignation in 1971. Powell became an early voice in the struggle for civil rights during his years in the ministry and in Congress.

Career in the Church

Powell did not fit the mold of the typical African American minister; he was drawn to nightlife and attractive women. Yet however unusual or even outrageous his activities were, the members of his church and community forgave him without question. His concern for his community was what commanded this overwhelming loyalty. During the Depression, he became a civil rights activist before civil rights became a national issue. Powell could be found organizing picket lines, mass meetings, rent strikes, and other protests against policies that denied African Americans equal opportunities for jobs, housing, or political representation. From 1941 to 1945 he was actively involved in a weekly newspaper, *The People's Voice*. Possibly realizing that the vote was the most effective way to produce change, Powell decided to run, as an independent candidate, for the New York City Council in 1941.

Career in Politics

Powell was elected to the U.S. Congress in 1944, serving first on the Indian Affairs, Invalid Pensions, and Labor Committees. In 1947 he was seated as a member of the Education and Labor Committee; he also served on the Committee on Interior and Insular Affairs from 1945 to 1961. During his initiation period in the House of Representatives, he took the advice of noted Speaker of the House Sam Rayburn to ease into the situation and spend time learning the rules. Rayburn sensed that Powell had a great future. The congressman's private social life, however, was a target of criticism. His marriage to Isabella Wash-

Adam Clayton Powell, Jr. *(Archive Photos)*

ington Powell deteriorated into divorce. His second wife was café society entertainer and jazz pianist Hazel Scott. At his church, he was not censured for this apparent breach of behavior. He was so admired by his constituents that he was forgiven without qualification.

His political life soon began to show signs of change. His impatience with the status quo could not be contained, and he became an agitator against lynchings, discrimination, and segregation. Until Powell's election, segregation pervaded even the halls of government. Nevertheless, Powell got the dining room and the barbershop in the Capitol to begin serving him. He managed to persuade racist congressmen from using ethnic epithets in sessions of Congress. Whenever there was an opportunity to protest, he seized it. Realizing the power available to him, he began to use the legislative process to his advantage. The "Powell amendment" led to the nullification of any bill that appropriated federal funds for a state or locality that continued discrimination in its agencies.

In 1960, Powell began to chair the powerful House Committee on Education and Labor. The chairmanship marked the high point of his career, for he was able to be influential in both John F. Kennedy's New Frontier program and Lyndon B. Johnson's Great Society program. Many social programs that would affect all Americans were involved: the setting of minimum wages, antipoverty programs, and the National Defense

U.S. congressman Adam Clayton Powell, Jr., with supporters in 1967. *(AP/Wide World Photos)*

The House Committee on Education and Labor

By 1960, Adam Clayton Powell, Jr., had enough seniority in the House of Representatives to qualify for the chairmanship of the powerful House Committee on Education and Labor. Some members of Congress attempted to deprive him of the chairmanship for a variety of reasons; Powell angrily retorted that the real reason was simply that he was a powerful black men. As chairman of the committee, Powell was at the zenith of his political career, and his accomplishments were impressive. He was able to oversee the approval of bills that would enhance the lives of the poor and hungry. He provided greater funding for public education on the elementary and secondary levels, and for public libraries. He also attempted to rid unions of discriminatory practices. Such measures were not entirely successful, but even partial victories were celebrated.

Education Act, which would help high school and college students

Career's End

Powell's career began to unravel later in the 1960's, however. He had continuing tax problems with the Internal Revenue Service and was accused of fraud, mishandling federal funds, and accepting kickbacks. He was unsuccessful in defending himself against such charges. Powell was expelled from Congress in 1967. In 1969 the U.S. Supreme Court ruled this action unconstitutional, and it was reversed. He was fined $25,000 to repay the kickbacks. However, by this time Powell showed little interest in working in Congress. He spent most of his time out of the country, on the Caribbean island of Bimini. His record of attendance in Congress became so poor that he lost the faith of his constituents. He lost the primary election in 1970 to Charles Rangel. Two years later, he died at the age of sixty-three.

Adam Clayton Powell, Jr., holding a press conference in 1966. *(Archive Photos)*

Bibliography

Anderson, Jervis. *This Was Harlem: A Cultural Portrait, 1900-1950.* New York: Farrar Straus Giroux, 1982.

Chapelle, Tony. "Adam Clayton Powell: Black Power Between Heaven and Hell." *The Black Collegian Magazine First Semester Super Issue.* 1997.

Coombs, Norman. *The Black Experience in America.* New York: Twayne, 1972.

Hamilton, Charles. *Adam Clayton Powell, Jr.: Political Biography of an American Dilemma.* New York: Atheneum Press, 1991.

Haygood, Wil. *King of Cats: The Life and Times of Adam Clayton Powell, Jr.* Boston: Houghton Mifflin, 1993.

Maude M. Jennings

Colin Powell

Born: April 5, 1937; New York, New York

U.S. military leader, Gulf War strategist (1990-1991)

Colin Luther Powell (KUH-lihn LEW-thur POWL), son of Jamaican immigrants, was educated in the New York City Public Schools, graduating from the City College of New York. In 1958, upon completion of a college Reserve Officer Training Corps (ROTC) program, Powell received a commission as an army second lieutenant. He served two tours in Vietnam from 1962 to 1963 and 1968 to 1969. In 1971 he received a master of business administration degree from George Washington University. In 1972 he was chosen to be a White House Fellow. Later, after a series of military commands, Powell served as a national security adviser to President Ronald Reagan from December, 1987, to January, 1989. He then rose to become the twelfth chairman of the Joint Chiefs of Staff, Department of Defense, from October 1, 1989, to September 30, 1993, under Presidents George Bush and Bill Clinton. During the course of his career, Powell received several U.S. military decorations, including the Defense Distinguished Service Medal, the Army Distinguished Service Medal, Soldier's Medal, Bronze Star Medal, and the Purple Heart. He married Alma Vivian Johnson of Birmingham, Alabama, and together they had a son, Michael, and two daughters, Linda and Annmarie.

Colin Powell *(U.S. Air Force)*

Hard Lessons in Vietnam

Though formally educated by the college ROTC program, Colin Powell's two tours of duty in Vietnam proved to be his true schooling in military management and provided the foundation for his future success. In the war, he suffered a wound from a punji trap—a spike coated with poison. Powell also survived a helicopter crash. He heroically pulled his commander, Major General Charles M. Gettys, from the wreckage despite suffering a broken ankle in the accident. Having sacrificed so much personally, Powell was critical of the personnel management errors he observed. During the war, he expressed disdain for self-promoting career officers who distributed award ribbons to other soldiers for routine duties. Drawing upon these and other experiences, he later developed his own personal code, "Colin Powell's rules," which consists of thirteen guiding principles of conduct.

Chairman of the Joint Chiefs of Staff

The Goldwater-Nichols Act of 1986 increased the powers of the chairman of the Joint Chiefs of Staff in order to establish a clear line of authority with respect to military command decisions. Prior to this law, the Joint Chiefs essentially worked as a committee. This situation had created confusion and turf wars among the separate branches of the military. Therefore, when General Powell was confirmed as chairman in 1989, he became the president's "principal military adviser" and one of the most powerful chairmen of the Joint Chiefs in history. At age fifty-two, he was the youngest person, the first African American, and the first ROTC graduate appointed to that post. Approximately twenty-four hours after assuming his new role, Powell was confronted with a crisis involving a potential uprising against the chief of the Panama Defense Forces (PDF), Brigadier General Manuel Noriega. Later that fall, the situation intensified when a U.S. Marine lieutenant was shot and killed by PDF soldiers. On December 20, 1989, the United States invaded Panama in a military operation supervised by Powell called Operation Just Cause. American forces captured Noriega and restored civilian rule to the country. Powell fully showed his skill as a military commander later in his term during the Gulf War.

After the Gulf War

In October, 1994, the Times Mirror Center for the People and the Press published a report on public opinion in which Colin Powell was named as an American hero by several different groups of U.S. citizens with very diverse political and religious beliefs. At that time, his strong popularity with the American people led to speculation that he might seek the presidency in 1996. Though he was extremely popular with the general public, few seemed to know much about Powell's political ideology. Critics charged that the military had insulated him from controversial issues and that his support would fade once he addressed public policy issues. Powell himself continued to fuel interest in a potential presidential bid by staging a multiple-city book tour in order to promote his 1995 autobiography, *My*

The Intermediate Range Nuclear Forces Treaty

During the time that Colin Powell headed the U.S. Army's V Corps in Frankfurt, Germany, the idea of using tactical (short-range) nuclear weapons to repel a possible Soviet invasion was discussed and considered a possibility. Powell became keenly aware that the use of tactical nuclear weapons would be one of the most significant military decisions since the World War II bombing of Hiroshima, Japan, by the United States. He understood that artillery-fired atomic projectiles (AFAPs) would endanger the civilian population in Germany. In addition, it would most certainly trigger a Soviet retaliation.

Powell's thinking on the use of tactical nuclear weapons crystallized when he became national security adviser to President Ronald Reagan. Reagan's counterpart in the Soviet Union, Mikhail Gorbachev, was eager to trim his country's defense budget by reducing intermediate-range nuclear weapons, or INF missiles. The Soviets would give up their SS-20 missiles, he proposed, if the United States eliminated its army's Pershing II missiles and its air force's ground-launched cruise missiles. As Powell stated in his autobiography, "The prospects brightened that we could get an INF treaty; and that meant that for the first time since the dawning of the atomic age, a class of nuclear weapons would be destroyed." Both leaders signed the INF treaty in 1987.

The American Gulf War Strategy

In 1990 Iraqi leader Saddam Hussein invaded and occupied the tiny oil-producing country of Kuwait. This action prompted the United States to send forces to the region in an operation known as Desert Shield. As chairman of the Joint Chiefs, General Colin Powell prepared military strategy in Washington, D.C., while General Norman Schwarzkopf commanded troops on the ground in Saudi Arabia. U.S. president George Bush formed an international coalition of countries that opposed the Iraqi invasion. The United Nations authorized the use of economic and military actions to restore Kuwait's sovereignty. Iraq ignored a January deadline to retreat from Kuwait, and Operation Desert Shield became Operation Desert Storm. In a memorable news briefing, General Powell, succinctly describing the military strategy to be used against the Iraqi army, said: "First we're going to cut it off, and then we're going to kill it." Vietnam veterans Powell and Schwarzkopf were united in their desire to minimize U.S. casualties, so they fashioned a massive thirty-eight-day air strike and bombing campaign to destabilize the Iraqi military prior to movement by ground forces. This Gulf War strategy was so successful that President Bush called off the ground assault after one hundred hours of action. Powell and Schwarzkopf achieved their objective of limiting American combat deaths, as U.S. casualties totaled 148.

American Journey. During these trips, mass confusion arose as to whether Powell would seek the Democratic nomination, enter the Republican primaries, run as an independent, or sit out the campaign entirely.

Despite high popularity and the formation of an impressive "draft Powell for president" organization, Powell ended the drama and held a news conference in which he announced that he would not be a candidate. He cleared up some of the questions concerning his political beliefs by declaring that he was a member of the Republican Party. Another draft-Powell presidential movement formed in preparation for the 2000 election, but the retired Powell expressed his contentment with

Chairman of the Joint Chiefs of Staff Colin Powell in a relaxed moment with military personnel in Saudi Arabia during preparations for Operation Desert Storm. *(Reuters/Jonathan Bainbridge/Archive Photos)*

private life. He stated that he had little desire for the rough and tumble of political campaigns. Powell remained active in service to the nation as chairman of America's Promise, a not-for-profit organization dedicated to the mobilization of resources for American children in need. He was also a member of the board of directors of the United Negro College Fund and the board of trustees of Howard University. Likewise, he served on the board of governors of the Boys and Girls Clubs of America and the board of the Children's Health Fund.

Bibliography

Brown, Warren. *Colin Powell.* New York: Chelsea House Paperbacks, 1992.

Powell, Colin L., and Joseph E. Persico. *My American Journey.* New York: Random House, 1995.

Roth, David. *Sacred Honor: Colin Powell, the Inside Account of His Life and Triumphs.* New York: Zondervan, 1996.

Woodward, Bob. *The Commanders.* New York: Pocket Books, 1992.

John W. Cavanaugh

Pu-yi

Born: February 7, 1906; Beijing, China
Died: October 17, 1967; Beijing, China

Last emperor of China (1909-1911) and figurehead emperor of Manchukuo (1934-1945)

Pu-yi (PEW-YEE), also known by his reign name, Xuanton or Hsuan-tung (SHWAHN TOONG), was the eldest son of the second Prince Chun. Prince Chun was the brother of the childless Emperor Kuang-hsu. Pu-yi was chosen to succeed Kuang-hsu by the empress dowager, Tz'u-hsi (or Cixi), and he ascended the throne when he was barely three years old at the end of 1908. He reigned as Emperor Hsuan-tung between 1909 and 1911.

Pu-yi *(National Archives)*

Abdication and Restoration

Late in 1911, an uprising organized in Wuhan by Sun Yat-sen's United League (later called the Kuomintang, or Nationalist Party) spread rapidly through central and southern China. The regent of the Qing Dynasty (or Ching Dynasty, also known as the Manchu dynasty) decided to abdicate on behalf of the boy emperor.

Under the "Articles of Favorable Treatment" of the abdication, signed on February 12, 1912, the Hsuan-tung emperor was to vacate the imperial palace in Beijing (Peking), but he retained his title and accompanying honors, received an annual allowance from the Chinese Republic, and retained the summer palace outside Beijing as his residence. In 1917, without his knowledge, the eleven-year-old Pu-yi was "restored" to the imperial throne for eleven days by a promonarchist general. No punitive action was taken against him for the failed restoration.

In 1918, on orders of the president of the Chinese republic, an Englishman named Reginald Johnson was appointed Pu-yi's tutor. Johnson gave him a modern education and an English name, Henry. In 1922 Pu-yi married two Manchu noblewomen: Wan-jung, who became empress, and Wen-hsiu, who received the rank of imperial concubine. He lived in the imperial palace until expelled by General Feng Yu-hsiang in November, 1924. In 1925 he and his wives moved to a mansion in the Japanese concession in Tianjin. In 1929 Wen-hsiu left Pu-yi's residence and requested a divorce, an unprecedented act by an imperial concubine. The request outraged her own family and wounded Pu-yi's pride. He was forced to agree to a divorce in 1931. Wen-hsiu became a schoolteacher. She died in 1950.

Puppet Emperor of Manchukuo

His feelings wounded by real and perceived indignities under the republic, Pu-yi began secret contacts with Japanese officials in Manchuria on the subject of his restoration around 1928. After the Japanese Kwangtung Army stationed in Manchuria (called the Northeastern Provinces in China) instigated an event called the Manchurian incident on September 18, 1931, to conquer the region, serious talks began between Pu-yi and Doihara Kenji, head of the secret-service section of the Kwangtung Army.

Pu-yi in 1932, riding to his inauguration as head of state of Manchukuo. *(National Archives)*

On November 10, Pu-yi arrived in Japanese-occupied Manchuria in a Japanese ship and accepted the position of chief executive of the Japanese puppet state called Manchukuo. Its capital city was Changchun, renamed Hsinking (or new capital). When Manchukuo was declared a constitutional monarchy in 1934, Pu-yi became emperor, under the reign name K'ang-te.

Pu-yi paid a state visit to Japan in 1935 to thank the Japanese for their crucial "assis-

Manchukuo

Manchukuo, or land of the Manchus, was the name given to the puppet state Japan established after taking the region from China during 1931 and 1932. Pu-yi became first its nominal head of state, then Emperor K'ang-te of Manchukuo during its existence as a constitutional monarchy under Japanese control between 1932 and 1945. It collapsed upon the defeat of Japan in World War II, and Manchuria was returned to China.

In an interview granted to H. G. W. Woodhead, a British writer and newspaper editor, in 1932, Pu-yi stated that he had gone to Manchuria of his free will. He reaffirmed this statement when interviewed by the Lytton Commission of Enquiry, sent by the League of Nations to investigate the circumstances surrounding the creation of Manchukuo. Pu-yi further stated that Manchukuo was an independent nation and that he had the support of his people. The Lytton Report, unanimously adopted by members of the League of Nations (except for China and Japan, which could not vote on the issue), condemned Japan's actions in Manchuria and rejected the contention that Manchukuo was either independent or established by the general popular will. Except for Japan, Nazi Germany, and Fascist Italy (Japan's Axis allies during World War II), no state recognized Manchukuo. Manchukuo joined the Axis alliance, called the Anti-Comintern Pact, in 1939.

The film *The Last Emperor*

Part of the brainwashing process in Chinese communist prisons was the writing and rewriting of autobiographies by the prisoners until they had produced accounts that satisfied the authorities. Pu-yi's draft autobiography, *From Emperor to Citizen*, which was published in 1964 and related his misdeeds, was certainly begun during his prison years. It became the basis for a 1987 Bernardo Bertolucci film entitled *The Last Emperor*. The film, which won nine Academy Awards, compresses some sixty years of Chinese history into two hours and forty minutes. In a general sense, the film is historically accurate. However, experts who have studied the process and conditions under which Chinese communist prisoners underwent "thought reform" agree that the film presented a far less grim state of affairs than actually existed.

tance" to Manchukuo. He made another visit to Japan in 1940. As emperor, Pu-yi played no role in politics and was entirely controlled by the Japanese—who also held every position of importance in Manchukuo. He had no children by his wife, who became addicted to opium and was kept in seclusion, by Wen-hsiu, or by the secondary consorts he had taken. Under Manchukuo's Japanese-inspired law of succession, the throne would pass to Pu-yi's younger brother Pu-chieh. In 1937 Pu-chieh married Hiro, daughter of Prince Saga and second cousin to the Japanese emperor.

Prisoner

In August, 1945, Pu-yi renounced the Manchukuo throne when he learned that Japan had lost World War II. He attempted to flee to Japan but was captured by Soviet troops before he could do so. Empress Wan-jung, who had been left behind, died in 1946. Pu-yi spent the next five years as prisoner in Khabarovsk in the Soviet Union, except for a short trip to Tokyo in 1946 to testify at the trial of top Japanese war criminals at the Tokyo International Court. In testimony during eight sessions, he stated that he had been a puppet of the Japanese and that he had been forced to do everything. He repeated these assertions when he testified at the war crimes trials of Japanese officials who had served in Manchukuo in the 1950's.

The Soviet authorities handed Pu-yi and his associates to the newly established communist government of the People's Republic of China in August, 1950. He remained at various prison camps located in Manchuria until released in 1959, along with some other "war criminals and counter-revolutionaries," in a special amnesty granted by Mao Zedong. He arrived in Beijing in 1960 and began work in the city's botanical garden. In 1963 he was appointed to a research position in the Historical Section of the National Political Library. He died of cancer in 1967 at the age of sixty-one.

Pu-yi was a truly pathetic antihero. He lived his life as a pawn, first of his relatives and other members of the Manchu court, then of the Japanese imperialists, and finally of the Chinese communists, who allegedly "brainwashed" him into a new man.

Bibliography

Morton, William F. *Tanaka Giichi and Japan's China Policy*. New York: St. Martin's Press, 1980.

Power, Brian. *The Puppet Emperor: Life of Pu-yi, Last Emperor of China*. London: Owen, 1986.

P'u-i. *The Last Manchu: The Autobiography of Henry Pu Yi, Last Emperor of China*. Translated by Kuo Ying Paul Tsai and edited and introduced by Paul Kramer. New York: Putnam, 1967.

Jiu-Hwa Lo Upshur

Muammar al-Qaddafi

Born: 1942; Sirte, Libya

The political leader of Libya (from 1969)

Muammar al-Qaddafi (muh-ah-MAHR ahl-kah-DAH-fee) was born in a tent in the Libyan desert into the seminomadic Qaddadfa tribe of Arabized Berbers. After attending primary and secondary schools, where he already became known as an agitator on behalf of Arab unity, he entered the military academy in 1963. Upon graduation in 1965, he spent six months at two British army schools specializing in signals. He was commissioned in 1966 and assigned to a base near Benghazi. Much earlier, however, he had already joined the secret Free Officers' Movement. As its leader on September 1, 1969, Qaddafi orchestrated the bloodless coup that toppled Libya's aging King Idris. Together with his fellow officers in the Revolutionary Command Council (RCC), he ruled his country much as his idol, former President Gamal Abdel Nasser of Egypt, had done. Qaddafi married twice and had several children.

Qaddafi's Foreign Policy

As chairman of the RCC and commander in chief of Libya's armed forces, Qaddafi pursued policies to eliminate Western influences in his country, to promote Arab unity and support the Palestinians, and to oppose Israel. He achieved the first by closing down British and American bases and expelling the Italian and Jewish civilians left over from colonial times. He also "nationalized," or took over, Western assets. He pursued his second goal by tireless efforts to merge, federate, or make other associative arrangements with Egypt, Sudan, Syria, Algeria, Tunisia, Morocco, and Mauritania. None of his overtures succeeded.

Because of his opposition to imperialism and the United States' support for Israel—as well as his nationalization of U.S. property—relations between Qaddafi and the United States were strained. Washington frequently accused him of aiding and abetting terrorism. During the Cold War, another irritant was Qaddafi's major purchases of Soviet weapons and use of Soviet advisers. He also sided with such U.S. adversaries as the Sandinista regime of Daniel Ortega in Nicaragua and that of Fidel Castro in Cuba. In 1981 and 1989, the U.S. Navy shot down Libyan jets defending Qaddafi's "line of death" in the Gulf of Sidra, over whose entirety he claimed Libyan sovereignty.

The Libyan Economy

Libya is a major oil producer and exporter. Its wealth allowed it to amass a huge weapons arse-

Muammar al-Qaddafi in 1969, shortly after overthrowing Libya's King Idris. *(Archive Photos)*

nal, to finance foreign adventures, and to influence other countries' policies. Oil revenues also made possible social reconstruction and economic development. Because of Libya's huge oil and gas reserves, Qaddafi developed a sizable petrochemical industry, including fertilizer production; Libya was suspected of producing toxic gases and other chemical weapons as well.

Work on Qaddafi's infrastructural centerpiece, the Great Man-Made River Project, intended to help Libya achieve food self-sufficiency, industrial growth, and a secure urban water supply, began in 1984. The $25 billion project was designed to bring water from underground aquifers in the Sahara Desert to the northern population centers and cultivable land areas.

Qaddafi's Political Approach

Qaddafi's enemies, both inside and outside the Arab world, came to characterize him as ruthless and maniacal. In contrast, his supporters admired his longevity in office, the simplicity of his personal life and integrity, and his religiosity and constant reaffirmation of Libya's Islamic nature. Many also approved of his unwillingness to accept a double standard of diplomatic and military behavior—one for the world's major powers and another for all other countries.

However, his shifting of sides, depending on which party was more amenable to his policies, made him notorious. For instance, at times he supported Soviet policies and bought Russian

Libyan leader Muammar al-Qaddafi speaking at the 1996 Arab Summit in Cairo, Egypt. *(Reuters/Mona Sharaf/Archive Photos)*

Qaddafi's Conflicts

Muammar al-Qaddafi's conflicts have involved numerous adversaries and have taken many forms. After reducing the physical and economic presence of Westerners in Libya, Qaddafi used his well-equipped but undertrained armed forces to occupy Chad's northern uranium-rich Aouzou Strip, over which he had claimed Libyan sovereignty. The Libyans were finally repulsed with heavy losses, especially when France entered the fray. In 1994 Libya accepted the World Court's ruling that the Aouzou Strip belonged to Chad.

Qaddafi's four-day border war with Egypt in 1977—the result of long-standing hostility between himself and Egyptian President Anwar al-Sadat—also resulted in the defeat of Libyan forces. Qaddafi's 1979 expedition to Uganda in support of its embattled president, Idi Amin, was no more successful. Qaddafi has also used nontraditional means in attempts to export revolution, combat American power, and aid dissident groups around the world. He has not hesitated to employ economic intimidation of impoverished African nations. Qaddafi's steadfast opposition to Israel increased after Israel shot down a straying Libyan passenger airliner over the Sinai Desert in 1973. He has also fought Libyan dissidents abroad and plots against his regime and his life at home.

weapons, but at others he denounced communist atheism and refused to grant the Russians port facilities along Libya's extensive Mediterranean coastline. He also engineered cloak-and-dagger operations, even in friendly Arab countries.

In May, 1998, Muammar al-Qaddafi adjusts his traditional clothing after leading the first Friday noon prayers of the Muslim year in the capital of Chad. *(Reuters/Aladin Abdel Naby/Archive Photos)*

In 1999 Qaddafi surprised many in the West by allowing the extradition of two Libyan suspects in the 1988 terrorist bombing of a jetliner over Lockerbie, Scotland. After lengthy negotiations between Qaddafi, U.N. officials, and others, it was agreed that the suspects would be surrendered by Libya for trial in the Netherlands under Scottish law. In agreeing to this arrangement, Qaddafi was undoubtedly trying to gain credence in the international community, where many leaders had long considered him an outcast. In response to the deal, the United Nations suspended its sanctions against Libya.

Bibliography

Arnold, Guy. *The Maverick State: Qaddafi and the New World Order*. London: Cassell Academic Press, 1997.

Blundy, David, and Andrew Lycett. *Qaddafi and the Libyan Revolution*. Boston: Little, Brown, 1987.

El-Kikhia, Mansour O. *Libya's Qaddafi: The Politics of Contradiction*. Gainesville: University Press of Florida, 1997.

Vandewalle, Dirk, ed. *Qadhafi's Libya, 1969-1994*. New York: St. Martin's Press, 1995.

Peter B. Heller

The Green Book

Muammar al-Qaddafi's ideological testament and definition of Arab socialism was published in three volumes between 1975 and 1978. These writings extended his earlier "cultural revolution," intended to turn the country of Libya over "to the people." In *The Green Book* Qaddafi rejects Western-style democratic institutions such as parliaments and political parties as being unrepresentative and divisive. Rather, he opts for mass participation through people's committees and popular congresses. Second, he shuns the conditions of servitude inherent in a system of production where those who toil are exploited by those who profit. He proposes a "third way" in which the producer is a partner, not a wage earner, and in which a home dweller is also a landlord, not a renter. Third, he defines the ideal community as a nation or nation-state with a shared history, common heritage, and a sense of a common destiny. Qaddafi emphasizes the equal rights of women in many areas as well as their natural role in motherhood.

Manuel Quezon

Born: August 19, 1878; Baler, Philippines
Died: August 1, 1944; Saranac Lake, New York

First president of Philippine Commonwealth (1935-1942), head of Philippine government-in-exile (1942-1944)

Manuel Luis Quezon y Molina (mahn-WEHL lew-WEES KAY-sohn ee moh-LEE-nah) was born in the province of Tayabas, later renamed Quezon in his honor, on the east coast of the island of Luzon. His father was a former soldier in the Spanish army who had settled down to teach school. His mother was also a schoolteacher. When Quezon was nine, his parents sent him to Manila to study, first at a Dominican school and later at the prestigious University of Santo Tomás, where he studied law.

The Philippines was a Spanish colony until 1898. Quezon's family had sympathized with Spain during the struggles between Spain and Filipino advocates of independence. After the United States defeated the Spanish (in the Spanish-American War) and occupied the Philippines in 1898, however, Quezon joined the nationalist guerrillas who fought to be free of the Americans. Leaving his law books, he joined with the forces of the nationalist leader Emilio Aguinaldo. Quezon rose to the rank of major. After Aguinaldo's capture, Quezon surrendered to the Americans. He was jailed for six months on suspicion of killing American prisoners and was then released for lack of evidence. He returned to law school and completed his degree in 1903.

Cooperation with the Americans

After finishing law school, Quezon returned to Tayabas. There he came to know American officials and became convinced that cooperation with the Americans was the best way to achieve independence for his country. With support from these foreigners, he ran for governor of Tayabas in 1905. After serving in this office for two years, he was elected to the Philippine Assembly, the country's new legislative body.

Quezon's obvious abilities and his willingness to work with the United States enabled him to rise rapidly. Quezon and a rival, Sergio Osmeña, became the two most influential individuals in the new Filipino political system. Quezon and Osmeña joined forces before the 1907 election to the Philippine Assembly and brought a variety of factions together to form the Nationalist Party, which would dominate Filipino politics for decades. In 1909, the U.S. Congress authorized nonvoting positions for two Filipino representatives in the U.S. House of Representatives, one to be

Manuel Quezon *(Library of Congress)*

The Philippine Senate in the 1930's

In 1916, the U.S. Congress created a new bicameral legislature in the Philippines, modeled on the U.S. government. Sergio Osmeña became speaker of the House of Representatives, and Manuel Quezon became president of the Senate. The Senate (upper house) consisted of twenty-four members, all but two of whom were popularly elected. The two nonelected senators were appointed by the American governor-general. The Nationalist Party, which elected Quezon as its head in 1922, won all but one seat in the Senate in the first election as well as eighty-three of the ninety seats in the House of Representatives. The major party opposing the Nationalists, the National Progressive Party, offered only a weak opposition. Thus, as both head of the dominant party and Senate president, Quezon was the most powerful individual in the Philippine government.

By the 1930's, it had become increasingly evident that the United States would grant independence to the Philippines. Debate now generally centered on the terms of independence. In 1933, the U.S. Congress passed the Hares-Hawes-Cutting Independence Bill over the veto of President Herbert Hoover. Quezon, however, opposed the bill: It contained a provision that would allow the United States to maintain military bases in the Philippines after independence, and the Philippine senate president believed that this would be inconsistent with true independence. Quezon used his influence to persuade the Philippine legislature to reject the Hare-Hawes-Cutting bill.

chosen by the U.S. governor of the Philippines and the other appointed by the Philippine Assembly. Quezon convinced the legislature to give him the position.

In Washington, D.C., Quezon argued that the Philippines should be granted independence. His advocacy encouraged the U.S. Congress to pass the Jones Act in 1916, promising that the Philippines would eventually receive independence. The act also gave the Philippines greater self-government and created a two-house legislature based on the American model. Following passage of this act, Quezon returned to Manila and won election to the new Philippine Senate. He served as president of this body until the creation of the Philippine Commonwealth in 1935.

Manuel Quezon (third from left), at the time president of the Philippine senate, heading the Philippine independence mission to the United States in 1924. *(Library of Congress)*

President of the Commonwealth

As Senate president, Quezon pushed for the granting of independence by the United States on terms that he and other Filipinos would find acceptable. In 1934, the U.S. Congress passed the Tydings-McDuffie Act, a piece of legislation strongly favored by Quezon. The Tydings-McDuffie Act provided for the creation of a commonwealth government that would govern the Philippines for ten years under American advice and direction. At the end of the ten-year period, the Philippines was to become an independent nation. On September 17, 1935, Quezon was elected president of the new Philippine Commonwealth.

Land reform was one of President Quezon's most pressing concerns, since many of the peasants in the Philippines were landless sharecroppers who worked the lands of large landowners. One of his strategies for dealing with the problem was the resettlement of people from the northern islands on the southern island of Mindanao. Quezon also attempted to fight corruption in the Philippine government, although political corruption continued to be a major difficulty for the country even after independence. With the assistance of his special military adviser General Douglas MacArthur, Quezon reorganized his country's military.

Manuel Quezon won a second term as president of the commonwealth in 1941. The following year, Japan invaded the Philippines as part of its strategy during World War II. Quezon fled to the United States. In the United States, he served as head of the Philippine government in exile. Quezon died of tuberculosis in the United States before the Philippines achieved the independence he had sought.

Quezon's Contributions and Limitations

Manuel Quezon is justly remembered as one of the principal founders of the modern nation of the Philippines. However, there were some limitations to his achievements. He was unable to overcome the problem of political corruption. He had opposed the establishment of U.S. military bases in the Philippines, but a treaty between the two countries established bases after Quezon's death. Perhaps most seriously, his policy of settling Christian northerners in the Muslim south eventually led to a Muslim separatist guerrilla movement.

Bibliography

Friend, Theodore. *Between Two Empires: The Ordeal of the Philippines*. New Haven, Conn.: Yale University Press, 1965.

Gopinath, Aruna. *Manuel L. Quezon: The Tutelary Democrat*. Detroit, Mich.: Cellar Book Shop, 1987.

Gripaldo, Rolando M. *The Quezon-Winslow Correspondence and Other Essays*. Manila, Philippines: De Salle University Press, 1994.

Karnow, Stanley. *In Our Image: America's Empire in the Philippines*. New York: Random House, 1989.

Quezon, Manuel L. *The Good Fight*. New York: Appleton, 1946.

Carl L. Bankston III

The Settlement of Mindanao

After Manuel Quezon became president of the newly created Commonwealth of the Philippines in 1935, he began a policy of resettling people from the Christian north to the primarily Muslim island of Mindanao in the south. The commonwealth government created the National Land Settlement Administration (NLSA) to encourage migration. The southern island was sparsely populated, and the Quezon government believed that resettlement could give landless people the opportunity to farm their own land. Resettlement also seemed like a good way to develop the resources of the south and to bind it more closely to the emerging Philippine nation.

However, the Muslim southerners came to see the northerners as invaders, bent on taking away Muslim land and destroying the Muslim way of life. As resettlement continued during the 1950's and 1960's, it led to conflict between the Philippine government and the Muslims of Mindanao, eventually resulting in the rise of a well-organized independence movement in the Muslim region.

Yitzhak Rabin

Born: March 1, 1922; Jerusalem, Palestine (now Israel)
Died: November 4, 1995; Tel Aviv

Prime minister of Israel (1974-1977)

Yitzhak Rabin (YIHTZ-hahk rah-BEEN) and his younger sister, Rachel, were born into the Labor Zionist aristocracy, a service elite. His mother was Rosa Cohen, an activist who devoted her life to Zionist causes. Her husband, Nehemiah Rubitsov, was born in Ukraine but arrived in Chicago at the age of eighteen; there he worked as a tailor. He was mobilized by the American Legion to drive Turks from the Middle East. Yitzhak excelled in science at Kadoorie, a secondary school he attended, but after graduation he joined the Palmach, an illegal organization trained to protect Jewish safety in Palestine. In 1948 he married Leah Schlossberg, a German Jew, with whom he had a daughter, Dalia, and a son, Yuval.

The Six-Day War

Rabin was a brigade commander during Israel's war of independence and managed to open the road to besieged Jerusalem as well as capture surrounding neighborhoods. In 1950 he was named Israel Defense Forces (IDF) head of operations, and by 1964 he had been promoted to chief of staff.

Skirmishes with Syria intensified in early 1967, and the Soviet Union spread false rumors that Israel was massing forces and planning a major attack. Syria asked Egyptian president Gamal Abdel Nasser for help. On May 18, the Egyptian president ordered all U.N. troops out of the Sinai and massed eighty thousand Egyptian soldiers on Israel's southern border. A few days later, Nasser closed the Strait of Tiran to Israeli shipping. When it became apparent that the United States was not going to step in, Rabin realized that there was no alternative to war. The Egyptian troops had eight hundred tanks and 242 fighters and bombers, but none of the planes even had a chance to leave the ground. At 7:45 A.M. on June 5, Israeli planes destroyed runways and radar stations and wiped out combat planes. As the Israeli Defense Forces swept through the Sinai, the paratroop brigade captured Arab suburbs. By the morning of June 7 Israeli paratroopers had reached the Western Wall, uniting Jerusalem under Jewish control for the first time in two thousand years.

When the war was over, Israel had increased its territory: It controlled the Golan, the West Bank, East Jerusalem, the Gaza Strip, and the Sinai Peninsula. As a result, it also controlled a hostile population of more than one million. Rabin earned lasting acclaim as the chief of staff

Yitzhak Rabin *(Archive Photos/Consolidated News)*

The War of Attrition, 1970

After the 1967 war, Egypt and Syria rebuilt and strengthened their armed forces. A "war of attrition," essentially a series of border incidents, was waged by Egypt against Israel between 1968 and 1970. The fighting took place chiefly along the Sinai-Suez border, but there was a front along the Jordanian border as well. With its vast population and steady supply of Russian arms, Egypt kept up steady artillery attacks across the Suez Canal. Largely because of Yitzhak Rabin's prodding, the Israelis began to step up the level of their responses with bombing raids against Egyptian military and industrial targets. When the Soviet Union went so far as to move missile launchers into the Suez region, the United States issued a warning to Moscow and stepped up efforts to end the fighting. A cease-fire took effect in 1970, and the United States guaranteed that it would supply Israel with enough weaponry to maintain a balance of forces in the region.

who planned Israel's most outstanding military victory.

Ambassador Rabin

Yitzhak Rabin was appointed ambassador to the United States in 1968, a position he held for five years. He believed that Israel's fate was inextricably linked to the United States, and he had established a relationship with U.S. president Richard M. Nixon before Nixon became president. Rabin met Nixon at an American embassy dinner in Israel in 1966 and invited him on a tour of military installations in northern Israel. When Nixon became president, he remembered Rabin's hospitality.

Israeli prime minister Yitzhak Rabin standing at Israel's border with Jordan in 1994, looking back toward Israeli-occupied West Bank territory. *(Reuters/Jim Hollander/Archive Photos)*

After Israel won the Six-Day War, the Soviet Union supplied arms to the Arabs, who still believed that they could win a military victory. Rabin convinced the Americans that it was in their interest to help Israel's defense. In 1968 the United States awarded Israel $25 million in military credits; the figure had risen to $307.5 million by 1973. By the time Rabin left Washington, the United States considered Israel a strategic asset in the Middle East. Yet Rabin did not leave the ambassadorship without controversy. Near the end of Nixon's first term, Rabin made public remarks suggesting that the incumbent would be preferable to the Democratic nominee. The remarks caused an uproar in Washington,

The Assassination of Rabin

Yitzhak Rabin was not particularly looking forward to the peace rally of November 4, 1995. He had been booed and heckled at previous public speeches because of an explosion of opposition to his government's peace accords with the Palestinians. Nevertheless, Rabin was prepared to give a speech at the rally. The theme of the massive gathering at Tel Aviv was both propeace and antiviolence. At the center of Rabin's speech was the need to moderate the violent tone of political debate in Israel. After his ringing declaration of his dedication to the peace process, the audience responded enthusiastically with a vast wave of clapping and cheering. However, Yigal Amir, a twenty-five-year-old law student at Tel Aviv's Bar Ilan University, had been waiting for his chance to assassinate Rabin. As Rabin approached his car, Amir fired three times and hit Rabin twice. Rabin's murder shocked Israel and the world; it also underscored the deeply divided opinions among Israelis toward the peace process.

with the *Washington Post* running an editorial titled "Israel's Undiplomatic Diplomat." Still, at the end of Rabin's Washington duty, *Newsweek* named Rabin and Soviet envoy Anatoly Dobrynin "Ambassadors of the Year."

The Fall and Rise of a Leader

In 1974 Rabin was selected by the Labor Party as prime minister to succeed Golda Meir, who had resigned after the bitter Yom Kippur War of 1973. He was involved in every detail of the interim agreement with Egypt that the Israeli cabinet ratified on September 1, 1975. This agreement was the first written agreement between Israel and an Arab state recognizing the desire to make peace. After three years Rabin resigned when a public scandal disclosed that his wife, Leah Rabin, had held an illegal U.S. bank account.

Seven years later, Rabin returned to government as defense minister. On December 8, 1987, a traffic accident that killed four Palestinian laborers incited a spontaneous popular uprising in Gaza. The uprising grew into the *Intifada*, the Palestinian war of liberation. The Israeli Army reacted with excessive violence, which horrified the international public and damaged Israeli morale. In 1989 media reports emerged of a Rabin peace plan, which the Palestine Liberation Organization (PLO) rejected. By 1990 the *Intifada* had evolved into an activist campaign of small groups attacking Israelis with bombs. The PLO had gained power, and the Palestinians' struggle had degenerated into factional fighting and mutual suspicion.

After replacing Shimon Peres as party leader, Rabin led the Labor Party to victory in the June, 1992, election and became prime minister. Always wary of Yasir Arafat, Rabin started working toward the Oslo Peace Accord with secret talks in 1993. He shook hands with Arafat at the White House on September 13, sealing their joint Declaration of Principles, a framework for Palestinian autonomy in the West Bank and Gaza Strip. This agreement led to the Israel-Jordan peace treaty, signed in October, 1994, the year that Rabin shared the Nobel Peace Prize with Arafat and Peres. A year later, Rabin was assassinated in Tel Aviv.

Bibliography

Horowitz, David, ed. *Yitzhak Rabin: Soldier of Peace.* London: Peter Halban Publishers Ltd, 1996.

Rabin, Leah. *Rabin: Our Life, His Legacy*. New York: G. P. Putnam's Sons, 1997.

Slater, Robert. *Rabin of Israel*. London: Robson Books, 1977.

Sheila Golburgh Johnson

Hashemi Rafsanjani

Born: 1934; Rafsanjan, Iran

President of Iran (1989-1997)

Ali Akbar Hashemi Rafsanjani (ah-LEE AHK-bahr HAH-sheh-mee rahf-sahn-JAH-nee) was born into a fairly wealthy family of pistachio growers in the province of Kerman, in south central Iran. He began Shia Islam theological training as an early teen in local schools and progressed to the theological college in Qom. He became a student of Ruhollah Khomeini (Ayatollah Khomeini), who was later the leader of the 1979 revolution against the shah. Rafsanjani eventually achieved the rank of *Hojat al-Islam*, one rank below ayatollah. A father of five children, he also wrote several books of a historical nature.

Hashemi Rafsanjani *(Reuters/Juda Ngwenya/Archive Photos)*

Early Political Life

During his years at Qom, Rafsanjani sided with Khomeini and other clerics who protested Shah Mohammad Reza Pahlavi's monarchy, particularly his westernization of Iran. In 1963, spurred on by opposition to the shah's land-reform package called the White Revolution, Rafsanjani became politically active. After Khomeini was exiled by the shah, Rafsanjani remained in close contact, consulting him regarding political operations such as the creation of various fundamentalist Islamic organizations. In 1965 one of these groups was responsible for the assassination of Prime Minister Hassan Ali Mansur, and Rafsanjani was indirectly linked to the event. He served a short sentence in jail, one of several he would serve in 1967, 1971, and 1972, and from 1975 to 1978.

Role in the Revolution

Iran's revolution occurred in February, 1979. Rafsanjani had key roles in two Islamic organizations during this time: the Revolutionary Council, composed of Rafsanjani and the clerics who had built revolutionary forces over the years, and the Islamic Republican Party (IRP). His first post in the new provisional government, headed by Mehdi Bazarga, was as undersecretary in the Interior Ministry. His main accomplishment during this short, frenzied period was to encourage oil workers to break their strike and return to work, giving the government some amount of economic stability.

In 1980 Rafsanjani became very influential. Parliamentary elections placed many IRP members in key positions, and Rafsanjani won a seat in the Majles (parliament). He was elected speaker by the other members, probably because of his close relationship to Ayatollah Khomeini. Led by Raf-

Iranian president Hashemi Rafsanjani waves to reporters in 1997 three months before the expiration of his second term as president. *(Reuters/Aladin Abdel Naby/Archive Photos)*

sanjani, the Majles became a very powerful clerical body. In 1981 it forced the Islamic Republic's first president, Abolhassan Bani-Sadr, into exile. Rafsanjani's status among religious leaders rose in the early 1980's, especially after a series of bombs killed dozens of important IRP leaders. Rafsanjani gradually built a network of allies in high positions. He also handled political disputes, maneuvered his way through the political maze, and gained a reputation as a mediator.

Rafsanjani's Politics

Rafsanjani's political stance, hard to identify precisely, could perhaps best be characterized as pragmatic. While other clerics held fast to the purist ideology of the Islamic revolution, Rafsanjani was also concerned with Iran's economic health and other national interests. In 1983 he was among those who suggested opening a dialogue with the United States. In 1985 he struck a weapons deal with U.S. president Ronald Reagan's administration, resulting in Iran receiving arms for its war against Iraq.

In 1987 Rafsanjani defused the tension surrounding the idea of dissolving the Islamic Republican Party. In 1988 he was named armed

The Armistice with Iraq, 1988

In the last stage of the Iran-Iraq War, Iranian morale was low because of repeated bombings and attacks on oil-producing regions, Iraq's recapture of the Fao Peninsula, and massive losses of people and revenue. In July of 1988, Ayatollah Ruhollah Khomeini named then-Majles speaker Hashemi Rafsanjani as commander in chief of the armed forces. Rafsanjani drew Iran's military leaders together to decide on a course of action. They agreed that Iran could no longer continue fighting; Iraq had the economic advantage of Western and Arab support. Rafsanjani and then-president Ali Khameini met with the country's leaders, and by a majority vote they agreed to end the war. There was already an effective armistice agreement in existence; in July of 1987, the U.N. Security Council had drawn up Resolution 598, which called for a cease-fire and negotiations to mitigate the problems between Iran and Iraq. The barrier to acceptance of the resolution, once accepted by Iranian officials, was Khomeini, who held the final decision. On July 18, 1988, he made a statement to the Iranian people, saying that accepting the armistice was like taking poison but that it was in the best interest of the Islamic Republic.

The Tehran Association of Militant Clergy

This Iranian political group is an umbrella group consisting of hard-line conservative Shia Islam clergy. In general, they seek to continue Ayatollah Ruhollah Khomeini's ideology and believe that Iran's future lies in the absolute interpretation of *velayat-e faqih*. This doctrine holds that decisions should ultimately be made by the *faqih*, or supreme spiritual leader of the country. They oppose foreign investment and loans, and they are culturally very conservative. Their ideological opponents favor economic reform and improved relations with the West.

During the early 1990's, the Tehran Association of Militant Clergy held a majority of seats in the Majles (Iran's parliament). Then-president Hashemi Rafsanjani, a political pragmatist not aligned with the conservatives, severely depleted the Majles of hard-liners in 1992. In the 1996 elections, they lost overall control of the parliament. Their influence, however, remained strong; they stood behind many of the major political figures in Iranian politics such as Ali Akbar Nateq Nouri, the speaker of the Majles.

forces commander. He negotiated an end to the eight-year war with Iraq, even though Khomeini disliked the idea. In Khomeini's final years, the ayatollah served as spiritual and ultimately supreme leader, but Rafsanjani presented the political face of Iran to the world.

Presidency

Following Khomeini's death in 1989, Rafsanjani replaced Ali Khameini as president, while Khameini became spiritual leader. His challenges included the effects of the revolution and the war with Iraq on the economy, a continuing ideological split in the Majles, and the Iranian people's expectations of improved social conditions. Finally, Rafsanjani faced the challenge of ruling after Khomeini, a leader who kept disparate factions together and who possessed unparalleled levels of control and power.

Rafsanjani attempted economic reform, emphasizing industry and infrastructure in place of the Iraq war, which had for so long been the country's focus. He believed that Iran could not economically survive in an isolated condition and sought to expand the economy into a free-market system, stabilizing the exchange rates between Iranian and foreign currency. Rafsanjani surrounded himself with like-minded reformers by requiring the current Majles members to take a challenging written exam on Islam to retain their rights for reelection; this situation eventually caused many hard-line incumbents to move on.

Rafsanjani enjoyed popular support for some time, as Iranian citizens hoped that, after a certain period, the reforms would improve the economy. The middle and lower classes suffered, however, as government subsidies and high inflation made living difficult. Riots and violent attacks caused by rising prices, the demolition of squatters' shacks, and other related events occurred in the early 1990's.

In June, 1993, Rafsanjani was reelected to a second term. His campaign had promised voters continued subsidies on staples and had attempted to convince them that a vote for Rafsanjani was a vote for Islam. He won the election with 63 percent of the vote, considerably less than the previous term but more than his opponents, who were also members of the same regime.

During Rafsanjani's second term, he continued to allow the Persian side of the country's culture, suppressed by Islam, to return discreetly. He attempted to find a balance between pre- and postrevolutionary Iran and to create economic reform. Unfortunately, the country's optimism was shaken as foreign debt increased, oil prices remained low, and the cost of living greatly increased. Rafsanjani's parliament, which he had so carefully maneuvered to his favor, now showed little support for his reforms and began to view his tactics as threatening to the clergy's power over national matters.

Maintaining Leadership

In August, 1997, Rafsanjani left office after serving the maximum two terms permissible under the Iranian constitution. He continued to play a key role in Iranian politics as chairman of the influential Expediency Council. The council is a mediating body between the constitutional council and the Majles, and it serves as a group of experts who advise the current president.

Bibliography

Hunter, Shireen. *Iran After Khomeini*. New York: Praeger, 1992.

Lyle, Garry. *Iran*. Philadelphia: Chelsea House, 1997.

Mackey, Sandra. *The Iranians: Persia, Islam, and the Soul of a Nation*. New York: Penguin Books, 1998.

Xiomara Garcia de la Cadena

Fidel Ramos

Born: March 18, 1928; Lingayen, Philippines

President of the Philippines (1992-1998)

Fidel Valdez Ramos (fee-DEHL val-DEHZ RAH-mohs) spent most of his youth in central Luzon, the main island of the Philippines. In 1950, he graduated from the U.S. Military Academy, and one year later he received a master's degree in civil engineering from the University of Illinois. He began a forty-year career in the Philippine armed forces. He and his wife, Amelita Martinez, had five daughters.

In Marcos's Shadow

Fidel Ramos began his rise in the Philippine military by serving along with American soldiers in the Korean War. Later he was commander of the Philippines Armed Forces (AFP) contingent during the Vietnam War. In 1972, Philippine president Ferdinand Marcos, Ramos's second cousin, appointed Ramos to head the Philippine Constabulary, the country's national police. Ramos's primary job was to execute the Marcos-dictated martial law. Under Ramos's direction, the Philippine Constabulary arrested thousands of "enemies of the state."

Although he remained loyal to his president, Ramos eventually realized the harm that Marcos was doing to the country and sought ways of rectifying the situation. Following the assassination of Benigno Aquino on August 21, 1983, and the popular repudiation of the government, which was held responsible, Ramos began to remove himself slowly from Marcos's shadow. The determining factor in Ramos's change of allegiances came when the Agrava Commission released a report on the assassination which most observers saw as merely parroting the government's story of the event.

Marcos called an election for January 17, 1986 (later moved to February 7), in order to entrench his hold on his country before the "people's power campaign" of Corazon Aquino (Benigno Aquino's widow) could do damage to his presidency. When the votes were counted, both the Marcos and the Aquino forces claimed victory. With each passing day, tensions in the island nation grew, nearing civil war proportions. Ramos's loyalties to his country became apparent. On February 22, Ramos, along with the country's defense secretary, traveled to the Ministry of Defense in Manila and asked the military to join them in a stand against Marcos. Slowly, more and more of the military came to their side, and Ferdinand Marcos was forced to flee the Philippines, giving the reins of power to Corazon Aquino.

Leading to the Future

During the presidency of Corazon Aquino, Fidel Ramos continued to serve in the military. He

Fidel Ramos *(Reuters/Jeff Vinnick/Archive Photos)*

eventually rose to military chief of staff from 1986 to 1988 and secretary of national defense from 1988 to 1991. As during the Marcos years, Ramos was called to defend his president against domestic opposition, most notably a half dozen attempted coups against President Aquino's government. Ramos did not hide his own presidential aspirations, however. In December of 1991, Aquino was forced by law to step down as president. At this point, Ramos declared his candidacy. He formed his own political organization and finally won Aquino's support. Through hard campaigning, Ramos won the presidency, even though his opponents repeatedly reminded voters of his once close association with Marcos. He took office in 1992.

The presidency of Fidel Ramos, which ended in 1998 when he too was not allowed to serve a second term, was characterized by a drive to better the Philippines' faltering economy, work toward reforming the country's legendarily corrupt police force, and bringing peace with the rebel Moro Islamic Liberation Front. In addition, he increased the production of electrical power and aggressively encouraged international investment. In spite of his past ties with Marcos, President Ramos was able to maintain a high public approval rating.

Philippine president Fidel Ramos watches Muslim rebel leader Nur Misuari sign a peace agreement ending nearly twenty-five years of civil war between the government and the Moro Islamic Liberation Front. *(Reuters/Erik de Castro/Archive Photos)*

Bibliography

Lande, Carl H., and Mickey Waxman. *Post Marcos Politics: A Geographical and Statistical Analysis of the 1992 Presidential Election*. New York: St. Martin's Press, 1996.

Schirmer, Daniel B. *Fidel Ramos: The Pentagon's Philippine Friend, 1992-1997*. Durham, N.C.: Friends of the Filipino People, 1997.

Thompson, Mark R. *The Anti-Marcos Struggle: Personalistic Rule and Democratic Transition in the Philippines*. New Haven, Conn.: Yale University Press, 1996.

Tom Frazier

The Moro Islamic Liberation Front

One of the most challenging situations to confront Fidel Ramos's presidency was the rebelling Moro Islamic Liberation Front. This organization wanted the southern Muslim portions of the Philippines, especially Mindanao, to become an independent area. The front waged a two-decades-long battle for sovereignty. During these dangerous years, which reached their zenith in the 1970's, more than 100,000 Filipinos lost their lives and many more were forced to leave their homes.

Ramos signed an agreement with the front in 1996. It gave the rebels some of the sovereignty they wanted, especially participation in the economic development of the southern portion of the Philippines. This agreement met serious opposition from the Christian Filipino majority but it went into effect nevertheless.

Jeannette Rankin

Born: June 11, 1880; near Missoula, Montana
Died: May 18, 1973; Carmel, California

First woman member of U.S. House of Representatives (1917-1919, 1941-1943)

Jeannette Pickering Rankin (jeh-NEHT PIH-kuh-rihng RAN-kihn) was born on a Montana ranch, the oldest of seven children. Her mother was an elementary schoolteacher, her father a successful rancher and lumber merchant. She graduated from the University of Montana in 1902 with a degree in biology and also studied at the New York School of Philanthropy and at the University of Washington. She spent two terms as a Republican member of Congress and devoted the rest of her long life to antiwar activism and women's issues.

Jeannette Rankin *(Library of Congress)*

From Suffragist Student to Member of Congress

After enrolling at the University of Washington in 1909, Rankin worked in that state's suffrage campaign. In 1910 she met Minnie J. Reynolds, a suffragist and journalist from New Jersey who convinced Rankin that the suffrage movement and the antiwar movement should join forces. While not all suffragists became antiwar activists, Rankin did.

When she returned to Montana in 1911, Rankin worked on winning suffrage there as well as in New York, California, and Ohio. In 1913 she became field secretary for the National American Woman Suffrage Association, which lobbied for suffrage state by state. In 1914, Montana voted to grant the state's women the right to vote. Rankin had become an accomplished political activist and was well-known in her home state.

In 1916 she ran for Congress as a progressive Republican who supported suffrage, protection for children, prohibition, and peace. Her victorious campaign made her the first woman ever elected to Congress. She upheld her pacifist platform by voting against U.S. entry into World War I, a vote she later described as the most significant act of her life. Established as a suffragist and a pacifist, Rankin continued working on those issues throughout her first congressional term. When her term ended, she tried to become the nation's first woman Senator, but that effort failed. Montana voters were no longer comfortable with her pacifism. Leaving Congress, she turned to other methods for attaining her goals.

Rankin worked for women and children through the National Consumers' League and supported

Rankin's Antiwar Votes in 1917 and 1941

In addition to being the first woman ever elected to Congress, Jeannette Rankin was also the only member of Congress to vote against both World War I and World War II. She had not run as a pacifist candidate in 1916, but when President Woodrow Wilson asked Congress to approve a war resolution in 1917, she joined fifty-six others to oppose that resolution. She did not run for reelection at the end of that term, but she did run successfully again twenty years later. In 1941, when President Franklin D. Roosevelt asked Congress to approve a war resolution following Japan's attack on Pearl Harbor, Rankin voted "No." This time, hers was the only negative vote. It was a highly unpopular vote, and it kept her from being reelected. Her persistent pacifism reemerged during the Vietnam War, however, earning renewed esteem among that era's antiwar protesters.

protective labor laws under the Sheppard-Towner bill. She also launched a Mississippi Valley campaign to improve working conditions for women. Her antiwar efforts ranged from the global to the local. She participated in the Second International Congress of Women, joined the Women's International League for Peace and Freedom, supported the Kellogg-Briand Pact to outlaw war, lobbied for the Women's Peace Union, which advocated amending the Constitution to outlaw war, and worked with the National Council for the Prevention of War.

In addition to global and national antiwar efforts, Rankin founded the Georgia Peace Society near Athens, Georgia. That organization served as home base for her pacifist activities until World War II. In 1939 Rankin's home state of Montana opposed U.S. involvement in that war, and Rankin launched a successful campaign for a belated second congressional term. Montana's opposition ended, however, when Japan attacked Pearl Harbor in December, 1941. When Congress voted to enter the war, Rankin cast the only negative vote. This vote was to end her congressional career.

Rankin persisted with antiwar work until the end of her life. She studied the activities of Mohandas Gandhi in the 1940's and opposed the Korean War in the 1950's. Jeannette Rankin Brigades demonstrated against the Vietnam War in the 1960's. At eighty-eight, she considered running for Congress on an antiwar ticket, but poor health stopped her. She died of a heart attack in Carmel, California, in 1973.

Bibliography

Davidson, Sue. *A Heart in Politics: Jeannette Rankin and Patsy T. Mink*. Seattle, Wash.: Seal Press, 1994.

Meiman-White, Florence. *First Woman in Congress, Jeannette Rankin*. New York: J. Messner, 1980.

O'Brien, Mary Barmeyer. *Jeannette Rankin, 1880-1973: Bright Star in a Big Sky*. Helena, Mont.: Falcon Press, 1995.

Susan MacFarland

Jerry John Rawlings

Born: June 22, 1947; Accra, Volta Region, Ghana

Ruler of Ghana beginning in 1982, elected president in 1992

John Jerry Rawlings (JON JEH-ree RAW-lihngz) was born the son of a Ghanaian civil servant and a Scottish father who left Ghana before his birth. With her civil servant's pay, Rawlings's mother was able to provide for an excellent education for him at the well-respected Achimota school, where he received a general certificate of education. After attending the Ghana Military Academy, Rawlings joined the Ghanaian Air Force in 1967. As one of the new nation's most promising young pilots, he was commissioned a lieutenant in 1969. By 1978 he had been promoted to the rank of flight lieutenant.

A Voice of the People

By 1979 Rawlings had become involved with a group of young military officers who were planning a coup against General Fred Akuffo. Rawlings and the others demanded that all government officials be held accountable for their actions, especially widespread corruption. His outspoken criticism of the government and call for change struck a chord with the people of Ghana. Rawlings soon emerged as their voice. In an effort to force positive change, Rawlings led a coup attempt on May 15, 1979.

The expected support for their cause failed to emerge, and the group surrendered to military authorities. Rawlings and the other officers were court-martialed on May 28 and imprisoned. Following the failed coup and the court-martial proceedings, Rawlings was freed from military custody by his supporters during a second coup. Rawlings immediately announced the establishment of the Armed Forces Revolutionary Council (AFRC), which would rule until free elections could be held throughout Ghana.

The People's National Party

Although many doubted his sincerity, Rawlings insisted that he had no intention of holding on to power indefinitely. Elections for the return of civilian rule proceeded as scheduled. The result was a dramatic victory by Hilla Limann's People's National Party. Limann was installed as president on September 24, 1979, and the AFRC was dissolved in a bloodless transfer of power. Few had expected Rawlings to give up control of

Ghana's president, Jerry John Rawlings (right), with U.S. congressman Charles Rangel in 1995. Rawlings was in New York celebrating the fiftieth anniversary of the United Nations. *(AP/Wide World Photos)*

the government willingly. The fact that he did so endeared him further to the people of Ghana.

Limann lived in constant fear that Rawlings, who was much more popular, might lead a new coup against his government. This threat was made plausible by Rawlings himself, who made several speeches critical of the Limann government. As tensions mounted, Limann made every effort to discredit Rawlings and undermine his popularity. In an extremely desperate move, the government stripped Rawlings of his commission. Frustrated with the failures of the Limann government, Rawlings seized power in a coup during January of 1982. His popular support resulted in only slight resistance by military units. He justified the armed intervention by stating that the Limann government had failed to halt corruption or improve the economy.

The Provisional National Defense Council

The Provisional National Defense Council (PNDC), which replaced the parliament as the supreme governing authority, initially consisted of three soldiers and three civilians. Some time later it was expanded to a sixteen-member civilian administration, with heads of ministries called secretaries. Most were well-known leftist activists who were popular with workers and looked to Cuba and Libya for models of governance. One leftist-populist model borrowed from Cuba and Libya was the People's Defense Committee, an attempt to involve the general populace in governance. Similar committees were established to oversee agricultural and business activities throughout Ghana. Rawlings soon discovered, however, that the committees often abused their power and heightened intertribal conflicts. By December of 1984 he had restructured the committees and limited their power. It was becoming increasingly apparent that his Marxist experiments were floundering.

Rawlings was eventually convinced by his conservative finance minister, Kwesi Botchwey, to align with the West and to adopt more conservative economic measures. Frugal and sparing budgets were passed beginning in 1983, and Ghana was forced to accept stringent International Monetary Fund conditions along with the

The Coup of 1979

Following their failed attempt to overthrow General Fred Akuffo in May of 1979, Jerry John Rawlings and his followers were court-martialed. Nevertheless, the general public increasingly viewed Rawlings as speaking for them. Rawlings used the court-martial proceedings as an opportunity to denounce government corruption. He openly accused government officials of extorting money from the people. Inspired by his dedication to positive reforms and fearing that he would be executed, junior officers and soldiers freed Rawlings from military custody in a second coup during the first week of June. This time Rawlings used a radio station to announce the establishment of the Armed Forces Revolutionary Council (AFRC), which he said would rule Ghana until a freely elected government was prepared to rule.

Rawlings emerged triumphant. Along with the sixteen-member AFRC, he ruled by decree. The goal of the populist regime was to eradicate corruption and the establishment of a new order, but few of the members had any idea of how to accomplish that goal. Calls for "Death to swindlers!" by demonstrators supporting the AFRC resulted in the execution of a number of former government leaders, including three former heads of state, during the brief 112-day AFRC rule prior to the return of civilian government.

Jerry John Rawlings in Independence Square in Accra, Ghana, with U. S. president and first lady Bill and Hillary Rodham Clinton. *(AP/Wide World Photos)*

devaluation of its currency. Domestic food production increased dramatically during the 1980's but did little to improve economic stability. Several coup attempts tried to oust Rawlings and the PNDC during the mid-1980's, but the number began to diminish as the economy improved in the early 1990's.

In an effort to legitimize its power—and its lengthy hold on power—the PNDC instituted local elections throughout the country during 1988 and early 1989. Voters selected individuals who could represent them in eighteen district assemblies, a move toward local and national parliaments. Voter turnout was low, at 59 percent, indicating voter skepticism regarding the true intent of the elections. By 1991 Rawlings announced his intent again to allow legal recognition of political parties. Seven parties initially filed for registration with the government. He followed with a call for a National Consultative Assembly to prepare a draft constitution.

Rawlings announced his candidacy for the presidency of Ghana just prior to the 1992 deadline for qualifying. He easily won the 1992 election in a landslide and was sworn in as president of Ghana on January 7, 1993. During his first term in office, Ghana was plagued by an ethnic war in the north. While the war disrupted his efforts to

The 1992 Elections in Ghana

Many international observers doubted whether Rawlings would willingly give up his power after indirectly managing and manipulating Ghana's political system since the coup of 1979. Even those who believed that he might willingly relinquish power thought that his mere presence would make governing impossible for any party elected. Few were surprised when Rawlings announced his intent to run for the office of president, but his landslide victory in the presidential election of 1992 surprised everyone. He received 60 percent of the vote cast, more than all his opponents combined. The National Democratic Congress, his party, won all but ten of the two hundred seats in the parliamentary elections.

improve the quality of life for most Ghanaians, Rawlings was able to maintain his popularity with voters and win his 1996 reelection campaign. In 1997 Rawlings led the nation's fortieth-anniversary celebration of independence, during which he stressed unity and the need to achieve the goals of the founders. Stated objectives of his second term included the diversification of Ghana's energy resources along with the improvement of health and education services.

Bibliography

Gutteridge, William Frank. *Africa's Military Rulers: An Assessment*. London: Institute for the Study of Conflict, 1975.

Nugent, Paul. *Big Men, Small Boys, and Politics in Ghana: Power, Ideology, and the Burden of History, 1982-1994*. New York: Printer, 1995.

Petchenkine, Youry. *Ghana: In Search of Stability, 1957-1992*. Westport, Conn.: Praeger, 1993.

Donald C. Simmons, Jr.

Ronald Reagan

Born: February 6, 1911; Tampico, Illinois

President of the United States (1981-1989)

Ronald Wilson Reagan (RO-nuhld WIHL-suhn RAY-guhn) was born to Nelle and John Reagan, a shoe salesman. After graduating from high school in Dixon, Illinois, he attended Eureka College. There he studied sociology and economics while playing football and acting in school plays. Upon college graduation, he became a radio sports announcer. In 1937 Reagan began a career as an actor, appearing in more than fifty films over the next two decades. Perhaps his most famous role came when he played "the Gipper" in *Knute Rockne, All American* (1942). He also served as president of the Screen Actors Guild from 1947 to 1952 and from 1959 to 1960. His first marriage was to actress Jane Wyman; they adopted two children, Maureen and Michael. In 1952 he married Nancy Davis. They had two children, Patricia and Ronald.

The Acting Governor

As his acting career began to decline in the 1950's, Reagan became a spokesman for the General Electric Company. His political ideology changed from the liberal Democrat he had been to a conservative Republican. His popularity as a conservative speaker led to his being encouraged to seek public office, and in 1966 he successfully ran for governor of California. He was reelected in 1970. He was a generally popular governor but was known more for his conservative rhetoric than his accomplishments.

His success in electoral politics in California and his strident conservatism with regard to the role of government in society led supporters to encourage him to seek the presidency. In 1968 he made his first bid for that office, losing the Republican nomination to Richard M. Nixon. In 1976 he sought the Republican nomination against incumbent president Gerald R. Ford. He was a serious contender that year, but he narrowly lost the nomination.

The Reagan Revolution

In 1980 Reagan won the Republican nomination for president and defeated incumbent president Jimmy Carter in a landslide during the general election. Reagan garnered 51 percent of the popular vote to Carter's 41 percent and independent candidate John Anderson's 6 percent. Reagan's success was the product of two issues: the perception that President Carter had weak leadership skills and the poor state of the American economy. Reagan's promises to reduce the

Ronald Reagan *(Library of Congress)*

size of the national government and lower taxes as a method of improving the economy appealed to many voters. Carter's inability to end the Iranian hostage crisis during the campaign only contributed to the notion that he was an ineffectual leader.

During his first term in office, Reagan put his conservative ideology to work. He persuaded Congress to enact a major tax cut in 1981. The government also reduced spending on a variety of social programs while increasing the military expenditures of the United States dramatically. The economic results of the 1981 law were mixed. On the negative side, the nation went through an economic recession in 1982, while the reduced taxes lessened government revenues and led to a greatly increased national debt. The distribution of income in the United States became more top heavy: The wealthiest Americans became better off, whereas most Americans did not benefit significantly from the tax cuts. On the positive side, after 1982 came a long period of economic growth, and inflation rates dropped dramatically. In terms of social programs, Reagan proposed reducing the increases in government transfer payments to the poor and transferring responsibility for welfare policy to the states, proposals that met with limited success.

In foreign policy, Reagan took a hard line as an anticommunist, moving with reluctance toward arms control with the Soviet Union. He authorized the U.S. military invasion of Grenada, a small Caribbean island, in 1983 for the purpose of ousting its communist government. Mean-

U.S. president Ronald Reagan (left) and Soviet leader Mikhail Gorbachev drink a toast at a White House state dinner in December, 1988. *(Archive Photos/Consolidated)*

The Iran-Contra Affair

In 1985 President Ronald Reagan had a number of foreign policy problems confronting him. Two of these were that Americans were being held hostage in Lebanon by Shiite Muslim terrorist groups and that a leftist leadership had power in Nicaragua. In order to confront these two problems, Reagan turned to his National Security Council (NSC), headed by Robert McFarlane at first and then by Admiral John Poindexter. The NSC sold arms to Iran in the mistaken belief that by doing so they could secure the release of the hostages in Lebanon. They pursued this action despite the specific U.S. policy of refusing to bargain with terrorists.

Some of the proceeds from the sale of the arms to Iran were diverted to help rebels (the Contras) who wished to overthrow the leftist government of Nicaragua. These sales were in violation of a law known as the Boland Amendment. The transfer of money was overseen by Colonel Oliver North, an NSC staff member. Both Poindexter and North were fired for their knowledge of these activities and were later prosecuted for their role in the affair. President Reagan denied knowledge of the affair but was chastised by a commission led by former senator John Tower for his lack of executive oversight. The affair damaged Reagan's public image.

while, he initiated a major buildup in American weapons, focusing on a defense system called the Strategic Defense Initiative (SDI).

On the personal front, Reagan emerged as a popular leader. Soon after his inauguration, he was shot and wounded by John W. Hinckley, Jr. His shooting united the nation in horror against needless violence, and his speedy and complete recovery contributed to a feeling that he was a man of vigor.

U.S. president Ronald Reagan speaking at the signing ceremony for the Civil Liberties Act of 1988. The act authorized compensatory payments to Japanese Americans who were held in internment camps during World War II. *(Ronald Reagan Library)*

The Second Term

Reagan handily defeated Walter Mondale, the Democratic nominee, for reelection in 1984. During his second term Reagan continued to push his conservative agenda. He persuaded Congress to overhaul the U.S. tax code in 1986 and continued to press his military buildup. Reagan's second term was not as successful as his first, and in late 1986 it was learned that the Reagan administration had shipped arms to the radical fundamentalist government in Iran as a means to secure the release of American hostages in the Middle East. Some of the profits from the

The 1987 Nuclear Arms Reduction Treaty

President Reagan negotiated a treaty with the Soviet Union in 1987 that was designed to lessen the threat of nuclear war by reducing the number of intermediate range nuclear missiles in Europe. The treaty, known as the INF treaty, called for dismantling, over three years, 2,619 missiles. Teams of observers from both countries were given the right to inspect certain operating bases so that they could verify that missiles had been destroyed. The treaty was signed by President Reagan and Soviet General Secretary Mikhail Gorbachev on December 8, 1987. The treaty represented a major step in the thawing of the Cold War.

sale were diverted secretly to organizations opposing the Marxist Sandinista government in Nicaragua. While Reagan denied knowing about these illegal activities, his administration lost some of its luster as it reached its conclusion.

The Reagan Legacy

Reagan left office as a popular president, well-liked by the American public for his affable personality and quick wit. His accomplishments as president were many, and the economic prosperity in the United States as he left office contributed to the notion that his had been a successful eight years. The fall of the Soviet Union soon after he left office seemed to vindicate his policy of military buildup.

Bibliography

Cannon, Lou. *President Reagan: The Role of a Lifetime*. New York: Simon and Schuster, 1991.

Johnson, Haynes. *Sleepwalking Through History*. New York: Norton, 1991.

Reagan, Ronald. *An American Life*. New York: Simon and Schuster, 1990.

Schmertz, Eric J., Natalie Datlof, and Alexej Ugrinsky, eds. *Ronald Reagan's America*. 2 vols. Westport, Conn.: Greenwood Press, 1997.

James W. Riddlesperger, Jr.

William H. Rehnquist

Born: October 1, 1924; Milwaukee, Wisconsin

U.S. Supreme Court justice (1972-1986) and chief justice of the United States (named 1986)

William Hubbs Rehnquist (WIHL-yuhm HUHBZ REHN-kwihst) grew up in a politically conservative home headed by a paper salesman. After serving with the army air corps during World War II, Rehnquist attended Stanford University, from which he received both a B.A. and a master's degree in political science. After receiving a second master's degree in government at Harvard University, he went back to Stanford to study law, graduating first in his class in 1952. He then clerked for Justice Robert H. Jackson at the U.S. Supreme Court and in 1953 married Natalie Cornell, with whom he had three children.

William H. Rehnquist *(Office of the Supreme Court)*

A Republican Activist

Rehnquist settled in Phoenix, Arizona, where he worked in private practice and became active in local Republican politics. During the 1964 presidential election, he campaigned for Republican candidate Barry Goldwater and became acquainted with another local political activist, Richard Kleindienst. After Kleindienst joined the administration of President Richard M. Nixon as deputy attorney general, he helped Rehnquist land a position as head of the Justice Department's Office of Legal Counsel in 1969.

Serving as assistant attorney general, Rehnquist was outspoken and articulate in representing the Nixon administration's opposition to many of the liberal policies resulting from rulings of the Supreme Court under the leadership of Chief Justice Earl Warren (1953-1969). One such policy is known as the exclusionary rule, prohibiting the introduction in criminal trials of evidence obtained in violation of the Fourth Amendment's ban on illegal search and seizure. Nixon had appointed Chief Justice Earl Warren's successor, Warren Burger, to reverse what conservatives saw as the liberal excesses of the Warren years. However, the Burger Court had in fact consolidated and even extended the Warren Court's expansion of civil liberties.

A Conservative Agenda

Upon the retirement of Justice John M. Harlan in 1971, President Nixon named Rehnquist to the Supreme Court as his replacement. During his confirmation hearings before the Senate Judiciary Committee, Rehnquist came under heavy criticism for opposing various integration measures, such as school busing, during his activist days in Phoenix. The committee's most pointed questions, however, concerned a memorandum that Rehnquist had written opposing school desegregation in the *Brown v. Board of Education* case (1954). In the end, however, Rehnquist's nomination was confirmed, and on January 7, 1972, he took his seat on the high bench.

As an associate justice, Rehnquist pressed his conservative agenda. During his early years on the Burger Court, he was often the only dissenter, but by the time Burger retired in 1986, the Court had grown increasingly conservative, and Rehnquist had become the Court's intellectual leader. Not surprisingly, Republican President Ronald Reagan appointed Rehnquist as Burger's successor.

Rehnquist came to the job of chief justice with considerable administrative skills and a clear political agenda. He continued to argue persuasively for those positions he had taken early in his career: restriction of the rights of criminal defendants, support for the death penalty, protection of private property, enlargement of states' rights,

Both William H. Rehnquist (left) and Lewis F. Powell were sworn in as U.S. Supreme Court judges in 1972. Rehnquist was named chief justice in 1986. *(CNP/Archive Photos)*

The Rehnquist Confirmation Debate

When a young William Rehnquist had clerked for Justice Robert Jackson, he prepared a memorandum to help the justice prepare for the Supreme Court's discussions about the *Brown v. Board of Education* (1954) school desegregation case. In that memo, Rehnquist expressed opposition to desegregation. He stated that he believed the "separate but equal" doctrine of the case *Plessy v. Ferguson*, which had been the law of the land since 1896, "was right and should be reaffirmed." The memo surfaced at Rehnquist's Supreme Court confirmation hearings in 1971, causing considerable controversy. Rehnquist convinced the Senate Judiciary Committee that the memo represented Justice Jackson's views rather than his own, and his nomination was confirmed 68 to 26. The memo was again the subject of debate when Rehnquist's nomination as chief justice came before the committee in 1986, together with allegations that he had harassed African American voters in Phoenix years earlier. Once again, however, the Senate confirmed Rehnquist's appointment, although at 65 to 33 the vote was slightly narrower than it had been in 1971.

overturning the right to abortion, and reversing affirmative action. In general, the Supreme Court he headed succeeded where the Burger Court had failed: It narrowed many of the Warren Court's more liberal rulings. For example, although the Rehnquist Court, as of 1998, had not overturned *Roe v. Wade* (1973), it significantly restricted a woman's access to abortion.

Rehnquist found himself in the headlines in 1999 for an unusual reason: After the U.S. House of Representatives voted in 1998 to impeach President Bill Clinton, Rehnquist became the second chief justice in U.S. history to preside over a U.S. Senate impeachment trial of a president.

Bibliography

Davis, Sue. *Justice Rehnquist and the Constitution*. Princeton, N.J.: Princeton University Press, 1989.

Irons, Peter H. *Brennan vs. Rehnquist: The Battle for the Constitution*. New York: Knopf, 1994.

Savage, David G. *Turning Right: The Making of the Rehnquist Court*. New York: Wiley, 1992.

Lisa Paddock

George Houston Reid

Born: February 25, 1845; Johnstone, Renfrew, Scotland
Died: September 12, 1918; London, England

Prime minister of Australia (1904-1905)

The family of George Houston Reid (JOHRJ HEW-stuhn REED) emigrated from London, England, to Melbourne, Australia, in 1852, when he was seven years old. As a young man he was ambitious; he served in the colonial Treasury between 1864 and 1878, acted as secretary to the attorney general of New South Wales in 1878, and began a law practice in Sydney a year later. He practiced law for only one year, however, before he entered politics.

George Houston Reid *(Library of Congress)*

Establishing the Commonwealth of Australia

In 1880, Reid was elected to the Legislative Assembly of New South Wales. He took the position of minister of public instruction in 1883, a post he held until 1899. Bent on social reform and economic recovery through increased education, he proposed legislation and implemented successful programs for technical education and endorsed evening university lectures. Popular among his constituents, in 1894 he was elected premier of New South Wales.

As premier, a position he held until 1899, Reid sought reform. He introduced a successful new financial accounting system. In keeping with his policy of government nonintervention, he also allowed the civil service to stand alone without political interference. He helped win New South Wales's approval of the formation of an Australian federation. In 1900, the continent of Australia's population exceeded four million people, and there were 10,000 miles (16,000 kilometers) of railroad track linking the country. An increasing sense of Australian identity was emerging throughout the provinces. These nationalistic passions fueled a desire for an Australian federation. As a result, the British Parliament passed the Australian Commonwealth Act in July, 1900.

On January 1, 1901, the Commonwealth of Australia was established. That same year, Reid, a leading figure in the federation movement, was elected to the first Parliament of the Commonwealth of Australia, which included New South Wales, South Australia, Victoria, Western Australia, Tasmania, and Queensland as constituents. In the first federal Parliament (1901-1904), Reid steered the Free Traders' opposition to Alfred Deakin, leader of the Liberal Party.

Prime Minister

In 1904, Reid was the leader of the opposition party in the Australian House of Representatives.

In August of that year, he united with Deakin and the Liberal Party to defeat the Labor Party. A coalition government was formed with Reid as prime minister. As prime minister, he was instrumental in designing and establishing an economic recovery program for Australia, utilizing a program of free trade and laissez-faire economics. Reid argued that the economy would function and regulate itself without government controls or intervention. He also legislated for, and utilized, taxes intended to bring about the demise of huge land monopolies. The coalition ministry lasted only until 1905. Reid then acted as the opposition leader in Parliament from 1905 to 1908, the year he retired from Australian politics. His retirement was brought about by conflict resulting directly from his role as a free trade advocate continually battling the surging tide of Australian protectionism.

Upon his retirement, Reid returned to England in 1909, where he was made a knight of the British realm. At this time he was also named Australia's first high commissioner to London. During the same year, he took up a seat in the British Parliament's House of Commons representing St. George, Hanover Square, in London. He served until his death in 1918. Reid is prominent in Australian history as a figure who helped forge the Commonwealth of Australia and establish it as an independent and prosperous modern nation.

Bibliography

Crisp, Leslie Finlay. *George Houston Reid: Federation Fathers; Federal Failure*. Canberra: Australian National University, 1979.

McMinn, W. G. *George Reid*. Melbourne, Australia: Melbourne University Press, 1990.

Miller, Murial. *George Reid*. London: Summerhill Press, 1987.

M. Casey Diana

The Free Trade Movement

Australia's first federal government was formed in 1901. For its first few years, the major parties were the Free Traders, the Protectionists (also called the Liberals), and the Labour Party. The Free Traders opposed government regulation of business, particularly the imposition of tariffs. The Protectionists favored tariffs intended to protect Australian businesses from foreign competition. Australia's first Parliament was led by the Protectionists, under Edmund Barton (1901-1903) and then Alfred Deakin (1903-1904). George Reid led the Free Traders in their opposition status. In 1904, Reid was elected prime minister when the Free Traders came to power. A year later, the Protectionists returned to power. Both as prime minister and as a leader of the Free Traders as an opposition party, Reid battled ceaselessly against protectionist policies. In 1909 Deakin formed an alliance between the Protectionists and the Free Traders, creating the Fusion Party to oppose Labour. By then the Free Traders had actually accepted an amount of government regulation.

Internationally, the free trade movement had been a powerful force in Europe since the mid-nineteenth century. Eighteenth-century economist Adam Smith had established a framework for the movement in his 1776 study *An Inquiry into the Nature and Causes of the Wealth of Nations*. Free trade rebelled against mercantilism, the economic policy that necessitated government involvement or regulation in nearly every facet of trade. Smith argued that the economy functions according to a self-regulating natural law and that governments should therefore not be involved in trade at all.

Louis Renault

Born: May 21, 1843; Autun, France
Died: February 8, 1918; Barbizon, France

French jurist and diplomat, winner of 1907 Nobel Peace Prize

Louis Renault (lew-EE reh-NOH), the son of a bookseller, demonstrated academic brilliance from an early age. He completed preparatory work at the Collège d'Autun before entering the University of Dijon to study literature. He then studied law in Paris, where he earned three degrees, culminating with his doctorate in 1868. At all stages, he earned the highest academic honors. He became a faculty member at the University of Paris in 1873, where he first taught criminal law and later international law. He was offered the Chair in International Law at the Sorbonne in 1881, which he kept until his death in 1918.

Louis Renault *(The Nobel Foundation)*

Scholarly Career

Renault was a prolific writer. His books include *Introduction to the Study of International Law* (1879) and the nine-volume *Treatise on Commercial Law*, written with Charles Lyon-Caen between 1889 and 1899. He published hundreds of contributions in scholarly publications, lectured extensively, and directed the work of many graduate students. As a teacher he influenced a generation of students who went on to shape French diplomacy in the twentieth century.

Entry into Diplomacy

The French government soon began to rely on Renault's expertise. As a professor he had become involved in unraveling tangles in international commercial law relating to such things as the international transfer of intellectual property. In 1891 he became a legal consultant to the French Foreign Office and served as France's leading representative at many international meetings involving diverse issues such as military aviation, the international regulation of obscene materials, the abolition of white slavery, and reorganization of the International Red Cross.

Main Achievements

In 1899 the czar of Russia, Nicholas II, proposed convening an international conference at The Hague in the Netherlands to study disarmament and the peaceful resolution of international disputes. The conference met from May 18 to July 29, 1899. Although German opposition made

The Hague Conference, 1907

Although formally convened by Russia's Czar Nicholas II, the Hague Conference of 1907 was based on a suggestion made by Theodore Roosevelt, president of the United States. It met from June 15 to October 18, 1907, and was attended by delegates representing forty-four nations. While delegates failed to agree on proposals designed to limit armaments, they agreed to establish several protocols involving the conduct of war—covering such things as the rights of neutral powers, the status of enemy merchant ships, and shelling by naval vessels. The conference also adopted a resolution calling for compulsory arbitration of international disputes. Its most important contribution was the establishment of the principle that international disputes should be resolved by regular conferences. This idea contributed to the creation of the League of Nations after World War I.

genuine progress toward disarmament impossible, the conference succeeded in establishing a panel of judges who could serve as arbitrators, if asked, for nations involved in disputes. Renault's contributions to the Hague Conference of 1899 was extensive, and he was the principal author of the final report. He was named as one of the twenty-eight arbiters available to help resolve disputes, and nations involved in international disputes chose him as an arbiter more often than any other member. His presence dominated the second Hague Conference in 1907.

Renault received numerous honors for his work toward international peace. France inducted him into the Legion of Honor and the Academy of Moral and Political Sciences. A number of foreign nations honored him with decorations and honorary doctorates. As a result of his work at the Hague Convention, he was awarded the Nobel Peace Prize in 1907 along with Ernesto Teodoro Moneta, the Italian president of the Lombard League of Peace. In 1914 Renault was elected president of the Academy of International Law created at The Hague in 1914.

Renault died in harness—still working at age seventy-four. He taught at the Sorbonne on February 6, 1918, and went to his country house in Barbizon to rest. He died on February 8, 1918. Although honored throughout the world, Renault wanted to be known as a man who was "a professor at heart."

Bibliography

Davis, Calvin D. *The United States and the First Hague Peace Conference*. Ithaca, N.Y.: Cornell University Press, 1962.

_______. *The United States and the Second Hague Peace Conference: American Diplomacy and International Organization, 1899-1914*. Durham, N.C.: Duke University Press, 1976.

Hale, Oron J. *The Great Illusion, 1900-1914*. New York: Harper & Row, 1971.

Taylor, A. J. P. *The Struggle for Mastery in Europe, 1848-1914*. Oxford, England: Clarendon Press, 1954.

C. James Haug

Janet Reno

Born: July 21, 1938; Miami, Florida

First woman to be named U.S. attorney general (named 1993)

The father of Janet Reno (JA-neht REE-noh) was a Danish immigrant and police reporter for the *Miami Herald*. Her mother was an investigative reporter for the *Miami News* who built the family's house with her own hands. In 1960 Reno graduated from Cornell University; in 1963 she graduated from Harvard Law School. Never married, Reno strongly committed herself to children's and women's rights and became well known for her organizational abilities, integrity, and no-nonsense approach to hard work. In 1995 she was diagnosed with Parkinson's disease.

Legal Firsts for Women

Reno was a member of the generation of women who broke new ground in the legal profession. At Harvard, she was one of only sixteen women enrolled in a class of 544. She faced discrimination at Harvard and then in the job market: Several large Miami law firms refused to hire a woman associate. Beginning her career in private practice in a smaller firm, she soon became interested in politics. In 1967, her work as Gerald Lewis's campaign manager ensured his election to the Florida House of Representatives. In 1971 she received her first political appointment as staff director of the Judiciary Committee of the Florida House of Representatives, where she modernized the court systems.

In 1972 she was defeated in her bid for a seat in the state legislature, but in 1973 she was hired by Dade County state attorney Richard Gerstein's office of the Eleventh Judicial Circuit of Florida. There she successfully reorganized the juvenile court. In 1976 she became the first woman partner of one of Florida's most prestigious law firms. In 1978 she replaced the retiring Gerstein for the remainder of his unexpired term, becoming the first woman in Florida to hold the position of state attorney.

First Female Florida State Attorney

Reno's abilities were tested early, when a race riot erupted after five white officers accused of police brutality were found not guilty by an all-

U.S. attorney general Janet Reno appearing before the House Judiciary Committee, testifying about the government's actions in the Branch Davidian siege. *(AP/Wide World Photos)*

white jury. Because her office was responsible for prosecuting the policemen, she had to work hard to repair her reputation with the African American community. Despite this early setback, her successes as state attorney included many firsts: developing a domestic violence intervention program, aggressively pursuing fathers for child support, and establishing a special drug court in which first-time nonviolent offenders were sent to rehabilitation. Because she preferred rehabilitation to incarceration, critics charged that she had a lower-than-state-average conviction rate and that she was not aggressive enough in pursuing drug-trafficking and public-corruption cases, preferring instead to let the federal courts take on these cases. Nevertheless, Reno was reelected as state attorney five times.

First Female Attorney General

On February 11, 1993, President Bill Clinton nominated Reno as the first female attorney general of the United States. Reno's abilities were again quickly tested when the conflict between the Branch Davidians and federal authorities erupted outside Waco, Texas. The Davidians, led by self-proclaimed messiah David Koresh, had stockpiled an arsenal in their compound, and it was alleged that sexual abuse of women and children was occurring there. FBI agents ap-

Janet Reno conferring informally with U.S. president Bill Clinton. *(Library of Congress)*

Militias

When Janet Reno ordered the assault on the Branch Davidian compound, it inflamed many people who belonged to militias—private armies engaged in paramilitary training to prepare for what members see as an inevitable war with the federal government. While secret hate groups of the past such as the Ku Klux Klan focused on white supremacy, the new militias are more concerned with the federal government as a threat to weapons ownership and individual freedom. Militias disseminate their extremist messages and literature at gun shows, on Web sites, and on local cable television and talk-radio shows. On April 19, 1995, the second anniversary of the FBI's tear-gas attack at Waco, Timothy McVeigh and Terry Nichols, who had connections with Michigan-based militias, bombed the Alfred P. Murrah federal building in Oklahoma City, killing 169 people. After this and other high-profile militia cases, legislation called the Antiterrorism and Effective Death Penalty Act of 1996 was enacted to fight domestic and international terrorism.

proached the compound, and the Davidians opened fire. A tense stand-off began that lasted for weeks; attempts at mediation were unsuccessful. Then, in April, 1993, Reno, after careful deliberation with various law enforcement specialists, ordered the Federal Bureau of Investigation (FBI) to fire tear gas into the compound. Instead of surrendering, cult members set fire to the compound, resulting in the deaths of eighty-six adults and children. Visibly affected by the disaster, Reno went on television and took responsibility for the debacle, winning the respect of many Americans.

Reno became known for her integrity and hard work and for resisting politically expedient solutions in favor of in-depth analysis of such events as the Waco stand-off and the World Trade Center bombing. She is representative of many women of her generation who accomplished firsts in their fields through determination and personal sacrifice.

Bibliography

Anderson, Paul. *Janet Reno: Doing the Right Thing*. New York: John Wiley & Sons, 1994.

Lindop, Laurie. *Political Leaders*. New York: Twenty-First Century Books, 1996.

Meachum, Virginia. *Janet Reno: United States Attorney General*. Springfield, N.J.: Enslow, 1995.

Lisa-Anne Culp

Syngman Rhee

Born: March 26, 1875; P'yongsan, Korea
Died: July 19, 1965; Honolulu, Hawaii

First president of South Korea (1948-1960)

Yi Sung-man (YIH SOONG MUHN), the baptismal name of Syngman Rhee (SIHNG-muhn REE) was born into an aristocratic family in 1875. At that time the tradition-minded Choson Dynasty of Korea (1392-1910) was at the end of its long existence. Having nearly run its course, the dynasty was on its last legs, too weak to reform itself or to resist foreign aggression.

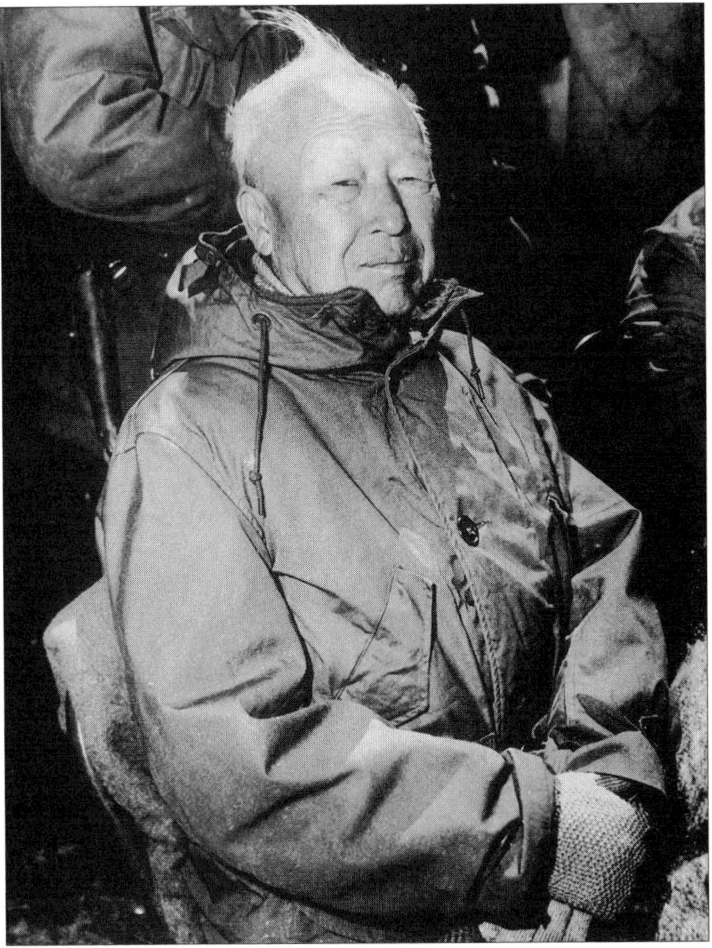

Syngman Rhee *(Archive Photos)*

Early Career

Rhee was one of the few Koreans at the time who sought the Western-style education provided by American Methodist missionaries. He also became involved in a reform movement, the Independence Club, which led to his arrest in 1898 at the age of twenty-three. While he was in jail, he wrote *The Spirit of Independence*, first published in 1906. Upon his release, he traveled to the United States, where he received a B.A. from George Washington University and an M.A. from Harvard University. He received his Ph.D. in political science from Princeton University in 1910, the same year that Japan annexed Korea.

Rhee returned to Korea in 1910 to work for the YMCA but left after two years to go to Hawaii. He had been invited there by nationalist leader Park Yong-man to help educate the children of the seven thousand Korean plantation workers who had gone there between 1903 and 1905. As the first Korean to receive a doctoral degree in the United States, he commanded a great deal of respect from a people whose Confucian training had always revered education.

The Nationalist Movement

Within a few years of his arrival in Hawaii, however, he had fallen out of favor with the Methodist Church, with whom he had been working, as well as with other nationalist leaders. The situation led him to establish his own church—the Korean Christian

Church—and his own nationalist organization—the Dongjihoe, or Comrades Society. The Comrades Society competed with Korea's main nationalist organization—the Kungminhoe, or Korean National Association. Thus was the Korean community rent into factions. Throughout, Rhee sought without success to win the American government over to the cause of Korean independence. Because Japan and the United States were allies, there was no change in U.S. policy.

The Korean nationalist movement was bolstered by anti-Japanese uprisings in Korea in 1919 known as the March First Movement. The factions temporarily set aside their differences to create a Korean provisional government and the Korean Commission in Shanghai to prepare for an independent Korea. Rhee was elected president of this government-in-exile. However, independence did not come, and the bickering soon resumed between Rhee and other leaders. By 1921 Rhee had returned to Hawaii and the nationalist movement had subsided.

The 1940's

When the Japanese attacked Pearl Harbor in December, 1941, Rhee once again sought the support of the United States. The United States noted that there was still no unity in the Korean nationalist community and declined to support Rhee. When Japan was defeated in 1945, Korea was occupied by an American military government. It was then that Rhee finally succeeded.

In the early postwar period, the Cold War against communism and the Soviet Union led the United States to divide the Korean peninsula to isolate the communists in North Korea. In South Korea, only the most conservative leaders could find fertile ground, and Rhee was a conservative anticommunist. Others who were more moderate were either arrested or frozen out of the po-

The Korean Commission

The Korean Commission was born in the aftermath of the uprising known as the March First Movement of 1919. A Korean provisional government was established in Shanghai, China, and the Korean Commission was created in the fall of that year. Headed by Kim Kyu-Sik, its goal was to influence members of the American government and other foreign powers to support the cause of Korean independence from Japan. The commission sponsored a number of publications designed to publicize the plight of Korea. While these publications did spread the word of Korea's situation, the commission was unable to influence the foreign policies of the major powers, including the United States and Great Britain, who were allies of Japan. When the provisional government in Shanghai collapsed in 1921, so did the Korean Commission, although it was not officially dissolved until 1925.

Symptomatic of the collapse were the financial issues faced by the Korean nationalist movement. Syngman Rhee headed the Washington branch of the Korean Commission and began to authorize the sale of bonds to support the cause of Korean independence. This money was sent to Shanghai even after events there had led to the ouster of Rhee as commission president. Rhee, in the United States, ordered that no more money raised by the Korean Commission be sent to Shanghai. Others in the movement argued that the commission was under the jurisdiction of the Shanghai government in exile and that Rhee could not unilaterally halt the flow of money. In addition, members of the Shanghai government-in-exile alleged that money had been collected from Koreans in the United States but that no accounting had been made of the proceeds.

The Spirit of Independence

Syngman Rhee was imprisoned in Seoul for seven years, beginning in 1898, for his political activities with the Independence Club. Another prisoner encouraged him to write about the principles of the independence movement in order to educate and inspire all Koreans. Rhee had to make ink from dye smuggled into the prison and write in secret; his writings were then smuggled out. In its published version, his book, *The Spirit of Independence*, consisted of forty-seven chapters, thirty-four written in prison. Reflecting Confucian ideas, Rhee interprets democracy primarily in terms of citizens' duties and responsibilities rather than their rights and privileges. The manuscript was smuggled overseas and printed in Los Angeles in 1906 and again in Honolulu. *The Spirit of Independence* became tremendously influential in Korean nationalist politics and was reprinted many times after Korea's liberation from Japan in 1945. Its place in Korean history has been compared with the place of the writings of Tom Paine and Thomas Jefferson in American history.

litical process. The result was that Rhee easily won a 1948 election, making him the first president of South Korea.

The Presidency

Rhee, an anti-Japanese nationalist before the war, had by this time transformed his nationalism into a desire to unify the country by destroying the communists in the North. Relations worsened between North and South, and in June, 1950, North Korean forces under Kim Il Sung launched an attack against the South, initiating the Korean War. The war lasted from 1950 to 1953. The United States aided Rhee and South Korea, while China and the Soviet Union aided the North. Although Rhee wanted to eliminate the North, the United States sought only to push the North Koreans back behind the 38th parallel, the previously agreed-upon line dividing North and South Korea.

During the war, Rhee was reelected to a second four-year term in 1952, but criticism began to mount. Rhee responded by accusing politicians who

South Korean president Syngman Rhee in 1952, touring the front during the Korean War. *(Archive Photos/American Stock)*

Syngman Rhee with fellow Korean nationalist Kim Kyu-Shik c. 1919, the year Kim Kyu-Shik went to the Paris Peace Conference to appeal for Korean independence. *(The Korea Society)*

opposed him of being communists and by banning newspapers that ran critical editorials. Rhee was presiding over an economically destitute nation with an authoritarian government. Hungry to maintain his power, Rhee had the constitution altered so that he could run for a third term in 1956. He won amid charges of voting irregularities. When he was elected for a fourth time in 1960, students took to the streets demanding democracy. The United States persuaded Rhee to step down and provided him with air transportation to Hawaii. He died there in 1965.

Bibliography

Allen, R. C. *Korea's Syngman Rhee: An Unauthorized Portrait*. Rutland, Vt.: Tuttle, 1960.

Chong-Sik Lee. *The Politics of Korean Nationalism*. Berkeley: University of California Press, 1965.

Oliver, Robert T. *Syngman Rhee and American Involvement in Korea, 1942-1960: A Personal Narrative*. Seoul, Korea: Panmun, 1978.

_______. *Syngman Rhee: The Man Behind the Myth*. New York: Dodd, Mead, 1954.

Wayne Patterson

Joachim von Ribbentrop

Born: April 30, 1893; Wesel, Germany
Died: October 16, 1946; Nuremberg, Germany

Foreign minister of Nazi Germany (1938-1945)

Ulrich Friedrich Willy Joachim Ribbentrop (EWL-rihk FREED-rihk VEE-lee yoh-AH-kihm RIH-behn-trop) was born on April 30, 1893, in the German town of Wesel on the Lower Rhine. His father was stationed there as an artillery lieutenant. Ribbentrop worked in Canada from 1910 to 1914 and then earned an Iron Cross for his World War I service. In 1920 he married Anna Elizabeth Henkell, daughter of a wealthy Wiesbaden wine merchant. He attained the "von" (fon) in his name by having a sixty-two-year-old aunt adopt him. In 1929 Ribbentrop was a successful wine merchant. Four years later he was Adolf Hitler's most loyal sycophant, and in 1946 he was hanged as a war criminal.

Joachim von Ribbentrop *(Archive Photos)*

The Prewar Years

Ribbentrop joined Hitler's National Socialist (Nazi) Party in 1932, and his slavish devotion to Hitler soon made him a useful tool in foreign affairs. After election to the Reichstag (the German parliament) in 1933, Ribbentrop accepted his first significant appointment, as disarmament commissioner, in 1934. He used the post as a means to hobnob with leaders in France, England, and Italy. His attempts to cultivate ties with England continued when Hitler named him a roving ambassador, and he was instrumental in concluding a 1935 Anglo-German Naval Agreement that was quite favorable to Germany.

This success earned Ribbentrop a grant of ten million Reichsmarks, which he used to staff and maintain his own personal government bureau. In July, 1936, Hitler appointed Ribbentrop ambassador to England. Four months later Ribbentrop signed the Anti-Comintern Pact with Japan. Spending little time in London, where he was commonly regarded as a buffoon, Ribbentrop was delighted to be made the Third Reich's foreign minister in February of 1938.

Career as Foreign Minister

Ribbentrop's tenure as foreign minister was marked by his eagerness to anticipate Hitler's schemes and help bring them to fruition. His insistence that the British would not fight back

German foreign minister Joachim von Ribbentrop, at right, with British prime minister Neville Chamberlain in Munich, 1938. *(Library of Congress)*

encouraged Hitler to execute the Anschluss and then to attack Czechoslovakia. In May, 1939, Ribbentrop signed an agreement (called the "pact of steel") with Italy's foreign minister, Count Galeazzo Ciano. This agreement was a minor accomplishment, however, compared with the protracted discussions with the Soviet Union that culminated in the Nazi-Soviet Nonaggression Pact of August, 1939. This pact is often described as Ribbentrop's greatest foreign-policy success.

Two years later, Ribbentrop was working diligently on Hitler's plan to invade the Soviet Union. From then on, until

The Anschluss

The Anschluss is the name given to Adolf Hitler's forced union of Austria with Germany in March, 1938. This union had long been a major objective of the Nazi führer, who had written in the second paragraph of his autobiographical *Mein Kampf* (1925-1927): "German Austria must be restored to the German Motherland." In the so-called July Agreement of 1936, Hitler had accepted Austrian sovereignty in exchange for Austrian chancellor Kurt von Schuschnigg's promise of recognition for Austria's Pan-German National Opposition Party. In mid-1937 Hitler appointed a trusted adviser, Wil- helm Keppler, as special liaison between Hitler and his Austrian minister, Franz von Papen. Schuschnigg named Arthur Seyss-Inquart, a Viennese lawyer and Nazi sympathizer, as overseer of a policy admitting Austrian Nazis to official appointments. By the time Joachim von Ribbentrop became German foreign minister in February, 1938, Hitler's preparations for the Anschluss were virtually complete.

When Schuschnigg met with Hitler on February 12, Hitler harangued the Austrian chancellor brutally with threats of force. He made Schuschnigg sign an agreement providing for the duplicitous Seyss-Inquart to be made interior minister of Austria, for the National Opposition Party to be given parity in Austrian political life, and for the freeing of German political prisoners held in Austria. With Ribbentrop in London trying to placate the alarmed British, Hitler kept up the pressure on the despairing Schuschnigg. Hitler forced him to cancel a planned plebiscite on Austrian independence on March 9 and to resign two days later. On March 12, 1938, German troops entered Austria, and on March 14 Hitler was in Vienna with Ribbentrop at his side.

When German troops marched into Austria in March, 1938, the Anschluss was complete and Austria was effectively part of Germany. *(National Archives)*

the end of World War II in 1945, he spent most of his efforts trying futilely to keep the collapsing German war machine going. After the war, the Allies found Ribbentrop hiding in Hamburg and arrested him as a war criminal. He tried to defend himself at the Nuremberg war crimes trials, but his shallow arguments could not conceal his complicity in Hitler's campaign of genocide or his compliance in killing Allied prisoners. Ribbentrop was found guilty of war crimes, and he was the first of ten prisoners to be hanged on October 16, 1946.

Bibliography

Bloch, Michael. *Ribbentrop*. New York: Crown, 1992.

Conot, Robert E. *Justice at Nuremberg*. New York: Carroll & Graf, 1983.

Ribbentrop, Joachim von. *The Ribbentrop Memoirs*. London: Weidenfeld and Nicolson, 1954.

Schwarz, Paul. *This Man Ribbentrop: His Life and Times*. New York: Julian Messner, 1943.

Weinberg, Gerhard L. *The Foreign Policy of Hitler's Germany*. 2 vols. Chicago: University of Chicago Press, 1970, 1979.

Frank Day

Hyman G. Rickover

Born: August 24, 1898, or January 27, 1900; Makow, Poland, Russian Empire (now Poland)
Died: July 8, 1986; Arlington, Virginia

U.S. military leader, advocate of nuclear submarines

Hyman George Rickover (HI-muhn JOHRJ RIH-koh-vur) was the son of Russian Jewish immigrants who immigrated to the United States when he was six years old. His father was a tailor in Chicago and, as a boy, Rickover supplemented the family's income by working as a messenger. In 1918 he gained admission to Annapolis. There he managed to weather four years of rabid anti-Semitism mainly by studying in his room. Rickover graduated in 1922, and for nearly two decades he filled a number of routine sea and land assignments. His excellent reputation as an engineer and a problem solver resulted in appointment as head of the electrical division of the Bureau of Ships in Washington, D.C., in 1939.

Hyman G. Rickover *(Library of Congress)*

The turning point in Rickover's destiny—and that of the U.S. Navy—occurred in 1946, when he was one of a handful of officers chosen to study at the Manhattan Engineering District at Oak Ridge, Tennessee. The Manhattan Engineering District was the agency responsible for the Manhattan Project—developing and testing atomic weapons. Here Rickover gained practical knowledge of the new science of atomic energy, and he began crusading for its application to sea power.

Visionary

As early as 1946, Rickover was promoting the idea of atomic-powered submarines to the chief of naval operations, Admiral Chester W. Nimitz, and within a year he had maneuvered himself into serving as both chief of the nuclear power division at the Bureau of Ships and head of the naval reactor branch of the Atomic Energy Commission (AEC). He then cleverly orchestrated simultaneous development of a nuclear submarine and the atomic plant to power it. Moreover, Rickover had a direct hand in designing and constructing all the essential components, which, when tested in March of 1953, worked perfectly. His backroom stratagems and technical innovations culminated in the successful launching of the USS *Nautilus*, the world's first atomic-powered submarine, in January, 1954. It was a brilliant technological accomplishment, coming only ten years after the first atomic reaction, and the Navy promoted him to rear admiral in July, 1953.

The USS *Nautilus*

At the time of its commissioning in 1955, the submarine *Nautilus* was unlike any submersible craft in the world. In contrast to the submarines of World War II, with their bulky conning towers and protuberances, Rickover's brainchild was sleek and smooth to promote high speed and silent running. At a length of 320 feet, it displaced 4,091 tons, yet it could maintain an underwater speed of 23 knots indefinitely because of the atomic reactors on board. In 1958 the *Nautilus* became the first submarine to sail across the entire North Pole under the ice. It also set many other distance and endurance records.

Indispensable

No sooner had atomic-powered submarines proved feasible than Rickover sought to apply the same technology to surface ships. He also supervised the design and construction of the United States' first atomic energy plant for civilian use at Shippingport, Pennsylvania, in 1958. Rickover was considered so indispensable to national security that in 1961 his term of service was extended beyond the mandatory retirement age of sixty-one. He remained director of the division of nuclear reactors for another twenty years. The outspoken admiral also made known his displeasure with the American school system.

In 1965 he accepted the Atomic Energy Commission's Enrico Fermi Award for his work in nuclear power, and in 1973 he gained promotion to full admiral. In January, 1982, Rickover was finally forced to resign on the orders of Secretary of the Navy John Lehman. He had given sixty years of conscientious service to the nation. Rickover died in Arlington, Virginia, on July 8, 1986, one of the most contentious, controversial, and visionary figures of naval history.

Rickover's Impact

For three decades the brilliant, acerbic, and combative Rickover was the United States' leading nuclear engineer. Through unceasing efforts, he overcame Navy bureaucracy and laid the groundwork for the world's first nuclear-powered submarine. Crass and obnoxious—and usually right—he was truly the "father of the nuclear navy." The nuclear craft he pioneered in the late 1940's have become standard equipment for the major navies of the world.

Bibliography

Bradford, James C., ed. *Quarterdeck and Bridge: Two Centuries of American Naval Leaders*. Annapolis, Md.: Naval Institute Press, 1997.

Duncan, Francis. *Rickover and the American Navy: The Discipline of Technology*. Annapolis, Md.: Naval Institute Press, 1989.

Polmar, Norman, and Thomas B. Allen. *Rickover*. New York: Simon & Schuster, 1982.

Rockwell, Theodore. *The Rickover Effect: How One Man Made a Difference*. Annapolis, Md.: Naval Institute Press, 1992.

John C. Fredriksen

Matthew B. Ridgway

Born: March 3, 1895; Fort Monroe, Virginia
Died: July 26, 1993; Fox Chapel, near Pittsburgh, Pennsylvania

U.S. military leader in World War II and the Korean War

Matthew Bunker Ridgway (MA-thew BUHN-kur RIHJ-way), the son of a World War I colonel, was born into the military and graduated from the U.S. Military Academy in 1917. After Mexican-border duty, he returned to West Point. He taught Spanish and was athletic manager under General Douglas MacArthur, then superintendent there. Ridgway held assignments in Nicaragua, Panama, and the Philippines, and he studied at the Infantry School, the Command and General Staff School, and the Army War College.

World War II and After

When World War II began, Ridgway was promoted to brigadier general and commanded the 82nd Infantry Division, which he converted into an airborne division. He inspired his men by personally training them in parachute and glider attacks. He directed paratrooper jumps into Sicily and advanced northward until his division was reassigned to England. Ridgway and the 82nd Airborne dropped behind German lines in France the day before D day in June, 1944, and helped the Normandy invasion succeed. Ridgway commanded the 18th Airborne Corps, the 30th Infantry Division, and the 7th Armored Division, and he led a paratrooper drop beyond the Rhine River. He crossed the Elbe River with his paratroopers, infantry, and tanks and contacted Russian troops near Denmark (May, 1945). Often exposed to enemy fire and once wounded by a German grenade, Ridgway was revered by his troops for his courage, compassion, and integrity.

Ridgway, now major general, was deputy supreme commander of the Mediterranean theater of operations (1945). In London after the war, he made recommendations to General Dwight D. Eisenhower during U.N. General Assembly meetings. In particular, in 1946, Ridgway recommended that there be an international U.N. force to deter aggressors. In Panama, Ridgway commanded American forces in the Caribbean. He was the U.S. Army's deputy chief of staff when the Korean conflict began.

Korea

When the American Eighth Army commander in Korea was killed, Ridgway, now a lieutenant

Matthew B. Ridgway *(National Archives)*

general, was sent to replace him. Ridgway rejuvenated the dispirited 8th Army, which had been savagely mauled by Chinese Communist soldiers in "human waves." He regrouped the 8th Army, rallied U.N. troops, and pushed Chinese forces north. General MacArthur was supreme commander of Allied Powers in Japan, U.N. forces in Korea, and U.S. forces in the Far East. President Harry S Truman vetoed MacArthur's unwise desire to widen (and perhaps globalize) the war by including anticommunist Taiwanese troops and advancing to the Yalu River. In April of 1951, Truman replaced MacArthur with Ridgway. Before the armistice was signed, Ridgway, now a full general, was in Europe.

The Cold War and Retirement

Ridgway succeeded Eisenhower, soon to become president, as supreme commander of the Allied forces of the North Atlantic Treaty Organization (NATO). Ridgway combined military and diplomatic skills in planning defenses and dealing with tensions among leaders of NATO's fourteen member countries. His last assignment was army chief of staff, commanding all forces in the Far East and Europe (1953). He later called this duty his toughest and most frustrating assignment. After increasing arguments with the Department of Defense and with his military and naval colleagues, Ridgway retired in 1955. He disagreed with Eisenhower, whom he thought was relying exces-

Matthew Ridgway (center) in Korea, accompanying General Douglas MacArthur on a visit to the front lines. *(National Archives)*

Succeeding Two Legends

General Douglas MacArthur was in command of U.N. troops in Korea when in 1951 General Matthew Ridgway arrived to lead the demoralized U.S. Eighth Army. He converted a defeated military unit into an aggressive one, dubbed "Operation Killer." When President Harry S Truman disagreed with MacArthur about widening the war and removed him, Ridgway became head of the U.N. command in the Far East, headquartered in Tokyo. Before the armistice was signed at Panmunjom, Korea (July, 1953), Ridgway had replaced General Dwight D. Eisenhower as supreme commander of Allied Powers in Europe. In the span of fourteen months, Ridgway replaced two legends—MacArthur and Eisenhower.

sively on nuclear weapons with insufficient conventional military strength to make "massive retaliation" workable. He also vehemently opposed proposals that the United States become involved in the Vietnamese conflict.

After retiring, Ridgway was a business executive with Colt Industries and then, until 1967, with the Mellon Institute of Industrial Research. Throughout the 1960's he deplored escalation of the Vietnam War. In 1968 he urged President Lyndon B. Johnson to seek peace. Ridgway, who died at the age of ninety-eight, is viewed by historians as one of the most intelligent, daring, and articulate corps commanders the U.S. Army has ever produced.

Bibliography

Blair, Clay. *The Forgotten War: America in Korea, 1950-1953*. New York: Times Books, 1987.

Ridgway, Matthew B. *The Korean War: How We Met the Challenge, How All-Out Asian War Was Averted, Why MacArthur Was Dismissed, Why Today's War Objectives Must Be Limited*. Garden City, N.Y.: Doubleday, 1967.

_______. *Soldier: The Memoirs of Matthew B. Ridgway*. New York: Harper & Brothers, 1956.

Smith, Robert. *MacArthur in Korea: The Naked Emperor*. New York: Simon and Schuster, 1962.

Soffer, Jonathan M. *General Matthew B. Ridgway: From Progressivism to Reaganism, 1895-1993*. Wesport, Conn.: Praeger, 1998.

Robert L. Gale

Mary Robinson

Born: May 21, 1944; Ballina, County Mayo, Ireland

First woman president of Ireland (1990-1997)

Mary Teresa Winifred Bourke Robinson (MEH-ree teh-RAY-sah WIH-nih-frehd BURK RO-bihn-suhn) was born the daughter of two doctors, Aubrey and Tessa Bourke. Raised in the west of Ireland, Robinson was an outstanding student at Trinity College in Dublin, receiving B.A. and L.L.B. degrees. In 1967-1968, she studied at Harvard Law School in the United States, where she earned an L.L.M. degree and was greatly influenced by the spirit of dissent and activism on campus.

At the age of twenty-five, Robinson became the youngest law professor at Trinity College. The Trinity College district sent her as their senator to the Seanad, the upper house of Ireland's parliament. She was the youngest senator in the country as well as the first woman and first Roman Catholic to represent her district. In the following year, 1970, she wed Nicholas Robinson, a political cartoonist for the *Irish Times*. The couple had three children: Tessa, William, and Aubrey.

Mary Robinson speaking at the fiftieth anniversary of the United Nations in 1995. In 1997 Robinson was named U.N. high commissioner for human rights. *(Reuters/Eric Miller/Archive Photos)*

A Champion of Human Rights

During her twenty years as a senator, Robinson fought steadily for women's rights, equality for homosexuals, and legalization of divorce. She championed reproductive rights, introducing the first bill to make contraception legal and legislation concerning abortion. In 1985 Robinson resigned from the Labour Party in protest against the Anglo-Irish Agreement, which she felt was created by the prime ministers of Ireland and Britain and forced upon the people of Northern Ireland.

Although Robinson was not affiliated with a political party, the head of the Labour Party proposed her as a candidate for the presidency in 1990. The office of president had long been regarded as a reward for elder statesmen. The Irish constitution accords no power to the president, who has no duties beyond living in a white house in Phoenix Park in Dublin and serving as a symbol of the nation. Robinson broke with tradition by spending three months campaigning; she toured the country by bus, meeting people from all classes. In a surprising upset, Robinson was elected as the first woman president of Ireland and was inaugurated on December 3, 1990.

President Robinson's Crusades

While in office, Robinson championed the causes of several special groups: women, travelers (a poor, nomadic ethnic group), and the Irish "diaspora" (people forced to emigrate from Ireland into other countries to survive). During her occupancy, Robinson kept a light burning in the window of the presidential mansion to welcome home those who had emigrated.

Stretching the limits of her office, Robinson began a campaign of reconciliation. She visited Northern Ireland and shook the hand of Sinn Féin leader Gerry Adams, starting a trend that led to his acceptance by other leaders. Robinson also became the first Irish president to visit the queen of England.

Irish president Mary Robinson viewing the Liberty Bell while in Philadelphia in 1994. *(Reuters/Steven Falk/Archive Photos)*

Robinson extended her range by visiting famine-ravaged Somalia in 1992. Outraged by the horrors she saw, Robinson reported the plight of the Somalis before the United Nations (U.N.). Her action led to the first U.N. intervention in a member's internal affairs for humanitarian reasons. Robinson later viewed refugee camps containing citizens of Rwanda fleeing their civil war. She brought before the world their suffering and the fate of one million massacred Rwandans. Continuing her diplomatic mission, Robinson traveled around the world, giving special attention to areas where Irish emigrants had settled.

Under Robinson's leadership, Ireland experienced unprecedented growth and change. The country caught up with its European counterparts socially and economically. Renewed Irish pride led to an interest in traditional Irish culture. On September 12, 1997, eleven weeks before the end of her seven-year term, Robinson resigned as president to accept the position of U.N. high commissioner for human rights.

Bibliography

Horgan, John. *Mary Robinson: A Woman of Ireland and the World.* Niwot, Colo.: Roberts Rhinehart, 1998.

Siggins, Lorna. *The Woman Who Took Power in the Park: Mary Robinson, President of Ireland, 1990-1997.* Edinburgh: Mainstream Publishing, 1997.

Carol Fox

U.N. Commissioner for Human Rights

Mary Robinson brought with her to the position of U.N. high commissioner for human rights a proven concern for the peoples of the world. She inherited an office that was considered highly ineffective. It had an inadequate budget and a small, demoralized staff. As a European, Robinson was viewed with skepticism by many emerging countries. However, she established a rapport, especially in African nations, by stressing that the Irish have felt the effects of colonialism and famine, much as the countries of Africa have. Robinson has shown tenacity and determination, confronting representatives of nations as diverse as China and the Congo about human rights violations.

Erwin Rommel

Born: November 15, 1891; Heidenheim an der Brentz, Württemberg, Germany
Died: October 14, 1944; Herrlingen, near Ulm, Germany

German military leader during World War II

The father of Erwin Johannes Eugen Rommel (AYR-veen yoh-HAH-nehs oy-GAYN RO-mehl) was a schoolteacher, and his mother was the daughter of the former president of the Württemberg government. Rommel joined the army in 1910 and went to officer's military school in Danzig (Gdansk). He was commissioned as a lieutenant in 1912, and his regiment went to war in August of 1914 at the beginning of World War I. The next year he married Lucie Maria Mollin and was first decorated for bravery (receiving the Iron Cross). The Rommels had one child, Manfred, who became mayor of Stuttgart after World War II. By the end of World War I, Rommel had distinguished himself for bravery and been promoted to captain.

Erwin Rommel *(Library of Congress)*

The Outbreak of World War II

Rommel remained in the military after the end of World War I and quickly rose through the ranks. When World War II began in 1939, Rommel was promoted to major-general and commanded Adolf Hitler's bodyguard for the duration of the Polish campaign. During the German invasion of western Europe, Rommel commanded the 7th Panzer Division with daring and used innovative tactics such as employing antiaircraft guns as antitank weapons. His division was dubbed the "Ghost Division" because of its rapid movements and its frequently unknown whereabouts. After the fall of France, Rommel was recalled to Berlin and promoted to the rank of lieutenant-general.

Command of the Afrika Corps

In February of 1941, Rommel was appointed commander of the Afrika Corps, which was sent to rescue the Italian army in Libya. The Italians, reeling from a series of defeats by the British, had been pushed out of Egypt and were disorganized and demoralized upon Rommel's arrival. From February to April of 1941, using surprise attacks and ingenious tactics, Rommel gained a series of victories against the British, who retreated to their Tobruk stronghold. After a year of battles, Tobruk surrendered in June, 1942. Rommel pressed his advantage and pushed the British back to defensive positions at El Alamein, Egypt.

El Alamein

In the summer of 1942, Adolf Hitler ordered Erwin Rommel to attack the Suez Canal and Cairo, Egypt. Despite Rommel's pleas to the contrary—his forces were exhausted and greatly outnumbered—he followed orders and attacked in June. After initial success, British resolve and lack of supplies for German troops halted the offensive at El Alamein, 150 miles (240 kilometers) west of Cairo. By mid-July, Rommel's troops established defensive positions, ending the first engagement.

On October 23, 1942, British troops commanded by Bernard Montgomery unleased an attack against the German-Italian forces. With greatly superior numbers—230,000 troops versus fewer than 80,000—the British routed Rommel's forces. By November 6 the British victory was complete. El Alamein proved to be the turning point in the African theater of war, leading to the inexorable retreat of Rommel's forces and their eventual surrender six months later.

German commander Erwin Rommel with the Fifteenth Panzer Division in Libya in 1941. *(National Archives)*

In October, however, the British launched an offensive against Rommel's greatly outnumbered forces, pushing them back to Tunis, recapturing Tobruk along the way. The November entrance of American troops into Africa made the situation hopeless for the German-Italian forces. Rommel was recalled to Germany in March of 1943, and the remnants of the Afrika Corps surrendered to the Anglo-Americans two months later.

Later Career

In December of 1943, Rommel was given command of the German defenses from Holland to Bordeaux, France, against the expected Allied invasion. He was away, celebrating his wife's birthday, when the invasion occurred. In July, 1944, Rommel's automobile was attacked by British planes, and Rommel suffered serious head injuries. While recuperating in a hospital, he was implicated in the July plot to overthrow Adolf Hitler. (His role in the plot has been highly disputed by historians.) Given the choice of a public trial or suicide—which would protect his family—he chose the latter course and died on October 14.

Rommel left behind a legacy of military genius: The British admiringly called him the Desert Fox for his wily battle tactics. Rommel, the youngest man promoted to the German rank of field marshal (in 1941), was also known as a man of high honor and chivalry who, in Christian conscience, treated prisoners well and opposed Nazi atrocities.

Bibliography

Fraser, David. *Knight's Cross: A Life of Field Marshall Erwin Rommel*. New York: HarperCollins, 1994.

Macksey, Kenneth. *Rommel: Battles and Campaigns*. New York: Da Capo Press, 1997.

Rommel, Erwin. *The Rommel Papers*. Edited by B. H. Liddell-Hart. New York: Da Capo Press, 1998.

Paul J. Chara, Jr.

Eleanor Roosevelt

Born: October 11, 1884; New York, New York
Died: November 7, 1962; New York, New York

First Lady of the United States (1933-1945)

Anna Eleanor Roosevelt (A-nah EH-leh-nohr ROH-zeh-vehlt) was a child of socially prominent parents, a niece of Theodore Roosevelt, and a distant cousin of Franklin Delano Roosevelt, who would become her husband. Because of her mother's early death and her father's alcoholism, she spent a lonely childhood until she went to boarding school.

At fifteen she was sent to Allenswood, an English girls' school, where she became an outstanding student and committed citizen. In 1905 she married Franklin D. Roosevelt, a young man with political ambitions. They had six children: Anna, James, Franklin (who died in infancy), Elliot, Franklin, Jr., and John. In 1910, when Franklin began his career in politics, Eleanor also moved into public life—first as a political wife, then as a reformer on her own.

Years of Preparation

Even before her marriage, Eleanor Roosevelt had been interested in social reform. She worked with the Junior League teaching settlement house children and with the Consumers' League, helping to investigate women's working conditions. Her first experiences with poverty influenced her commitment to improve the lot of the less fortunate. In 1913, when Franklin Roosevelt was appointed assistant secretary of the Navy, the family moved to Washington, D.C. When the United States became involved in World War I, Eleanor threw herself into war-related work. She organized the Red Cross canteen and the Navy Red Cross. Besides knitting, entertaining troops, and serving food to servicemen, she visited soldiers in the hospital and raised funds for a recreation center for wounded veterans. While serving others, Eleanor also developed her own political skills and organizing talents.

During this period, Eleanor learned that her husband was having a romantic affair with her social secretary, Lucy Mercer. Although she offered him a divorce, Franklin and Eleanor determined to remain together, prompted both by the potential political damage of a divorce and by the realization that together they made a forceful combination. The episode convinced Eleanor that she would have to find her life's fulfillment from work and friendships outside her marriage.

Franklin ran unsuccessfully for vice president

Eleanor Roosevelt *(Archive Photos)*

in 1920, and the next year he contracted polio. As a result of these events, Eleanor became active both in the Democratic Party and as a supporter of women's issues. She served in the League of Women Voters and in the Women's Trade Union League. With a group of women friends, she created a furniture crafts factory on the grounds of the Roosevelt estate at Hyde Park. There they published the *Women's Democratic News*. She and her associates bought a private girls' school, Todhunter, in New York City, where Eleanor taught three days a week until after she became First Lady.

Eleanor Roosevelt at the 1942 International Student Assembly in Washington, D.C., pictured with a Chinese

She also became involved in party politics, both as a representative for her husband during his illness and as a spokeswoman for social reform. She organized Democratic women, spoke in behalf of candidates, and supported women's election to office. When her husband was elected governor of New York in 1928 and president in 1932, she helped to ensure women's backing for the Democratic ticket. In turn, she advocated the appointment of women to public office. Among those she brought to her husband's attention was Frances Perkins, who became his secretary of labor, the first woman ever appointed to a presidential cabinet.

First Lady

During the Great Depression, the First Lady found ample opportunities to act as an advocate for the poor and unfortunate and to support equal rights for African Americans and for women. She traveled around the country to cities,

The Universal Declaration of Human Rights

On December 10, 1948, the United Nations (U.N.) overwhelmingly approved the Declaration of Human Rights, described by Eleanor Roosevelt as a "Magna Carta for mankind." The U.N. General Assembly gave Roosevelt a standing ovation, indicating their recognition that she deserved credit for its passage. She had succeeded in getting a diverse group of nations to draft a statement that transcended Cold War tensions as well as religious and cultural differences.

After months of debate over whether human rights belong to individuals or are conferred by the state, the document ultimately began with the statement that "all men and women are born free and equal." The declaration, which has ultimately acquired the binding force of international law, commits nations to respect civil, political, and economic rights of citizens.

My Day

From 1936 until shortly before her death, Eleanor Roosevelt wrote a regular newspaper column entitled *My Day*. The column began with descriptions of daily life at the White House and came to include commentary on books, plays, popular culture, and ultimately, national and world events. Roosevelt wrote in the first person, and the column bore the unmistakable stamp of her personality. Once she even refused the president's offer to contribute a column in her place. She donated her newspaper salary to charity.

Eleanor Roosevelt described complex issues in terms designed for ordinary people, using the column both to reassure Americans during the turmoil of the Depression and World War II and to stimulate support for free expression during the McCarthy era. No matter how busy her schedule, she seldom missed a deadline. Much of the public's affection for Eleanor Roosevelt came from knowing her through her unpretentious column.

farms, and coal mines, serving as the president's "eyes and ears," never failing to meet and empathize with people experiencing poverty and unemployment. She spoke for the "forgotten" Americans and helped them speak for themselves. A favorite tactic was to bring a spokesperson for a reform cause to the White House, where they would be seated next to the president, making Franklin a captive audience.

Eleanor Roosevelt in 1949 hosting Indian prime minister Jawaharlal Nehru (right), Nehru's sister, ambassador Vijaya Lakshmi Pandit, and his daughter (far left), future prime minister Indira Gandhi. They are pictured at the Roosevelt estate in Hyde Park, New York. *(National Archives)*

Eleanor Roosevelt emerged from her sheltered and privileged background to develop a lifelong commitment to equal rights for black Americans. She used the visibility of her position to stand up publicly against segregation and discrimination. In 1939, at the segregated meeting of the Southern Conference on Human Welfare, the First Lady placed her chair in the center of the aisle between the black and white sections. She publicly resigned her membership in the Daughters of the American Revolution when that group refused to permit black singer Marian Anderson to perform at their Constitution Hall. Eleanor Roosevelt arranged for Anderson to give a concert at the Lincoln Memorial before seventy-five thousand people. Beyond such symbolic gestures, she lobbied for legislation to make lynching a federal crime and to eliminate discrimination in the armed forces. During World War II, Eleanor Roosevelt worked to ensure that women would participate fully in the mobilization and that the social reforms begun during the New Deal of the 1930's would not be abandoned because of the military emergency.

"First Lady of the World"

After Franklin Roosevelt's death in 1945, Eleanor turned much of her attention to issues of international peace and cooperation. From 1945 until 1953 she served as an American delegate to the United Nations and as chair of the committee that drew up the 1948 Declaration of Human Rights. She traveled widely, demonstrating her concern for victims of war and oppression, and she helped to shape public opinion about international issues through her daily newspaper column, her massive correspondence, her frequent public appearances, and her radio broadcasts. She remained an active Democrat and supporter of civil rights and women's issues. Her last public role was chairing President John F. Kennedy's Commission on the Status of Women.

Eleanor Roosevelt redefined the roles of political spouse and First Lady to include championing social causes and using her public role to place such reforms on the national agenda. She served as a role model because of her courage, compassion, and tenacity. To the international community, she represented the moral and humanitarian face of American foreign policy.

Bibliography

Cook, Blanche Wiesen. *Eleanor Roosevelt*. New York: Viking, 1992.

Hoff-Wilson, Joan, and Marjorie Lightman, eds. *Without Precedent: The Life and Career of Eleanor Roosevelt*. Bloomington: Indiana University Press, 1984.

Lash, Joseph P. *Eleanor and Franklin*. New York: Norton, 1971.

_______. *Eleanor: The Years Alone*. New York: Norton, 1972.

Roosevelt, Eleanor. *The Autobiography of Eleanor Roosevelt*. New York: Harper & Row, 1984.

_______. *Empty Without You: The Intimate Letters of Eleanor Roosevelt and Lorena Hickok*. Edited by Rodger Streitmatter. New York: Free Press, 1998.

Mary Welek Atwell

Franklin D. Roosevelt

Born: January 30, 1882; Hyde Park, New York
Died: April 11, 1945; Warm Springs, Georgia

President of the United States (1933-1945)

His peers at Harvard University would not have predicted high office for Franklin Delano Roosevelt (FRANK-lihn DEH-lah-noh ROH-zeh-vehlt), the amiable, if apparently frivolous, scion of a prominent New York State family. Yet for Roosevelt, privilege brought with it a deep sense of the obligations that accompany it. After briefly practicing law, he decided on a political career. In 1905 Franklin married distant cousin Eleanor, and their marriage developed into an extremely effective political partnership.

Franklin D. Roosevelt *(Library of Congress)*

Political Apprenticeship

Roosevelt first ventured into office as a New York state senator, winning election in 1910. His articulate opposition to New York City machine politics brought him the attention of the national Democratic Party. During World War I, he served as assistant secretary of the Navy, the same post his illustrious relative Theodore Roosevelt had once held. In 1920 Roosevelt earned the nomination for the vice presidency, running with James M. Cox. The times were against the Democrats, however, and the Cox-Roosevelt ticket lost to Warren G. Harding's campaign for a return to "normalcy." Struggles with polio kept Roosevelt out of the national spotlight for much of the 1920's, but with Eleanor's help he worked tirelessly to revive a Democratic Party racked with ethnic and regional splits. In 1928, eyeing the presidency, Roosevelt won election to the powerful governorship of New York.

In 1929 the Great Depression plunged the country into economic turmoil. Roosevelt seized upon his party influence and the unpopularity of President Herbert Hoover and ran an effective 1932 presidential campaign. His pledge of a "New Deal" contrasted sharply with Hoover's perceived lethargy, resulting in a landslide win for Roosevelt. In his inaugural address he told anxious Americans that they had "nothing to fear but fear itself." This was not the last time his skillful phrase-making reassured the nation.

Dealing with the Depression

Never a deep ideological thinker, Roosevelt possessed great talents for synthesizing information and motivating subordinates. The New Deal reflected his instinctive leadership style, and subordinates frequently felt at cross-purposes with one another. The New Deal was less a coherent or unified program than a rambunctious onslaught against the Depression. Opponents perceived chaos in the whirl of legislative energy and experimentation, but most Americans saw the flurry of activity as an appropriate strategy during the crisis.

Roosevelt's second-term campaign faced important political challenges. Business leaders condemned the New Deal as socialistic. At the other end of the spectrum, demagogues such as Huey Long, the flamboyant senator from Louisiana, advanced more radical plans that appealed to some Americans. In 1935 the U.S. Supreme Court declared key pieces of New Deal legislation to be unconstitutional. Roosevelt responded first with an unpopular reorganization of the Democratic Party. Then, in 1937, he proposed to add five justices to the Supreme Court—his infamous "Court-packing" plan—and thereby to shift the Court's political balance. Many leaders denounced Roosevelt and warned that his attempt to consolidate power foreshadowed a dictatorship. Roosevelt won a resounding victory in 1936, but his second term was plagued by political vulnerability.

World Crisis

Global events intervened, however, as the rise of fascism in Germany and Japan occupied the nation's attention. World War II broke out in Europe in 1939, and by 1940 Roosevelt was promising Britain's prime minister Winston Churchill that the United States would support England against the Nazis. One important agreement was the lend-lease plan, whereby the United States loaned war material to Britain under generous terms. Roosevelt ran for an unprecedented third term in 1940, arguing that an executive change was ill-advised as war threatened. In early 1941, as it became apparent to Roosevelt that the United States would probably be forced to enter

The New Deal

Franklin D. Roosevelt's presidency commenced with the so-called First Hundred Days, during which Congress passed an avalanche of New Deal legislation. For instance, the Agricultural Adjustment Act addressed farm overproduction by paying farmers not to produce beyond a set quota. The National Industrial Recovery Act tried to stabilize business by establishing rules of competition within particular industries. The administration fought poverty with programs such as the Public Works Administration, which employed the jobless on building projects, and the Civilian Conservation Corps, which created jobs in conservation efforts.

The next wave of legislation came in 1935, and much of it reflected the more partisan nature of Roosevelt's second term. For example, the Works Progress Administration was a wide-ranging effort to provide relief for the poor and to sponsor a variety of cultural projects in theater, photography, history, and music. Legislation such as the Wagner Act protected unions and the rights of workers to collectively bargain. The Social Security Act created federal pensions for retired people. Banking and tax reform, holding-company regulation, and other minor pieces of legislation more radically attacked the Depression.

Most historians conclude that the New Deal did not end the Depression. Some argue that the programs were inherently flawed and thus ineffectual; others counter that the New Deal conceded too much to political opponents and foundered in compromise. For many Depression-era Americans, however, the New Deal offered a crucial glimmer of hope.

Polio

Until 1953, when Jonas Salk discovered a vaccine for polio, the paralyzing disease often struck children. In 1921, while swimming, thirty-nine-year-old Franklin D. Roosevelt contracted the poliomyelitis virus. Though he struggled to regain his ability to walk, he was largely confined to a wheelchair for the rest of his life. His wife Eleanor felt that his polio helped him become more empathetic to others' suffering.

Roosevelt neither hid nor publicized his disability. His speeches were usually delivered as he stood behind a podium, legs locked into place by heavy braces. A deferential press corps typically refrained from photographing the president in his wheelchair. Moreover, illustrations of the president, as in political cartoons, often depicted him standing or running. Consequently, many Americans never knew that the person they looked to for strength during difficult times was himself disabled.

the war, he gave a speech listing the "Four Freedoms"—freedom from fear, freedom from want, freedom to worship, and freedom of speech— that summarized his vision for the postwar world. The Four Freedoms soon became the banner of America's war aims, another example of the president's remarkable powers of inspiration.

U.S. president Franklin D. Roosevelt giving one of his famous "fireside chats" over the radio. *(Franklin D. Roosevelt Library)*

When the Japanese navy bombed Pearl Harbor on December 7, 1941, the United States declared war on Japan. Roosevelt now actively assumed the role of commander in chief, and his leadership helped unify the country as it forged the military-industrial machine that guaranteed victory for the Allies. By 1944 the rigors of more than a decade in the presidency and the burdens of guiding America's war effort had visibly affected Roosevelt's health. Nevertheless, he ran for a fourth term. Political opponents fretted that Roosevelt was turning the presidency into his personal domain, but for many Americans Roosevelt was virtually the only president they had known. He won again in convincing fashion. However, in April, 1945, at his retreat in Warm Springs, Georgia, Roosevelt suffered a fatal stroke.

Franklin D. Roosevelt signing the Lend-Lease Act in March, 1941, to provide aid to the European nations fighting Germany in World War II. *(National Archives)*

Assessment

Though Franklin D. Roosevelt inspired enmity from Americans opposed to his legislative agenda—some of his critics sneeringly referred to him as "that man in the White House"—many Americans saw Roosevelt as an icon of paternal concern. His well-honed political instincts enabled him to resist threats from both the Left and the Right, and they allowed him both to define and to occupy the majority position. He was the first chief executive to use the mass media effectively; his radio "fireside chats" brought Roosevelt into Americans' living rooms, producing a deep personal attachment to the president. Further, his witty and informative press conferences endeared him to reporters, upon whom he often relied to publicize the New Deal. The party alignments that Roosevelt helped fashion structured American political life for decades. His New Deal programs questioned the American belief in strict self-reliance, bequeathing a political tradition that demands energetic government to address social problems. Above all, for his millions of supporters, Franklin D. Roosevelt symbolized hope to a nation challenged with depression and war.

Bibliography

Burns, James MacGregor. *Roosevelt: The Lion and the Fox, 1882-1940*. New York: Harcourt Brace Jovanovich, 1956.

_______. *Roosevelt: The Soldier of Freedom, 1940-1945*. New York: Harcourt Brace Jovanovich, 1970.

Goodwin, Doris Kearns. *No Ordinary Time: Franklin and Eleanor Roosevelt, the Home Front in World War II*. New York: Touchstone, 1994.

McElvaine, Robert S. *The Great Depression, 1929-1941*. New York: Times Books, 1993.

Schlesinger, Arthur M., Jr. *The Age of Roosevelt*. 3 vols. Boston: Houghton Mifflin, 1957-1960.

David J. Snyder

Theodore Roosevelt

Born: October 27, 1858; New York, New York
Died: January 6, 1919; Oyster Bay, New York

President of the United States (1901-1909)

Born into an aristocratic New York family, Theodore Roosevelt (THEE-o-dohr ROH-zeh-vehlt) was of Dutch descent. He suffered from asthma as a child, and his father, whom he idolized, urged him to develop his body. Therefore Roosevelt spent much of his life in strenuous physical activity. A voracious reader of wide-ranging interests, he also authored many books. The first, a study of the naval war of 1812, was begun while he was a student at Harvard University. In a move that was unusual at the time for someone of his social background, he went into politics, serving in the New York Assembly as a Republican.

Preparation for the Presidency

His kinetic energy, his glasses, and his flashing teeth immediately made Roosevelt a lively subject for cartoonists. His first wife, Alice Lee, died in childbirth. Partially to forget this tragedy, he took up ranching in South Dakota's Black Hills. Continuing to write, notably *The Winning of the West* (1889-1896), he also pursued politics, running unsuccessfully for mayor of New York City, serving as civil service commissioner under Benjamin Harrison and Grover Cleveland and as New York's police commissioner. In 1897 President William McKinley appointed him as assistant secretary of the Navy.

When events in Cuba led to war against Spain in 1898, Roosevelt organized a volunteer regiment, the Rough Riders, and became a national hero. Though his reputation was that of a radical reformer, New York's Republican machine supported him for governor because of his popularity. In 1900, against his better judgment, he accepted the vice presidency. When President McKinley was assassinated in September, 1901, Roosevelt, only forty-two, became the United States' youngest president.

A Modern Presidency

Roosevelt transformed the presidency. The White House, which he officially named, became the focus of national attention. Roosevelt had remarried, to Edith Carow, and the antics of the six Roosevelt children captivated the country. It was Roosevelt himself, however, who dominated the headlines. His political philosophy was that of a constructive conservative. Living in the West

Theodore Roosevelt *(Library of Congress)*

had given him knowledge of the lives of ordinary Americans, and he believed that the nation's future depended upon the betterment of all its citizens. He was no economic leveler, but he expressed disgust at the shortsightedness and greed of the new industrial class.

No immediate changes were made to the McKinley cabinet, but Roosevelt soon made two major policy departures. During a nationwide coal strike, when the mine owners refused to negotiate with the miners, Roosevelt, unlike his predecessors (who had used troops to crush strikes), mediated a resolution between the two sides. This was the first time that the federal government had been both active and neutral in such an industrial dispute. Roosevelt also instituted an antitrust suit against the Northern Securities Company, a J. P. Morgan conglomerate. His objection was not to big business as such, but to what he considered illegal or immoral actions. Although he was praised as a "trustbuster," it was not size but behavior that mattered to Roosevelt.

In 1904 Roosevelt was reelected president in his own right, afterward announcing that he would not be a candidate in 1908, a statement he possibly came to regret. His second term was as eventful as the first. Emphasizing the conservation of natural resources, Roosevelt established bird sanctuaries and national parks, and constructed irrigation projects. Although he loved the wilderness and counted naturalists John Muir and John Burroughs among his friends, Roosevelt's goals were more to conserve for the benefit of future generations than pure preservation. In the last year of his presidency he organized a national conservation conference for state governors. No president did more to protect the nation's inheritance than Roosevelt.

Foreign Affairs

Roosevelt was also an activist on the world stage, having a greater awareness of international issues than many presidents. When Panama revolted against Colombia in 1903, the new country was recognized immediately by the United States—too quickly for some. Roosevelt officially recognized Panama because he wanted

The Bull Moose Party

By the second decade of the twentieth century, the progressive reform movement was at high tide. For many Americans, William Howard Taft, Theodore Roosevelt's successor, was too legalistic, cautious, and lacking in leadership qualities. Seeking an alternative for 1912, many Republican progressives turned to Roosevelt.

Although Roosevelt was far more popular among the voters, Taft controlled the Republican convention. The progressives abandoned the party and nominated Roosevelt as the candidate of the new Progressive Party, or the Bull Moose Party, named for Roosevelt's remark that he felt as strong as a bull moose. Moral fervor predominated, with Roosevelt claiming, "We stand at Armageddon and battle for the Lord." The party's radical platform advocated increased democracy through the use of initiative, referendum, and recall. It also supported the popular election of senators, national presidential primaries, government regulation of economic monopolies, and numerous social justice measures including women's suffrage and workers' protection.

Roosevelt did not expect to win, particularly after the Democrats nominated New Jersey's progressive governor, Woodrow Wilson. Nevertheless, he campaigned hard until he was shot in Milwaukee by a potential assassin. Wilson won, but the Bull Moose Party finished second, the best result by any third party in American history.

Theodore Roosevelt (center, hands on hips) in 1898 with the Rough Riders, standing atop San Juan Hill in Cuba. *(Library of Congress)*

The Rough Riders

Theodore Roosevelt long sought to test himself in battle. Some biographers have suggested that he wished to compensate for his father's failure to serve as a soldier in the Civil War. When the war with Spain began in 1898, President William McKinley gave Roosevelt permission to form the First U.S. Cavalry Volunteers, nicknamed Roosevelt's Rough Riders. An all-American contingent, it included cowboys, miners, lawmen, and Native Americans from the West and Ivy League athletes and upper-class equestrians from the East. The Rough Riders got to Cuba and into combat—but without their horses. In the Battle of San Juan Hill, they distinguished themselves, earning a fabled place in American lore.

the long-discussed Panama Canal built to link the Pacific to the Atlantic. As he later said, he "took" Panama. While widely popular, this action was also among his most criticized. For Roosevelt himself, it was the single action of which he was most proud.

Although supposedly overly bellicose, Roosevelt was awarded the Nobel Peace Prize in 1906 for his mediation that helped resolve the differences between the belligerents in the Russo-Japanese War. American relations with Japan were a concern, partly because of the many Cali-

U.S. president Theodore Roosevelt (left) with naturalist John Muir at Glacier Point, above California's Yosemite Valley. Conservation was among Roosevelt's most important concerns. *(Library of Congress)*

fornians who discriminated against Japanese immigrants and their descendants. The "gentlemen's agreement" by which Japan and the United States would each restrict emigration to the other country was Roosevelt's attempt to ameliorate the issue.

To end European intervention in Latin America, particularly the Caribbean, Roosevelt issued the Roosevelt Corollary to the Monroe Doctrine. It made the United States the effective police power in the area, a development later criticized in Latin America. Symbolically, Roosevelt's dynamic foreign policy culminated when he sent the U.S. fleet around the world as an expression of America's coming-of-age.

Post-White House Years

After endorsing William Howard Taft as his successor, Roosevelt spent a year on safari in Africa and being feted in Europe. Taft was no Roosevelt, either in policies or personality, and Roosevelt again sought the presidency in 1912 as the Progressive, or Bull Moose, candidate. He won more votes than Taft but lost to Democrat Woodrow Wilson. Roosevelt's exploration of Brazil's River of Doubt permanently damaged his health. With the outbreak of World War I, Roosevelt urged American preparedness, hoping to again lead volunteers into battle. It was not to be, but his four sons served. The youngest, Quentin, died in combat. Preparing to run again for the presidency in 1920, Roosevelt died in January, 1919, one of the United States' most beloved and most significant presidents.

Bibliography

Brands, H. W. *T. R.: The Last Romantic*. New York: Basic Books, 1997.

Harbaugh, William Henry. *Power and Responsibility*. New York: Farrar, Straus and Cudahy, 1961.

Miller, Nathan. *Theodore Roosevelt: A Life*. New York: William Morrow, 1992.

Morris, Edmund. *The Rise of Theodore Roosevelt*. New York: Coward, McCann & Geoghegan, 1979.

Eugene Larson

Elihu Root

Born: February 15, 1845; Clinton, New York
Died: February 7, 1937; New York, New York

U.S. secretary of state (1905-1909), winner of 1912 Nobel Peace Prize

Elihu Root (EH-lih-hew REWT), lawyer and American elder statesman, was the son of a mathematics professor at Hamilton College in Clinton, New York. Root graduated from that same college as valedictorian in 1864, and he completed law studies at New York University in 1867.

Early Career in Law and Politics

Root set up practice in New York City, a place rife with post-Civil War corruption, notably in the form of William Marcy "Boss" Tweed. Root's practice fared well, and he soon gained a reputation as a hard-working, dedicated advocate who excelled in the courtroom. He quickly trebled his father's income as a professor. His brush with politics came early, participating as an assistant defense counsel in one of the many cases brought against Boss Tweed. Although Root's role in this 1873 trial was minimal, later his political opponents used his defense of the infamous Tweed as political ammunition against him. Root's practice grew to representing banks, railroads, and large corporations. He enjoyed great success in the courtroom and was widely known in New York's social circles. He married Clara Francis Walen in 1878.

Elihu Root *(The Nobel Foundation)*

Local politics became an important part of Root's life early in his career in New York City. He participated regularly in the local Republican Party and joined the Union League Club. He supported young Theodore Roosevelt's bid for mayor of New York. The two became close political associates from that point on. As mayor and later as police commissioner, Roosevelt enjoyed having Root on his advising team. Both became active in New York State politics, though Root often opposed the state Republican Party boss, Senator Thomas C. Platt.

National Politics

In 1899 President William McKinley asked Root to serve as his secretary of war. Root, an advocate of international law and supporter of utilizing lawyers as administrators, was perfect for the position despite his lack of military experience. He had earlier turned down an invitation to participate in the peace negotiations with Spain after the Spanish-American War of 1898.

Principal among Root's duties was the administration of the new American possessions gained from the war, notably Cuba and the Philippines. Each presented difficult issues and problems. In Cuba, Root supported Cuban independence and self-government under a strong centralized system. These things were achieved with the collaboration of General Leonard Wood, the American military governor of Cuba. Root also was instrumental in drafting the Platt Amendment, which guaranteed an American presence in Cuba after Cuban independence. In the Philippines, Root had to deal with a widespread and bitter rebellion against American rule. Atrocities reigned on both sides. Working closely with the American civilian governor, William Howard Taft, Root curbed the unnecessary violence and brought an end to the revolt.

Root also busied himself with reforming the military, mainly the Army. He established the Army War College and put into effect a fair staff-line rotation system for officers to replace the antiquated, corrupt system of permanent postings. Root became secretary of state in 1905 after the death of John Hay. He continued Roosevelt's "good neighbor" policy in Latin America but tried to stay away from the frequent "dollar diplomacy" schemes that large corporations used to control Latin American governments. He worked tirelessly for hemispheric peace and was awarded the Nobel Peace Prize in 1912 for his efforts. In 1909 Root was elected by the New York legislature to represent that state in the U.S. Senate. There he spent less time on legislation and more time trying to sooth the growing rift between his two friends Roosevelt and Taft. Both threatened to split the Republican Party, thereby ensuring a Democratic victory in the 1912 presidential election. Root failed to bring the two together, with Roosevelt leaving the party to form his Bull Moose Party. Democrat Woodrow Wilson was elected president.

In April, 1917, Wilson appointed Root to head a high-level bipartisan commission to explore Russia's economic, military, and social conditions after the revolution there in March, 1917. Noting the tremendous strain that World War I was placing on Russia, Root's commission advised economic support of the fragile new democracy. Wilson ignored the commission's recommendations, mainly because he distrusted the Republican Root. Wilson had sent the commission as a token show of support for the revolution. Despite this affront, Root supported Wilson's efforts in Paris in 1919, where European nations gathered to draft a peace treaty after World War I. Root objected only to the resulting Treaty of Versailles's Article X, which stipulated military support of member nations of the new League of Nations. Root feared that this provision could embroil the United States in more European conflicts.

The Battle for the World Court

Established in 1920, the Permanent Court of International Justice, or World Court, served as the judicial branch of the League of Nations until the founding of the United Nations International Court of Justice in 1945. Largely the work of American lawyer and statesman Elihu Root and British jurist Lord Phillimore, the Court comprised fifteen judges from various nations. The Court ruled mainly in international disputes and some human rights cases. The United States refused to join the World Court or be bound by its rulings, mainly because the U.S. Senate had rejected the League of Nations and the Treaty of Versailles. Root campaigned for American membership but could not overcome isolationist attitudes in the post-World War I United States.

The Tweed Ring

Organized and run by political boss William Marcy Tweed, known simply as Boss Tweed, the Tweed ring of New York City was one of the most powerful and corrupt political organizations in American history. Tweed's network of city officials, Democratic Party underlings, and business associates ruled New York City for almost twenty years. It left a political taint on the city for several decades thereafter. Tweed built his power base as a city alderman and congressman during the 1850's. As supervisor of New York City elections, he abused his authority to gain political friends and dependents. While his machine rebuilt the city's infrastructure and made other municipal improvements, debts increased dramatically as Tweed took huge kickbacks from contractors and city officials. Tweed's power eroded as the city's financial situation worsened. Thomas Nast, cartoonist for *Harper's Weekly*, drew accusatory caricatures of Boss Tweed that further eroded his authority. Tweed was brought to trial in 1871 for misdemeanor charges and was sentenced to one year in prison. The state of New York sued Tweed for several million dollars in kickbacks in 1875. Tweed broke bail and was later arrested in Europe. He died before his trial could begin. Tweed's political legacy was one of municipal corruption and payoffs.

In 1920 Root played a major role in forming the new Permanent Court of International Justice, or World Court, as part of the League of Nations. Always an advocate for international law, Root urged U.S. participation in the World Court despite the country's absence from the league. His effort to gain American membership failed. By now considered an "elder statesman," Root was called upon to serve on various commissions, both national and international. He died in New York City at the age of ninety-one.

Bibliography

Jessup, Philip C. *Elihu Root*. New York: Dodd, Meade, 1938.

Leopold, Richard William. *Elihu Root and the Conservative Tradition*. Boston: Little, Brown, 1954.

William Allison

Nellie Tayloe Ross

Born: November 29, 1876; St. Joseph, Missouri
Died: December 19, 1977; Washington, D.C.

Governor of Wyoming (1925-1927), the first elected woman governor in the United States

Nellie Davis Tayloe Ross (NEH-lee DAY-vihs TAY-loh ROS) was the daughter of a merchant and farmer in Missouri and a mother who died when Nellie was young. Largely self-educated, she married William Bradford Ross, an attorney, in 1902. The couple lived in Wyoming and had four sons, one of whom died in an accident. While her husband took part in the affairs of the state's Democratic Party, Nellie Ross was active in club work. In 1922 William Ross became Wyoming's governor. He died in October, 1924, with two years of his term yet to be served.

Nellie Tayloe Ross *(Library of Congress)*

The First Woman Governor

Wyoming law required that a special election be held, and the Democrats nominated Nellie Ross. She limited her campaign to issuing public letters, and she promised the voters to show that women could succeed in high state offices. She defeated her Republican opponent by eight thousand votes. Because she was sworn into office on January 5, 1925, she became the nation's first woman governor, beating Miriam Amanda Ferguson of Texas by only two weeks. Ross gained national attention, and her performance was watched closely.

In office, Ross confronted a Republican legislature but asserted the prerogatives of her position with vigor. She enforced Prohibition and achieved a certain amount of banking reform. Intraparty battles hurt Ross's election chances in 1926. She was an ally of Joseph C. O'Mahoney, a Roman Catholic. This alliance led Republicans in Wyoming to allege that an "invisible government" was running the statehouse. Opponents also charged that reelecting Ross would enable her to appoint O'Mahoney to the U.S. Senate should the elderly Republican incumbent, Francis E. Warren, die in office before his term ended in 1930. Republicans also contended that the governorship was no place for a woman. Ross lost her bid to remain governor by a margin of 1,300 votes.

Ross remained active in politics. She served as vice chair of the Democratic National Committee in 1928 and was a strong supporter of Alfred E. Smith. Her leadership position allowed her to campaign on behalf of a greater role for women in the Democratic Party. These commitments led her to a friendship with Eleanor Roosevelt. When Franklin D. Roosevelt became president in 1933, Ross lobbied for women to receive federal appointments.

Director of the Mint

President Roosevelt named Ross to be the director of the U.S. Mint, and she took up her duties on May 3, 1933. The Great Depression of the

1930's had reduced the work of the mint, and Ross headed a bureau with a small workforce. During her tenure she dealt with the surge of gold into the United States that occurred during World War II and with an improving economy. She supervised the coinage needs of wartime. The zinc-coated penny, a conservation measure, was not popular with most Americans. Ross left office in 1953 after having managed about two-thirds of all the coinage in the mint's history to that time. During her later years, Ross, in her trademark hats, was a highly sought-after speaker. She died at the age of 102.

A Symbol of Female Progress

Fate pushed Nellie Ross into the national spotlight, but she lived up to the demands of the Wyoming governorship with efficiency and style. Nellie Tayloe Ross was much more than a "first" in American women's history. She was also a genuine pioneer in the annals of American feminism who expanded opportunities for women in and out of government.

Bibliography

Brown, Mabel E., ed. *First Ladies of Wyoming*. Cheyenne: Wyoming Arts Council, 1990.

Larson, T. A. *History of Wyoming*. Lincoln: University of Nebraska Press, 1978.

Ware, Susan. *Beyond Suffrage: Women in the New Deal*. Cambridge, Mass.: Harvard University Press, 1981.

Lewis L. Gould

Nellie Tayloe Ross as director of the U.S. Mint; she served from 1933 to 1953. *(National Archives)*

The U.S. Mint

The U.S. Mint began its operations in 1792 in Philadelphia, and operations stayed in that city when Washington, D.C., became the national capital. Over the years Congress established various branch mints; with the exception of the one now operating in Denver, Colorado, none achieved permanent status. Silver (1794) and gold (1795) coins were minted from the outset, but sometimes in its early stages during the 1820's the mint lacked the precious metals it needed to operate. The mint stopped making gold coins in 1934. Through the Coinage Act of 1873, Congress created the Bureau of the Mint in February, 1873, within the Department of the Treasury, and the bureau continues to operate the mints that make coins in Philadelphia and Denver, the assay offices in New York City and San Francisco, and the depositories that hold bullion at Fort Knox in Kentucky (gold) and West Point, New York (silver).

Gerd von Rundstedt

Born: December 12, 1875; Aschersleben, Germany
Died: February 24, 1953; Hannover, West Germany

German military commander during World War II

Born into a Prussian family with a tradition of military service, Karl Rudolf Gerd von Rundstedt (KAHRL REW-dohlf GAYRT fon ROONT-shteht) seemed foreordained for a military career. He attended cadet schools at Oranienstein (1888) and Lichterfelde (1890) and was commissioned as an infantry lieutenant in 1893. During the period before World War I, von Rundstedt obtained advanced military schooling and served primarily as a staff officer.

Early Military Career

During World War I, von Rundstedt held staff positions, first at division level, then at corps level, on eastern and western fronts. Though ranking no higher than major, he acquired a reputation for expertise in logistics and for professionalism.

After World War I, he was given both headquarters staff assignments and field assignments. He received steady promotions, commanding both a cavalry division and an elite commando group. He kept a watchful eye on new developments in technology as well as tactics. He was promoted to general of infantry (1932). Two years later he attempted to retire but was persuaded to remain. During Germany's massive military buildup under Adolf Hitler, von Rundstedt's expertise and experience were needed. In 1938, after promotion to colonel general, he retired, with the understanding that he could be recalled.

Army Group Commander

Before the German attack on Poland in September, 1939, von Rundstedt was recalled to as-

German field marshal Gerd von Rundstedt, in command of coastal defenses in western Europe from 1942 to 1944. *(Library of Congress)*

The Battle of the Bulge

The Battle of the Bulge was the name given by Anglo-American forces to a German winter offensive. Code-named "Watch on the Rhine," the attack was launched on December 16, 1944, through the Ardennes Forest into Belgium and Luxembourg. It sought to drive a wedge between British and American armies and capture Antwerp. Even if it failed, the Germans hoped to stall the Anglo-American advance. The plan, formulated before von Rundstedt took command on September 5, 1944, called for two armies under generals Sepp Dietrich and Hasso von Manteuffel to assemble secretly and make a rapid advance of approximately 150 miles (about 240 kilometers). Von Rundstedt made only minor modifications but sought delays for troops and equipment to be properly positioned.

The initial force, approximately 250,000 men, consisted of several divisions of veteran soldiers and others—the others composed largely of underage and overage conscripts. To have a chance of success, the Germans knew they would have to rely on surprise and inclement weather that would keep Allied planes grounded. Although the advance was rapid, the attackers failed to reach their initial objectives. During the first day, American resistance stiffened at key points, notably Bastogne. Beginning on December 23, clearing skies brought Allied warplanes to the attack, and American ground forces began hammering the salient (the "bulge" in the German lines) on both flanks. On December 25, a counterattack by the Second Armored Division forced a German withdrawal near Celles, Belgium, after an advance of approximately 50 miles (80 kilometers). By January 16, 1945, the German units had withdrawn to a line near their beginning point. When the battle ended on January 28, German losses included eight hundred tanks, one thousand warplanes, and more than 100,000 soldiers.

American soldiers captured by Germans during the Battle of the Bulge, the surprise German drive into Allied positions led by Gerd von Rundstedt in December, 1944. *(National Archives)*

sume the role that he held for much of the war: army group commander, in charge of operations involving hundreds of thousands of troops. He led Army Group South into the brief battle that overwhelmed Polish defenses. Von Rundstedt became recognized for his reliance on capable staff officers, for his ability to grasp the complexities of an attack plan, and for expedient deployment of forces.

During the invasion of France in May, 1940, he

American infantrymen firing on German troops during the Battle of the Bulge, December, 1944. Although it was well-conceived, the German attack near Bastogne, Belgium, failed quickly. *(National Archives)*

commanded the divisions that swept through the Ardennes into Belgium and across northern France. As in Poland, victory was rapid, with light casualties during the unstoppable German Blitzkrieg. For his leadership he was promoted to field marshal in 1940. In 1941 von Rundstedt assumed command of Army Group South for the invasion of Russia, code-named "Operation Barbarossa," initiated on June 22, 1941. His million-man army advanced toward Ukraine and its capital, Kiev, the Don River Basin, and the Caucasus region. Following victories in Ukraine, bad weather hampered troop movements. After units fighting near the Black Sea retreated in order to strengthen their lines, he was relieved of command.

Command in the West

In March, 1942, he was sent to France to command forces defending western Europe, then threatened by an Allied invasion. He set about planning strategy and building coastal defenses. Von Rundstedt's strategy called for reserve divisions to be brought from the interior to meet a coastal invasion. When the Allies invaded Normandy on June 6, 1944, his measures proved ineffective. Removed from command in July, 1944, he returned to a period of inactivity. In September, 1944, he was recalled to command the armies committed to the Battle of the Bulge, Germany's final western offensive. Although the December attack was a well-conceived, tactical surprise, it quickly failed.

After the war, von Rundstedt was held captive by the British while the Allies searched for evidence of his involvement in war crimes. He was eventually released after charges against him were dropped, partly for lack of credible evidence and partly because of his ill health and advanced age.

Bibliography

Blumentritt, Guenther. *Von Rundstedt: The Soldier and the Man*. London: Odhams, 1952.

Keegan, John. *Rundstedt*. New York: Ballantine, 1974.

Messenger, Charles. *The Last Prussian: A Biography of Field Marshal Gerd von Rundstedt, 1875-1953*. London: Brassey's, 1991.

Stanley Archer

BIOGRAPHICAL ENCYCLOPEDIA OF
20th-Century World Leaders

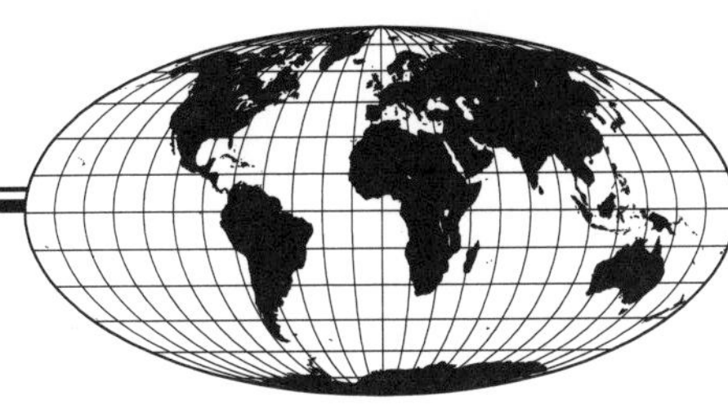

Index

In the following index, volume numbers and those page numbers referring to full articles appear in **bold face** type.